WINGATE COLLEGE LIBRARY

973.2
H

The
History of North America

GUY CARLETON LEE, Ph. D.

OF

Johns Hopkins and Columbian Universities, Editor

JEAN TALON

PIERRE FRANÇOIS RIGAUD DE VAUDREUIL

LE MOYNE LONGUEIL

After the original paintings in the Château de Ramezay, Montreal.

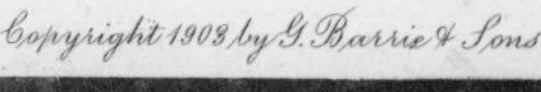
Copyright 1903 by G. Barrie & Sons

The Colonization of the South: Volume Three of The History of North America.

BY PETER JOSEPH HAMILTON. Author of: *Rambles in Historic Lands; Colonial Mobile; Mobile,* in *Historical Towns of the South* series; *Rights and Duties in time of War,* contributed to *Taylor's International Law,* etc., etc.

ILLUSTRATED WITH PORTRAITS, MAPS, ETC.,
FROM AUTHENTIC SOURCES

Philadelphia
PUBLISHED FOR THE HOME UNIVERSITY LEAGUE BY
GEORGE BARRIE & SONS

WINGATE COLLEGE LIBRARY
WINGATE, N. C.

COPYRIGHT, 1904, BY GEORGE BARRIE & SONS

Entered at Stationers' Hall, London.

EDITOR'S INTRODUCTION

This volume of The History of North America is the first of three, by different hands, having for their subject Colonization. Its scope is coterminous with that of the most fascinating field of American history. There is in the story of the colonization of the South a glamour of romance that does not attach to any other period in the up-bringing of what is now the United States.

The records of the colonization of New England, and of its constituent parts, are filled with pages that are of the most vital importance in the study of the social, economic, and constitutional growth of these United States; but few of them, however, thrill the modern reader. This because the men and women of Plymouth and Massachusetts, of Hartford, New Haven, and the Providence and Rhode Island Plantations are too nearly akin, despite their manners that jar upon our modernity, to the men and women of the present day. It is hard to throw around them the aureole of romance. True is it that, thanks to New England's second-greatest poet, the drapery of imagination has enfolded, and mayhap obscured, the characters of Standish and Alden and other worthies whose names will ever dwell in our memories; yet, nevertheless, Romance refuses to clothe the stark realism of New England with the mantle of fancy. It gives her, ungrudgingly, the maximum of credit for her share in nation building, but it has ever denied to

24298

her the attractiveness that comes from mystery, the glamour that is the offspring of myth.

The history of the colonization period of the Middle States, if we except the conflicts between the Long House and the whites, and the struggle between the pertinacious Claiborne and the representatives of Lord Baltimore, has little upon which romance can fasten. In truth, the importance of the record of the colonies and provinces in that portion of America bounded on the north by the St. Lawrence and on the south by the Potomac is one of politics, save for the Indian troubles and the struggles between rather pusillanimous colonists to get possession of this or that bit of promising wilderness.

Men and women with commercial or agricultural training came to the Middle colonies on business bent. They were strictly commercialists; they had well-defined plans of settlement. They knew something of the conditions that awaited them; they knew more of the methods by which success might be wrested from adversity. Their contribution, as colonists, to American progress is the substantial one; nevertheless, there is little or nothing about it, when it is considered broadly, that is roseated by romance.

The South and the Southwest, however, amply supply the lack which we note in the history of the colonization of New England and the Middle States. The territory that lengthened northward from the Mexican Gulf and the Rio Grande to where the Potomac and Ohio leashed its onward stretch or the trackless plains of the Middle West halted its earliest pioneers was the home of romance. It had from the first years of westward voyaging been a land of mystery, a land where it was asserted, and believed, that gold and precious stones might be had for the gathering, and where spices and perfumes abounded. Within its confines were thought to be wonderful cities with walls of gold, fountains that gave perpetual youth to those who laved themselves therein, and gardens in which might be partaken the delights of Eden. Exploration, as we have seen in the first volume of this history of North America, had done much to dispel these golden dreams; yet, despite the knowledge gained in the period through which moved the figures of Cortés, De Soto, and Coronado, the minds of men still invested the South with an unreality that centuries of knowledge hardly took from it. The romance of the elder fables was replaced by that arising from the projects whose phantasies again and again influenced the impressionable and imaginative Latin of the colonization era.

There are substantial reasons for this continuing romance. The New England colonies were of exceedingly limited area; the Middle colonies could not pretend to vast stretches of territory; but the South was, seemingly, limitless. Hundreds of miles to the north it stretched, and westward its bounds were unknown thousands of miles from the landing place of the first colonizers. Deep were its mysteries. Dark forests harbored widespread and numerous tribes of strange savages. In its swamps lurked animals to Europeans unknown, and its waters held fish of astonishing qualities. Over its vast prairies roamed beasts that excited terror or stirred admiration. Climate, too, was not without its influence, and upon the newcomers fell the spell that has universally enthralled those who dwell beneath Southern skies, and the Spirit of the Land took the European invaders captive. Then, too, these first colonizers were not as the men of the North. They did not come to plant gardens, to till fields, to follow the kine to pasture. Theirs was not the intent to build homes. In the opinion of the nations that first contended for its possession, the South was a land to be exploited. Their colonists came upon it as soldiers; they established garrisons, they proposed to get by trading, if they must, but by force if they could not otherwise obtain it, sufficient of the products of the country to reward their enforced sojourn in a wild land. Passages to Cathay were objects more attractive to endeavor than was the cultivation of crops. Diamond reefs and gold mines claimed more attention than mechanical pursuits, and the fur trade was ever the mainspring of frontier activity.

Many of the first colonists reaped what the earlier explorers had sown, a harvest of hate, a terror that caused them to spend more time in subjugation and conciliation than they had first deemed necessary; and others brought upon themselves, by deceit and misapplied force, the antagonism of the native tribes. But with years came experience, and with experience, wisdom; and soon we find the tribes coming into subjections called alliances. In such a period, with such colonists, romance was inevitable. The history of Southern colonization is full of it. Spaniards and Frenchmen, Georgians, Carolinians, and Virginians, all give their share. Conflicts between struggling nations; vast commercial enterprises rivalling the most gigantic of modern capitalistic aggregations in importance; colonization projects that have never been equalled; expeditionary plans that have few compeers; loves that altered the course of colonial history—all these things are bound up with the record of Southern colonization.

In the present volume the great men of the past live again. We range the forests with soldiers and hunters of France and Spain, and seek, as it were, to further the ambitious schemes of conflicting commanders. We sail with colonists that Raleigh sent, and we labor under the rule of the Virginia Company. We are with Oglethorpe and his associates in his Georgian enterprise. But the days of the soldier gave way to the days of the planter; the agriculturist displaced the trapper; the stock raiser, the hunter. The ambitious schemes by which control of waterways was of the greatest importance, because of the carriage of furs, gave place to plans for making the most of the lands available for the raising of tobacco.

The struggle for possession of the southern territory was stilled in the greater struggle to form self-supporting and self-governing colonies. With the supremacy of the English came the dominance of the material and orderly. Even in the South in the later period of colonization we find the realities of life crowding out romance. Whether in Virginia or the Carolinas, in Georgia or the Floridas, or in the far country beyond the Appalachians, the spirit of endeavor is aroused and the way prepared, as is foreshadowed in the later pages of the work before us, for the struggle that is to be described in the volume devoted to the Revolution.

The author has made much of his opportunities. He sets before us the history of the years of colonization in a manner deserving of large praise. With skill and judgment he has given us of the romance, and yet he presents naught but the romance of fact, as he sets before us the activities of the three contending nations and the triple methods by which they pursued their colonial policies. In all this he has, because of his use of source material, and of his wide knowledge of the subject, been able to draw a picture that is fresh and of unusual interest. He has given us a chapter in history that has never been adequately presented. The author is peculiarly fitted by inclination and study for the task of preparing this present volume. His residence in the heart of the South, his intimate acquaintance with its records and those of Spain, France, and England, and his devotion to the period of which this volume treats, have given him a *zeitgeist* that enables him to make an illuminating exposition of the history of Southern Colonization, and because of this I take pleasure in giving the present volume its place in THE HISTORY OF NORTH AMERICA.

GUY CARLETON LEE.

Johns Hopkins University.

AUTHOR'S PREFACE

THE tension preceding the Civil War, the war itself, the problems growing out of it, have prevented the calm thought necessary to the study of Southern foundations. Southern men had other duties, Northern men had not the incentive for such investigations. It would seem, however, that to-day the times are propitious and that the work whose result is contained in the present volume is the task of the hour.

In interest this study will yield to none. It begins with the first attempts by the leading European nations to plant themselves in America; it then exhibits the conflicts of these colonies; it ends with the success and growth of one race. It hinges, so to speak, about Florida, Virginia, and Louisiana, and is a record of the evolution harmonizing the claims which these names represent,—a record of diplomacy, intrigue, and war. Only in connection with the Southern colonies can be understood the power and pertinacity of Spain; for she looked on Raleigh and Ribault, Jamestown, Charlestown, and Savannah alike as intruding on her domain of Florida. Only so, also, can be appreciated the work of La Salle and Iberville, in the teeth of both Spaniard and Englishman; for Louisiana included the whole Mississippi valley, ruled from Mobile, New Orleans, and Fort Chartres, developed by Law and his *Compagnie*. The problem set before the French and Anglo-Saxon races in America was: Whether the Mississippi valley should develop into a French colony, Louisiana, in touch through the Great Lakes with Canada and ruled from the Gulf; or whether it should be a hinterland for British expansion over the Alleghanies from the Atlantic colonies. Trade rivalry played a great part in the solution, but war was, as usual, the final arbiter. Louisiana was the prize of the Seven Years' War not less than were Canada and India. True, the Englishman did only half of the work; he won only the territory east of the Mississippi and afterward even lost Florida back to Spain. But this advance of the Latin at the expense of the Anglo-Saxon is itself a study the more valuable because almost anomalous, and the long life of Spanish Louisiana is a curious subject too much ignored as a factor in American development. For the Latin institutions were not less marked than the Anglo-Saxon.

The Southern colonies present a field of conflict of civilizations found in the same degree nowhere else. Mr. Freeman once said that the history of the panhandle by which Alabama and Mississippi reach the Gulf had perplexed him more than any other district on the earth's surface. The whole Northwest and Southwest are thus within the scope of our investigation, for they were Virginian, Carolinian, or Georgian. Under its charter of 1606 Virginia extended from thirty-four to forty-five degrees of latitude. The curious overlapping of the Plymouth and London subcompanies had no practical result, on account of the collapse of the former enterprise. The gradual carving of other colonies out of Virginia left a large residuum to her in the northwest, but to the south Carolina was not so much carved out as cut off from Virginia, carrying the southwest along with her. Even more than the valleys west of the Alleghanies, the colonies between the mountains and the sea deserve attention, for there grew up Americans out of the English, Scotch, Irish, French, and Germans who came in successive waves, to take root in different spots. It was the Englishman, that wonderful colonizer, who gave the speech and form to the civilization; but it was a civilization modified by absorbing other elements and by the new ground upon which it was worked out. The intermingling of races of different stages of culture produces a mongrel, slow, or unfruitful growth: to some extent the intermarriage of Latin and Indian in Central and South America illustrates both the possibility and slowness of such an advance. In North America we shall find the form assumed to be a leadership of the natives by the French, contrasting with the antipathy of the English toward them. On the other hand, from Babylon and Egypt down, the clashing and intermixture of races at the same degree of advance has produced a higher result, has pushed on human progress. We usually think of the Atlantic settlers as homogeneous, and so indeed they became; but in the days of colonization Scotchmen and Englishmen were not the same, the Scotch-Irish different yet, while all these long regarded the Huguenots and Germans as foreigners. The Englishman in the South assimilated them all, but became himself modified in the assimilation. In the process the presence of Latin and Indian foes kept him at a tension and produced a special form of that adaptability to environment which marks all life, and differentiated the American even from his own ancestral English.

Not only was this race change going on during our period, but in time the natural tendency of Anglo-Saxons to self-government became accentuated by the different interests of the colonies and the mother country. At first it was the great struggle of the liberal Virginia Company with the Stuart kings, then the natural friction between an English proprietor or governor and the local assembly, all important, for all beginnings are, and important too in the political training thus given. In course of time, colonial interests prevailed over ancestral attachment, an American or continental feeling superseded old traditions—and the Revolution came.

The plan of the series forbade the division of this volume into books, but informally the material falls naturally into five parts. The first would relate to the Spanish, French, and English Beginnings, and embrace the first three chapters. A second part would cover British Colonization in the Seventeenth Century, particularly Virginia and Carolina, and their institutions. A third part would concern itself with Louisiana in all its extent, from La Salle to the royal governors, as found in Chapters IX to XIII. The fourth would cover the time of Conflict of Latin and Teuton, in trade and war, with a view of Georgia founded at this period. The concluding part, from Chapter XIX on, would have to do with the Growth of the Anglo-Saxons after the Peace of Paris, not neglecting to look also at the Latin expansion and at the Americanization which prepared the way for the Revolution.

Such is the varied story here portrayed, marked chronologically by the settlement, conflict, and development of races; at any given epoch showing within each race, in cross section as it were, the interplay and growth of its institutions—of politics, religion, social and industrial life.

Instead of limiting our view to Jamestown and Plymouth, therefore, we can see that over against Jamestown should be set St. Augustine and Mobile, the cradles of Spanish Florida and French Louisiana, which also were to help to make up America, and that, even among the British, second only to Virginia in influence was Carolina. Indeed, while in breadth the Southern character may owe more to Virginia, in intensity it looks to Carolina. The later commonwealth of Georgia had an independent English origin, while Kentucky and Tennessee were the second growth, the new start beyond the mountains, of the new Americans, and all three are needed to round out colonization and colonial life.

It is true that when we roll up our map America is but half won. The Indians hold much of the valley east of the Mississippi, the Latins claim all beyond, as well as all on the Gulf. But the Indian lived on sufferance, and the Spaniard was not yet felt to be in the way. Latin and Teuton have been hereditary foes, but Louisiana and Florida were not yet coveted by the Anglo-Saxon; the era of colonization must first give place to one of revolt from England.

In writing this book original sources have, as far as possible, been consulted and liberal use has been made of the accumulation of colonial documents which has for years been going on. If it is possible to write a more satisfactory history now than a quarter-century ago, much is due to the labors of Alexander Brown,—whose incapacitation is a blow to American research,—of Bruce, of Courtenay, and of the lamented McCrady, of C. C. Jones, Waddell, Garrison, of Brymner, Margry, Gayarré, and others, and of historical societies and students. And Heaven bless the local antiquaries, laboring for love of their work and getting no other reward! But for them little history could be written, for little material would be preserved from which to write it. The historian, coming after, sifts their work, gives it the proper perspective,—and enters into their rest. All honor to a too little appreciated kind of patriotism! I have met many of these men and women in my explorations and travels, as well as known them by their works, and I have found them as instructive as the sites they guard from Jamestown to New Orleans. Indeed, I may add, *quorum pars sum*, and I have found that the detailed study of one field has proved the best possible preparation for understanding the others and their relation to each other.

For Spanish and French times I have acquired much new material, in maps and documents, from Spain and France; and the study of British Florida, that interesting if abortive British colony, is almost original, based on the Haldimand Papers and much manuscript material in England. It may not be amiss to add that John Fiske urged the author to take up this as a valuable and neglected field. It is hoped, therefore, that the present volume will tend to unify the beginnings of Southern history and institutions, to show, at least in outline, what a great part was played upon this stage, and how much of American history finds here its genesis or explanation.

PETER JOSEPH HAMILTON.

Mobile, Alabama.

CONTENTS

THE

COLONIZATION OF THE SOUTH

HAMILTON

Copyright, 1903,

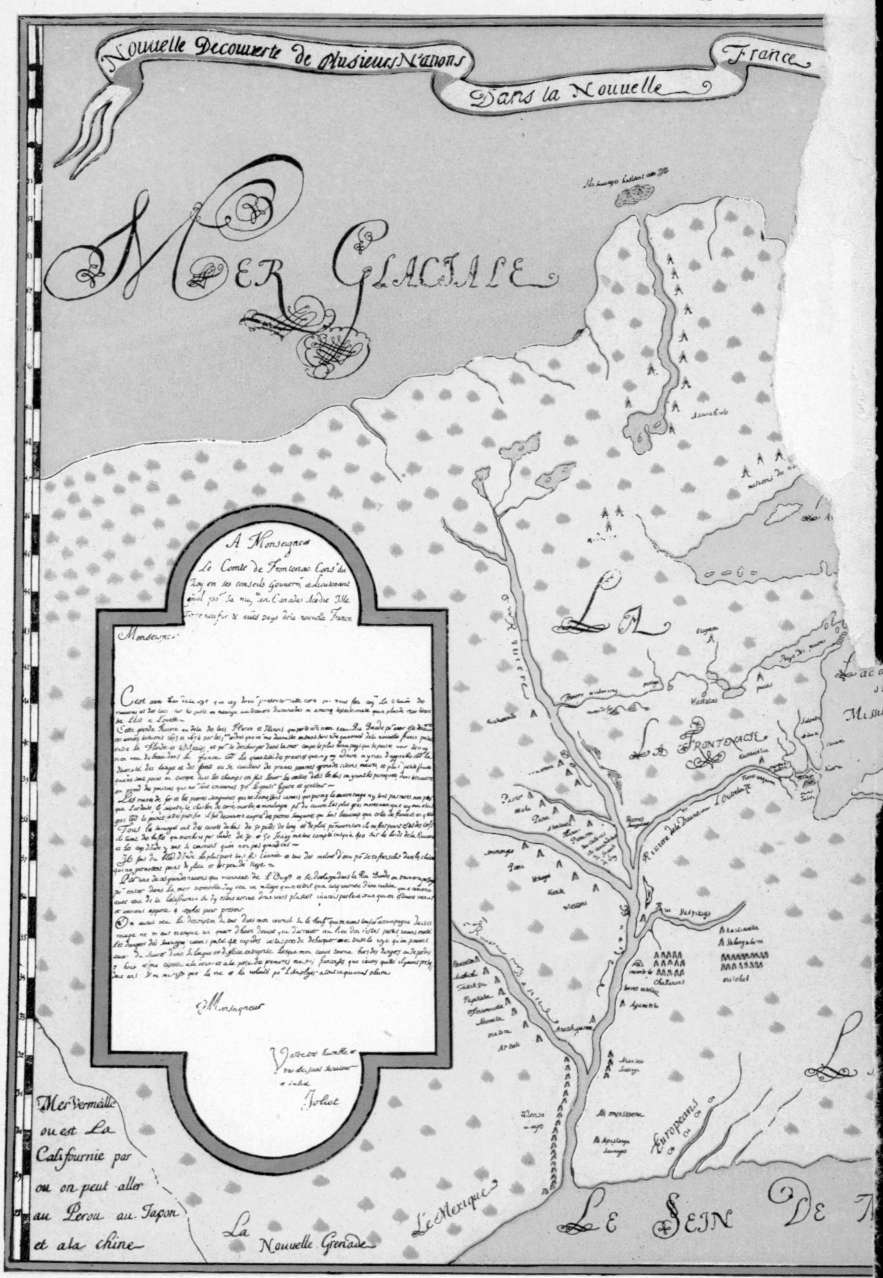

Joliet's map of the Mississippi, dated 1674. *From the*

e Barrie & Sons.

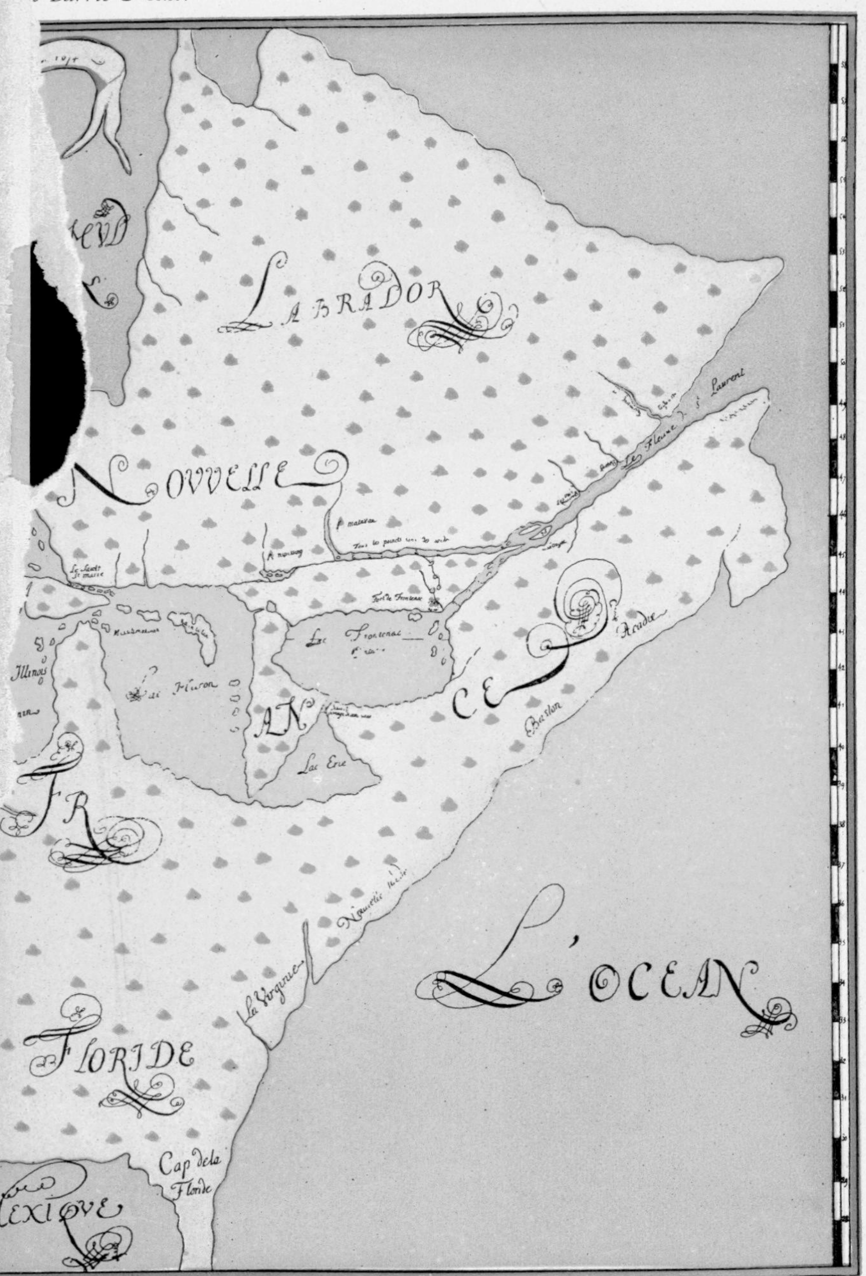

riginal in the Ministère des Affaires Étrangères, Paris.

CHAPTER I

THE SPANISH SETTLEMENT OF FLORIDA

THE restless energy of the Crusades, whether toward the Orient, the south of France, or the south of Spain, led to the adventurous voyages which resulted in the discovery of America, and the gradual exploration of that continent caused hopes of further developments. The energy of discovery was to be transmuted into the energy of colonization. What had been found must be held. From the first, in the more valuable lands of the west there had been settlements. Despite all the endeavors of Spain and Portugal to keep their knowledge to themselves, other countries had learned something. Mediterranean sailors flocked to other ports and carried information with them.

Colonization was no new thing. Every country of Europe was a mixture of old and new races; for the fall of the Roman Empire had been but the colonization of barbarians in the southern countries and on a vast scale. And history was full of it in the past. In prehistoric times, the Phœnicians had created Greece by colonizing her harbors. In classic times, Greece had colonized the south of Italy, and, later, Roman settlements were a recognized means of spreading and perpetuating Roman influence and civilization. More than one city in Europe even derived its name from such colonies. The Teutonic Knights founded Prussia in the same manner. It was the love of novelty, reinforced often by the pressure of overpopulation, compelling overflow into new fields. But colonization had, prior to the fifteenth century, almost always been forcible and had assumed the form of conquest. It was due to coveting the property of some race that was thought to be better off, and was made easier by the fact that civilization either enervates, and so renders its possessors subject to invasion by ruder races, or puts into their hands arms and science which enable them to conquer races lower in the scale. When love of adventure is joined with need of new possessions and with superiority in arms to the possessors, *væ victis!* Such things make up the staple of history, and America was to be no exception.

But America, at least, contained no races fit to cope with Europeans of the sixteenth century; and while at first there were wars of conquest, full of cruelty, they were in South and Central America soon to be terminated in favor of the Spaniards, and in North America to play a subordinate part to commerce. Ancient colonization was a form of conquest; modern, while nominally religious and guided often by crusading zeal, was to be at heart commercial and finally to assume the form of mercantile enterprise. Columbus had hoped to open up the way to the Indies for Spanish commerce, but an important, if secondary, object in his mind was the conversion of the heathen to the true faith. The same spirit prevailed throughout the Spanish exploration of the West Indies and continental America. The monks were no less active than the soldiers in the voyages which subdued Hispaniola and Cuba, as well as in those later on the continent. The presence of the precious metals in large quantity soon made Mexico and Peru the principal objective points of Spanish effort, although the West Indian islands remained always important as ports of call and as commanding the Gulf of Mexico and adjacent seas, as well as for their own products. Cuba had early succeeded Hispaniola as the principal island settlement of Spain, and Havana was the most important of the Gulf ports. From Cuba had been conquered Mexico in 1519, and Mexico in turn became the leading Spanish colony in the New World. It was even called New Spain. Brazil was Portuguese, and Peru could be reached better from the Pacific; so that while the treasure galleons of Spain came to the Isthmus of Panama for their freight of precious bars and ingots, these were brought to Nombre de Dios by mule trains overland from Panama, where they had been collected by fleet from Peru and elsewhere on the Pacific. The result was that on the eastern coast of America Mexico was the leading country, and its harbor of Vera Cruz, at first called San Juan de Ulloa, a port of greater importance even than Cartagena and all other ports after Havana. The importance of Vera Cruz, however, was due to the fact that it was the nearest port to the City of Mexico, for in the early explorations Panuco, the Tampico of to-day, was even better known. Following the Gulf Stream, the homeward route of the Spanish vessels, whether from Panama or Mexico, was by Cuba and not far from the east coast of Florida.

The country named Florida by Ponce de Leon embraced all the territory from Chesapeake Bay to beyond Mississippi River, as well as the peninsula of Florida, but it is a strange as well as an interesting fact that the Spanish explorations produced few good maps, while the accounts of the voyages are so stilted and confused as to make it difficult to identify the peoples or places visited. It would seem to be true, however, that from the earliest explorations the tribal arrangements of the natives were but little unchanged. The Muskhogees occupied the territory from what we call Alabama River almost or quite to the Atlantic Ocean, with an offshoot called the Seminoles extending down into Florida, at whose southern extremity were also the Carlos and Tequestas. West of the Muskhogees were the Choctaws, extending to the Mississippi on the west and to the Gulf at Mobile and Pensacola at the south. There were numberless other small tribes, however, especially near the coasts, whose affinities are difficult to establish, and who for all practical purposes may be regarded as independent. Such were the Apalaches, the Timuquas, and the Yamasis and

Yamacraws further north on the Atlantic. It was perhaps fortunate that the larger tribes lived in the interior and that the newcomers, until they became powerful themselves, had to do mainly with the smaller ones on the coast. For the chiefs of the Choctaws, Creeks, Cherokees, Catawbas, and other great nationalities exercised much more power than the chiefs in the northern part of what has become the United States, and hostility on their part would have made colonization even more difficult than it was.

The Europeans found a degree of barbarism to their advantage, for it is a mistake to think of native America as a wilderness. Although the southern Indians were hunters and required much territory for that purpose, their women were agriculturists and raised vegetables that have ever since remained staples of the country. Maize, peas, squash, and the like were found in abundance. Each of the great tribes had several groups or towns, of scattered wigwams to be sure, but fairly well fixed. If a particular locality became exhausted, they moved to an adjacent spot, retaining the same name and institutions. Cosa, or Coosa, for instance, on the upper Coosa River, had been established for centuries, and many other towns can also be mentioned. Hunting and warring expeditions made some kind of communication necessary, and between neighboring villages were trails and roads, mere bridle paths perhaps, but passable and well known. Such there were also between neighboring tribes, and, taking the country as a whole, there was no great difficulty for the natives to travel by these routes to and from any quarter. These paths or trails were often circuitous; for, as a rule, they followed watersheds, that travellers might be spared the toilsome passage of swamps and the danger of swimming unfordable rivers. The early explorers generally used these roads and trails, and their routes may yet be discovered by making a closer study of the Indian highway system.

In course of time, the Spaniards turned their attention to the mainland of America washed by the Gulf of Mexico and the Atlantic Ocean. They had made their own the West Indies, Central and South America, and were now to explore and in a measure settle the vast country to the north before the other nations of Europe awakened to the importance of Columbus's landfall. They sought gold and in so doing they ran roughshod over the natives, but it is a mistake to think all of them ruthless and cruel. Most of the accounts which have come down to us of the Spanish conquest were written by enemies, and inspired often by religious as well as national hatred, although even the Spaniard Las Casas draws a black enough picture of the havoc wrought. By a study of the reports of the explorers and those who were with them we may get a truer picture of what they did. It will be a scene often harsh enough to modern eyes, but its actors were not modern men. They were Spaniards fresh from the creation of their own country by expulsion of Moors and Jews, proud of their king and looking down on all other countries, and especially filled with zeal for converting to the true Catholic faith the idolaters of the New World. They were determined that within the limits claimed by their monarch there should settle no heretics to disturb the orthodoxy of themselves and ruin the simple-minded natives. This is the keynote of the Spanish rule in North America.

Exploration fades so imperceptibly into colonization that we must recall the names of some Spanish explorers. Of those prominent in the beginning of Florida after the unfortunate Ponce de Leon, who named it, six stand out preëminent. The first is Pineda, sent out by the Spanish governor of Jamaica, who sought the strait supposed to connect the Gulf with the Pacific and thus, after all, provide a water route to China and the other Indies. Instead, he found a bay which he named Espiritu Santo, with a neighborhood thickly populated, for there were no less than forty native settlements within a short compass. Then came De Ayllon, who was more than an explorer. He was granted the government of all the lands he should discover, and discovered and named more than he lived to govern. The first who definitely planned the colonization of Florida was Panfilo de Narvaez, the first who bore the title *adelantado* of the country from the river Palmas to the southern cape of the peninsula, and this under an *asiento* of 1526. So far successful was he thought to be at home that the next year King Philip II. named a governor, or *regidor*, for the first pueblo established by Narvaez. We know his sad story. So far from settling Florida, he was to take to the sea again at Appalachee, and on it to meet his fate; while his follower, Cabeza de Vaca, almost found his on the island of Malhado, and yet, after fleeing from the Charruas to the Abaraes and other Indian tribes, lived to enter Mexico with a few men at last. The next year came the *asiento* with De Soto for the conquest and colonization of the same province, followed by the appointment of at least one *regidor* for a pueblo established by him. His explorations do not now concern us except that they were intended as a basis for colonization. He designed a city on or near the Mississippi as a capital or centre of influence for the Spaniards, but before it was built he ended his life in the charmed limits of Florida.

Here we may pause a moment to remember that while these barren attempts were being made to the north, the mining districts of Central and South America were still pouring their treasures into Spain and building up a lucrative trade with each other. If the other nations of the world had not been active enough to discover the wealth of the west, at least individuals from them made efforts to share in the commerce of the Spanish Main. English and French ships brought and carried away goods from the West Indian islands, and from the cattle trade and smoked beef of Santo Domingo acquired the name *buccaneers*, soon to be of a more sinister meaning. Shut out by law, they entered by force, and received no little encouragement from the Spanish colonists and sometimes from the officials themselves. This trade of freebooting gradually drew to it the most daring spirits of Protestant Europe.

The Calvinists of France, the Reformed of Holland, and the Protestant English forgot their own quarrels in a chance to unite against the hated Spaniard, break his rules, and seize his treasure. In an era when war was almost incessant, the buccaneers became important and occupied a different position from that of pirates now. There was a species of honor among them, and even the Spaniards learned to speak of them with respect. On their side, the Spaniards made no scruple of capturing, imprisoning, and even killing them, thinking thereby to do God service while striking a blow for their monarch. Even in 1549 an English ambassador was able to make out a long list of vessels, cargoes, and sailors captured and still detained in Spain in this manner; and as time went on, the business was more and more profitable and popular. The French at first seemed to have taken the lead, and in a capture of Havana not long afterward put men, women, and children to the sword with such cruelty as to furnish an excuse, but not a reason, for one of the most hateful events in Florida's story.

A Spanish treasure fleet was wrecked by a tropical storm off the mainland, and the viceroy of New Spain, Velasco of good memory, sent Villafañe to investigate. He did not find the treasure, but he became acquainted with the Florida coast and this led directly or indirectly to another plan for colonizing the mainland of North America. The details of De Soto's expedition were well known, and the efforts now made were not so much with the view of finding gold as of preëmpting the land from foreign occupation and of securing harbors which would protect the plate fleets and afford a basis for operations against the buccaneers.

In 1555 came the retirement of Charles V.; and he was succeeded by Philip II., who was equally painstaking, if less brilliant. The Council of the Indies won his assent to appointing Don Luis de Velasco, viceroy of New Spain, to carry out definitely the conquest and colonization of Florida. Velasco prepared three ships, supplied everything necessary, and for destination he selected the land of Cosa as that most praised by the survivors of the expeditions of Narvaez and De Soto. Thus we find that these explorers had not lived in vain, for they determined where was to be the first definite attempt at colonization; for although at some point De Soto had established a pueblo with *regidores*, and at Cosa had left at least two men, nothing had lasted but a memory. And now, in 1559, Velasco made Tristan de Luna captain-general of his *armada* and of Florida, and sent with him Juan Ceron as master of camp, and fifteen hundred soldiers, besides women and children. Of the twelve captains, we are told that half had been in Cosa in the previous expeditions. The army marched to Vera Cruz, where final instructions were given and the fleet set sail. On August 14th they landed at a port which they called Santa Maria, with a good bay, and Tristan sent back glowing despatches. He explored along the coast and up the river, when a terrible hurricane dispersed and wrecked the entire fleet, with loss of everyone aboard; but, undismayed, he sent his *sargento maior* with four companies to penetrate further, for with no means of retreat he must press forward to reach the fertile land of Cosa. They proceeded forty days through uninhabited land to Gran Rio, probably Alabama River, which they followed, and found a pueblo abounding in maize. By an interpreter they learned that it was called Nanipacna, and had formerly been larger until destroyed by men resembling themselves. Thus by poetic justice the Spaniards had reached a solitude created by Spaniards! Tristan, on receiving word, came with all his forces by river and land, and on his arrival named the place Santa Cruz de Nanipacna. So large a party soon ate up all the supplies. The men had to live on bitter acorns, mashed first in salt and then in fresh water, while their women and children could eat only leaves and shoots of trees.

Where Nanipacna was situated is perhaps uncertain, but the indications point to the Mauvila of De Soto, and, at all events, Tristan determined to leave its desolation and seek for Cosa. To blaze the way, he sent his *sargento maior* and two hundred soldiers, and with them went two priests. The accounts of the distance vary, but may be reconciled by supposing that they wandered around for two hundred leagues before reaching the river Olibahali, with huts and villages of the Indians on its banks. Then they came to the principal pueblo of the province of Cosa, with its twenty houses; and the Spaniards, acting for once with moderation, were well received. They learned that De Soto's deserters were long since dead, and, alas! the priests could make little progress in converting the natives. Instead of going back to Tristan, however, the *sargento maior* was persuaded to assist the warriors of Cosa against a tribe called Napochies, who had recently revolted. Invading the country about the Gran Rio, the allies found it deserted and that the Napochies had taken refuge near the river called Ochechiton. This the invaders forded waist deep, and the firearms of the Spaniards brought the rebels to terms, so that tribute of fruits and the like was again arranged. Meantime, Tristan had deemed his advance party dead, and with his eight hundred people returned to port, leaving directions buried in a pot. The distress was so great that Feria, one of his priests, obtained permission to seek aid in Cuba, and receiving none there went on to Vera Cruz. On the other hand, the *sargento maior* finally reached the coast; but his men so exaggerated the hardships of the journey that no one thought further of going to Cosa. Tristan seems to have occupied his time largely in trying to enforce discipline, and the records are filled with accounts of his severity. At least one soldier was punished with death, and many others were condemned, although they were so numerous that it was impossible to carry out the sentence. Ceron was the leader of the opposition, and it was only after five months that, taking advantage of Palm Sunday, Father Anunciacion managed to secure concord. A dramatic scene it must have been when upon the elevation of the Host the general softened and asked pardon of those whom he had offended; for Ceron and the others were also on their knees, and a thorough reconciliation was effected.

Their encampment was in effect the first Spanish colonization of Florida, and its exact location would be a matter of considerable interest. It is generally thought of as the origin of Pensacola, but if so the settlement was certainly much nearer the Gulf than the present city. Pensacola Bay was always afterward known to the Spaniards as Santa Maria, and there is little reason to doubt that this colony was located somewhere between the bays now known as Mobile and Pensacola. No mention is made in the sources of any permanent works, although it was characteristic of the Spaniards to build of solid materials; and it is quite possible that some rude remains, and in particular a canal affording an easier outlet from Mobile Bay to the Gulf, may date from this time. It is indeed probable that in addition to the port first occupied the colony had another site, for we read that they finally proceeded overland on horses to a different harbor; but, at all events, the two were not far apart, and the rude peninsula between the two bays named probably embraced the scene of Tristan's colonization.

The result of Father Feria's mission was that Villafañe came as Governor of Florida, with special instructions to explore the eastern coast, and upon his arrival there were long and earnest discussions as to carrying out the old enterprise. Some desired to make a road to New Spain, but the upshot was that Villafañe took off most of the colonists, famished and discouraged, and landed them at Havana. Only Tristan and some personal adherents remained, sending word to the viceroy how to make the colony effective, and finally even Tristan received command to return. This he did with great reluctance and embarked for Havana, whence he passed to Mexico. And when he sailed came the end of the first definite colonization of the mainland of Florida. It had not resulted in a permanent settlement, nor in securing a port effectual for the protection of the coast and plate fleets against foreigners and buccaneers. Its three years' duration had only thrown a little light upon geography and natural history and named one or more harbors on the north coast of the Gulf.

Passing around to the Atlantic coast, however, Villafañe, in the name of the king, took possession of the coast and point of Santa Helena, already named by De Ayllon and to become famous in after days. But there was for the present no thought of further settling Florida. The Spaniards came to think of it as haunted by evil spirits, and a decree of the king seemed to sanction their dread by prohibiting every form of expedition to the country. The only improvement Tristan had made on the ill success of his predecessors was in escaping with his own life.

In the meantime there was preparing in France an expedition to contest Spain's right to this very country of Santa Helena, now Port Royal in South Carolina; and with an easy identification of the Protestant French with the freebooting corsairs, Spain was to attempt their extermination. The expedition of Ribault can better be told in another chapter, but here must be noted the work of his opponent in other and more creditable lines.

The year that Pineda was discovering the bay of Espiritu Santo there was born at Avilés, near the north coast of Spain, Pedro Menendez, called De Avilés to distinguish him from others of the name. He served as a cabin boy, and early acquired that love of the ocean which has made him one of the heroic figures of Spanish history. To him, says an admirer, Spain owes a monument, history a volume, and the Muses an epic. Early employed at sea, he once saved Charles V., went to England with Philip II. at his marriage, and became a great sailor in the Atlantic service of his country. The business of the buccaneers had grown so much and become so well organized that about this time it was usual for treasure ships coming from America to set out only at certain seasons of the year and under the guard of men-of-war. Of this *armada* Menendez was made captain-general, and won the hearty approval of Velasco in America

WINGATE COLLEGE LIBRARY
WINGATE, N. C.

and of King Philip in Spain in his efforts against the buccaneers. He was not so acceptable to the Casa de Contratacion at Seville. This institution was founded in 1503 to handle matters pertaining to the growing trade with America, and gradually it obtained or assumed extensive powers connected with navigation. There is no doubt that it facilitated the upbuilding of the Spanish marine, and it was the envy of other countries. Its selection of admirals, or of generals, as they were still called, had lately been somewhat unfortunate, however, and this was in part the reason for the king's taking this appointment to himself. The Casa hampered Menendez all that it could, but in the end he was successful.

From the fateful year 1565 date not only the capitulation and *asiento* for Menendez's colonization and conquest of Florida, and an inventory of the formidable *armada* prepared for that purpose, but a number of decrees and regulations affecting the subject. The settlers were to import and export for ten years without duties what was necessary for their well-being, while Menendez received several benefits himself. Thus he was granted twenty-five leagues square in Florida forever, a license to transport thither free of duty five hundred slaves, a *cedula* gave him the right of two *pesquerias* [fisheries], one of pearls and the other of fishes, and he was to participate in all the profits, mines, and quarries. Thus rewarded in advance, and yet in such a way that his reward would be valueless unless he was successful, he set sail, and, touching at Porto Rico, on August 28th, St. Augustine's day, he saw the land of Florida.

In the early days of September he landed soldiers and colonists while manœuvring in stormy weather before attacking the Huguenots at Fort Caroline; and while he was fighting there, his representatives were building a fort. Padre Mendoza remained, and says that they were well received by the Indians, who gave them a large house, belonging to a cacique, situated near the river, and that the Spaniards built an intrenchment around it, in which they mounted bronze guns. Gradually, a palisaded fort, triangular in shape, arose nearly opposite the inlet by which he entered, and a short distance below was the beginning of the town, named St. Augustine, from the day of arrival in Florida. Bayous bounded the settlement to the north and south, but the site was sufficiently high to secure the place from inundation, while opposite it the long, low island of Anastasia, sandy and covered with a short growth of oaks and underbrush, protected it from the force of ocean storms.

After his sanguinary success over the French and the settlement of St. Augustine, Menendez departed for Cuba to obtain supplies. Here he found himself hampered by Osorio, the governor, and only by pledging his jewels and decorations could he obtain the means he needed. The next year he explored the coast further to the north and south. De Ayllon had gone over somewhat the same route forty odd years before, enslaving the natives and naming places; and now Menendez acted in a more statesmanlike manner, and founded several settlements. His activity extended from far up the Atlantic coast, possibly Chesapeake Bay, which was known even to De Ayllon as Santa Maria, to the extreme southern coast of Florida, whose islands were already called Martires from the number of explorers whose lives were sacrificed by the natives. Menendez discovered a safe harbor, which he considered of great importance for shipping and especially for the plate fleet from Mexico, and entered into a treaty with the Indians, who called themselves Carlos; but he does not seem to have made a permanent settlement among them, unless the fort of San Anton is to be regarded as such. It is recorded that this fort had one hundred soldiers and guarded the Cape of Martires and the Bahama channel. The Indians were warlike, friendly rather to the French, which must have been due to the buccaneers, or to the French in the neighboring island of Santo Domingo, where they were increasing in number. The furthest settlement to the north seems to have been Santa Helena, where Menendez built the fort of San Felipe, with one hundred soldiers. This was a favorite colony of the Spaniards, both on account of the beautiful location of the port and of the friendliness of the Indians.

These were outlying posts, and after the destruction of San Mateo by Gourgues the others lay principally in the immediate neighborhood of St. Augustine. The fort at the town itself was then also called San Agustin, the principal post of Florida, designed especially to guard the Bahama passage. Somewhat below was a block house, or similar structure, with fifty soldiers, at the inlet of Matanzas, so named from the slaughter of the Huguenots, and further yet was Nocoroco, between the waters leading to Matanzas and those to Mosquito Inlet. The remaining fort named in the archives was San Pedro on the island of Tacatacoru, some twenty leagues from St. Augustine, guarding San Mateo and the Bay of Ballenas, both good ports.

All these forts were in the shape of triangles and were made of wood and earth, supplied with the necessary artillery and soldiers. They were the origin and the defence of the Spanish settlements. From them went out an influence among the Indians, and gradually other colonies, which in the palmy times of Spain amounted to a very real colonization of Florida.

For our present purposes what we now know as Pensacola and Appalachee may be left out of account, for the one had been abandoned and the other was less a Spanish post than the seat of a flourishing tribe of Indians, whose influence was rather upon nomenclature than on colonization. Among the smaller settlements may be mentioned Santa Lucia, or Ais, peopled and fortified by Menendez in the same year as St. Augustine, and San Juan de Pinos somewhat nearer, of about the same date, both dependencies of the capital. All told, the Spaniards were to count the province or colony of Carlos in the south; St. Augustine, in the east; Guale, in what we call Georgia, which was somewhat later to have as a capital St. Simon; Orysta, about Santa Helena; and

Chicora, extending indefinitely to the north. Their claim was not only that De Ayllon discovered Chicora, but that in 1521 he had commenced to colonize it under his patents. Certain it seems that at some time, more likely in that of Menendez, there was a Spanish settlement near the Bay of Santa Maria at what was afterward called Jamestown Island, where lived Spaniards and their slaves.

Next to St. Augustine the principal settlement was that at Santa Helena, whose history also goes back to De Ayllon, who named it. Menendez fortified it and was often there. A plan shows that Fort San Felipe lay on the river and was shaped something like a boat. In the rear, connected by gates, was a building comprising sleeping apartments, protected of course, while in front was a triangular platform, with cannon mounted on carriages, and outside are buildings, one for women and having two stories. The drawing is rude and somewhat symbolic, but the size of the houses and the presence of women indicate a permanent settlement. From the fort of San Felipe, Menendez wrote at least one lengthy and important letter to the Spanish monarch, and it was from there in 1566 were undertaken the two expeditions of Juan Pardo for the better knowledge of the country. He left Santa Helena with two hundred and forty-eight soldiers, and after great hardships arrived at a place called Guatari, on Savannah River, but was recalled by a letter stating that the fort was in danger of attack by the French. His relations with the natives were more kindly than usual with the Spaniards, and they showed some disposition to embrace the Catholic faith and acknowledge the sovereignty of Spain. Therefore, Menendez sent him out a second time, with instructions to convert the natives and build necessary forts. On this occasion he proceeded two hundred and sixty leagues and lacked a few days' journey of reaching the frontier of New Spain, being well received by the chiefs. He mentions Cossa, Tasquiqui, and Trascaluza,—the last the westernmost place in Florida,—so he must have crossed the paths of De Soto and Tristan. To secure what he had gained he built at the request of the natives the forts of Joado, Guiomae, Lameco, Cauchi, and Guatari, returning successfully to Santa Helena, where he made full written reports. Unfortunately, subsequent events blotted out the remembrance of his discoveries, and we cannot now locate many of the places he mentions, but he was in the Tennessee mountains and traversed what is now called Georgia, Florida, Alabama, and Mississippi. The expedition impressed Menendez, for almost his last plan was to build a palace in Guatari, or at Canos, near Santa Helena and equally praised by Pardo.

Menendez himself explored St. John's or San Mateo River for fifty leagues, to such purpose that on future occasions the Spaniards became the arbiters in the Indian disputes despite the old leaning of the natives toward the French. It is remarkable that they had such defective conceptions of that river. It rises far to the south, runs northwardly a few miles west of St. Augustine, some of its waters almost interlacing with those of the Suwanee leading to the west coast, and thus forms a means of communication with much of the peninsula. The early maps give no indication of its course; they sustain the impression that with the exception of Pardo, and possibly of Menendez himself, the Spaniards explored only a short distance from the coast.

Menendez was indefatigable in his efforts for Florida. In 1568 he had been made Governor of Cuba, and in Havana he effected reforms and improvements, among them instituting a college where Florida and other Indians were educated. He appreciated the necessity for obtaining laborers instead of gentlemen, but in 1573 the need for colonists forced the government to send also from Mexico and other colonies those who had been condemned to banishment, deserters, and even galley convicts. We read, however, even in this same year of fifty men with their families who were to come from Asturia in Spain, one hundred from the Azores, fifty from Seville, and one hundred Portuguese laborers, marking a gradual and steady inflow of population into the new colony. The expenses were paid by money sent from New Spain, thus avoiding the dangers of carrying the bullion to Spain and back again; at one time four thousand ducats were ordered; at another, Vera Cruz was to remit Menendez annually a certain sum.

In this year the boundaries of Florida were extended westwardly to Panuco River, and among the last-recorded wishes of Menendez was that he might go back to Florida to spend his days in saving souls. He never quite gave up the idea impressed on him by the learned Urdaneta that there extended from the Bay of Santa Maria to the waters of China a strait through Florida. Many tales were told of this passage, and Menendez never ceased to impress upon his king the necessity of seizing and fortifying it before some other nation found it out. But there is a limit to the activity of even a Menendez; and while at the head of the greatest *armada* Spain had assembled up to that time, destined possibly for England, he died at Santander, September 17, 1574.

Despite this event, the colony of Florida, gradually developing into several districts, became more and more firmly established. None of Menendez's successors equalled him, and in the several forts from time to time we find distrust if not dissension. Francis Drake in 1586 was even able through the treachery of deserters to attack and destroy St. Augustine, and the garrison with the inhabitants took refuge in the old fort of San Mateo. But Drake gained little spoil, and the Spaniards immediately rebuilt and reoccupied the place. We have plans of what it looked like a few years later. Thus, there is one of a square fort, with platform, embrasures, and mounted cannon, and to the rear is a separate division for munitions, also fortified. A striking feature of this rather crude drawing is the representation of the sentinels, all pacing away from the sea. Those to the north are called day guards, and those toward the town, night. They look as if they are on dress parade, each with hand on sword, and a heavy arquebus on the right shoulder. The uniform seems to be a jaunty one of shoes and hose, doublet and coat, while a hat with feathers completes the attire. Spears are seen leaning against the walls or in a crotch, and arquebuses stand to one side in a rack, indicating the arquebusiers and lancers of that day. The boats, too, are characteristic, if more symbolical than correct in details. Each is three-masted, with ratlines, and carries one cannon in front and three at the side. Their pennants are two-pointed, and the masts, like the houses, show crosses at the top.

From the same year, 1595, dates a large plat, differing in some details and showing more of the surrounding country. Thus, the fort is triangular, but with bastions at the angles, while five hundred paces away is the little town, with boats tied to a rude plank wharf. We find a fortified *cuerpo de guardia*, the house of the general, a church with four or more bells in a detached belfry, and to the rear, not far from San Sebastian Creek, we see where live the Augustinians. There seems to be a palisade along the beach, and much of the land back of the buildings is taken up with gardens. Behind the fort a thousand paces is the Indian pueblo of Nombre de Dios, of huts, some with roofs and some rounded, and across the San Sebastian, near the Augustinians, is another Indian settlement, bearing the name of Sebastian. Beyond we find only bayous, marshes, and woods, indicated by symbolic marks for trees and grass.

It is interesting to study the Spanish method of colonization. It is natural, in taking possession of a new country, for the occupation to be at first military and then gradually to change into civil. We see this in the old division of the Roman provinces. When first conquered they were under military rule and known as imperial provinces; while after the country had become quiet and civilized, they were turned over to proconsuls and called senatorial. The American conquest of the Philippines presents the same picture. With the Spaniards, however, the procedure hardly got so far, for the occupation cannot fairly be said ever to have progressed beyond the military condition. It is true that a distinction between the military and political departments was known. The military occupancy was called a *presidio*, governed by a commandant of varying titles, while a civil or political settlement was called a *ciudad*. But even where there was no real danger of warfare the soldiers predominated, and the same man was often both civil and military governor. Particularly was this true of the widely scattered settlements in Florida. The government may be said to have been practically military throughout, and military in the sense and under the regulations of Charles V.; for Spain never progressed beyond his standard, and subsequent kings sought merely to adapt this rather than make new rules to suit the time. Add to this the fact that the age of Charles V. was the Golden Age of Spain. It seemed unpatriotic to attempt to improve on it.

There was one aspect of Spanish civilization which was not military. No people in Europe were more religious and none were more devoted to Catholic rites and doctrines. The country had practically been created by the crusade against the Moors, and as a consequence the priesthood acquired power unexampled in the rest of Europe. Heresy of all kinds, Jewish or Protestant, was relentlessly crushed out. A type of character was formed which considered purity of belief the greatest thing in the world. To modern eyes it created a zeal which was not only one-sided, but cruel; and yet therein was the secret of its success. Its rulers sought to merit heaven by making earth a hell. With the soldier went the priest, and no expedition in search of American gold departed without instructions and means for the conversion of the savages. If they did not conform, they were to be killed or enslaved, for to the Spanish mind this was a lesser evil. To this effect was the proclamation of Narvaez. For if slain they would at least not contaminate others. And yet it may well be that history has laid more stress on the harsh side of the Spanish conquests than is deserved. It is impossible to read the story of the fathers who accompanied the colonists and devoted their lives to the conversion of the natives, without a feeling of admiration. They abandoned everything that was dear to man, with the aim and hope of doing good to the ignorant and often cruel natives of the New World. While priests always accompanied the soldiers, soldiers did not always go along with the priests. In the outlying districts near every fort there would gradually be built chapels for the natives, and these were centres not of religious work alone. The fathers would teach the Indians whom they could influence how to cultivate the soil and the simpler forms of handiwork and manufacture, for their method with the Indians was the same in Florida as it was in Texas and California. The defect was that they did not teach them self-reliance. If left to themselves, these converts generally starved or relapsed into barbarism. And yet at least one whole tribe became thoroughly Christianized, a tribe of importance in many ways. The Apalaches had suffered from De Soto and had seen Narvaez build his craft on their shores, and later they had enjoyed the ministrations of the devoted Spanish priests. Their greatness is attested by the fact that they have given their name to a bay and several rivers, and even to the eastern continental range of America, whence they obtained gold. They were to be the chief fruits of Spanish efforts to civilize the natives.

At the beginning there were three missions of more or less importance. The first was in 1566, when the Franciscans began their work. Of them Father Martinez, who was one of the best known, was killed by the Indians near the river St. John's while exploring the coast in a small boat. Two years later others divided themselves among the missions of Carlos, Tocolaga, Tequesta, Orysta, and Guale, but they were to attain little success. In 1570 there was a third expedition, and then we have a long letter from one of the padres who had been in Orysta, almost giving up hope of converting the savages; for they were too migratory and resented anything said against the Devil. The next year a renegade neophyte named Luis led his savage kinsmen and killed eight or more padres, some dying in the celebration of the Mass, some while blessing their murderers. Of course, Menendez severely punished the offenders, but the cause of religion almost stood still. A short time before, the Theatines had begun to labor in Guale and Santa Helena, and were able to report much pleasure at the progress of Christianity in that direction. Dominicans and Franciscans also worked at different points on the coast and in the interior, and the Franciscans built the convent in St. Augustine, which lasted throughout the Spanish rule. And yet, despite the large number of converts in Guale, true savages still, they, near the end of the century, revolted and slaughtered all the good padres. It would be a sad pleasure to detail the perseverance of the missionaries under such sufferings—sufferings unsurpassed anywhere. Ultimately they won the hearts and, we may trust, the souls of many; but at the beginning the Indians seem to have visited on them, fearlessly going about unarmed on their sacred missions and doing only good, the hatred which men of the Stone Age had learned for those who wielded weapons of iron. And yet, we must remember that the cruelty and cunning which we find and detest among the Indians was but that generally found among savages of their grade of culture. With the improvement of weapons and customs comes the improvement of morals, and it is always difficult for the civilized man to judge fairly those lower in the scale. The Spanish soldiers made no such attempt, but some of their leaders did, and the priests were beyond praise.

The Spanish relations with the natives about them differed entirely from that of the English when they later settled further north. It has been suggested that the Indians influenced the English more by being their constant enemies, and thus enforcing vigilance and energy, than in any other way. To the south, we have the anomalous fact that the Spaniards treated the natives with more harshness and yet ultimately secured the greater influence over them.

Slavery was not unknown among the Indians themselves, and when the Spaniards made servants of natives captured in war it was not felt to be unusual or oppressive. The same thing is done to this day in Africa, and has been practised in the beginnings of all history. In Florida the system had few of the cruel features seen in the Spanish islands. The worst the foreigners did with the natives was to make them bear burdens and cultivate the soil, while in the West Indies they were divided up by *repartimientos* and forced to work in the mines, where their spirits drooped and they died like sheep. There it was that the humane bishop Las Casas conceived the plan of importing from Guinea negroes to do the work which the native Indians were unable to endure. Thus it was that negroes were brought to the Western Hemisphere. The seed planted produced a much larger tree than the bishop intended, and he lived to regret giving the advice; but at least it did some good to the Indians, and, despite Isabella, was ultimately adopted by the government for the development of its American colonies. Although it started in the West Indies, the system ultimately spread to the continent, and in Florida as elsewhere we early find negro slaves.

The industries of the colonists were governed by the circumstances surrounding them. Agriculture was a necessity. The vegetables and fruits most favored were those native to the soil, and adopted from the Indians; but oranges and figs the Spaniards brought with them, by way of the West Indies. Carpenters and masons were equally necessary; but few other industries existed. As might be expected, therefore, the government and church buildings were substantial, while there were few or none of any pretensions in private hands. It is the forts, the *cabildos*, and churches which have survived and are representative of the Spanish times.

Thus Florida had been firmly won and the Spanish power was supreme, not only around the Gulf of Mexico, but in the islands and passes which guarded its entrance, and this was ever the aim of Spanish policy. It was not so much greed of territory, although that is human and not less Anglo-Saxon than Latin, but it was the patent necessity of protecting what for the time being were the most valuable countries of the world and of keeping possession of so much of the mainland as might make them secure. No passage to China had yet been discovered, but neither the Spaniards of this age nor other nations for almost a century to come could be certain that the great bays of the Atlantic coast, like the Chesapeake, did not, after all, run through to what was called the South Sea. The first conflict was with the French while St. Augustine was being founded, and then came a longer struggle with England. The country had been won by Spain in her prime, and was to be defended step by step with tenacity as long as any of it should remain to her.

CHAPTER II

FRENCH FLORIDA

France has played a great part in the history of Europe for so many centuries that it seems strange to think of her as not taking the lead in colonization. During the time of formation of nationalities through the growth of the kingly power at the expense of the nobles, she enjoyed the advantage of having such kings as Louis XI. and his successors. The trade from the East had never ceased, even during the Middle Ages, passing mainly through Venice, Genoa, Germany, and the Rhine country to the north, while some came through Marseilles and the Rhone region, developing Provence and the east of France. The growth of Paris—the nucleus of modern France—was due largely to its nearness to Flanders, with which the Seine, and thus indirectly the Rhone, readily communicated by portages,—a system of transportation which the French were so largely to make use of in a new world. The Low Countries, next after the mines of America, made Charles V. The prominence of France in the Crusades and her nearness to the Moors permeated her with the new learning and new science; and when the religious ferment began, nowhere was it more gladly received and more consistently thought out. Marot translated the Psalms in a version which immediately became popular, and Lefevre made the Gospels familiar in the French tongue. It would seem as if everything was ripe for France to assume the leading rôle in the changes taking place in religion and discovery. But French civilization was fundamentally Latin, and commercial ties through Marseilles and the south were strong with the Mediterranean countries. It was not unnatural, therefore, for the French awakening to show itself internationally interested in Italy, the seat of the old religion and civilization, whose mediæval development had been into numerous republics, which in their old age had become rich but warring principalities. The invasion of Italy by Charles VIII. in 1494, marked not by blood, but by chalk, had concentrated French enthusiasm on conquest in that direction rather than in discoveries of as yet doubtful utility in the western seas. And yet, as Charles V. of Germany and Spain had interests in the same quarter, Francis I. became involved in a death struggle with the emperor, who used the products of his American mines to deprive France of her new influence in Italy as well as to keep her out of the west. The reign of Francis was a great one for his country in intellectual and religious respects, despite the defeats abroad, and the reign of his son Henry II. continued its traditions. War with Spain lasted almost incessantly, but the line began to be drawn at home against the adherents of what was called the Reformed religion. They began to be called Huguenots, and met with discouragement and disfavor in every way that the Church and State could show. Religious persecution commenced, and the cruelties in Spain were not left uncopied; and yet, influenced more especially by John Calvin at Geneva, the Reformed grew in numbers, zeal, and influence. It became uncertain whether France would ultimately be Reformed or Catholic. Great families were converts to the new faith, and among them the Châtillons and Montmorencys were more or less openly its advocates.

Of course, with its vast influence and wealth at stake, the old religion was not slow to do all possible to suppress the new. The queen, the famous Catherine de' Medici, with true Italian zeal for her church and unscrupulousness of methods, and the semiroyal family of Guise, with its able duke and astute cardinal, came to the front on the Catholic side; while Gaspard de Coligny, of the Châtillon family, was even more than the lukewarm Bourbons the leader of the Reformed.

Both Guise and Coligny filled high offices of State. Coligny was not only in the army, but was made Admiral of France and as such cast a careful eye abroad over French commerce. For years the sailors of Dieppe had made voyages to South as well as North America. Even in 1504 the French had been in the port of Bahia, and five years later Brazilian savages had been shown in Rouen; while Verrazano in 1524 and Cartier ten years later voyaged to North America for Francis I. French captains, like all others of the day, were sometimes piratical, and one even sacked Pernambuco. The policy of Francis I. had been vacillating, but in 1543 he declared the western sea to be open to his subjects. During the middle of the reign of Henry II., Coligny thought that, despite Portuguese claims, it would be a good plan for French commerce and influence to settle a colony in Brazil, while the troubled state of France from religious causes seemed to make it easy to find recruits. So in 1555 he sent out under Villegagnon, a monk, an expedition for that purpose. Disputes and the cruelty of their commander soon completed the ruin of the colony, and despite reinforcements it was finally abandoned after four unhappy years. Villegagnon went home, but his successor was hardly better, and the Portuguese at last found means to destroy such of the French as had not returned.

Meantime much had happened in France. In 1559, Francis II., husband of Mary, the child Queen of Scots, ascended the throne, to die almost immediately, and to be succeeded the next year by his brother, Charles IX., under whom civil and religious dissensions were to reach their height. The Guises lost their influence, for Catherine, powerless and neglected in the time of her husband, was determined to rule in the name of her sons. The result, however, was that she had to court the influence now of the Catholic, now of the Reformed party. Looking back with the light of after history, it seems clear that France, from its origin and institutions, could not become other than Catholic, and it appears strange to us that such a clear-headed man as Coligny could not see this. The Reformed religion prevailed in the west and south of France, possibly one-third of the country, while the rest, including Paris, remained faithful to the old teaching. But this developed only later. At first the ferment was everywhere and one could hardly tell where it was strongest. To its adherents the new teaching was so clearly that of the Bible that they could not believe it would not finally prevail. Even among the old faith were many who recognized abuses and hoped for a Gallican Church, which, somewhat like that of England, while independent of Rome, would be broad enough to shelter Frenchmen of all shades of religious belief.

The Admiral of France was one of the last to give up this hope, and yet the present dissension and suffering were such that, despite the failure of the Brazil experiment, he sought another refuge for such of the Reformed as would care to exile themselves. And the new attempt would have also another object, for it was quite statesmanlike to make the parties at home forget their differences by uniting against a common foe abroad. From the time of Francis I. there was no question that the principal enemy of France was Spain, and Spain's preponderance was such that through family alliance, and even actual possession, her king had territories on both sides of France and held that country almost in a vice. Add now to this the fact that Philip II. was anxious to intervene in the religious dissensions and was ready to pour forty thousand tried troops into France to aid the Catholic side. It is true that the Reformed could call on England and on German princes, but the result would be civil war. This actually happened, but it was as wise as it was patriotic to try to avoid this and unite France against Spain. After differing religionists had fought alongside, their respect for each other would surely lead to some compromise satisfactory to both. The admiral had commanded in Picardy as well as in Paris, and was later to urge that the Spaniards be attacked in the Low Countries, their most valuable possession. Expansion in this direction has been the dream of France for ages, and in a measure it may be said to have begun with Coligny. But the time was not ripe, and his more definite plan was to settle a colony in what was known as Florida, which would take Spanish attention and efforts away from France, and at the same time unite all Frenchmen against the common foe.

This time Coligny selected a Huguenot to command, Jean Ribault by name, to whom also we are indebted for an account of the expedition in the shape of a report to the admiral. The party was made up of soldiers, gentlemen, and workmen, all Protestants, and a few of them survivors of the Brazil experiment. On February 18, 1562, they sailed from Havre, and, after waiting on the weather, boldly attempted a direct course instead of going like the Spaniards by way of the West Indies. On April 30th they sighted Cape Cañaveral, which they patriotically called Cap François, and sailed on northwardly, charmed with the perfume and beauty of the scene. On the 1st of May they discovered a magnificent river, increasing in depth after they passed the bar, and from the day they named it the May. They spent some time in intercourse with the natives, whom they found almost naked, painted with devices in blue, red, and black, but pleasant and hospitable in their manner. They were armed with bows and lances, the strings being of leather, and the arrows of reed tipped with fishes' teeth. At an appropriate place the French erected a column of stone engraved with the arms of the King of France, and two days later sailed to the north, finding a number of harbors and islands, to which they gave names. One of the rivers was that which they knew of already as the Jordan, for although there was at this time no Spanish settlement on the Atlantic, much of the coast had been named by

De Ayllon and others after him. The expedition of Ponce de Leon had, it is said, been undertaken to discover the river Jordan, wherein he could bathe and become young again. Ribault had no such purpose, but took possession in the name of the king, erecting another column, engraved like the one set up in the river May. He mentions the province of Chicora, called by him Checere, whose name is mentioned by De Ayllon as of Indian origin. The Jordan, with its harbor, which he named Port Royal, was that named by De Ayllon as Santa Helena, and in this very year taken in possession by Villafañe for the King of Spain. Ribault seems to have known or cared nothing for this, and, delighted with the vines and other vegetation, he made a settlement there of thirty gentlemen, soldiers, and mariners. They built a fort on the north side of an island in an exposed situation, naming it Charlesfort. Then in June he sailed northwardly, exploring to the fortieth degree, when on account of stormy weather he returned with his fleet to France.

The Indians were friendly and brought the colonists game, vegetables, and fruits in abundance, and even silver from the mountains, so that the summer passed agreeably; and yet there was the same neglect of the future that there had been in Brazil. Having sown nothing, there was nothing to reap, and when the winter came they almost starved. Fire destroyed their houses, and dissension their peace. Pierria, who was in command, hanged one mutineer and banished another, but finally the colonists rose and murdered him. No help or even news had come from France in a year, and they set to work to fell trees and build a rude vessel to return home. For tar they used resin, for ropes vines, for sails their own clothing, and with characteristic improvidence they took insufficient provisions. During a calm in the middle of the ocean they finished their last supplies, and cast lots who should die to furnish a meal to the survivors. The one whom Pierria had banished was the unfortunate man, and thus they subsisted until, in sight of England, a privateer rescued them and took them to London.

They had not been forgotten, but the hopes and plans of the admiral for war against Spain had been frustrated. Hardly had the Edict of January, 1562, recognized the rights of the Reformed and allowed them to worship according to their own belief, when Guise stumbled on a praying congregation at Vassy and massacred them out of hand. The result was the civil war which the admiral had done so much to avoid. France became instantly two hostile camps, with Guise as leader of the Catholics, Coligny of the Reformed. The superior generalship of Guise prevailed at Dreux, despite the assistance sent by Elizabeth of England, but the assassination of Guise shortly afterward turned the scale again in favor of the Protestants. The influence of the one man whom all France, Catholic and Reformed, could trust restored peace again, and he was once more in position to push his Florida project.

In May, 1564, therefore, Coligny fitted out a larger expedition. He sent three ships containing gentlemen, soldiers, volunteers, and workmen under Laudonnière, who had been in Florida with Ribault. Everything testified to the admiral's thoughtfulness. There was even an artist to draw views of the country. Next month they arrived in Florida and this time landed on May or St. John's River, and there on a little triangular island they built Fort Caroline.

The first thing of interest in the history of this new colony was their relation with the Indians. As usual there were native wars, here between tribes ruled by the caciques Outina and Saturiwa. Instead of remaining neutral or definitely taking one side or the other, Laudonnière vacillated, and finally incurred the enmity of both. But at least they explored the country, and the artist, Le Moyne, made interesting and valuable sketches of the land and people. Many of these have been preserved, and are invaluable. The history of Brazil and Charlesfort was repeated in more than one particular. There were jealousies and mutinies; the mutineers seized ships in the stream and turned pirates, of whom one set were captured and the others met with such misfortunes that they were glad to get back to the fort. But even then was much to be desired. Despite Le Moyne's pictures of native agriculture, or perhaps because the Indians deemed it women's work, again the French neglected to till the soil, and again they almost starved. They lived on boiled roots rather than catch the many fish swimming before their eyes. Such disregard of opportunities lying around we find continually. They were brave and energetic, and the only explanation is that the trades of soldiers and workmen were so different that the higher would not in any extremity condescend to do the work of the lower class, although they could unite to build a boat in which to escape.

Hatred of Spain, as we shall see, was not confined to Frenchmen. Elizabeth was too cautious to oppose Philip openly, but we shall find that her favorite expedient was to let loose privateers whose profits she could share and whose depredations she could disown. A pioneer in these days was John Hawkins, one of the first of the hardy adventurers from the southwest of England. Among his early voyages had been some to catch slaves on the west coast of Africa and sell them at a great profit in the West Indies. This had shown him the wealth and weakness of the Spanish system, and as a buccaneer he had become notable in the southern seas. It was at this time of distress for the French colony that he visited it, in returning home from one of his expeditions. He proffered assistance, and the French eagerly embraced the opportunity to repair to Europe. Hawkins sold them a ship and provisions and they were almost ready to start, when Ribault hove in sight with seven vessels and six hundred soldiers, the tangible proof of Coligny's care. Return was now given up, and everything was changed into plans for permanent occupation and extension of the colony.

Picturesquely our story now turns from the English privateer and the French colonists to the court of Spain. Philip seems to have realized the trap into which the admiral was drawing him: he learned of the Huguenot colony, and, instead of treating it as made by the French state, he determined to regard it as a nest of pirates, and heretics at that, whom he would exterminate with his own soldiers. He would then be ready afterward to settle scores with France, if necessary; but through his agents at the French court, and through the unscrupulous queen-mother Catherine herself, that was not to be needed. There seems little doubt that she acquainted the Spanish court with what was going on in Florida and was not at all reluctant to have Philip settle the question in his own way. And his way was to send out an expedition of twenty-six hundred men under Menendez over to Florida.

Now came the tug of war. The fleets had raced across the ocean, each eager to reach the goal before the other. A French vessel had captured one of Menendez's fleet in the West Indies, and from despatches learned the Spaniards' plans, of which word was sent to Ribault, although Menendez had sailed through new and dangerous passages to avoid detection. On St. Augustine's day, August 28, 1565, Menendez sighted Florida, and not fifty miles away Ribault was anchored off the bar of the river May. The conflict was inevitable, for Spain claimed by discovery and settlement all Florida to the Chesapeake, and France under Coligny was equally committed to the claim that the land was unoccupied and open to colonization by Frenchmen. Menendez, conveniently confounded the Huguenots with the buccaneers, and a privateering expedition from Charlesfort not only gave color to the position, but had also been the cause of the Spanish court's knowledge of the French settlement in America. During the manœuvring which now ensued, Menendez announced to the French in the St. John's that he was captain-general to the King of Spain and had come to hang all Lutherans whom he found there—a fact testified to by Mendoza, the chaplain of the fleet, and practically by Menendez himself in his report to the king. A storm dispersed the two fleets, and the Spaniards withdrew in good order to the river Seloy.

The genius of Menendez was seen in his appreciation of the effect of the surroundings. Convinced that the storm would detain the French fleet for several days, if it did not wreck it, he marched at once with sufficient force to attack Fort Caroline on the river May. The shallowest of the streams forded reached up to the knees, the dense forests impeded their advance, and when they arrived in sight of the fort they had to remain all night in water up to their waists. On September 19th the Spanish assailed the fort at a time when the sentinels had retired from their posts on account of the weather, and the greater part of the garrison were still in bed. It was a complete surprise. What then ensued is the subject of dispute. According to the French, but twenty escaped, among them Laudonnière, and the rest, including women and children, were slaughtered without mercy. According to Mendoza and Menendez, one hundred and forty were killed, and the women and children under fifteen were spared, while three hundred scaled the walls and took refuge either in the forests or on the six ships in the river. Some certainly escaped to sea. The capture of the fort yielded pikes, helmets, arquebuses, and shields,—for although gunpowder had come in, armor had not gone out,—besides clothing, biscuits, flour, wheat, and other supplies. Six cases of Lutheran books which were found were promptly burned, and, the nearest saint's day being St. Matthew's, the name of the fort was changed to San Mateo.

Menendez was, of course, received like the conqueror in his new settlement of St. Augustine, but there was still the question of the French fleet. Would Ribault outride the storm and with his well-armed vessels and hundreds of soldiers and sailors return to wreak vengeance on the Spaniards? The question was soon answered. Some Indians reported that a French vessel had been wrecked to the south, and Menendez promptly sent men in boats and then went himself. From the top of a tree he saw the enemy on the other side of the inlet. Mendoza says that his general was enlightened throughout by the Holy Spirit, and that his zeal for Christianity was so great that all his troubles were but repose for his mind. At all events, his religion was soon tested. Securing an interview with a Frenchman, he found that the enemy had not eaten bread for eight or ten days, and, what is more, says Mendoza, they were all Lutherans; whereupon he made known the slaughter at Fort Caroline and sent word they must surrender or he would put them to death. After some parley, Menendez refused tempting ransoms offered for a return to France and announced that "he would make no promises, and that they must surrender unconditionally and lay down their arms; because if he spared their lives, he wanted them to be grateful for it; and if they were put to death, that there should be no cause for complaint." The officer with whom he was negotiating thereupon brought all their arms and flags and surrendered the force unconditionally. Finding that they were all Lutherans, Menendez ordered them all to be put to death. The tender priest, however, had what he called bowels of mercy and succeeded in persuading Menendez to spare those who were found to be Christians. Unfortunately there were only ten or twelve of these, for to Mendoza the word meant Roman Catholics, and all the others had their throats cut [*degollados*] because they were Lutherans and enemies of the Holy Catholic faith, on Saturday, St. Michael's day, September 29, 1565. The French account was that they were bound and one by one marched up to a line which Menendez drew in the sand with his cane, and on reaching it were stabbed to death. Thus forty men massacred almost two hundred.

A day or so after, Menendez learned that Ribault and the rest of his men had been seen, and so set out with one hundred and fifty soldiers, well equipped, and from Anastasia Island he saw the French where their companions had been. Ribault sent word that he had three hundred and fifty men and was marching for Fort Caroline, and Menendez replied that he had captured that fort and put the garrison to death. An interview followed, Menendez receiving Ribault and his party cordially, offering them refreshments. These Ribault declined on account of the death of their companions, but did take some wine and preserves. High ransom was offered again, but declined, and finally Ribault delivered up royal standards, weapons, and his official seal, and surrendered at discretion one hundred and fifty who were willing to surrender on the terms of being mercifully treated, but the remainder departed in another direction. The prisoners were brought over in boats ten at a time, bound, on the pretext that they were to be marched to St. Augustine by a few guards, and distributed among the bushes behind the sand hills. Ribault and his officers were similarly treated. On being asked if they were Lutherans, or Catholics, Ribault replied that they were Lutherans and began singing the psalm *Domine memento mei*, and afterward, realizing his fate, said that, as they were of earth and to earth must return, twenty years more or less were of no consequence. Thereupon Menendez gave the signal and all were put to death like their comrades, except the fifers, drummers, trumpeters, and four men who were Catholics, making sixteen in all.

It would seem unnecessary, if not impossible, to make this picture blacker, and yet defenders of Menendez wax indignant over certain touches which they say the French have added. Thus the French declare that the Spaniards hacked the corpses before burning them and that Menendez put up the inscription on trees near by: "Slaughtered not as Frenchmen, but as Lutherans." Whether he wrote this or not may be uncertain, but it was the professed motive of his action. Another story is that Menendez had Ribault flayed and sent his stuffed skin to Europe for exhibition, and that he gave pieces of his beard as presents to different friends. The defenders of Menendez say that he did not conceal the massacre at Fort Caroline, and held out no hopes. A dispassionate reading of the facts recorded even by his brother-in-law, Solis de Meris, leaves this doubtful. Menendez surely knew that the French surrendered relying upon his mercy, and even at St. Augustine he met reproaches. To this day the name of the inlet recalls the slaughter. Those of the French who had not surrendered prepared to resist attack; and Menendez, to avoid the possible losses incident to a conflict, accepted their surrender on terms and sent them to the galleys.

The tale thrilled Europe with horror. Even Catherine was compelled to demand explanation of Spain, although the demand was evaded and she was easily satisfied. Not so the Huguenots. What would have been their course in brighter days we can well imagine; but for the present France was convulsed again with civil war. Soon was to come the battle of St. Denis, where Coligny, outnumbered, effected a famous retreat, then the hollow Peace of Longjumeau, and next the recognition of the religious division of the country by the virtual selection of La Rochelle as the Huguenot capital. In 1569 were the defeat of Jarnac and the death of Condé; but they were followed by the rapid recuperation of Coligny, for he, like his son-in-law and successor William the Silent, could make as much out of a lost battle as others out of a victory. So here he wrested victory from defeat, and by his unexpected march from the south in 1570 dictated almost at the gates of Paris the Peace of St.-Germain-en-Laye. This had every assurance of being lasting, for it was a full recognition of the rights of the Huguenots, and, better yet, was secured by their holding four important cities, among them La Rochelle, whose position on the sea made it accessible to foreign aid, while its strength by land made it all but impregnable against domestic attack.

Revenge for the Florida massacres could not be expected from the government, and it was left to a private chevalier, De Gourgues, to effect it. Of this exploit there remains an account, called *La Reprinse de la Floride.* His summary of the situation was that the Spaniards thought the New World created only for themselves. At his own expense and what he could obtain from friends he fitted out three small ships, carrying eighty sailors and one hundred arquebusiers, and sailed on August 2, 1567, from Bordeaux.

They finally arrived off the river May and got in communication with Satirona, as De Gourgues calls him, and other Indians whom they found hostile to the new occupants of San Mateo. After reconnoitring, an attack was made upon two small forts at the mouth of the river, which were captured, and then upon San Mateo itself. It was a case of surprise again, but with the position of the actors reversed. The French rushed with the Spaniards into the latter fort, while on the outside the savages prevented the escape of the garrison, and De Gourgues avenged the slaughter of his countrymen by slaying almost all within and hanging the rest. One of the victims confessed to having hanged five Frenchmen. The fort itself was injured by an accidental explosion due to Indians firing a train, and then with the other two wrecked of set purpose, De Gourgues saving much of the artillery. The French story goes on to say that De Gourgues, imitating Menendez, put up an inscription with the words: "I do not this as to Spaniards, but as to perfidious people, thieves, and murderers." The Frenchmen are inconsistent in relating that this inscription was affixed to the same tree on which Menendez had placed his, for their other account was that this had occurred at the time of Ribault's capture on Anastasia Island; but this would not seem to be material. The revenge was complete and poetic in its justice.

He considered he had too few troops to march on St. Augustine, and, after promising the Indians that a new colony would be established within twelve moons, he returned to his fleet and then sailed for France. The Spaniards point out that he chose a time for his attack when Menendez was not in Florida. While his expedition was rather a raid than a *Reprinse de la Floride*, it was warmly hailed in France, and on his return to La Rochelle he was received with enthusiasm. The indignation of Menendez and Spain may readily be conceived, and only the influence of Coligny kept De Gourgues from punishment by the court.

Such was the end of French Florida. The dream of establishing a Protestant state in America, which might be an asylum for the Huguenots unwelcome at home, was not to be realized. In France they were to remain to work out their own destiny for a century to come. The far-seeing Coligny himself died in the massacre of St. Bartholomew, in 1572, murdered by Charles IX. goaded on by the unscrupulous Catherine, and civil war prevailed between the Huguenots and the League until a new Calvinistic leader thought Paris well worth a Mass and became a convert to Catholicism. By that time the opportunity for settlement in Florida had passed, and Henry IV. had all he could do in reuniting France. He succeeded in healing the wounds of civil war and almost brought prosperity to his people, but no colonization toward the South marked his reign. The Huguenots had their rights and guarantees at home from the Edict of Nantes of 1598 until Louis XIV., but of French Florida naught remained but the stone with the arms of France, long worshipped by the Indians, but now washed away, and the name of Caroline, the origin of that of future colonies and States. The immediate contribution of the Huguenots to colonization was not to be their own settlement in America, but rather the universal hatred against Spain which their sufferings evoked and the inspiration they gave to their fellow Protestants beyond the Channel.

CHAPTER III

RALEIGH FOUNDS VIRGINIA

ENGLAND had not shared in full the European development. For although her civil wars happily ended before Cabot's discovery, and the religious dissension was stilled by Henry VIII. and Edward, there came a reaction under Mary, and, against the wish of her subjects, England was drawn, through the queen's marriage, into the sphere of Spanish influence. But national tendencies were too strong, and with the accession of Elizabeth in 1558 began a new era. The Spanish discoveries in the New World, the Portuguese acquisitions in the Orient, came at the time when economic questions like the closing of the monasteries and the eviction of small landholders for the purpose of raising sheep turned loose a large and restless population. A national navy had been begun by Henry VIII., but it was still small, and yet, although the Spaniards dominated the sea, by a happy instinct the newly aroused British energy turned to it. The world to the west seemed divided between Spain and Portugal quite as the Bull of Alexander VI. designed, and if the English wished to reach the East it must apparently be by sailing to the northeast or to the northwest. Endeavors in the former direction led to the discovery of Archangel and the foundation of the Muscovy Company; efforts to the northwest led to the voyages, among others, of Frobisher and Gilbert. The difficulties of the Arctic route in both directions caused the gradual abandonment of the Russian enterprise and the search for a more southerly route through

America to the Indies. At first the new continent was not valued for itself. It was an obstacle in the way of commerce with the Orient, and, when it was found to be in the way for all time, the efforts of other countries were directed to finding deposits of precious metals to rival the Spanish acquisitions further south.

Conflict was inevitable. The Spaniards claimed all the New World as the Indies, explored it northwardly almost to what is now New York, and in a measure settled it even to Chesapeake Bay. Religious antagonism played its part. England became more intensely Protestant in proportion as Spain endeavored by fair means or foul to subject her, although for a long time state policy forbade hostilities. Spain was too powerful, and England not yet conscious of her own strength. The most that could be done officially was quietly to encourage private enterprise. Privateering, shading into buccaneering, became a recognized trade, and after a while even the queen had an interest in the business. Her share was secret, to be sure. If she furnished money to fit out vessels, this was not divulged; and so, if the Spaniards captured the fleet, she disclaimed all knowledge of its undertakings. If, as generally happened, a cargo of Spanish goods and precious metals was brought into Plymouth or other English port, she received her full share of the proceeds. It was very convenient for all concerned, for without royal connivance a vessel could hardly be fitted out; and yet, internationally, the government was completely ignorant and left the privateers to their own fate when captured. It was an odd sort of morality, but we are dealing with the age of Elizabeth and not of Victoria and Edward VII. In the new development thus coming from the seas, it was natural that the southern parts of England should feel the first impulse. London had not then acquired that overwhelming preponderance which now makes it the centre of every movement. The southwest counties were very influential, and after Cabot's Bristol, long almost a free city, Plymouth and Dartmouth, even more than the old Cinque Ports, were the leading commercial places of the kingdom. Devonshire and the adjoining counties contributed to the history of that day great figures, the product of mixed English and Celtic blood and of inspiring surroundings. Thence came Drake and Hawkins, the Gilberts and Walter Raleigh. In no quarter of England was there greater hatred of Spain; than these men there were none to assail more heavily her supremacy. Religious hatred had its share, of course. Where there was daily fear of an uprising of Catholics in favor of the Spanish Philip or the Scottish Mary, Protestantism and patriotism became almost synonymous. Eventually religion and politics were dissociated, for Raleigh was to declare that it was Spanish supremacy and not Spanish religion which he hated; but at the first the two went together, and Drake could attack Nombre de Dios and the Spanish Main in America with a crusader's zeal, and deem in seizing the Spanish plate ships and treasures that he was rendering God service. Even earlier, when Hawkins, with a more commercial instinct, had captured negroes off the coast of Guinea and sold them to the Spanish colonists, he hated Spain as heartily. Francis Drake was knighted in 1580, on his return in the *Golden Hind* from his famous three years' circumnavigation of the globe; but it was less love of science than emulation of Spanish success in the Pacific that urged him on, and only seven years later he was at Cadiz, singeing the Spanish king's beard.

Of somewhat different temper were the Gilberts, and to Sir Humphrey is due the first effort at English colonization in America. After some time spent in exploration, he obtained from Elizabeth a patent which, in consideration of his colonizing Newfoundland, gave him various commercial and other privileges. The geography of America was being only gradually revealed, for the English knew even less than the Spanish, and Gilbert looked forward to large returns in precious metals and the like. The most important point about his enterprise historically is that he took possession and made sundry grants of land. It was unsuccessful, like almost everything else he undertook; still he had not only shown that one is as near heaven on the sea as on the land, but that Englishmen too could found homes in the New World as well as in the Old. His lamented loss in the *Squirrel* in 1583 only opened the way for the broader mind and greater resources of his half-brother, Walter Raleigh.

Raleigh was one of the great men of the world's history. He was great as a soldier, as a sailor, as an explorer, as a writer; great in his life, and even greater in his death. He served in France under Coligny and then in Ireland against a Spanish invasion, and soon became a favorite of the queen, herself one of the greatest of problems. A woman with all the whims and passions of her sex, capricious and jealous, she yet set bounds to love, and usually chose the best men for her public offices. She could love Leicester as only a woman could, and yet keep Burleigh at the head of the State. Raleigh she would never advance beyond knighthood, despite her unquestionable affection; but while she could not permit him to leave England for long, even after the event which broke off her personal relations, she learned in time again to employ his great talents. Among the gifts which she showered upon him in their earlier days was her patent for exploring and settling America, the counterpart of the one to his half-brother, and founded on it. Under it he had full power to take, fortify, and colonize any land not already possessed by Christians, with full rights of ownership and disposition of soil within two hundred leagues of the settlements he might make within six years. He had the power of establishing laws as near as conveniently might be to the laws of the realm, and not opposed to the Church of England. For herself the queen only reserved a royalty of one-fifth of the precious metals discovered. It is true that the patent was only a license to act, for she had no vested right that she could grant, and Raleigh was to meet all expenses, but, at all events, this paper gave him an international status. The Spaniard would no doubt contest the right to settle in the Indies and in undefined Florida, embracing almost all America in the temperate zone; but at least he would not be able to treat the colonists as pirates, and would have to negotiate with England rather than exterminate them as he had the Huguenots. It was not long before the queen was to announce that she would not recognize the papal gift or even a claim from discovery if not followed by permanent occupation. Her growing sea power and her aid, even if capricious and ill-directed at times, to the revolted Dutch made Protestant England a country which even Spain must reckon with and respect almost as much as France, more powerful but more distracted. Their conflict might come in the narrow waters of Europe, or on and across the great ocean so little known, and yet already the scene of commercial and warlike rivalry for the English and Spanish, and soon also to be a field for the newborn Dutch.

In the early expeditions to the west the ships usually went first to the West Indies. We ordinarily think that this was due to Columbus's discovery of them attracting attention in that direction. This is partly true, but Columbus did not discover them because they lay in the latitude of Spain, from which he sailed. Lisbon is in the latitude of Washington; and, in point of fact, if Columbus had not met a flock of parrots flying southwestwardly and followed them, he would have landed somewhere on the east coast of what is now the United States. As geese saved Rome, so parrots prevented this country from becoming Spanish. The fact is that voyages were by way of the West Indies even after the east coast of America was well known, and the reason must be sought in the fact that the ships of those days were sailing vessels and had to follow the winds and currents. An examination of a chart of the Atlantic will show that during much of the year there is a fairly constant wind and current from the latitude of Spain southwardly past the Canaries and thence over to the West Indies, while from there the Gulf Stream and winds go northwardly along the east coast of America and by the Azores over to the coast of Great Britain again. In other words, the winds and currents run roughly in the shape of a circle or ellipse,—westwardly on the southern limb and eastwardly on the northern, with the Sargasso sea of weed in the neutral centre. In course of time, mariners learned by taking advantage of cross winds to pursue a northern route, as did the French chevalier, De Gourgues; but the usual way was to proceed from England southwardly past the Canaries, where vessels might water, and then by way of the West Indies, where they might refit, and thence on to America. The western trip would by these means take from thirty to forty days, besides what might be spent in watering and refitting. It was wise to make a study of conditions in advance.

Therefore, Raleigh prudently sent out an exploring expedition before he undertook a colony. It consisted of two ships under Arthur Barlow and Philip Amadas, the former of whom has left an account of this voyage of 1584. Crossing on a southerly line, they saw land in July. Coasting to the north, admiring semitropical views and odors, they entered an opening and took possession of an island which was called Roanoke. After a while they met the natives of the country, in particular Granganimeo, the brother of the king, and also some women. Their relations with the Indians were kindly in every way, forming a strong contrast to later history. Of natural products they noticed especially the tall red cedars, crops of maize and peas, the supply of game, and in September returned to England, taking with them two Indians named Wanchese and Manteo.

Then Raleigh sent a fleet of seven ships conveying one hundred and eight colonists. The expedition was under the command of Sir Richard Grenville, and the colony when established was to be governed by Ralph Lane, both brave men of experience and ability. They stopped first at the Spanish island of St. John, and then at Hispaniola, where they were well received, in June ran up the American coast, and, despite what appears to be the treachery of their Portuguese pilot, landed without loss near Roanoke.

Plan of San Augustin de la Florida, *circa* 1595. *Traced from the original, especially for this work, by D. Pedro Torres Lanzas, Chief of the Archives, from the hitherto unpublished original in the Archives of the Indies, Seville.*

Naturally they spent some time in exploring the mainland, going as far north as Secotan, but unfortunately getting into unnecessary conflict with the natives. In August, Grenville sailed back with the fleet, and the colony was left to itself. We have materials for quite a full history of the experiment in the diary of one who accompanied Grenville forth and back, letters of Lane to Raleigh and Richard Hakluyt, the account of Thomas Hariot, and other papers. Lane says that they were much pleased with the country, which was healthful and productive, needing but horses and kine, and the natives he described as most courteous, desiring especially coarse clothing and red copper. "All the kingdoms and states of Christendom," he continues, "their commodities joined in one together, did not yield more good or plentiful whatsoever for public use is needful or pleasing for delight." He was not so satisfied with his colonists themselves, for then, as for so long after, the mistake was made of thinking that ruffians would make good settlers.

The site of the settlement was near the northeast corner of the island, where may still be traced the winding ditch which marked a camp forty yards square, apparently of palisades with bastions at the corners and salients between. It was a resort rather than a place of residence, for it was too small to live in; and the colonists devoted their time to exploration instead of agriculture, depending upon the natives for supplies. They seem to have got to the Chesepians on Elizabeth River, near our Hampton Roads, and, threading the maze of waters of this coast, in the spring explored from Albemarle Sound westwardly up the river Chowan. Following information derived from Menatonon, king of the Chawanoks, Lane conducted an expedition up the river Moratoc, or Roanoke, to find a pearl fishery, precious metals, and a passage to the Great South Sea, with the intention of moving his colony over to that other coast. The party pushed on for about two hundred miles up the river, subsisting at last on their two mastiffs boiled with sassafras leaves, but they did not find the Pacific, the pearls, or the precious metals, and had to return to Roanoke. The most tangible result of the expedition and its incidents was the fixed hostility of Pemissapan, the father and successor of Granganimeo. One would suppose that peaceful relations with the natives were essential to a small band coming to explore and settle a new country, and would be cultivated, particularly after the cordial reception given to Barlow and Amadas, and Lane's own opinion of the neighboring tribes; but war followed, and it was only by bravery and something like treachery that the English were victorious.

This was the time of Francis Drake's dash on Santo Domingo and Cartagena, and it so chanced that after capturing St. Augustine he came by with his large fleet. After some hesitation, Lane and his colonists accepted Drake's offer to take them back to England. They went aboard in such bad weather as to lose most of their books and goods, but sail they did and Roanoke was left deserted. Sir Richard Grenville soon arrived with supply ships, and spent some time searching for the settlers and exploring; and rather than lose what had been done, he left fifteen men well supplied with provisions and himself returned with the fleet to England. The history of these fifteen is a blank. Some bones were afterward found, and subsequent comers heard that the colonists had suffered the penalty of Pemissapan's vengeance.

It was not in Raleigh, however, to give up as long as his means held out, and, in fact, his next expedition was the most promising of all, for in the following year he sent out one hundred and fifty settlers, including seventeen women, under John White, a man of experience in the previous attempt. Against his judgment White was persuaded to take possession of the old fort on Roanoke Island. Exploration was again undertaken, this time in a more friendly manner, and in it they were largely aided by Manteo, who had now returned, and was baptized and given the title of Lord of Roanoke and Dasamonpeake. Five days later was the more important event of the birth of the first English child, Virginia, to Ananias Dare and his wife Eleanor, the daughter of John White. Some progress had been made, and when it seemed proper to send home a report of the condition of affairs it was determined that White himself should go. On November 8th he reached Southampton, having with him Wanchese, who was in Bideford church baptized a Christian, but soon died and was also buried there. The settlers left at Roanoke to build up an English colony had the promise of White's early return with instructions and supplies.

Lord Bacon tells us, looking back perhaps to this event of his own day, that the beginnings of states are the most instructive studies, because then is determined the whole course of future development. Interesting indeed would it be could we trace in detail the government and institutions of this first real English colony in America. It presented many features differing from the later enterprises. It came at a time when the final forms of English institutions were themselves uncertain. Indeed, in this time of conflict with Spain abroad and Catholicism at home it was doubtful whether there would be any England remaining as an independent State. Everything was in flux, and yet, although they came out under a private patent more as tenantry on the land of their overlord, Walter Raleigh, and for the purpose of finding gold or other treasure and making homes, these men under Lane and White were Englishmen through and through, Englishmen of the age of Elizabeth. The very fact that they came without fixed laws would make those they established the more characteristic of the age. It is true that the settlement under White was of a civil nature, for he and twelve others were incorporated as the governor and assistants of the city of Raleigh, and met in council and directed the government. But the colony was small and all in one place, so that there was no opportunity for the development of the distinguishing feature of Anglo-Saxon institutions,—local self-government. And the Indian hostilities afforded little opportunity to develop more than military law. The colonists were almost all soldiers, and this gave the tone even to those who were not. Precisely what did happen, however, is not known. The final loss of the colony has made everything obscure.

For the time was not auspicious. Spain had suffered so much at the hand of England that she was preparing retribution. Elizabeth had assisted revolt in the Netherlands with men and money. Drake had captured plate ships from America and scourged the Spanish Main and the South Sea. The Pacific, hitherto Spanish alone, was now through the capture of maps and information laid open to the English. English buccaneers swarmed everywhere. Florida, claimed and colonized at such cost, was actually invaded by Raleigh. And the insult at Cadiz made the situation unendurable. The Invincible Armada followed.

It is almost impossible at this day to realize the situation. While such seamen as Hawkins and Drake had lost their fear of the Spaniard, to the nation at large, as to Europe generally, Spain represented everything that was powerful, cruel, and hateful. There was almost universal panic, as there always has been in England at the idea of invasion, and the fear of Jesuits and civil war was added to that of the Spaniard himself. The famous action in which Lord Howard of Effingham, assisted by Drake and other English sailors, drove off the Armada, and the next succeeding event when, as the English firmly believed, the Lord arose and scattered His and their enemies, are not for us to tell. But that time of trial directly affected the colony in America. Raleigh sent out Grenville with a fleet, and then White with two small vessels, which were turned back by this invasion, the latter after some privateering. Neither men nor ships could be spared from home. Looking back now, we can see that the Spanish power was crushed by this defeat; but of this, Englishmen of the day could not be certain for years to come. It was no time for colonizing, and the settlers were left to themselves.

Exactly what became of them no one ever knew. When White finally arrived, a year after the Armada, he found Roanoke deserted. Whether they were massacred, and among them Virginia Dare, like the earlier settlers, we do not certainly know. Subsequent tradition so declared and that only two boys were spared to grow up with the natives. At all events, it was afterward fancied that some of the Indians in that vicinity were of a lighter complexion than the rest, lending probability to the report that these two had intermarried and become the ancestors of a fairer race.

Standing on a hilltop a landscape will spread like a map before us. We can see the prominent points, the heads of streams, the rocks, the coast—everything lies in proper perspective. Thus looking back upon history, we can see the importance of events which are hid from participants and onlookers. We can hail the Roanoke settlement as the beginning of English colonization in America. To the Englishman of that day this was not so clear. Except so far as he was interested in Raleigh's fortunes or connected with the lost colonists themselves, the event made no great impression. For the moment all were too busy with the thought of the Spanish repulse at home to care much about what happened in America. But while the public were perhaps not interested, the matter was vastly important to Raleigh himself. He had spent £40,000, much of his fortune, without result. In 1589 he found it expedient to assign to John White, Sir Thomas Smythe,—a name to become familiar,—and others the privilege of the Virginia trade, and thus joined with his past colonizing the name of one who was later, under different circumstances, to take up his work. Had he wished to continue his schemes, two events in the near future made it almost impossible. In 1591 came the daring battle in the Azores of his trusted lieutenant, Sir Richard Grenville, with an overwhelming Spanish fleet. While the Spaniard conquered, he did not triumph. Grenville was killed and his vessel destroyed, but no braver and hardly a more famous combat is recorded in

England's long naval story. Then, only a year after, came that marriage of Raleigh with Elizabeth Throckmorton, which banished him from court. Queen Elizabeth was past fifty, and this maid of honor twenty-two. The queen would not wed a subject like Raleigh, but, if he was to retain her favor, neither must he marry a subject, and must keep himself a bachelor for her sake. The exact relations between the knight and the maid of honor are doubtful, if not dubious; but at least Sir Walter made the best amends he could and married the young woman, even though he must have felt it would cost him the favor of the queen. At all events, the result was that he lost means and influence, and for the next few years remained in quiet at Sherborne, the Dorset place so closely associated with his history. He remembered America, for he often spoke of it; but of his enterprise there were left only some maps bearing the barren name Virginia. Elizabeth had given the name, but little else, and the lasting colonization of America was not to be reckoned among the glories of her reign.

CHAPTER IV

VIRGINIA UNDER THE COMPANY

WITH Elizabeth passed away the age of the sea kings. With James began a more commercial era. It is true that the intellectual and religious activity of the earlier reign continued and soon concentrated itself on political subjects, from which concentration came a restlessness which reached its climax under the second Stuart, although its mutterings were not indistinct under the first; but in the time of James I. trade and commerce absorbed much of the energy of the awakened English.

Napoleon was to call them a nation of shopkeepers, but it was not ever thus. During the Middle Ages trade developed in guilds or unions of workmen, such as goldsmiths, mercers, and many other occupations. In time these associations were to fetter industry, but at first they protected it from the violence of the period. We have seen that the growth of kingly power under Henry VII. and Henry VIII. was accompanied by great economic changes, and that the surplus population thus freed from land was both a cause and a means of England's suddenly acquired greatness by sea. We have now rather to look at the domestic side of these changes. The overpopulation due to the dissolution of the monasteries and the increase of sheep pastures was to be an argument and an incentive to colonization, but at first these changes brought about the movement over sea for quite different objects. Although colonization was the result, a reaching out after new trade routes came earlier. The older centres were insufficient for the expanding industries of England, of which the chief were connected with wool, for cotton was as yet almost unknown.

The use of woollen clothing is so common that we seldom think of its beginnings, and yet the raising of sheep, the principal source of wool, is not universal. The finest wool came from Spain, and England almost from the time of the Romans produced a great deal. During the later Middle Ages, tin, hides, and wool were the chief exports of the realm, the last going for manufacture mainly to the Netherlands, that hive of industry; for England's supremacy in clothmaking is of quite modern growth. The kings attempted to regulate this export, sometimes even forbidding it, on the notion of the day that a nation was rich in proportion to what it kept at home rather than to what it sold or exchanged abroad. They established markets, or staples, from which alone the business should be carried on. In course of time, the merchants engaged in this export of wool became known as Staplers, and as long as the manufacture of cloth in England was unimportant they did a large business and had great influence. During some of the wars on the continent, however, Flemish and other weavers were brought over, and then began a rival commerce. England was to be more than an agricultural and a pastoral country, with incidental handicrafts; manufacturing was to be added to her other industries, and in time to become the chief of all.

Thus arose the famous corporation known as the Governor, Assistants, and Fellowship of the Merchants Adventurers of England. Their origin is mediæval and their scene of activity mainly the continent of Europe, where they from time to time had sundry "Marte townes" and ports. Their great commodity was woollen cloth, of whose export for a long time they had a monopoly; and at fixed seasons their fleet sailed from England in convoy of men-of-war, somewhat as, later, did the plate fleet of Spain from America. Their rules were numerous and strict, and as far back as the discovery of America they had been recognized by Acts of Parliament. In the beginning, English commerce with the continent was handled by Italians, the Hansa, and the domestic Staplers, but the Fellowship of Merchants Adventurers now gradually superseded the others in the trade to the Low Countries. The Fellowship regulated prices by regulating the supply, and instituted a stint whenever necessary. Were a port hostile, trade was diverted elsewhere. Ultimately the Fellowship drove out the Staplers, and in the sixteenth and seventeenth centuries the Merchants Adventurers were in their prime.

Although these companies took no part in the colonization of America, yet they showed the way in which commercial enterprises could be carried on, and furnished a model for their organization; while their monopoly of the continent led to search for other markets, and ultimately the guilds at least were to aid the cause by contributions. America had been discovered in the attempt to reach the Indies, the objective point of all early expeditions, and attempts to the northwest and northeast through the Arctic Ocean were unsuccessful. It is true the Muscovy Company imported timber and naval stores from the Baltic and Arctic seas, but the rigor of the climate left these open only part of the year, and Drake's circumnavigation of the globe revealed the feasibility of a new route to the East. The result was the adventuring in 1599 of £30,000 in that trade and next year the formation of the East India Company, a trading corporation managed from the first largely by London merchants, among whom was specially prominent Sir Thomas Smythe. He was the first governor of the Company, and about a hundred of his fellow members were afterward interested in the Virginia enterprises.

The year after the Spanish Armada, the Rev. Richard Hakluyt published a book of travels by Englishmen, and nine years later he began his more famous work, *The Principal Navigations, Voyages, Traffiques & Discoveries of the English Nation, made by Sea or Over Land*, and these books soon had plenty of company. It is said that there were even during the reign of Elizabeth at least one hundred and five authors of books or tracts concerning maritime and colonization affairs. The Azores were well known, being the port of call of many fleets to the west as well as the scene of battles, and Newfoundland was regularly visited for its fisheries and claimed by both France and England. Among those sailing to the west at different times were Bartholomew Gosnold, George Somers, Gabriel Archer, and Christopher Newport; and their patrons were Shakespeare's patron the Earl of Southampton, Lord Cobham the fatal friend of Raleigh, Sir Ferdinando Gorges, as well as Sir Walter Raleigh, whose interest now was centred more especially in Guiana. It seems strange to us to think of Guiana as a proposed colony for the English, and yet we must remember that the whole world was then opening before them. They did not know which part was better suited to their genius, and, in fact, only time was to tell. At first they sought Russia and Newfoundland, then Guiana and the East Indies, and only later were they to appreciate the commercial importance of Virginia. And this was a broad name in those days. Just as the Spaniards claimed all of temperate America under the name of Florida, the English were disposed to claim as Virginia all from the peninsula of Florida up to the regions of Newfoundland. In course of time, a compromise line was to be drawn, but at first America and Virginia were to the British almost synonymous. Thus a voyage in 1605 of Captain George Weymouth to what we now call New England was considered an expedition to Virginia; and when he returned in July he brought back five natives, who attracted even more attention than the crocodiles and wild bears from Hispaniola which Newport presented to King James. A treaty of peace with Spain was finally ratified on June 15, 1605, purposely leaving obscure the question of boundaries in America, but rendering it possible to make settlements without armed conflict, and the Indians brought back by

Weymouth but whetted the curiosity of the English. Adventurers, we learn from Ben Jonson's play, *Eastward Ho!* were still ready to sell away competent certainties to purchase with any danger excellent uncertainties, and in this same play we have our first Virginia colonel. They still dreamed of gold, for the piece represented the natives as using it for domestic vessels and street purposes, while rubies and diamonds were gathered by the seashore and given to children.

Sir Walter Raleigh had been received very coldly by the new king, and a leading man of the new colonization was to be the Lord Chief Justice, Sir John Popham. For although it seems that in some sense Gosnold was the first mover of the plantation and interested Edward Maria Wingfield, John Smith, and others, it was not much advanced until some of the nobility, gentry, and merchants were enlisted also. There had been already in the time of Henry VIII. "The Mysterie and Companie of the Merchant Adventurers for Discoverie of Regions, Dominions, Islands, and Places unknown," different from the Adventurers in wool; but they had not much success, and the new company to be formed was for more strictly commercial purposes. Its beginning was an agreement between Weymouth and Sir John Zouch for a "marchante voyage" to Virginia, but it was at last realized that such an enterprise as colonization should be undertaken by public authority. A paper giving reasons for raising a fund for the support of the colony in Virginia justly says "that private purses are cold comfort to adventurers and have ever been found fatal to all enterprises hitherto undertaken by the English by reason of delays, jealousies, and unwillingness to back that project which succeeded not at the first attempt." There was reason for haste, because Henry IV. had already found France pacified sufficiently to begin looking to America again, and had granted to De Monts a patent to inhabit Acadia, described as Virginia north of forty degrees. In England the Gunpowder Plot no doubt delayed matters, and only recently have we learned the keenness with which Pedro de Zuñiga, the Spanish ambassador at London, watched and reported on the plans for new attempts at colonization.

Finally in April, 1606, a charter, drawn by Popham and revised by Coke, passed the seals, naming as grantees Thomas Gates, George Somers, Richard Hakluyt, Edward Maria Wingfield, Thomas Hanham, Raleigh Gilbert, William Parker, and George Popham. While the instrument is expressly spoken of as a license and patent, it was characteristic of the new king that it should be very different from patents granted by Elizabeth. That sovereign had confided extensive powers to the undertakers in each instance, reserving to herself only certain rights of sovereignty and an interest in the products, while the learned and pedantic James preferred to regulate all details himself. It was evident that he did not embrace colonies abroad within the humble plan which he afterward said he conceived on coming to England of sitting still seven years in order to learn the laws of this kingdom before venturing to make new ones. He divided the adventurers into two colonies, the first being composed of the London petitioners, who should operate between the thirty-fourth and forty-first degrees of latitude; and the second comprising the men of Plymouth, Bristol, and Exeter, whose field lay between the thirty-eighth and forty-fifth degrees. These respective colonies should have dominion for fifty miles north and south from their settlements, as well as a hundred miles to sea and a hundred miles inland, but were not to build within one hundred miles of each other. Each should have a council with a seal showing the king's arms and portraiture, while in England there should be a superior council to control them both, also with a seal, all nominated by James. Power was given to build settlements, defend themselves, coin money, control trade, import goods without duty for seven years, and the king agreed to patent to their nominees lands colonized, to be held as of the manor of East Greenwich in the county of Kent, in free and common socage and not in capite, thus in effect preventing military tenures in the colonies. There was also a wise provision forbidding piracy, and, possibly by inadvertence on the part of the king, possibly by wisdom on the part of the adventurers or Coke or Popham, there was inserted the famous provision which is the foundation of American liberty and institutions. It is the paragraph numbered fifteen, reading as follows: "Also we do, for Us, our Heirs, and Successors, Declare, by these Presents, that all and every the Persons, being our Subjects, which shall dwell and inhabit within every or any of the said several Colonies and Plantations, and every of their children, which shall happen to be born within any of the Limits and Precincts of the said several Colonies and Plantations, shall have and enjoy all Liberties, Franchises, and Immunities, within any of our other Dominions, to all Intents and Purposes, as if they had been abiding and born, within this our Realm of England or any other of our said Dominions."

The councils might order all matters according to such laws, ordinances, and instructions as should be in that behalf given and signed with the king's hand or sign manual and pass under the privy seal. Had this patent continued in full operation, therefore, it might have played a great part in favor of royalty in the civil wars which were to come; but modifications will concern us at a later period. For the present, the king drew elaborate instructions in November for the government of his loving subjects in Virginia. He did permit the councils to fill vacancies and to select their own presidents, but this latter provision, putting the presidency at the will of the actual majority, was to work badly. He directed that Christianity was to be preached among the colonists and the natives. Jury trial was preserved, offences defined, and the local councils constituted into courts for trying and punishing all cases. Judicial proceedings were to be summary, without writing, with the exception of the judgment, which was to be signed by the president and the members of the council acting. Trade was to be regulated by keeping everything in joint stock, and there should be a "cape merchant" to take charge of all commodities, and it was the royal "will and pleasure that all subjects in said colonies and plantations should well entreat the savages and use all good means to draw them to the true service and knowledge of God, and that all just, kind, and charitable courses should be holden with such of them as would conform themselves to any good and sociable traffique dealing" with British subjects, all under such severe pains and punishments for infringements as should be inflicted by the president and council.

The initiative for the northern enterprise was thus to come from the southwest of England, and to be under the patronage of the lord chief justice. The other was to have its headquarters at London, the patron being no less a person than Robert Cecil, Earl of Salisbury, the principal secretary of state. The basis of this division is not clear, but it would seem likely that the neighborhood of the fisheries of Newfoundland, which were well known and visited by the west of England mariners, may have been the attraction in the first case. Whoever the patron and whoever the originators of the plan, the active man in the former colony was Sir Ferdinando Gorges, the governor of Plymouth, and on August 22, 1606, the *Richard* sailed from there under M. Henry Challons to go to the North Plantation of Virginia. Two months later a second ship was sent out, under Thomas Hanham as commander and Martin Prynne of Bristol as master, to second Challons and his people. Hanham and Prynne returned the next spring with valuable reports as to the coast of North Virginia, but Challons was less fortunate, for in November his vessel was captured by the Spaniards in the West Indies. The western adventurers were not discouraged, and soon sent out another expedition, but, with the death of the chief justice not long afterward, the enterprise languished, and it was left for the London people to make the first real settlement in America.

London at this time had a population of nearly three hundred thousand, although from 1603 to 1611 it was suffering from a visitation of the plague, of which, particularly in the earlier days, thousands died. This was to be a factor in colonization, as it reinforced the distress caused by the stringent poor laws and the dread due to the administration of criminal laws naming three hundred capital crimes, and caused many people to leave England. The disorganization of labor in the country drove multitudes to London, and, now that peace was succeeding the troublous times of Elizabeth, trade and commerce were waxing important and building up the capital. Although beginning their operations later, the promoters of the first colony, or the London Company, as they were generally called, were much more successful than their brethren of Plymouth.

Of the many expeditions to America, none after Columbus was more important than that of the *Sarah Constant* under Captain Christopher Newport, the *Goodspeed* under Captain Bartholomew Gosnold, and the *Discovery* under Captain John Ratcliffe, Newport being in general charge. Drayton marked the occasion by penning an ode to "Virginia, earth's only paradise," and on December 30, 1606 (N. S.), the vessels sailed from London. There was no dearth of instructions. There were orders and directions by the Council for Virginia, among them prescribing that Newport should have sole charge and command at sea and that the names of the local council would be found in secret instructions to be opened on arrival. Exploration was to be carried on for at least two months and such place selected for a site as would be a safe port at the entrance of the navigable river running furthest into the land. In fact, if the river had two branches, the one should be selected which bent more toward the northwest, for that way they would sooner find the other sea, which was not supposed to be far from the Atlantic. Before it was reached they were specially instructed to examine any high lands or hills, and with pickaxes try if they could find minerals, for the South Sea and precious metals were still special objects of desire.

Detained off the Downs and south coast of England by adverse winds until the 18th of February, they reached the

Canaries in March, and the island of Dominica early in April. They then saw in succession Guadeloupe, Nevis and Mona, taking water more than once. After a severe storm which providentially drove them past the fatal Roanoke they sought, the little fleet at four o'clock in the morning of May 6th entered Chesapeake Bay, and were soon ravished with the sight of fair meadows, goodly tall trees, and fresh water running through the woods. They landed, and named the cape after Henry, Prince of Wales. That night they opened their sealed orders and found the local council to consist of Gosnold, Wingfield, Newport, John Smith, Ratcliffe, John Martin, and George Kendall. As directed, they began exploring the bay and tributary rivers, naming the largest for King James, although it was already called Powhatan by the Indians, and were much disappointed at the shallow water until, rowing over to a point of land, they found a deep channel, which put them in such good comfort that they named it Cape Comfort. May 14th they finally selected their "seating place," where the ships could lie so near the shore that they were moored to the trees in six fathoms. The spot chosen was a peninsula, and there the trumpets sounded, the admiral struck sail, and the rest of the fleet came to an anchor. The colony disembarked, and every man brought ashore his particular store and furniture, together with the general provision, to protect which they measured off a fortification and began in the name of God to raise a fortress. When finished it was a triangle, having three bulwarks at the corners like a half-moon, with three or four pieces of artillery mounted in them. Toward the river and landing, the fort was four hundred and twenty feet long, and on the other sides three hundred feet each; in the centre a *corps de garde*, chapel, and storehouse. The houses faced the palisades, with a street between. The Rev. Mr. Hunt was the minister, and there were regular religious services held, with a sermon every Sunday when practicable. Unfortunately, possibly as a result of Roanoke, the Indians from the first were not friendly, and the fort was built none

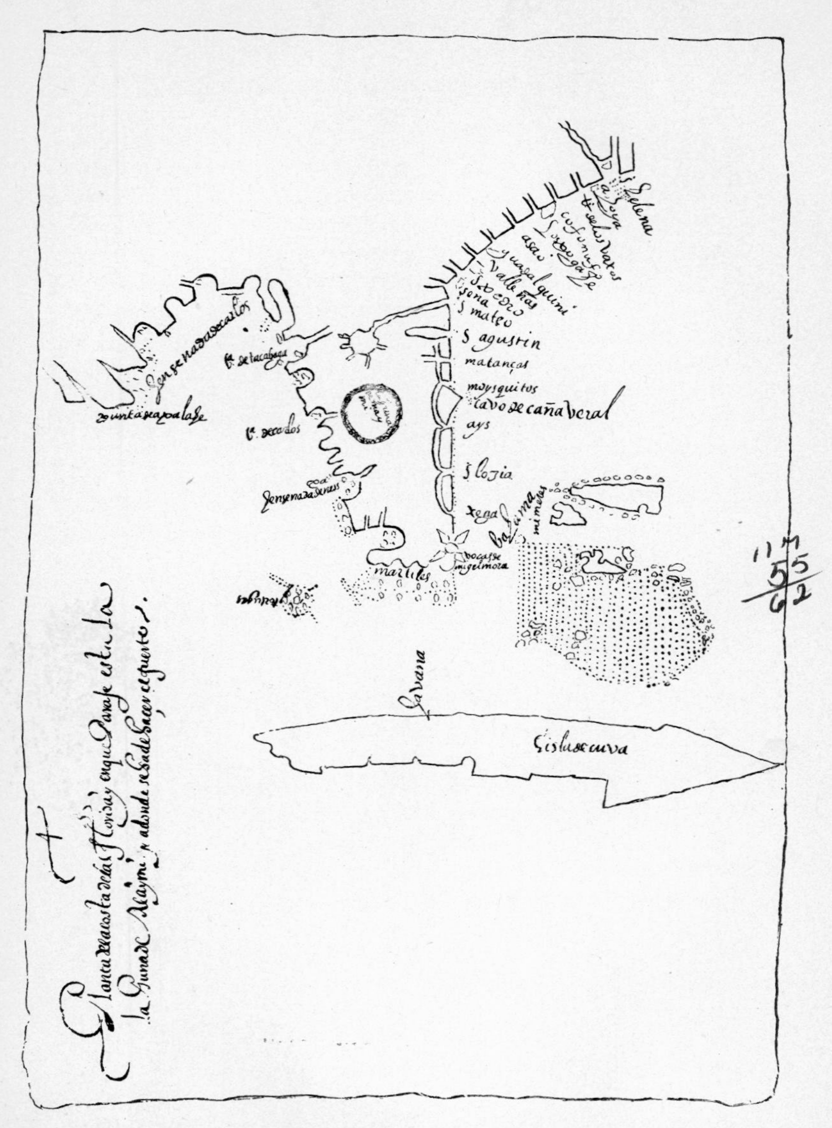

Map made in 1599, showing Cuba, the Bahamas, and Florida, with the Laguna de Maimi, "where a fort is to be made." *Traced from the original, especially for this work, by D. Pedro Torres Lanzas, Chief of the Archives, from the hitherto unpublished original in the Archives of the Indies, Seville.*

too soon. The English, sooner or later, in all parts of the world have proved themselves superior to the natives, but they often begin in a blundering sort of way. Their colonists have seldom been numerous enough to conquer the savages into submission at once, like the Spaniards, while their manners have always lacked the conciliatory tone which has made the French so welcome, particularly in America.

It seems strange that every expedition heretofore sent to the New World by other than the Spaniards should have selected an island for settlement. The French had done so in Brazil, at Charlesfort, and Fort Caroline; the English, three times at Roanoke. All these settlements had been unsuccessful, and largely so because they condemned the colony to an insulated existence, out of touch with the mainland, its people and its advantages, and Jamestown was to be only partially an exception. The real reason, of course, was a feeling of dependence upon the sea and a fear of the savages. Even the Spaniards knew more about the coast than they did of the interior, but there were no English explorers who like De Soto and Tristan plunged resolutely into the forest and left the coast far behind.

Wheat was sown at Jamestown, and not long afterward potatoes, "pumpions," melons, garden seed, and West Indian oranges and "cotton trees" were planted, while mulberries, cherries, vines, gooseberries, strawberries, raspberries, groundnuts, and other plants were found native to the soil. Of course, they sought for gold, and curiously enough they found a real piece. Captain John Martin even got together a whole barrel of "fool's gold." He was a practical man and one of experience in American voyages, although mistaken in this instance. Exploring was not neglected, and the natives were a constant source of surprise and interest—if also fear.

Newport left in the *Sarah Constant* July 2d, with Virginia's first exports, the supposed gold and real clapboards. He took the *Goodspeed* along, leaving the *Discovery*, a pinnace of twenty tons, for colonial use. The colony, consisting of one hundred and four persons, was face to face with its future. Hardly had he left when a messenger came, offering peace from the Great Powhatan. Early accounts all call him thus, but it would seem that his name was Wahunsonacock, and he was chief of the Powhatan tribe of Indians, living ten miles from Jamestown on the Putin Bay of York River—itself an abbreviation of "Powhatan." The Indians remained friendly for a while, supplying corn and meat; and it was fortunate, for with the summer began the sickness which for years to come was so fatal to the English. It is generally spoken of as "the seasoning period," but the proportion that survived was hardly forty per cent, especially at the beginning. This summer they lost forty men, including Gosnold on September 1st. From that time on, to illness was added dissension. Kendall was put in prison, and after the death of the "cape merchant," Studley, Captain John Smith acted in his place. September 20th, Ratcliffe, Smith, and Martin deposed Wingfield and made Ratcliffe president, and not long afterward in some quarrel a man named Read struck Ratcliffe and was condemned to be hanged. It seems this did not take place, because he revealed a proposed mutiny of Kendall, who was shot instead.

Captain John Smith almost ranks with Mary Queen of Scots as a historical question and has been able to immortalize a prosaic name. On the voyage over under Newport he was a prisoner much of the time for some alleged insubordination, and as to his share in the movement afterward there is difference of opinion. Smith has left several accounts, which unfortunately differ somewhat from each other, but there was probably a basis of truth in even his wildest narratives. He was chosen by lot to command an exploring expedition, and with it proceeded up Chickahominy River, through the domains of Opechancanough, the unfriendly brother of Powhatan. Where the water became too low, Smith left his vessel and crew and went ahead in a canoe with Indian guides and two Englishmen. The crew were attacked and Smith lost his two companions, but saved himself, as he always did in personal encounters, by superior skill. He tied the Indian guide before him as a kind of shield, and but for a swamp would not have been captured. In his early history he tells us he had slain three Turkish champions in Hungary in single combat, and had more than once in captivity been befriended by beautiful women, and so we could not expect him to succumb finally to the savages of America. While he did not mention it in his first account, he did not fail after the princess had become famous in England to tell the interesting story of how he was rescued by the intervention of the child Pocahontas, who threw herself between him and the uplifted club of her savage father. He then beguiled his captors by showing the use of the compass, of his gun, and his civilized method of communicating with Jamestown by writing. Certain it is that he was released, and at Jamestown was in some way about to be called in question for the death of his two followers, when the arrival of Newport from England changed dissension into a measure of contentment.

Newport had made on July 29, 1607, a report to Salisbury, forwarded from Plymouth, in which he said that they had explored the back country for nearly two hundred miles and a river navigable one hundred and fifty miles. The land they found excellent and very rich in gold and copper, and of the gold they had brought "a say." He took up to London, in the course of August, a letter from the council in Virginia to the Virginia council in England, one from Robert Tindall to Prince Henry giving a "dearnall" of the voyage and a "draughte" of the river, Newport's relation of the discovery of the river, a *Description* of the new-discovered river and country of Virginia, and a *Brief Description* of the people, the last three probably written by Gabriel Archer, the recorder of the colony. The letter of the council claims that they had sown a good store of wheat, sent clapboards to England, built houses, and spared some hands for discoveries. The richest commodity at first was "sasafrix roots," whose special value in that day seems to have been for making with anise seed a beverage of merit for preserving health on long voyages. The river was full of sturgeon and other "sweet fish," the soil most fruitful, bearing oak, ash, walnut, poplar, pine, cedar, and other woods, some yielding gums of virtue for healing wounds and aches. They further refer to the "gold showing mountains," for expedition to which they asked immediate succors, "least that the all devouring Spaniard lay his hands upon them." Naturally, the first thing those interested did was to have the gold analyzed; and Sir Walter Cope, in a letter to Salisbury, expresses the keen disappointment of all that after trial four times by the best experience about the city it all turned to vapor. The Company met that same evening, and, despite being thus deprived of hope of any extraordinary consequence, cheerfully determined to send supplies. Newport, for his part, told Sir Thomas Smythe that he was resolved never to see Salisbury again before he should bring what he confidently believed he had brought. The new expedition was set on foot, and on October 4th the ships *John & Francis* under Captain Newport and the *Phœnix* under Captain Nelson left London for Virginia, having on board colonists, and also, unknown to the authorities, a spy named Francis McGuire in the pay of Spain. Newport arrived at Jamestown on January 12, 1609, but Nelson did not reach there for some time. Newport found only thirty-eight or forty colonists left and added to them nearly one hundred, having lost some on the voyage.

His coming relieved Wingfield and Captain John Smith from prison, and we have a mysterious hint that it prevented a parliament which Recorder Archer, who had been sworn a councillor by the president, had intended to summon. Exactly what this was we do not know, but it is the first intimation of a popular assembly in American history. Hardly had Newport arrived before Jamestown was burned, with nearly all the buildings in the fort, church, storehouse, and magazine included, besides the first library which we know of in America, that of the Rev. Mr. Hunt, unless Wingfield's trunk full of books, including a Bible, was earlier. The winter was a hard one and bore severely on all.

While Newport was in Virginia he explored somewhat with Smith, having also a conference with the Great Powhatan. Newport sailed for England on the 20th of April, taking with him Wingfield, Archer, McGuire, and others, and as papers the interesting chart made by Tindall of their explorations, Percy's *Discoveries*, White's *Description*, and the like. By Nelson, somewhat later, was sent John Martin and Smith's famous *True Relation*, accompanied by his chart of Virginia.

Exploration continued under Smith, with the special view of finding some way to the South Sea. The Indians said that the Potomac extended far up into the country until it met another river flowing to that ocean. This, of course, was not so, but points in some shape to a passage over to a branch of the Ohio and thus down to the Gulf of Mexico. It is only poetic justice that almost two hundred years later the plan of connecting the headwaters of the Potomac with those of an affluent of the Ohio by adequate communication was urged by the famous Virginian, whose veracity, unlike his predecessor's, has never been attacked; and thus does history join the names of two very different and yet almost equally famous Americans, Smith and Washington. Smith's exploration showed that there was no way of getting to the South Sea by water from Chesapeake Bay or by the rivers running into it, and after spending the summer in this way he returned to Jamestown. Then, as the term of Ratcliffe was expiring, Captain John Smith became president.

There is no question as to the energy of Smith, but he seems to have got on ill with his superiors and his inferiors alike, and the colony did not flourish under his administration. He, of course, lays the blame on the Company's management in England, and, no doubt, things would have been worse had he not been president. There were not many events during his term beyond constant acquisition of knowledge of the country and its natives, sometimes at the expense of the lives of colonists. A somewhat ludicrous incident connected with the Indians was the solemn crowning of Powhatan with a copper diadem received from King James, performed against Smith's will, on express instructions, with the idea of attaching the savage more firmly to the English interest. At this time, out of some three hundred colonists sent from first to last there were hardly more than eighty white inhabitants in the whole bounds of Virginia, a disproportion due to the inroads of disease, partly en route at sea, and more especially after arrival in Virginia. The summers were very fatal, due largely to malaria, and this to some extent was to continue until the inhabitants became acclimated; for quinine was unknown, and it was then simply a question of survival of the fittest. This was concealed in England, but it was one of the greatest difficulties with which the founders of the enterprise had to contend. It is only fair to remember that of the Indians brought to England at various times at least one half also died, showing that constitutions suited to one climate were not suited to the other. And yet, to some extent the colony was already of a settled nature. Marriages took place, the first being that of John Laydon with Anne Burras, although it is not certain exactly when was born their daughter Virginia, the first white child in Jamestown. The situation as a whole, however, was certainly not encouraging. In the summer of 1609 the colony had actually to be broken up by Smith, in part dispersed among the savages, in part to the coast, where they lived on oysters. This was not bad living, but the tradition has survived that it did not agree with the English, some of the men contracting a disorder which caused their skin to peel,—but it would hardly do to lay this on the innocent bivalves. In the fall the population had increased through other arrivals from England, and an indication of the spread of the colony as well as of the never absent fear of Spanish inroads is found in the building by Ratcliffe of a fort at Point Comfort.

Sassafras and clapboards were hardly sufficient returns for what had been expended, and none of the three things which the Company had required had been found,—there was no lump of gold, no South Sea, and there was no survivor from Raleigh's experiments. It would indeed seem as if the Virginia colony was not remunerative, and yet in some way from 1609 dates an enthusiasm which was to make the dream of colonization a reality. Sermons and pamphlets appeared, which interested the British public in Virginia. *Nova Britannia*, for instance, painted the new country in no neutral colors, for it was declared to be fertile and rich in timber and minerals, the natives loving, and the enterprise offering a great means of building up English shipping by trading thither. The population of England should thus find a vent and create a new market for English cloth, and raise again that ancient trade of clothing, so much decayed.

The principal persons interested in the enterprise perceived that the plantation went rather backward than forward, and held meetings at the residence of the Earl of Exeter and elsewhere in London. They concluded that the trouble arose from the form of government and from the length and danger of the passage. The latter could be remedied with fuller experience, but for the former they determined on a special charter. It was of great import that the drafting of this charter was by Sir Edwin Sandys, a leading advocate in Parliament of the popular rights now almost unconsciously coming to the surface, besides being a resolute opponent of Spain, although its final form was the work of Sir Henry Hobart, attorney-general, and Sir Francis Bacon, the solicitor-general. The petition was probably drawn in January, 1609, and was promptly granted by the king, but, as all planters and adventurers were to be named, it was not finally signed and sealed until June 2d. We are told that the incorporators of this charter were fifty-six city companies of London and six hundred and fifty-nine persons, of whom twenty-one were peers, ninety-six knights, eleven doctors, ministers, etc., fifty-three captains, twenty-eight esquires, fifty-eight gentlemen, one hundred and ten merchants, and two hundred and eighty-two citizens and others not classified. With it, as amended three years later, we are on firm historical ground, for now, if not with the patent which preceded, we have the beginning of popular government in America. The boundaries of the colony were to be two hundred miles north and south from Point Comfort, extending westwardly from sea to sea and eastwardly to embrace all islands within one hundred miles. This did not include all that was in the earlier patent, but there had been no settlement up to this time in what had been called the second colony, and so what was now incorporated was to be the basis of everything that might follow. Virginia embraced, and therefore this Company might yet control, the bulk of what is now the United States, extending from the thirty-fourth to the forty-fifth degree, inclusive, from near the present Atlanta to the northern line of the State of New York. Even the Pilgrim Fathers of later years settled within these limits.

An interesting and little-known fact connected with the colonization of Virginia is that the first patent was carried out by the original patentees themselves, while under the new charter the Company was to have the assistance of the guilds of London also. Of these there were thirteen great companies, being the Salters, Vintners, Drapers, Goldsmiths, Haberdashers, Skinners, Mercers, Grocers, Fishmongers, Merchant Tailors, Ironmongers, Clothworkers, and Stationers. The movement was started by a letter from the council and Company to the lord mayor, aldermen, and companies, stating the object of the enterprise and asking that the guilds or their members take bills of adventure of £12 10*s*. each, with special privileges to those adventuring large amounts. The lord mayor thereupon issued a precept to the masters and wardens of the several companies to consider the matter, and this led to important results. The records of some are lost, and others show very little, but, in one way or other, the Grocers, the Mercers, the Clothworkers, the Merchant Tailors, and the Stationers adventured from £100 to £200 at least. In fact, by the next year, it is said that "the noble men and companies of London" had adventured £5,000 together. When we remember that money was then worth five times what it is now, we can appreciate the value of the contributions thus made by the guilds. They were largely reinforced by subscriptions of knights, esquires, citizens, and others, many of them members of Parliament, under a circular of the Virginia council asking subscriptions for three supplies to settle "a foundation of annexing another kingdom to this crown," and from all these sources by 1610 £18,000 had been subscribed. It is not too much to say that but for these subscriptions the enterprise would have fallen through.

Under the new charter the Company had greater powers, and it set about its work with increased interest. It determined to have as governor some person higher in the social scale than heretofore, and so selected Thomas West, Lord de la Warr, whose name has been popularized as "Delaware." Nominally, he was to remain lord governor and captain-general until 1619, and he always took a deep interest in the enterprise. Practically, he did not reach America immediately, and remained there but a short time; and the actual government for most of the period was in the hands of his deputies, particularly Gates and Dale.

The Company sent out promptly enough in 1610 an expedition of nine ships and five hundred people under Sir George Somers and Sir Thomas Gates, with Newport in charge of the fleet. Unfortunately, this was dispersed by the tempest, and the *Sea Adventure*, bearing the new rulers, was wrecked in the Bermudas; and as none of those who actually arrived in Virginia had a commission to succeed Smith, things drifted along with no legal head. An interesting, if incidental, result of the wreck was the discovery and practical annexation of the Bermudas to the crown of England. They were henceforward long known as Somers

Islands, and sometimes by mistake spelled "Summer" Islands. The English found there hogs running wild, and thus subsisted despite the loss of so much, and managed finally to construct out of the wreckage two vessels that brought them safely to Virginia. This storm was the origin of Shakespeare's play *The Tempest*, performed a year or so after; for although the plot is Italian, Ariel and Caliban are fair samples of what the mariners of that day expected to find in unknown islands like "the still vexed Bermoothes." In fact, Caliban is about what the Caribs were pictured, for from that tropical region the name was taken, while the god Setebos comes from Patagonia.

Captain John Smith had returned to England, and Captain George Percy was the president of the council and in general command when Gates and Somers arrived in Virginia on June 2, 1610 (N. S.), the first anniversary of the signing of the charter under which they had come to act. Sir Thomas Gates, with a copy of the charter and his commission, went to the church, and by ringing the bell assembled the planters. The minister, the Rev. Richard Buck, offered a prayer; and after service Secretary William Strachey read the new commission, whereupon Percy surrendered the old one, the charter, and the seal. There were sixty old inhabitants present and one hundred and thirty-five new ones, among them nonconformists as well as members of the Church of England, including Stephen Hopkins, afterward one of the Pilgrim Fathers. The soldiers on guard were a company of veterans trained in the Netherlands, for Gates had certainly served under Maurice of Nassau and may have done so under his father, William the Silent, and was even at this time still in the service of the States General, and only lent or furloughed by them for this enterprise on the special request of King James. He assumed active charge, erected Forts Henry and Charles, in honor of the two princes, at the mouth of the river, and proceeded to make laws suited to the circumstances, setting them up on posts in the church.

The Company, on the discouraging return of the first part of their expedition of 1609, had published in England the broadside called *A True and Sincere Declaration*, citing the drawbacks to be overcome as three,—the dangers of the ocean passage, the barrenness of the country, and the unhealthfulness of the climate. The subsequent history of the colony was the amelioration of these difficulties, but for the present they seemed to Gates insuperable. He restored order, but could not restore spirits. After doing his best under existing circumstances, on consultation with the council he determined to abandon the country. The boats were provisioned and freighted, the ordnance buried, and every person taken aboard, Gates himself being the last; and they sailed, leaving Jamestown undestroyed. At this very time, De la Warr arrived in the bay with another expedition, and a message to Gates by one of his boats caused the fleet to turn back to Jamestown, where De la Warr himself arrived on Sunday, June 20th. As soon as he landed, he fell upon his knees and made a long, silent prayer. After hearing a sermon in the chapel, his commission was read; and he received from Gates the old one, the patents, and the seal, and assumed the government.

There was not to be any great improvement even under De la Warr for some time, but at least the devout character of the English showed itself prominently even here, for this was the time when the great translation of the Bible was in progress, and the Scrooby Independents had not taken all religion with them to Holland. Among his first acts the lord governor put in order the chapel, a building sixty feet long by twenty-four wide, with a steeple at the west end holding two bells. The chancel was of cedar, with the font like a canoe, the communion table of black walnut, and the pews and pulpit of cedar. De la Warr even decorated the building with native flowers from time to time. Daily the sexton rang the bell at ten o'clock, and in the afternoon at four, when prayers were had, and besides two sermons on Sunday there was one on Thursday.

When De la Warr went to church on Sundays he was accompanied by councillors, officers, and gentlemen, together with a guard of fifty halberdiers in his own livery and red cloaks. The lord governor sat in the choir, in a green velvet chair, knelt on a green velvet cushion before him, and so worshipped God with comfort and satisfaction. The private houses did not exhibit so much show, although they were comfortable and warmed with big wood fires in capacious fireplaces and chimneys. The laws instituted by Gates were approved, despite the apparent unreasonableness of some. One is mentioned forbidding throwing soapsuds into the street, the reason being that it was said that everybody in London who used that new invention or wore clothes washed with that article died of the plague.

Prompt measures were taken to obtain supplies from the Bermudas and also fish from North Virginia, and reports sent home. Delaware River and Bay were named for the governor, and attempts were made to reach the mountains to discover gold and silver, but these were unsuccessful. Instead, a fort was built at the falls, although ultimately, on account of sickness and massacres, the colony was again concentrated at Jamestown and Algernoune Fort at the mouth of the river. More to the point, as then believed, were the discoveries by Dr. Bohun of sundry remedies extracted from vegetables and minerals of the country. They did not, however, help the lord governor very much, and in April, 1611, he sailed for Mevis in order to benefit himself and other colonists with the warm baths. Unpropitious winds and currents carried them to the Azores instead, whence after a short stay they sailed for England.

Gates was left in command, and maintained the same policy. Domestic difficulties continued, and that the old fear of Spaniards was not ill founded is shown by the capture this year of Molina and several companions. They had more assurance than Ecija, and, sailing into the bay, took on board and detained several English, and were caught themselves in a similar trap on shore. They were to remain long in Virginia, and this detention of prisoners on both sides caused interminable negotiations between the two governments. Molina got letters to the Spanish ambassador in England at sundry times, one being sewed up in the sole of a traveller's shoe. While the Spaniards maintained that there was no ground for the detention, the facts as now known leave no doubt that Molina and his friends were really spies.

It was felt at home that the Company should have further powers, and, on a petition, held up for over a year on account of opposition, a new charter, or an amendment of the old charter, passed the seals on March 12, 1612. The principal changes were the extension of boundaries so as to include the Bermudas and giving the right to the Company to open lotteries for its benefit. Recognizing the harm which refugees from the colony had done, to the extent even of endangering the utter overthrow and ruin of the enterprise, which, to use the words of the charter, yet could not miscarry without some dishonor to the king and kingdom, the instrument went on to confer the power on the treasurer and the Company to apprehend any such people or send them back to Virginia to be there punished.

Under the amended charter there was to be, to use the name of a pamphlet of that day, *New Life for Virginia*. It came about in a very unexpected way, however, and almost contemporaneously with two deaths which threw almost all circles, political and colonial, into confusion. One was that of Henry, Prince of Wales, the other that of Robert Cecil, Earl of Salisbury. Through Cecil had been a continuity of effort in the direction of colonizing America from the time of Elizabeth, for we should recollect he was the son and successor of her Lord Burleigh. Another pamphlet, publishing of course only what the Company wanted known, was entitled *Good News from Virginia;* but, in point of fact, the really good news was not known until later. A definite means of subsistence for the colonists and of profit for the Company was being found at this very time, for it was in this year that John Rolfe, on some spot now forgotten, made his first good crop of tobacco, imitated from the methods of the Indians. The first imported into England was not esteemed, probably from imperfect curing, but by 1615 these difficulties were overcome and it was taken over in quantity. The result was that the future of Virginia was assured. It was not for two years yet that this same John Rolfe married Pocahontas; but her capture in March, 1612, accomplished perhaps by treachery, had a beneficial effect in that it kept Powhatan under more or less control, although he would not accede to the terms which the English demanded for her ransom. For the time being matters were not promising, and in September there sailed from Virginia the last ship that was to leave until July in the next year.

At first blush one is apt to undervalue these early struggles of the colony, somewhat as Milton looked at the contests of the little Saxon kingdoms when he compared them to the wars of the kites and crows. The frequent change of government, both in the Company's charter and the actual administration in America; the apparent inactivity of the colonists in useful occupations; the variation in population, due to so many coming and so many dying; the frequent famines of those who survived,—all these make up a recital full of incident, but apparently without purpose and without continuity. When we reach the period when tobacco is cultivated, and particularly when it becomes a staple crop, we feel we are on firm ground at last. And yet, time had not been wasted. The main difficulty was that at first the Company and its representatives were seeking some immediate return in the way of mines or precious commodities, and it was some time before the people settled down even to their own maintenance. The reason is not far to seek. They came to a new country, whose forests they admired, but which had to be cut away before they could cultivate; for, unfortunately, they did not settle in any of the places already cleared by the natives, possibly because of the early instructions not to dispossess the Indians. There had been a mistake in choosing Jamestown Island for the capital of the settlement, and even Henrico was not to be permanently its successor. The island was too small for building and agricultural purposes both, and the mainland at this point was thickly wooded. The frequent hostilities with the natives prevented the colonists from going far away from the fort, and the matter of felling and clearing the primitive forest was formidable. On this account they were largely dependent upon the Indians for a number of years. Captain John Smith we have known as an explorer, and this was necessarily the first work to be done in a new country; but he has equal claim to the gratitude of Americans in that he saw the necessity of agriculture and used all his power to develop it. He made the colonists chop down trees, often against their will, and instituted the cultivation of seeds, vegetables, and fruits. Of course, for a while it was all experimental and it was only slowly that they could learn what was suitable to the land and what was not. Wheat did not appear to flourish, running largely to stalk in the new and fertile soil, and thus it resulted that Indian corn became the principal crop, reinforced by native vegetables. We must never forget that this was not the settlement of freemen on land owned by them individually. It was a commercial enterprise, managed by a corporation in England, which could not appreciate to the full the difficulties or devise the best means for overcoming them. We must remember also that the times were still semi-feudal, and the emancipation of tillers of the soil had not progressed far even at home; so it was not unnatural for the Company to carry out quasi-feudal principles on its own account. The community system and similar utopian schemes have been attractive to man in all ages, but the joint stock system of the Company was carrying out the principle for the benefit rather of the proprietors in England than of the colonists in Virginia. This was a device by which a kind of Tontine period of seven years from the charter of 1609 was instituted within which there was to be no division of land or sharing of profits. The few grants of land during this time were exceptional. Commercially, the joint stock seemed to be the proper plan, for it enabled all capital, whether of adventurers of the purse or planters of the soil, to be kept together until something could be realized. But the disadvantage was that it took away the incentive of private ownership, which, socialists to the contrary notwithstanding, has been the secret of man's progress from the Stone Age down. This lesson could have been learned by observing the natives. These had only a rudimentary private ownership, and while this made the tribe strong for war it led the individual to be content with the bare necessities of life.

Possibly Captain John Smith was practically the founder of Virginia, and certainly that other disciplinarian Sir Thomas Dale was the restorer of the colony. Lieutenant under Gates, he was in Gates's numerous absences practically governor, and then governor in his own name afterward. He too was a soldier and a sailor. His rule has sometimes been thought of as a military despotism, but something of this sort was needed among the English as among the Latin colonies further south, and under him there was at least a more energetic policy at Jamestown. There had always been a common garden, where the colonists labored for the benefit of the Company, as there was a magazine, where the Company bought and sold at fixed prices, but Dale now allowed small private gardens for the individual colonists, with beneficial results. Under him came the end of the first joint stock and the beginning of private land owning. Those who had been laboring for the Company were released from their dependency and found themselves landholders, while shareholders in England received also one hundred acres for each share of £12 10*s*. The best part of the joint stock was the end of it, for now more land was cleared and more interest taken in its cultivation. We can hardly imagine any great impetus to tobacco culture if it had been all for the benefit of the non-resident Company. But even this improvement would hardly have come if Dale had not also extended the settlements. It was in his time that Henrico was established, and several pales built, extending from one body of water to another, particularly at Henrico and opposite Jamestown. These consisted of palisades, with something equivalent to a blockhouse at intervals, designed as a defence against animals, but more especially against Indians, thus giving great encouragement to agriculture and assisting in the gradual extension of the settlements. New Bermuda, for instance, was founded by Dale. Thus his administration was justly looked upon as the turning point in colonial history, and by many enactments and public documents the term "ancient planters" is limited to those who were in America "before the going away of Sir Thomas Dale." The last ship that brought over such immigrants was the *Treasurer* in 1615.

Samuel Argall succeeded Dale and arrived at Jamestown in May, 1617. As indicative of the new circumstances, we are told that so far had the importance of tobacco progressed that the very streets of Jamestown were then given up to its cultivation. In truth, the time had now come for official cognizance of tobacco. The Company ordained that it should sell in Virginia at three shillings a pound, a regulation which created much discontent, inasmuch as it then sold on arrival in England for four or five times this amount. As the population gradually increased, not only were new lands taken up for tobacco culture, but further settlements were made from time to time, as, for instance, Martin's Brandon. Among the laws ordained by Argall was one possibly recognizing a difference in the Indian outlook after the death of Powhatan, for it expressly provided that the savages should not be taught to use firearms. A very different regulation was that making churchgoing compulsory, for there was not yet any sharp division in practical piety between the Puritans and their fellow countrymen. In fact, in this very year 1618 was the sitting of the Synod of Dort, whose aim was greater unity of Protestant Christianity over all Europe, although the extreme Puritans had already found their position in

England uncomfortable. The year Jamestown was founded some went to Holland under Robinson, but they were now looking to the New World. They had already made sundry applications for land in Virginia.

Sir George Yeardley was appointed deputy-governor to succeed Argall, and a paper, one of the dearest to Virginians and most eventful in American history, was now sent out by the Company,—the Great Charter. It really was an ordinance by the Company, but conferred suffrage and the right of representation in a general assembly, which were to survive the Company itself. For it is one of the many instances we find in the history of comparative politics where a development occurs vastly out of proportion to its beginning; where that organism which we call a State irresistibly begins in a collection of men regardless of whether they are intended as a dependency of a trading company or of a mother country. Paper withes, whether these be labelled "charters" or what not, cannot bind a growing giant. An unwritten law has often more force than a paper constitution.

A contemporaneous instance of the birth of a new institution, unappreciated for years, but finally to prove its importance and to be extinguished only in the blood of generations unborn, is found in negro slavery. Like so many other things which have played a great part in the development of the human race, its origin can be traced, even in America, only with great difficulty. The usual account is that a Dutch man-of-war brought some slaves captured in the West Indies and sold them, probably at Jamestown. This may be true, but there seems reason to connect with the matter the ship *Treasurer*, owned by the Earl of Warwick and other members of the Virginia Company as a private adventure of their own. She was fitted out for legitimate purposes, and seems to have gone to the West Indies on business which in the time of Drake would have been legitimate, but in these piping times of peace was called piracy. Unpublished papers are said to indicate that she was the alleged Dutch man-of-war, despite the fact that the new governor officially reported that the *Treasurer* was coldly received and sailed away from Virginia. In some quarters this is regarded as a ruse designed to deceive Spain, for the subject of this expedition of the *Treasurer* required to be delicately handled and led to long negotiations. It is probable that the *Treasurer* had something to do with the matter, and at least gave information to the Dutch man-of-war which led to her calling at Jamestown, if she were not in fact the Dutch ship herself. So far as appears from the records, only one of the *Treasurer's* negroes, Angela, was landed in Virginia, and the rest were taken to the Bermudas, where they were put ashore for use on Warwick's lands.

Looking back, we can appreciate the far-reaching importance of the introduction of tobacco and of the beginning of negro slavery. The two were to react upon each other, each making the other more necessary. But this came only in course of time, and for a long while the presence of negroes was hardly appreciable. The Dutch ship seems to have brought nineteen or twenty, the *Treasurer* one, if they were different, and not until 1623 was there another imported, in the *Swan*, so that the census in 1624–1625 shows only twenty-two Africans. Two of these were children, although the records are too incomplete for us to know whether they were born in America or in Africa. One cause of this slow increase was that at first the two sexes were, intentionally or otherwise, kept apart, the men being in some settlements, and the women as a rule in others.

It must not be supposed that there was the slightest scruple on the part of any Englishman in connection with slavery. So far as they thought of it at all, all endorsed the reply which Hawkins is reported to have made to the reproaches of Queen Elizabeth, in which he averred that in bringing the negroes from their savage home to a Christian country he was doing them a positive benefit. In their condition on arriving in Virginia may be found one reason for their slow increase. They came as savages, not only ignorant of English, but in intelligence and habits little above the cattle whose labor in part they took over. It was long before they were to be regarded generally as human beings, in the full sense of the word. The first experiments with them would be made only by the more venturesome or progressive planters, as their qualities were unknown, while their savageness was apparent. But the Spaniards had led the way, and negroes brought from the West Indies had learned enough of agriculture and particularly of tobacco raising to show the value of such labor. The climate of Virginia differed from that of the West Indies, but as the best tobacco, that with which the Virginians were most in competition, came from those islands, it would soon be found imperative to employ the same methods in order to get upon an equality. Such was the economic necessity for negro slavery. At first, the negroes were known as servants, just as the indented whites from England, the legal difference being only in the term of their service. The word "slave" belongs to a later period than the rule of the Company, under which, as in fact during almost all the remainder of the century, the indented whites formed the mass of the laboring population.

The administration of Yeardley is marked not only by the Great Charter, the first legislature, and the introduction of negro slavery, but also as one of reaction from the rapacity of Argall, and one of general quiet and prosperity. The population was about eight hundred, divided into a number of settlements, themselves now combined in four great corporations, or cities. The first was the city of Henricus, embracing Henrico and thence westwardly on James River, bounded south by Dale's Pale; the second, Charles City, extending eastwardly on both sides of the James to the Chickahominy; the third, James City, embracing both sides of the James about Jamestown; and the fourth, Kiccowtan, extending thence to Chesapeake Bay. All were on the water, and more especially on James River, and thus convenient for trade with England and foreign countries. In point of fact, vessels came up to the wharves of the plantations to be loaded, which was a great advantage to commerce, although having in one respect a bad effect upon the colony. Every place being so readily reached by water, there was no necessity felt for building good roads, and, as a result, the road system remained primitive.

The boroughs from which the burgesses were to be chosen were more numerous than might be supposed. It is true the corporation of Henricus made up one borough, embracing the settlements known as Arrahattock, Coxendale, and Henrico, while, on the other hand, Charles City contained five electoral boroughs. One of these was made up of the plantations of Bermuda Hundred, Shirley Hundred, and Charles City; the second was Smith's Hundred; the third, Flowerdue Hundred; the fourth, Ward's Plantation, the last three being new settlements; and the fifth, Martin's Brandon, having a special patent, and on that account not to be recognized by the general assembly. The corporation of James City contained the four boroughs of James City, Argall's Gift, Martin's Hundred, and Lawne's Plantation, the last two being new settlements. Kiccowtan made up only one borough.

The legislative body was composed of the council of state and the General Assembly, and met in the church at Jamestown, Friday, August 9, 1619, there being twenty members of the assembly. The secretary of the council of state, John Pory, an ex-member of Parliament, was appointed speaker, the proceedings were opened by prayer, and all took the oath of supremacy. The speaker seems to have divided up the business in a convenient manner, and committees acted promptly. The Great Charter was considered and gave satisfaction, some details being the subject of representations to the Company, and was passed with the general assent and applause of the whole assembly. Their laws, as sent to England for approval, related to the treatment of Indians, the Church, planting corn, mulberry trees, flax, vines, and tobacco, to patents, tradesmen, the magazine, against idleness, gaming, drunkenness, excess in apparel, and to similar subjects. Rents and taxes were to be paid in commodity, there being no mint and no money, and therefore the price of tobacco was fixed at three shillings a pound for the best and eighteen pence for the second grade. All of less value was to be burned before the owner's face,—the first, and, as it proved, a temporary, inspection law. On account of the weather and of the illness of members, the assembly was soon prorogued and then dissolved.

For sickness still afflicted the colonists, particularly the newcomers; and in 1620, of twelve hundred people sent out to Virginia no less than one thousand died. It was almost of necessity that the Company turned to less desirable classes and imported some of the malefactors granted by the Privy Council. A lot of boys were also sent, called "Duty boys" from the ship in which they came; but the most interesting of the colonists were those due to the foresight of the Earl of Southampton. Many women had come before as wives and daughters, and even as colonists, but now they were imported systematically. From this time several cargoes of maids, and some widows besides, were sent over as wives "in order to make the men feel at home." To repay the outlay involved in this commendable enterprise, the colonists desiring helpmeets had to pay one hundred and twenty pounds of the best leaf tobacco per wife, and they do not seem to have been considered high at that.

A number of interesting provisions date from this time. For instance, the Great Charter directed that the officials should be supported out of the proceeds of the lands allotted to the several officers and distributed among the different boroughs, thus easing the inhabitants of taxes, and the governor in particular had the further advantage of the house at Jamestown previously erected by Gates. The education of the Indians was not neglected, for lands were set apart for a college, and collections were made in England to such good purpose that the bishops received there some £1,500.

On the whole, the term of Yeardley can fairly be regarded as closing the experimental period of the colony.

With the establishment of the Great Charter, the remunerative cultivation of tobacco, the institution of a general assembly, the as yet unappreciated importation of Africans, and the provision for home life in the systematic bringing over of women, we have reached a time of stability. England had at last learned how to colonize; but the great Virginia Company was, like many a mother, to die in giving life to her child.

CHAPTER V

THE END OF THE COMPANY

We have reached a time when it becomes possible in some measure to dissociate the Virginia Company from the history of Virginia. And yet, it would be a mistake to consider either by itself. When the Company began to lay more stress upon its political powers, it was doing so not only as a corporation for its own ends, but also for the country it was founding over sea. When such features were added to commercial functions, it came in conflict with the crown, and there was precipitated a battle between liberty and prerogative. In this the Company went down, but went down in a good cause and one which was ultimately to be victorious, first on British and then on American soil. Let us briefly trace the steps and do tardy justice to the Virginia Company.

Toward the end of the reign of Elizabeth the popular and intellectual agitation of earlier years was gradually changing into political channels. Thanks to the internecine strife of the nobility in the Wars of the Roses and to Tudor ability, royalty had overthrown the worst features of aristocracy, and a movement began looking to the enfranchisement of the people as against the crown itself. If they had the right of private judgment in religion, the same principle was sure to be applied sooner or later to politics. Elizabeth had the good sense with her last parliament to bow to the coming storm, although she could not tell what it meant or what shape it would take, nor could anyone of that day. To her, doubtless, it seemed to be only the opposition of her people to monopolies which she had granted and which worked hardship. Historians often make the mistake of thinking that Sandys and others had very definite political plans in view under her successor. The English people have never been extremists. At different times a strong current of thought, a *Zeitgeist*, has carried them in one direction or the other, but seldom has it been that a satisfactory compromise could not be reached by intelligent statesmen. If unrecognized and goaded beyond endurance, we shall find Jack Cades, Wat Tylers, Puritans, and Papists, but generally there may be a national church founded or a national parliament evolved which, if properly directed, will work out its own salvation with little friction. Unfortunately, the Stuart kings were not such directors. James I. had been so hectored in Scotland by the Presbyterians and the nobles that he determined to govern England with all the absoluteness of Elizabeth at a time when even Elizabeth had perceived that this method was out of date. His first parliament was loyal, as a first parliament is apt to be, and the Gunpowder Plot made it more so; and yet Bacon, aided by Sandys and others, found it necessary to draw up for the Commons a remonstrance against the conduct of the king toward them and to advocate toleration in Church and reform in State. This parliament did not last long, and the second was hardly more successful except in showing the rising tide of public opinion. On the 17th of June, 1614, the king dissolved the second, and got along without any other for seven years. During this time the Privy Council practically ruled for the king, while the Virginia Company, in its assemblies, numerously attended and composed in part of men prominent in public life, became to a large extent the rallying place for advocates of popular rights. On the religious side, such extremists as the persecuted Separatists of Scrooby found it necessary to withdraw to Holland; and after years of negotiation, some of them, to us known as the Pilgrim Fathers, were to obtain permission through Elder Brewster to settle in Virginia. Among their number in the *Mayflower* were members of the Company, including the governor.

It was almost inevitable that in course of time the Company should divide as to matters of policy. There can be no progress without debate, and no large body of men have ever been able to agree perfectly. It would probably have been true under any form of organization, but the charter of 1612 contained a provision relating to the internal government of the Company which made certain the growth of parties and factions. This was the institution of four "great and general courts of the council and company of adventurers for Virginia," to be held on the last Wednesday save one of the Hilary, Easter, Trinity, and Michaelmas terms, for the election of members of the council, appointing officers, and ordaining laws not contrary to the laws and statutes of the realm. These meetings are indiscriminately called assemblies and courts, and in them was debated everything relating to the business of the Company. The names so given have become the titles for the legislative bodies of America. Thus, in Massachusetts we have the General Court, and in Virginia the General Assembly, and upon these are modelled the representative bodies of most of the States.

The cleavage in the Company at first seems to have been between the aristocratic and commercial elements, represented more especially by Lord King, afterward Earl of Warwick, on the one side, and Sir Thomas Smythe and Alderman Johnson on the other. This related more especially to the objects of the enterprise, the factions being interested more in the governmental and the commercial aspects respectively. The beginnings of parties are always hard to trace, and they are particularly so in this instance on account of loss of records and lack of memoirs of the actors, but we find that there followed later an even more important division between the popular and royalist elements.

The former came to predominate, and ultimately the well-posted Spanish ambassador Gondomar warned King James that the Virginia courts were a "seminary for a seditious parliament." On the popular side the leader was Sir Edwin Sandys, and with him stood the Earl of Southampton, Shakespeare's friend, Sir Nicholas Ferrar, and others. The observant Spaniard told James that the first was dangerous, and the second popular; and Sandys was by others declared to have a "malitious hearte to the government of a monarchie." As in politics outside, these were known as the Patriots. The opposing party contained such men as Sir Thomas Smythe and Alderman Johnson, although among them ranged also some who were creatures of the king. One is apt to take sides with the Patriots, who seem to date back in some shape to the unfortunate Earl of Essex of Elizabeth's reign, but it must not be forgotten that among their opponents were many who as patriotically believed that royal government was, possibly at home, and certainly in the colonies, the best form of administration.

Patriotism is made up of a number of elements. Love of home and one's people enters largely, and in particular cases this will be accentuated by dislike of other nations. In England at the time of Elizabeth we have seen that religious differences and fear of invasion made Spain the most hated of all continental countries and that, even after the Spanish Armada and its results had lessened the fear of injury, the aversion increased through commercial rivalry. Lord Bacon, speaking of Spain, attributed that nation's greatness to four things: to wit, her long and admirably trained army, her religious unity due to expulsion of the Moors and ruthless suppression of heresy by means of the Inquisition, to the treasure which she so constantly drew from her American provinces, and to her alliance through family and other ties with the House of Austria, which controlled the Holy Roman Empire. In this hatred England was all but a unit, and one of the chief causes of the gradual estrangement between the people and the king was found in the friendliness of James for Spain. For a long time there was a plan for the marriage of his eldest son Henry, Prince of Wales, to the Spanish Infanta, and to this may be attributed in part the reluctance of the Spanish king to proceed to extremities in regard to the Virginia colony. After the death of Prince Henry came the marriage of Princess Elizabeth to the Elector Palatine, one of the leading Protestant princes of Germany, a popular measure to have important consequences in the future. And yet, so long as the second son of the king, Charles, now Prince of Wales, was unmarried, there was a chance, and in fact a plan, for him to marry the Infanta and thus connect, after all, the royal houses. It cannot be doubted that James was thoroughly in earnest about this match, but difficulties supervened, and he must have realized how unpopular it was. Although after a while Sir Thomas Smythe and some of the merchants seemed to have gone over to the court side and favored the alliance, on the other hand Sir Edwin Sandys and his colleagues were bitterly opposed to it. Sandys hardly made a secret of his belief that "if God from heaven did constitute and direct a frame of government on earth, it was that of Geneva," an idea equally distasteful to James and to the clergy of England, and Sandys is even said to have asked the Archbishop of Canterbury to give leave to the Brownists and Separatists of England to go to Virginia. The dread of Spain and the love of Geneva no doubt reacted upon each other in his mind, and ultimately he is said to have declared that he wished to erect a free popular state in Virginia, and he interpreted the charter to mean that the colonists there should have "no government put upon them but by their own consent."

From the first, the correspondence was vigorous between Zuñiga and his royal master as to the colony in Virginia, which the ambassador was anxious for the king to exterminate. Like his father, however, Philip was anxious and deliberate, but, unlike him, did not always carry his deliberations to a conclusion. The truth was that Spain had been badly crippled by the rising sea power of England and the revolted Netherlands, with the latter of whom, in 1609, Philip was forced to conclude the twelve-year truce which practically recognized their independence. Zuñiga succeeded in October, 1607, in having an interview with King James, and represented to him how contrary to good friendship it was to colonize Virginia, for it was a part of the Spanish Indies. The king answered that he had not particularly known what was going on, but that Virginia was a very distant country from where the Spaniards lived and he did not understand that the Spanish king had any right to it; that in point of fact it seemed to him to be a new region, discovered by his people just as the Spaniards had earlier discovered others. All the satisfaction the Spanish ambassador could obtain was that if the English went where under the treaty they should not go, the Spaniards could punish them. He says he was told by Salisbury that it seemed to him that the English should not go to Virginia, evidently on the idea that it was part of the Spanish Indies, but that the government did not feel at liberty to prevent their going or to command those there to return. Zuñiga urged the Spanish king to "drive these villains out from there, hanging them in short order,"—quite as had been done to Ribault and his interlopers. But if Salisbury ever assented to the Spanish claim that Virginia was part of the Indies, he must have done it to gain time, for the patent had been carefully drawn on the other theory. The probability is that the Spaniard's hope was father to the thought and that he mistook evasion for assent. There was friction between the two countries about the men of the expedition undertaken in 1607 by Challons to settle a colony in North Virginia, but who were captured by the Spaniards. The president of the Contratacion House at Seville closely examined them as to Virginia and its advantages, and tried to get maps from them, but apparently without avail. Of these Daniel Tucker, the cape merchant, or commissary, had been set ashore near Bordeaux; and when he reached England, there was a great stir in diplomatic circles over the matter. The English ambassador in Spain wrote fully, and it was discussed in Parliament, Bacon and Sir Edwin Sandys taking part in the debates. Negotiations lasted for years and did no little to keep alive the hostility of the two nations. In the summer of 1609, Ecija, by royal directions, explored the coast northwardly from St. Augustine and located the English in Chesapeake Bay, but did not interfere with them. For a long time it was exceedingly doubtful what course Spain would pursue in the matter, and the early founders of Virginia had every reason to expect armed interference with their projects, while on the other hand King James was inclined to peace. Even when the proposed Spanish match fell through, the death of Sir Walter Raleigh on the block showed the great influence still of Spain, for even Catherine de' Medici had not punished De Gourgues. Raleigh had languished in the Tower for many years, and his unfortunate expedition to Guiana had increased the hatred of him by the Spaniards, while it had lessened the interest of James. Truly, to use the words of his ill-fated brother, Humphrey Gilbert, "the wings of a man's life are plumed with the feathers of death." No act of James has injured him more with posterity, and it was universally reprobated in contemporary England; and yet, it is indicative of how times had changed that it could be permitted and how little, after all, Raleigh was to be missed in colonization. James so leaned to Spain that it was questionable whether the government would afford the colony adequate protection, and the Protestant English settled in Virginia had the experience of the Protestant French massacred in Florida ever before their eyes; for Spain claimed that Virginia was her province or district known as Orysta, and the Spanish ambassador at London advised that the English government would not interfere if the colonists were exterminated. Can one doubt what would have occurred if Menendez had been alive?

Events in England affected the history of the Company from the beginning, and particularly after the charter of 1612.

Just about that time Purchas, with the publication of his *Pilgrimage*, was beginning his contributions to literature and continuing the interest begun long before by Hakluyt, who was to die four years later, contemporaneously with the great dramatist who commemorated the *Tempest* of Gates and Somers. The Company now sold the Bermuda Islands for £2,000 to a corporation made up of some of its own members, thus leaving free play to its efforts for continental Virginia, and at the same time the Privy Council showed its interest by commending the lotteries authorized to the different trade companies of the kingdom. These were put into effect very soon, one of the principal being established at the west end of St. Paul's Cathedral. The London guilds subscribed with many others throughout England to this form of aid, and the lotteries so largely took the place of the bills of adventure of earlier days as a source of revenue that when the privilege was withdrawn in 1621 the loss was severely felt. By the infrequent parliaments also, Virginia colonization was favored, and this in spite of an injudicious speech on one occasion.

In 1616 we are told that Sir Thomas Smythe's health was such that Sandys was elected to assist him, although it was not until three years later that Sandys was made treasurer in fact, and John Ferrar succeeded Alderman Johnson as deputy, on which occasion there was used a "balletting" box. A few months later came the definite alienation of Sandys and Johnson. A more serious matter, however, was the rupture between Sandys and King James. The king on several occasions sent a list of men from whom he desired a choice should be made, and in 1620 the Company showed its independence by electing Southampton, a Patriot member of the Privy Council, who had not been named at all. This was possibly in the nature of a compromise, for at least it removed Sandys, whom the king declared to be his greatest enemy, even telling the Company to choose the Devil treasurer if it would, but not Sir Edwin Sandys. Southampton and Sandys acted together, so that the subsequent history of the Company may be said to be under the Sandys-Southampton administration; for, to the rage of James, in 1622 Southampton was reëlected over the king's candidates by a vote of one hundred and seventeen to twenty.

It so happened that the feeling of the Company's managers was intensified by the action of the king in regard to tobacco, which had become the chief product of the colony and in very truth saved it from abandonment. One would have supposed that the government would have welcomed this result and given the importations every encouragement. In fact, under James it did somewhat the opposite, and there is every reason to suppose that this was due to fear of offending Spain, whose colonies, particularly Trinidad, produced tobacco of a high grade and up to this time had controlled the markets of England as well as the continent. It was easy to say that tobacco was no necessity, and that even as a luxury it did only harm by injuring the health and means of the consumers. With this abstract question we have nothing to do, nor properly had the king. The fact was that from the time of Sir Walter Raleigh people in Europe had learned to use tobacco and value it, and with King James the policy certainly should have been, if his people must use it, to have it brought from his own colonies and not from those of Spain. The charter had authorized an impost of five per cent upon imports for twenty-one years, and this was bad enough. By 1619 the imports of tobacco from Virginia and the Bermudas were twenty thousand pounds, in 1622 forty thousand pounds, and in 1624 sixty thousand. The king not only wrote against the use of the article, but, instigated by Spanish influence, took measures to prohibit the introduction of more than fifty-five thousand pounds per annùm, while at the same time he allowed the introduction of the Spanish product. He even resorted at one time to the grant of a monopoly. The Company endeavored to meet his wishes by agreeing to a larger impost and making him a present of one-third of the product as a bribe besides, but finally felt compelled to have their crop taken to Holland for sale so as to get it out of royal control altogether. This was opposed by the government, but was persisted in for a time, Sandys declaring that while the Company's own cargoes might be subject to regulation, this did not apply to private planters, as they under the charter had the same rights as all Englishmen.

The king's hands were now strengthened by an occurrence which seemed indeed to show the necessity for some other supervision than that of the Company. Ever since the capture of Pocahontas there had been peace with the Indians, and it did not occur to the colonial officials that it could ever be otherwise again. Despite their own experience and that of other colonies, they did not realize the savage character. White traders and missionaries were among the natives, the natives were allowed free access to the white settlements, and measures were taken for their education and civilization. The whites even permitted them the use of firearms, so that they might do the hunting while the colonists devoted themselves more especially to the cultivation of tobacco. The influence of Pocahontas was gone, for she had sailed to England, to be much noticed and in 1617 to die there; and at religious ceremonies connected with the disinterring of Powhatan's bones there had been some threats of trouble, to which no attention was paid. The white settlements had grown until they extended from the bay up both sides of James River to Henrico, with outlying places at other points, and the number of boroughs and plantations indicates a settled and growing community. Berkeley Hundred had been established a short time, and among the last settlements we have Accomac and Newport News. Pory had even been sent to explore the river Chowan, and reported great forests of pine and a fruitful country,—an expedition harking back to Raleigh's colonies at Roanoke and forward to the Carolina movements later in the century.

There seemed to be the best feeling between the races. The Indians had been gradually dispossessed of the land, and their title was not recognized by the authorities; but there had been no occasion to define the limits or to make treaties on this subject. And yet the savages instinctively realized that the country was not large enough for the two races, and they resolved to cut the knot in their own way. Suddenly, in March, 1622, almost every settlement was assaulted at once in a well-planned massacre, participated in by many of the tribes. Probably four hundred men, women, and children were slaughtered, and the rest withdrew hurriedly to Jamestown and a few lower settlements. It was impossible for the fleeing and panic-stricken whites to carry their belongings with them; and although no negroes were killed, cattle and domestic animals of all kinds were butchered and improvements so far as practicable destroyed. Outside the palisaded forts the country was again a wilderness.

The Company minimized the reports and did all it could to repair the damage, but the distress was too great not to become known, and, unfortunately, just at this time Governor Butler was passing through Virginia on his return from the Bermudas and soon published his book *Virginia Unmasked*, telling the truth—and probably a good deal more. Nor was this all. The massacre interfered with planting the crops; and the succeeding fall and winter witnessed famine and sickness recalling the "Starving Time," for it is said that more people died during this season than had perished from the Indians. When spring came, there were only four or five hundred people left in the whole country, and the Indians had become daring enough even to attack a vessel, the *Tiger*,—a thing unheard of before. But soon the whites wreaked vengeance. When the corn was almost ripe, armed parties attacked the Indians and destroyed their crops and settlements with a ferocity that equalled that of the savages themselves. The result was beneficial to Virginia. The distress of the natives almost paralleled that of the colonists, and they retired into the interior, leaving much of the James and York River regions to the undisputed occupancy of the English.

The king, however, was not slow to seize so good an opportunity of balancing scores with the Patriots. He contended, and some who valued his favor also claimed, that the colony had not been a success under the Company management and that it should be restored to the shape in which it was before the charter of 1609 had been granted. If the management had been in the hands of the court party, as James had endeavored to secure on the occasion of several elections, this point would never have been raised; but having failed to get control of the Company, he now determined to abolish the corporation, and the dissension which broke out in pamphlets the next year between the new and the old officials only played into his hands. The Company was now really involved in trouble. Members hesitated about attending meetings, and it was not long before we are told two-thirds did not come. Some were even willing to surrender the charter, among them the Earl of Warwick, Sir Thomas Smythe, Alderman Johnson, John Martin, and Captain John Smith.

We have seen that with all his energy Captain Smith had not proved acceptable in the colonies, and during this time was in England. It is, perhaps, not important whether Pocahontas saved Smith or whether a great many things in his history are true. It may fairly be said that his adventures were hardly more incredible than many recorded by the early Spanish voyagers. If he exaggerated his own exploits, he did not do more than De Soto and De Ayllon, and his exaggerations were limited to his own adventures, while as an explorer he is far more accurate than his predecessors. The controversy which has arisen over him has a broader scope. Why he was not reëmployed we do not know. He does not seem to have paid up the share of stock for which he subscribed, although one would think his sufferings and his experience would have been of sufficient importance to entitle him to recognition, even after making a considerable discount on his narrative. The reason may lie deeper. Whether he intended it or not, his exaltation of his own times was a reflection upon the succeeding period when the Virginia Company was in charge. This may have made him unacceptable to the Company, while it probably made him a favorite with the court party. The dates of his publications point in this direction. His Oxford Tract came out in 1612, one of the darkest periods in the Company's annals; and his *Historie* appeared in 1623, in time to do damage to the Company and furnish many a text for their opponents, although it may be doubted whether the mere licensing of his works necessarily shows them to represent the royal view. Printing had become too much of a public necessity for it to be possible to publish arguments alone, and the system of censorship exercised could hardly go further than suppress works hostile to the crown. It is more likely that Smith's books were licensed because they contained nothing to which the king could object than that they were licensed because they were intended as an argument for the course the king desired to pursue. The Oxford Tract, for example, was published the very year that the king was signing a charter giving greater powers to the Company.

At all events, it was in 1623 that the king had the Privy Council investigate, and the Company through Sandys and others prepared and submitted papers in its own defence. On April 28th the king appointed a special commission in the matter, with Sir William Jones, late chief justice of the Irish King's Bench, as president. Southampton and Sandys were confined by the Privy Council in their own houses, whereupon the Company deferred the annual election, and in the absence of the leaders the burden of management fell upon Nicholas Ferrar. A provisional report of the commission in July was in favor of the earlier method of government.

The object of the king all this while is not certain. No doubt he desired to get rid of the Company, but it is not clear what disposition he would make of the colony. The

Patriots always claimed that James intended to give Virginia and the Bermudas over to Spain as a kind of dowry in case the Spanish match was arranged. In the autumn of 1623, however, this fell through, and thence on, at least, his plan seems to have been to preserve the colony under royal government. At all events, he required the Company to vote on surrendering its charter, and on October 30th its members declined by a large majority.

It became necessary finally for public reasons for James to summon a parliament; and as Sandys was elected a member from Kent, he was released and sat in this fourth parliament, beginning February 22, 1624. The plan now approved itself to the Company of reserving the whole matter for the parliament, in which it had a number of friends, Nicholas Ferrar, for instance, being a member for Lymington. On May 6th its petition was presented, calling Virginia "the child of the kingdom, exposed in the wilderness to extreme danger," and praying for assistance. A committee was appointed; but James wrote to the House not to trouble themselves with this petition, as he intended to settle the matter himself in the Privy Council. Silence greeted this message, but the matter was then and there permitted to drop.

On the 3d of November the Privy Council appointed Captain John Harvey and three others as commissioners to proceed to Virginia and report on the situation, while the Patriots in Virginia had sent John Pountis to England to support the Company. He unfortunately died at sea. The royal commission finally reported in favor of annulling the charter; and on June 26, 1624, this was done by *quo warranto* by Sir James Ley in the court of King's Bench. The contention of Attorney-general Coventry was that the charter was void because unlimited, and the Company could transfer to Virginia all the king's subjects and give them the right to govern themselves. Then the king immediately set to work to devise a plan of government for Virginia, seeking the assistance of the same people who had helped him to plan one for Ireland, but he died somewhat suddenly on April 6, 1625. His successor, Charles I., had always been on friendly terms with the Patriot leaders, and was induced to continue practically the original form of government; so that the success of James's effort was only partial.

During his different investigations and proceedings, King James, through his Privy Council, had ordered seized all known papers of the Company. From the fact that none of these have survived, the inference is justifiable that they were destroyed and that this was done by royal order. In point of fact, until recently the history of the Company has been almost a blank. Of course, the books and pamphlets published by it and about its work have been known. Before the charter of 1612 it had itself issued some twenty tracts and the like, and after that time an annual "declaration of the present state of the colony" was read at the Hilary term and afterward for some years printed; but from 1623 none of its printed matter survived, although manuscript books were numerous. For the different officers had records, of which the most important were letters from the royal officials, charters, laws, minutes, and acts, and what we would call stock books. It has been estimated that the original manuscripts would contain seven million words. In the spring of 1623 the Privy Council sequestered the court books, and then the commissioners ordered the Virginia and Somers Islands Companies to deliver at the inquest house adjoining St. Andrew's Church, in Holborn, all writings, the principal officers of both being then under arrest. After the charter was quashed, the king appointed a commission which at different times seized whatever remaining evidences there were of the Company's work. The Company appreciated the importance of its documents, and in the spring of 1623 was busily engaged in having them copied. Sir John Danvers copied the "lieger court books," that is, the acts of the general courts from 1619, while Ferrar did the same for all the court books and writings belonging to the Company, both sets being attested. In that summer

Danvers and Ferrar delivered the copies to the Earl of Southampton; and when the commissioners demanded these from him, he replied "he would as soon part with the evidences of his land as with the said papers, being the evidence of his honor in that service," somewhat as the managers of the Company asked the Privy Council "that howsoever your lordships shall please for the future to dispose of the Company, the records of their past success may not be corrupted and falsified." Before going to the Netherlands in the fall of 1624, Southampton sent the Danvers copies to his seat at Titchfield, in Hampshire, and delivered the Ferrar copies to Sir Robert Killigrew. Even the Ferrar copies have disappeared, but those made by Danvers passed with Titchfield to different proprietors, until in 1667 Colonel William Byrd purchased the papers at an executor's sale for sixty guineas. He brought them to America, where they were copied by Colonel Richard Bland, and both the Byrd and Bland papers were bought by Thomas Jefferson. Finally, they were purchased by Congress from the estate of Jefferson, and now the two volumes are deposited in the Library of Congress.

Such was the end of the Virginia Company. It had found the infant settlement hardly alive under the earlier patent, and persevered despite all discouragements within and without until the colony became self-sustaining. It is true that during the struggle with the king there had been few people sent over, but at least there was consequently little sickness in Virginia, and so the population was again at about eleven hundred. The cost was startling. These were all that survived out of five thousand six hundred and forty-nine people landed in America; and Captain John Smith is not alone in estimating the money spent first and last at £200,000, to be multiplied by five to reach the equivalent in current money. And yet, Virginia was a success. The plantations were to some extent palisaded, as was natural only two or three years after the massacre, but the houses were comfortable, originally often of logs and generally still of wood, although at least one was reported of stone. We are told there were five hundred and twenty-six tame swine, the woods being full of wild ones, and there were five hundred cattle and three hundred goats, although, strange to say, only one horse and one mare. In tobacco had been found a form of agriculture which, despite governmental interference and the fall of the Company, assured the future.

So far as we know, the Virginia Company never rose to the dignity of having, like the East India Company, its own house or building. In its earlier days we repeatedly learn that it met at the house of Sir Thomas Smythe, in Aldersgate Street, and after Sir Edwin Sandys succeeded Smythe it met in Sandys's house, which was on the same street. Sandys's abode was in sight of Aldersgate itself, by which King James had entered London on his accession in 1603, and on this account dear to him and made much of by his satellites. During the later years of the Company, he was remodelling Aldersgate as a kind of monument to himself and his great reign. On each side was a figure of James in royal state, carved in high relief, and there were also inscriptions from Holy Writ supposed to be appropriate to so august a monarch,—which need hardly surprise us if we will turn to the preface of the authorized version of the Scriptures published even earlier and still in common use. Near by, Sandys was erecting a very different monument to the Virginia Company and its persistent and finally successful attempt to found a free state in America; for, although during the troublous times meetings were sometimes held in the great hall of the Ferrar house, the places most connected with the Company were the residences of Smythe and Sandys.

A contrast has sometimes been drawn between the two great colonizing corporations of England which began their careers at almost the same time. The East India Company was organized as a trading concern pure and simple, its route being around Cape of Good Hope, and in it figured Sir George Somers, Sir Thomas Smythe, and others prominent in the Virginia enterprise also. It acquired a firm hold in India, and without any design to colonize found it necessary to secure land for its factories, and, being drawn into the conflicts of the native princes, gradually became stronger and stronger, acquiring the position of arbiter and finally of master. In the course of time, the trading company assumed political powers and ruled the vast Indian empire which only within the memory of people now living was transferred to the crown. On the other hand, the Virginia Company, while commercial also in nature, proceeded along the same paths in the Western Hemisphere, but developed political functions so rapidly as to assume rather a political than a trading form. It was not allowed to reach its majority of twenty-one years before the jealousy of the crown was excited and the Company abolished. So that the anomaly is presented of the East India Company developing a vast political structure out of a trading charter, and the Virginia Company losing even commercial power in an attempt to use its political rights. The reason for the difference is not far to seek. The governmental features of the East India Company grew up only gradually, hardly known to the crown at all, because far away in their operations and affecting only alien races. The Virginia Company, however, built up a colony of Englishmen, across an ocean, to be sure, but communicating at short intervals with England, and supervised by the king through his Privy Council.

Its downfall is only an example of success involved in apparent defeat. History not infrequently shows those whose death has effected more than their lives, and on the list surely ranks high the company whose claims embraced practically the whole of what is now the United States not then in alien occupation, who settled the first lasting colony, and whose plan looked forward not only to imperial growth but to a democratic state. Virginia has been the mother of presidents, but the Virginia Company was the mother of States, and, not unlike its forerunner Raleigh, nothing in its great life so became it as the manner of its death.

CHAPTER VI

THE OLD DOMINION

THE progress of any community depends upon its people and their environment. When one says "people," it means more than "race." The English race is active and progressive, but even the English were in the seventeenth century far behind the Dutch in many respects. The Dutch with no forests built ships and controlled the carrying trade of the world. The English could not compete with them. Even in agriculture, by a system of alternation of crops not understood in England, the Dutch had carried gardening to perfection and made their little country, reclaimed from the sea, the garden spot of the world. When the English settled Virginia, they did not send out even their best agriculturists. We have seen their story to be one of constant faction among the leaders and, at first, indifference or worse among most of the colonists; but at least from Dale's time the bulk of the people, after they became acclimated, were energetic.

The other element of progress we have said was environment. Excluding for the present government and dealings with the natives, the principal question concerns soil and its possible productions. In every country advance has been dependent upon producing more than can be consumed at home and thus paving a way for commerce. In early civilizations it is not material whether this surplus be metals, wood, or agricultural products which are merely carried off in bulk, leaving behind articles exchanged for them; but as development goes on, it is seen that more ingenuity and a higher civilization result where products exported are first changed into something different from their natural state, where what we call "manufactures" grow up. As long as America produced gold and silver for Spain, or tobacco for England, the style of civilization developed was rather that of caste, in which the great mass of population consisted of laborers, although the upper class reached a high degree of culture. Virginia can hardly be said, certainly not during the period now confronting us, to have passed beyond this agricultural stage. It is possible for a country to become great on the carrying trade alone, in carrying the products of one part of the world to be exchanged for the products of another, as was the case with the Phœnicians in ancient times, the Venetians in the Middle Ages, and with the Dutch and British in more recent days, the situation being modified in the last two instances, however, by other features. War alone will not in the long run secure mastery. The decline of Spain after a brilliant rise is an instance in point. An advancing nation may improve its position by force; but if a nation represents nothing but force, has no commercial or industrial ability, it will be unable to sustain the position which it may seize.

Virginia as a dependency of Great Britain could make no progress by war, except incidentally against the natives, and developed no disposition to build ships, or even to any extent to own them. We have seen that there were many reasons conceived for founding the colony, some of which materialized and others did not. As a place for sending surplus population, it was a success, even though at first probably four-fifths died of those who were sent. As a means of supplying the home country with things which it must buy abroad, it was not a success. Of the numerous results expected, at first we hear of nothing realized except sassafras and soap ashes. Precious metals there were none, and, although persistent and well-directed efforts were made toward the production of silk, wine, hemp, flax, pitch, and similar things, late in the century these were officially given up.

Virginia remained essentially an agricultural country. In considering it from this point of view, there are three subjects to engage our attention. These are: the land, including acquisition of title; labor, relating more especially to servants; and the products, which we shall find to be almost exclusively tobacco.

Land was a cheap article in the settlement of the country. Each adventurer, whether of the purse or person, was to receive one hundred acres, although at first there was a period of seven years within which there was no distribution. Besides this method of acquiring land, which may be considered as in the nature of a dividend, there were two others. One was the performance of some service which benefited the community; and thus ministers, officials, doctors, and others were frequently awarded bills of adventure, or shares, which passed to their successors or assigns. Probably the method by which in the long run the great bulk of the land was acquired, however, was what was called the "head right." Increase of population was so essential that persons bringing immigrants were granted fifty acres for each, provided only the immigrant remained three years. This head right was deemed so important that it was one of the terms sought and confirmed in the Articles of Surrender of 1652. The people imported were not necessarily free; they might be servants or slaves, and there is a record of one man who imported in different years three wives—fortunately only one at a time. A privilege of this sort was subject to abuse, the more especially as the records were imperfect and it was possible for clerks to give away lands for fees. Thus ship captains received grants for their crews, who did not stay, and this sometimes successively, in the several counties where they called. The clerks in the office of the secretary of the colony received in this manner from one to five shillings for each certificate, without taking any care to see that the laws were complied with. The method of procedure was to file this paper among the records of the secretary, and a second certificate or warrant was then issued requiring a surveyor of the county to seat the applicant. For a few years shortly after the fall of the Company, patents sometimes issued for a thousand acres; but it was seldom so much, and on the average from one to three hundred. There was no official surveyor in the earliest times. It seems as if one was intended in 1616, and one probably came with Argall, but the first whose name was known was Richard Norwood, from the Somers Islands, and the best known was William Claiborne. The right was conferred upon William and Mary College as one of its perquisites. Ultimately, there were surveyors for smaller districts, such as the counties.

Of course, as in all early surveys, there was overlapping and afterward litigation, and to correct this there was what was called "processioning." This meant that once in four years people of each neighborhood assembled and marched around the boundaries of the plantations, examining the marks and recutting blazes when necessary. Legislation connected with these matters originated the practice of allowing the successful claimant of the soil to buy the improvements of the one in possession at valuations fixed by jury, while if he did not avail himself of this privilege the person dispossessed had the right to buy the land from him at its value.

After fees were paid, patent received, and the patentee seated, the principal condition imposed was the payment of a quitrent, sometimes twelvepence per annum per acre. Collectors were appointed for this and other purposes, and in 1637 a treasurer was instituted for the colony. The subject of quitrents is a complicated one, the more especially as they varied from time to time and were not regularly paid.

Between private citizens there were deeds in the usual English forms, and these from an early date were required to be enrolled or recorded in Jamestown within a limited period. The same rule applied somewhat later to courts at other places as they were established.

We will recall that Captain John Smith says that he exerted himself strenuously to make the gentlemen who had come over labor with their hands. For instance, he made them plant maize, and earlier yet compelled them to cut down trees. In his time and for some years afterward it promised to be a question of developing an Anglo-American peasantry. Almost from the beginning there were sent over people who were to serve the Company for a certain length of time and then acquire their freedom and with it land and personalty. This may be said, in a sense, to have embraced almost everyone at the beginning, but after land was divided in severalty indented servants came all the more, now not to serve the Company, but the planters who needed labor. In 1619, we read that there were eight hundred and eleven servants introduced from England, besides one hundred children, and in 1628 between fourteen and fifteen hundred children were sent over to Virginia. The unrest and civil wars in England produced many of these servants, some being of good rank, but the bulk of them of the lower classes, and to them must be added some few criminals. These servants of both sexes brought with them the promise of future citizenship, for if they rose equal to their opportunities they would in a few years be not only independent, but able to progress. And yet, there was no difference between their condition for the time being and slavery proper. Their labor belonged to their masters, who were bound only to give the servants food and lodging and general attention. Still, the very fact that their term was limited, whether it be one year or ten or even longer, made their labor of less value. Ultimately, they would not be available, and the planter would have to look forward to other importations; for what would be true of his would be true of all other white servants. Thus the system of white service was not a success. It was both too much and too little in the nature of slavery. When we add to this the great mortality among such immigrants to Virginia, and the fact, gradually apparent, that the white man could not stand malaria and thus could not labor in low lands to advantage, we find a good reason, in fact the true reason, for the gradual spread of African slavery. Whatever be the truth as to the origin and brotherhood of man, the black savage captured in Africa had little in common with the European of the seventeenth century. The kinship was not admitted, for the African was deemed an animal, while his usefulness after he had been somewhat domesticated was clear. He could labor in the sun and in marshes with no injury to himself, and there throve; while, after the horrors of the middle passage were over, his condition in the new home was preferable to that in the old. Of course, it was the actual benefit to themselves that influenced the Virginian planters, but statistics show it was a long time before slavery amounted to much. The year 1619 marks an epoch as its beginning, but far too much stress has been laid upon slavery in early Virginia. In 1625 there were four hundred and sixty-four white servants and only twenty-two negroes, and even as late as 1671, while there were two thousand slaves, the white servants numbered six thousand.

African slavery was sure to come to Virginia at one time or other, because the main product of the country was tobacco; and the best tobacco was produced by competing Spanish colonies in the West Indies, where slavery had been known from an early period. A number of the negroes in Virginia bore Spanish names, showing that they came from this source; but a peculiarity of Spanish slavery was that although the Spaniards used by far the most slaves they did not import them. In the nature of the case they could not, for the terms of the demarcation made by Alexander VI. gave the coast of Africa to Portugal and the coast of America to Spain. The Portuguese were therefore naturally the first modern European slavers, and the *asiento*, or contract, for supplying the Spanish colonies with Africans was to be one of the prizes in the world contests of this

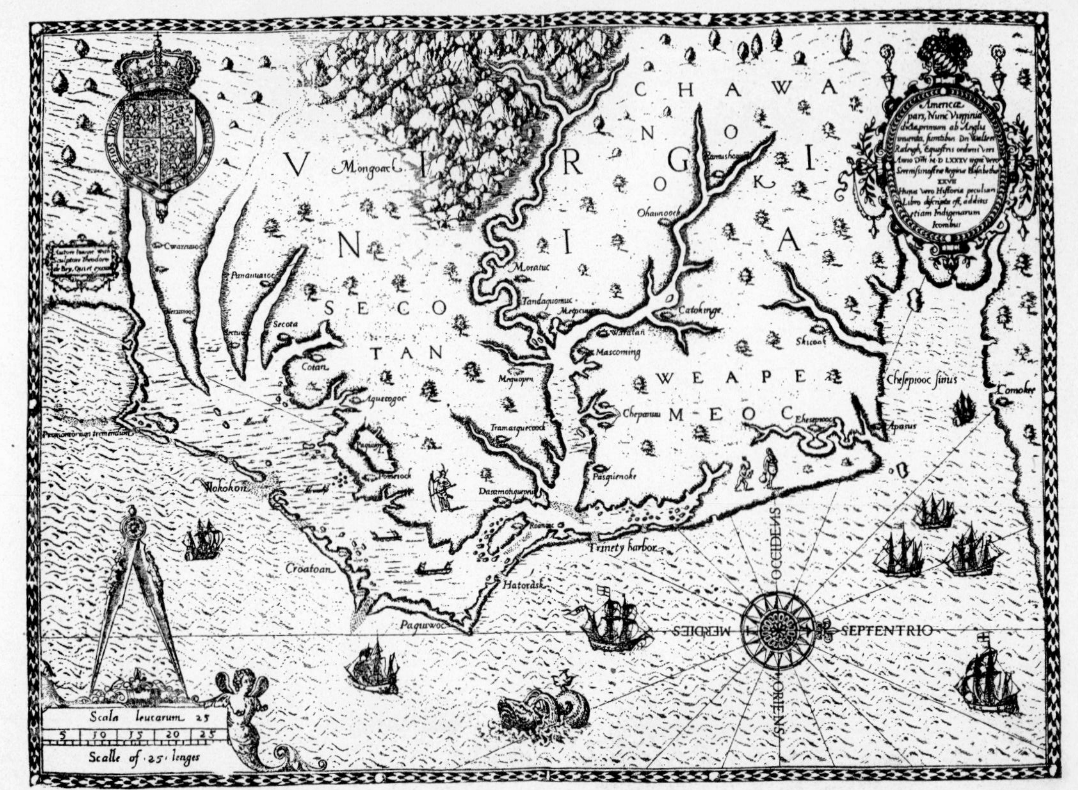

Map of Virginia drawn by John White, "who was sent thither speciallye and for the same purpose by Sir Walter Raleigh in the year 1585." *From the copperplate engraved by Theodore de Bry, which appeared in*

and the following century. No scruples were felt by Europeans of any nationality, unless the reproaches of Queen Elizabeth to Sir John Hawkins may be called such; and his reply was certainly the feeling of his age and others yet to come, when he justified slaving on the ground of removing the negro from heathendom to Christianity. The English government had in 1618 given the exclusive privilege of this trade on the Guinea coast to the Earl of Warwick and his associates; but the Dutch were for a long time the chief means of bringing Africans, and it was to meet this fact that the Royal African Company was chartered in 1622 to import slaves to the number of not less than three thousand a year into the English colonies. The Duke of York, afterward James II., was the head of this company. It does not seem to have been active in regard to Virginia before its new charter of 1672, and, in fact, it was not for ten years after this that the company became the principal importer of Africans. By that time there was also to some extent a domestic slave trade. In 1640 there were about one hundred and fifty Africans, commanding about £18 apiece; toward the end of the century, they were reckoned by the thousand, wealthy planters often owning from fifty to one hundred. In 1700, we are told that there were six thousand.

At first they were not baptized, the general feeling being not unlike that of a pious lady of Barbadoes, who declared one might as well baptize puppies. Instances to the contrary occur from an early date, and shortly after the Restoration the Council for Foreign Plantations took an interest in the slaves. The fear was entertained that when baptized they would cease to be slaves, on the idea that a Christian could not hold a Christian in bondage; but this was removed by the law of 1667, which provided that baptism should not change their legal status.

As a rule, the slaves seem to have been docile, happy, and well treated. There were runaways, of course, and these were severely punished. Meetings were prohibited, firearms not allowed, and there were many regulations, aiming to keep them in quiet subjection. Marriage was not legally recognized between them, although their pairing off was as far as possible respected. Illicit relations could not fail to exist to some extent between masters and the females, but this was severely frowned on by public opinion, and punishment was inflicted on both parties by law.

Black freemen were not unknown, and it would even seem that for a time they had the right of suffrage, although, if so, this certainly was taken away in 1723. In fact, in the last year of the seventeenth century the law required that all Africans when freed should be sent out of the colony, and the planter liberating a negro had to pay £10 for the expense thus incurred.

Although other things were undertaken, it was tobacco that seemed to succeed best, and in a short time this was the staple of the country. New land was cheap, and the subject of renewing and fertilizing old lands was hardly yet understood even in England; so that when it was found that tobacco exhausted the soil in three years, it was perfectly natural that the ground should be given over to wheat and maize, which did better then than on fresh soils, and that the planter should seek new lands further in the interior. Rolfe had discovered the valuable qualities of marl, but this was to be unappreciated for many years. Even the ease with which marshes could be drained and made fertile was overlooked from the facility with which new lands could be acquired, and, in point of fact, it was found that tobacco raised on marsh lands was coarser even if larger than that on drier soil.

At first the Company and King James decried giving so much attention to tobacco, and Charles I. was to regret that the industries of the colony should be built on smoke. But ultimately everyone recognized that Virginia meant tobacco, and tobacco meant Virginia. An attorney-general was to tell Blair: "Damn your souls! Make tobacco!" The home government treated it in a manner that was meant for encouragement. Thus, shortly after the fall of the Company, it was forbidden to cultivate this plant in England, and, although that from the West Indies was the finest in the world, a duty was imposed upon Spanish-grown tobacco. It is true these regulations varied at different times, and there were some that showed the encouragement to be meant only for the purpose of bringing something to England out of which England could reap a benefit. Thus there was a duty, a long time of two shillings, imposed upon the Virginia product, and after the Company was abolished the king thought seriously of making a contract with individuals for the privilege of buying and selling all of the article produced. Even the members of the old Company attempted to secure this contract, which existed for a short time in other hands, although yielding finally to the protests of the colonists. More serious were the requirements, dating from 1624, that all tobacco should be brought to England, and should be brought in English ships. The result of this was to restrict the market and thus do away with the competition of Dutch shipping.

Virginia had had the advantage not only of vessels trading to and from Holland, but also to and from New Amsterdam and other colonies in America. It is true that this commerce was to some extent kept up in a clandestine manner; but from now on it was against the law and became more and more difficult. Particularly was this so later in the century, when the Virginian authorities were required to keep a record of the amount shipped and in what vessels, and make a report to the home government. Different regulations were adopted from time to time in Virginia designed to improve the quality or restrict the quantity of the crop. Thus, as the prices fell, laws were passed that the lower leaves should not be used, and that the plants should bear certain proportions to the cultivators; as, for instance, three thousand plants at one time and fifteen hundred at another. The crop was exported either in bulk, that is, in loose parcels packed into the holds of vessels, or in hogsheads. The size of the hogsheads was defined; they ordinarily contained about five hundred pounds, but at one time they were made larger. The advantage of packing in bulk was that the cargo would be greater, there being none of the open spaces sure to remain between casks, and there were also some advantages not publicly mentioned. Thus, portions could be run ashore in unfrequented bays and places in England and sold without paying duty. A cargo in bulk could be sampled much more readily than when packed in casks. The first general inspection law was in 1630, when it was provided that mean tobacco should be burned and the offender prohibited from making another crop. Two or three years later, five places were designated as inspection points, where warehouses were erected in which the prime tobacco was stored, the low grades being destroyed. Shipments were made from these places; and although goods imported from England were at this time landed only at Jamestown, debts could be paid at the warehouses. In course of time, other points were given similar privileges, although it is not quite clear to what extent these laws were fully enforced. Taxes were imposed in Virginia to pay for the expenses connected with the inspection and shipment of tobacco, and in 1637 a custom house was established.

The great question was as to the result of these regulations. Did the crop pay the producer? He certainly could not be expected, and in fact could not be compelled in the long run, to produce something at a loss to himself for the benefit of others. About the period when inspection began, the price of tobacco in Virginia was less than one penny a pound, and the popular plan for bringing up the price was one which has not been unknown in later times and with other commodities. This was a general agreement for a "stint," or reduction in the quantity planted or produced. The price fluctuated from time to time, and under the Commonwealth was twopence a pound in Virginia and double that in England. It is to be remembered, however, that, fortunately, tobacco was not always the sole, although it was the principal, reliance of the colony. In 1634, when Virginia held a population of five thousand, there was such an abundance of corn produced that ten thousand bushels were spared to be sold to New England, and eleven years later we find cattle also sent there in large quantities. Cattle were exported also to Barbadoes from time to time and were to no small extent the making of that island. Only two years after this great abundance corn was so dear as to command twenty shillings a bushel, but not long after there was a general regulation allowing its export whenever it fell below twelve shillings.

In early Virginia the raising of cattle was important. The crops were fenced in, and the cattle grazed in the open. There are many instances of palisades or pales being built from stream to stream so as to furnish a large range for cattle. This herding led to some peculiar regulations. For instance, at certain periods of the year it was customary for owners to collect their stock and brand the young ones. Ultimately, this could not be done without first giving notice, so that all interested could see that one did not brand more than the produce of his own cows. The first law requiring the enclosure of land against cattle was in 1627, when in certain ranges, such as Hog and James City Islands, it was prohibited to run fences across narrow necks, and the owners had to enclose their own fields. In 1631, the requirement was made general, although there was some opposition to it, and these two enactments were the origin of the rule, common ever since in Virginia as well as in other parts of the South, by which the burden of fencing is placed upon the farmer instead of on the cattle owner.

From the beginning there were few roads, because the country was so intersected by watercourses that river communication was easier. It was not until 1632 that there was any systematic regulation; authority was then conferred upon certain officials to establish what roads might be needed, and it was not for thirty years that the laws as to their preservation became adequate. The first place in mind in road legislation seems to have been the church, next the courthouse, then the capital, and, lastly, communication between counties. The roads were to be forty feet wide, and the planters were compelled to supply laborers to the district surveyors. As the highways ran through large plantations, drawbars became usual, and, on account of the scarcity of iron for hinges and nails, it was long before gates superseded them to any extent. Ferries, of course, came with the roads, but they are first clearly mentioned in 1640, and a year or so later the assembly provided for free ferries. In the country, taverns were infrequent, and even in Jamestown high priced. They were the less needed, though, on account of the hospitality of the people. This was made the more possible by the abundance of game, and the more spontaneous from desire for the society and news of travellers. The custom led to the written law that unless contracted for in advance no charge could be made for entertainment.

On the fall of the Company, the Virginia Assembly had refused to produce the original public records for the inspection even of John Pory, their old speaker, when he came over as royal commissioner, and they stood the clerk of the council, Edward Sharpless, in the pillory and cut off part of an ear for furnishing a copy. And yet, during the Civil War in England, the sympathy of the Virginians was largely with the king; but there was no practical occasion for showing it. The Church of England was supreme, for, although we are told that there were one thousand Dissenters or Independents, say seven per cent of the whole population, many were driven out and found refuge in Maryland and New England. The colony had its reward. When a movement was on foot to reëstablish the old Company, King Charles, while at York in 1643, almost hiding from his enemies, made it clear by letter that he would not alienate Virginia from his "immediate protection," and, better yet, he addressed "our trusty and well beloved our Governor, Council, and Burgesses of the Grand

Assembly of Virginia,"—thus accidentally or incidentally, but fully, recognizing for the first time the Assembly instituted under the Company. It is sometimes said that Charles II. was proclaimed in Virginia, but the recognition is somewhat like his father's recognition of the Assembly. In 1649 the burgesses in their very first law declared the dead monarch to be "the late most excellent and now undoubtedly sainted king," and enacted that defenders of the "late traitorous proceedings" are accessories *post factum*, and further denounced punishment against all who shall question "the undoubted and inherent right of his Majesty that now is to the colony of Virginia, and all other his Majesty's dominions."

In 1652 Cromwell sent out a fleet, and a frigate appeared before Jamestown to demand its surrender. Berkeley prepared to resist, but there ensued a parley, for the commissioners found, as they reported, "a force raised by the governor and country to make opposition against said fleet." The conference resulted "in Articles at the Surrender of the Country," which was in the nature of a treaty, and "acknowledged a voluntary act, not forced nor constrained by a conquest upon the country." It was provided that the freedoms and privileges of freeborn people of England should continue; the Grand Assembly alone had the power of taxation; indemnity was granted as to all past opposition to Parliament; free trade was allowed with all the world, despite the Navigation Act lately passed; the prayerbook might continue in use for a year, provided whatever related to kingship be not used publicly; and all persons should take the oath of allegiance to the English Commonwealth, or have a year to dispose of their property and depart. It is true that some of these articles were not confirmed by the Long Parliament; as, for instance, the one providing that there should be no taxation except by the Assembly, but then the Long Parliament itself was broken up shortly afterward, and Cromwell seems to have respected the terms of the surrender. The supremacy of the Commonwealth was acknowledged in theory, and Berkeley and other king's men retired from public life. The Roundhead Richard Bennett was made governor by the Assembly, and the practical upshot of the whole matter was that the Assembly was recognized as the true source of authority in Virginia. Of course, the Assembly itself was, under the circumstances, made up largely of new men, but there was no persecution of anyone—unless lawyers be an exception. The trouble with them seems to have been that they were "mercenary," and acts were passed aiming at control of these very "subtle" people. In 1642 their fees were limited, three years later they were expelled from office, and then two years afterward they were forbidden to take fees at all—which should have been the end of them. In 1656 they were licensed again, but two years later they were forbidden anew to receive any reward or profit under a penalty of five hundred pounds of tobacco. The profession seems never to have died out entirely, however, and so their "subtlety" must have devised some way around these drastic laws.

The population had so spread as to form numerous settlements along the lower James and York Rivers and across the bay in Accomac. The burgesses had represented hundreds and plantations, but by 1634 the old hundreds were so populous as to be renamed "shires," eight in number; to wit: James City, Henrico, Charles City, Elizabeth City, Warwick City, Warrosquoyake, Charles River, and Accomac. Over each was a lieutenant, whose chief duty was to look out for the Indians. Nine years later the title "county" was substituted, and in ten years these were fourteen, bearing the names Henrico, Charles City, James City, Isle of Wight, Nansemond, Lower Norfolk, Elizabeth City, Warwick, York, Northampton (formerly Accomac), Northumberland, Gloucester, Lancaster, and the new county of Surrey. With a population grown to fifteen thousand, Virginia under the Commonwealth pursued her own way. We learn that there were then one hundred and fifty plows and three hundred horses, but oxen were almost universally the draught animals. The small number of plows was due to the fact that so much new ground was taken up every few years by the same tobacco planter, where roots and stumps did not permit the general use of the implement. At the beginning plows were not made of iron, but of wood with metal tips, and in course of time they were manufactured in Virginia.

The Commonwealth governors seem to have been good men, and there was no disturbance except about an old custom of admitting the governor and council to seats in the Assembly. In 1658 this law was repealed and Governor Matthews promptly dissolved the Assembly, but the members refused to be thus disposed of and actually proceeded to depose the governor and council. To raise as little opposition as possible, although at the same time to show that they were supreme, they made the same Samuel Matthews governor and captain-general. As Matthews promptly accepted, the trouble was at an end. Berkeley remained in close communication with Charles II., and had sent word that he would raise the royal standard in Virginia when there was a prospect of success. Charles then declined; but, after the death of Cromwell and that of Matthews, the Assembly in 1660 declared Berkeley to be the governor and captain-general of Virginia, prescribing that he was to govern according to English and Virginia law, call assemblies biennially, which were not to be dissolved without their own consent, and that writs should issue in the name of the Grand Assembly of Virginia. Berkeley thus went into office confessedly as the servant of the Assembly; but in May next came the Restoration, and Berkeley received a royal commission.

Of the renewed impulse toward colonization Virginia could hardly complain. Although it somewhat curtailed her boundaries to the north and south, it gave as neighbors Maryland and the Carolinas; but as to the grant of the Northern Neck to Arlington and Culpepper by the king while in exile there was good ground for protest. Instead of reserving public lands for public purposes, to be used to build up the colony, these were thus given away to favorites, who, in their turn, were to make no good use of them. Perhaps an even greater cause of complaint on the part of all the American colonies was the enforcement of the Navigation Act. This had been passed in 1651 by the Commonwealth as a war measure directed more especially against the West Indies, and was found to redound so much to the advantage of the mother country that after the Restoration the government not only reënacted it but enforced it against Virginia also. The result was to confine trade to British ships and to exclude Virginia from sending tobacco to foreign States except after paying English duties of two shillings per hogshead; and Virginia and Maryland together produced forty thousand hogsheads. Berkeley was too good a royalist to wink at any infraction, and gradually the hardships resulting caused general discontent.

If the Restoration injured the Virginians, it had also other results. The entanglement of Charles II. in the meshes of the policy of Louis XIV. is one of the strangest things in English history. It will be seen to have important effects in the Mississippi valley, but one of the most striking and indefensible results was the alienation of England and Holland. The two peoples were closely akin in race and in commercial traits, and yet Charles II. succeeded in dragging them into wars. The first lasted from 1664 to the Peace of Breda, three years later, and resulted in the permanent acquisition of New Amsterdam, under the title of New York. For Virginia it brought interruption and danger to shipping, and in the very year of the peace the Dutch sailed up James River, and, while the captain of the guardship *Elizabeth* was ashore at a wedding, destroyed seven merchant vessels and captured thirteen others, the *Elizabeth* being burned. There soon followed a second war, and during it there was another attack in Virginia waters by eight men-of-war, which destroyed eleven merchantmen. To these troubles was added a hurricane which blew down thousands of houses, and a deeper-seated injury yet was the venality more than suspected to prevail in public office.

As if all this was not enough, the increasing population and gradual extension of boundaries renewed friction with the Indians. Ever since the massacre there had been sworn enmity between them and the whites. In 1629 a law had been passed that the inhabitants should annually go three several marches on the Indians, to wit, in November, March, and July, and "do all manner of spoil and offence that may possibly be effected." A massacre is recorded for 1640, and four years later old Opechancanough had led an attack upon the colonists along the upper waters of the York and Pamunkey, killing three hundred; but Berkeley had captured him, and he was shot in the back at Jamestown by one of the soldiers. Such was the end of the last emperor, and it broke the power of the tidewater Indians. By treaty, the tribes were to remain north of York River, none coming south except as messengers, marked by badges of striped cloth, and, on the other hand, the whites were forbidden to go into the Indian country; but, as so often later, the latter rule was not enforced. However, there was no more danger from the Indians until, in 1656, the Richahecrians came from beyond the Blue Ridge and settled near the James River falls. The whites assumed that their mission was hostile, and attacked them, but were disastrously defeated, Colonel Hill being killed, as well as Totopotomoi and a hundred of the friendly Pamunkeys. The Richahecrians had enough of it, too, for they seem to have retired beyond the mountains. In 1670 the explorer Batte crossed the Alleghanies even to the New River district, and this, of course, aroused the jealousy of the Indians. Some years later, Doegs who committed outrages were pursued into Maryland, and, despite a flag of truce, some of them killed in an old fort where Washington now stands. Excitement prevailed all over Virginia, from the great planters in the tidewater country to the armed men in log cabins nearer the Blue Ridge. There were, it is true, old frontier forts, quasi-palatine grants of a quarter-century ago, but the colonists wanted rather to invade and cut off the Indians than to huddle behind defensive palisades. If the government would not take the war in hand, the people would do so themselves. All that was wanting was a leader.

It was quite appropriate that civil disturbances in which college men were to take the lead should be presaged by omens in classical style. The vivacious historian of the time, the unknown assemblyman from Stafford bearing the initials "T. M.," recounts that in the year 1675 there was a large comet every evening for a week or more, streaming like a horse's tail, westward; that flights of pigeons were nearly a quarter of the mid hemisphere broad, and of their length there was no visible end, while their weight broke down the limbs of large trees, causing the "more portentious apprehensions" because this had not been seen since the massacre of 1640; while the third strange appearance was swarms of flies, about an inch long and as big as the top of a man's little finger, rising out of the earth and lasting for a month. Necessarily, therefore, what happened was unprecedented.

Nathaniel Bacon, lately arrived from England, of gentle blood, and now hardly twenty-eight years old, was a member of the council, precipitate and impulsive, brave and eloquent; and so when the Indians killed his overseer, whom he much loved, and one of his servants, he vowed to avenge them. Savages, three to six in parties, were committing murders, usually at the sources of the rivers, the actual frontier of the time, although rarely burning or destroying property.

For some reason Governor Berkeley paid little attention to Indian matters, although frequently notified of the outrages committed by the savages. He would promise assistance, but never send it, until the report went abroad that he was interested in the beaver trade and that his agents actually sold ammunition to the Indians, and it was believed his idea was that "rebel forfeitures would be loyal inheritances." The people about the heads of the James and York at length acted together and chose Bacon as their leader against the Indians. Bacon made repeated efforts to secure a commission from the governor, and, failing in this, proceeded to war on his own account, destroying much property and killing one hundred and fifty of the enemy. Naturally, at the ensuing election for members of the Assembly he was unanimously chosen for one, but on arriving at Jamestown was arrested and his sloop destroyed. However, the governor, admitting that he was a gentleman, released him on his parole. Berkeley got him to confess his crime before the Assembly and then publicly forgave him, restoring him to his seat in the council. Bacon, nevertheless, sued him for the value of the sloop and won the suit. As soon as the Assembly took up the public grievances relative to revenues, collectors, and the like, the governor tried to confine their attention to Indian affairs. Friction was imminent over several matters, when "one morning early a bruit ran about the town, Bacon has fled." In a few days he returned with an army, and Berkeley tragically bared his breast and told him: "Here! shoot me, 'fore God, fair mark; shoot!" Bacon declined the opportunity, but insisted upon a commission against the Indians, and went before the Assembly to obtain it. He finally received it and marched against the enemy, when Berkeley summoned the militia of Gloucester and Middlesex, supposed to be loyal, and proposed to "follow and suppress that rebel." The militiamen walked out of the field and left the governor to himself, and thereupon he gave up the contest and sailed over Chesapeake Bay to Accomac.

Bacon, on hearing of the trouble behind him, marched promptly back. His chief advisers throughout were said to be one Mr. Lawrence, formerly of Oxford University, noted for wit, learning, sobriety, and a sable Venus, and also Mr. Drummond, lately governor of Carolina. T. M. says that thoughtful Mr. Lawrence was at the bottom of it all, but it seems as if Bacon was the head and front of everything himself. He summoned a convention at the Middle Plantation, afterward Williamsburg, and persuaded all to take an oath to aid the Indian war and oppose Sir William's designs, if he had any, to hinder the same, and to protect the general, army, and friends against any power that should be sent out of England, until the country's complaint be heard before king and Parliament. He also called an Assembly and sent an expedition against Berkeley at Accomac, but this was unsuccessful, and its leader, Captain Carver, was hanged on shore. Berkeley, taking advantage of Bacon's absence, entered Jamestown, but found his men would not serve against the general, on whose return the town was easily recaptured. Here it was that Bacon violated the laws of war as recognized even in that day by seizing the wives of his leading opponents, including Lady Berkeley, and standing them on the intrenchments he was erecting; but the success of what is called the "white apron" defence became famous. Berkeley fled again to Accomac; and to prevent Jamestown from being a "harbor for rogues" any more, Bacon burned the capital, Drummond and Lawrence setting fire to their own houses.

The situation was interesting. The lawful governor of Virginia had fled to the peninsula across the bay, which was thinly inhabited, and it may be a question whether the reinforcements he expected from England or the army which Bacon was quite sure to bring would reach him first. Bacon was master of all the mainland, and the first rebellion in America seemed almost ready to be dignified with the more complimentary term "revolution." Suddenly there came an event which changed everything. The malaria about Jamestown which had so hindered the early settlement of the country now did its fell work upon Nathaniel Bacon. His expeditions against the Indians were in wet weather, and finally he had to take to his bed, sick of fever and flux. Shortly afterward he died, October 1, 1677. He was succeeded by one Ingram, and an old annalist says that "the lion had no sooner made his exit, but the ape (by indubitable right) steps upon the stage." Whatever of fairness there may be in the comparison, certain it is that Berkeley took the offensive and soon the rebellion went to pieces.

Lawrence seems to have put stones in Bacon's coffin and sunk it somewhere in York River, beyond recovery; but if the governor could not find the dead man, he at least found a number of live ones to send after him. The last account of Mr. Lawrence himself was from an uppermost plantation, as with four others he marched away in snow ankle deep. T. M. thinks they cast themselves into a branch of a river, but it is possible they escaped the country. Drummond was not so fortunate, for he was captured. On hearing this, Berkeley came on shore from his ship, and, bowing low, said: "Mr. Drummond! you are very welcome, I am more glad to see you than any man in Virginia. Mr. Drummond, you shall be hanged in half an hour." To which the other answered, doubtless with as courteous a bow: "What your honor pleases." The governor was out of his reckoning only a little, for it seems to have taken two hours to have a court martial and erect the necessary gibbet.

The actual pacification of Virginia was carried out by three commissioners sent from England, Jeffreys, Moryson, and Berry, and they found it necessary rather to protect the late insurgents than to aid the governor, who treated even them with scant courtesy. A list of executions signed by himself, embracing Commonwealth soldiers and others, amounts to fourteen, but there seem to have been many more, enough in all, as report had it, "to outnumber those slain in the whole war on both sides." Charles II. said "that old fool has hanged more men in that naked country than I have for the murder of my father." His triumph seemed complete; but when he returned shortly afterward to London, his majesty, for some reason, did not receive him, and the governor died soon afterward. The commissioners succeeded in their task, and among other things made a lasting peace with the Indians by which the sovereignty of the king was acknowledged and they agreed to pay a quitrent of arrows.

The civil disturbances under Bacon led not only to the interruption of regular occupations, but to the destruction of stock and crops. Although tobacco was more largely planted than ever, within a few years there was acute distress, and the council and the Assembly petitioned the government for measures to compel cessation of planting. People had even begun to regret their large plantations and wish for the building of towns, so that other than agricultural industries might flourish. The petition was refused, no doubt because the revenues from Virginia amounted to £100,000 and the navigation of the kingdom would suffer, although the nominal reason was that if there was this cessation the Spanish, Dutch, and French colonies would supply the world and supplant Virginia entirely. In the year 1682 two Assemblies sat on the matter, but mob law was quicker and more efficient. The people commenced cutting down their own plants and those of their neighbors, the movement reaching its height in Gloucester County, where two-thirds of the tobacco in the ground was destroyed and two hundred plantations desolated. The soldiers who came over to repress Bacon's rebellion had to be used to suppress this economic disturbance. Tobacco fell to its lowest value; the next year, on account of the enforced stint, it brought better prices, and for a year or two to come the colony was reasonably prosperous and contented. A curious result was that in 1685 there was omitted in the instructions given to Lord Howard of Effingham the time-honored injunction to all previous governors, to encourage the production of silk, wine, hemp, flax, pitch, and pot ashes, and this from fear that the people actually would devote themselves to these things and thus lessen the growth of tobacco.

Before the end of the century Virginia had exported to England over fifteen million pounds of tobacco, but efforts were still made in other directions. Berkeley had succeeded in sending Charles II. three hundred pounds of silk, and

Sir Thomas West, third Lord De la Warr.
Founder of the first permanent English settlement in America. First Governor and Captain-general of Virginia, April 15, 1609.

After the painting in the State Library, Richmond, Virginia.

Charles, who was a good judge of women and other luxuries, praised the Virginia silk as equal to any he had known. Flocks of sheep became common about the time of the English Revolution.

It would be interesting to follow the planter through his daily life and with him to look through his house, with its large hall and rooms, gradually becoming more pretentious and in course of time filled with imported furniture and linen, and see him and his family, clothed more and more in silk and lace like his friends in England. Particularly was this true after the coming of the Cavaliers, between the execution of Charles I. and the year 1670, when the population advanced from fifteen to forty thousand, giving an entirely different and more cultured tone to Virginia. But this would take us too far afield. Suffice it that in the front of the home, called in the case of plantations the "great house" by whites as well as negroes, there was the "yard," generally enclosed by fences and containing the flowers and plants so dear to people of English descent. The prevalence of timber made wooden houses usual, although there were brick kilns from an early date, and bricks were long used for foundations and chimneys. Berkeley built his dwelling at Green Spring of brick, and Bacon burned three brick houses owned by the governor in Jamestown. Toward the end of the century such dwellings became more common, but the roofing was generally of cypress shingles, slate being unknown and tiles too liable to injury. Glass was used in windows, and paint was a common importation. It was the custom to import cloth of different kinds, pewter, and many other things in bulk, they being made up as they were needed. Plates, cups, and the like were of pewter, and, although case knives were usual, Virginia pioneers seemed to have been almost unacquainted with the use of forks. Silver plate frequently occurs, and Byrd at least thought it a good investment, as something tangible that would never decrease in value. While the lower classes used pine knots, the upper used candles, sometimes of beeswax, but generally perhaps of wax from the myrtle berry, common in the South.

From homes turning to churches, we learn that assemblies, after the Restoration, sent a clergyman to England to seek improvement in ecclesiastical affairs. The plan favored there was to make Virginia a bishopric, and it is said that a bishop was chosen. Certain it is that Dean Swift desired the position. The compensation of the clergy was not regularly paid, even in tobacco, and the size of the parishes made their ministrations difficult. The principal trouble was that the democratic vestries insisted on hiring or choosing their own pastors, and this custom was steadily and sturdily persevered in. Bishop Compton seems to have sent out a London preacher named James Blair to Virginia, who, after the Revolution, became his commissary, with duty to inspect and administer discipline. He was a Scotchman of ability, conscientious and thoroughly efficient, and his activity was not confined to Virginia, for Maryland was also much benefited.

Upon the English Revolution, whereby James II. was driven from his throne, William and Mary were proclaimed in April of the next year as Lord and Lady of Virginia, and Governor Lord Howard of Effingham was succeeded in 1690 by Francis Nicholson, who had been Governor of New York. He laid out a city at the Middle Plantation of Bacon's day and called it Williamsburg, and tried to arrange its streets in the form of W and M, in honor of the king and queen, but fortunately did not perfectly succeed. In 1691 the college of William and Mary was founded there, the second in America. There had been, as we know, an Indian college planned at Henricus, but George Thorpe, who designed it, was killed in the great massacre by the savages for whom he was laboring. There had been some schools, but it was left for James Blair to make the college a success. The burgesses sent him to England, and the king and queen granted their "well beloved in Christ" for his college a charter, land on the Pamunkey and elsewhere, a penny a pound on exports of tobacco, the office of surveyor-general with its fees, arrears of quitrents, and a burgess in the Assembly. The Bishop of London was first chancellor, and the institution was to render annually to the governor two copies of Latin verses on the 5th of November. Christopher Wren planned the building, and at the first commencement, in 1700, crowds were present even from other colonies. Fires occurred in 1705 and several times afterward; but on each occasion the college has been rebuilt. One of its fellows said that it was "a college without a chapel, without a scholarship, and without a statute, a library without books, a president without a fixed salary, and a burgess without electors." It is true that for long it was little more than a boarding school, and that even Blair had trouble with the propensity of young Virginians for horseracing and other unintellectual amusements. But he persevered, the college lived, and it remained the chief seat of learning in the colony.

Thus we reach the end of the century. The formative and experimental period had passed. Although founded on the cultivation of a single plant, and lacking the development which grows from city life, Virginia was firmly established, and in the struggle with its conditions was developing a high type of men. The substitution of William and Mary for James had plunged England into continental wars which were to bring great glory upon her through the campaigns of Marlborough, and the time was coming when her contest with France was to have marked results for the American colonies. For, contemporaneously, France was exploring the interior of America, and after the momentary Peace of Ryswick was to acquire a firm foothold behind the Alleghanies. As showing Virginia's growth also, the accession of Queen Anne at the beginning of the new century sprinkled the country with variations of her name. The counties of Princess Anne and Fluvanna, the rivers Rivanna, North and South Anna, and Rapidan recall the queen; but all this was still in the lowlands, in tidewater

Virginia. There was no thought as yet of the mountains and beyond, little even of the colonies growing up to the south. In 1705 Virginia slew her first and last witch, but to redeem that she then codified her laws, and in Beverly found a native and worthy chronicler of her history. Proud of the title of the Old Dominion, derived from her loyalty under the Commonwealth and from the motto on her seal, *En dat Virginia quintum*, ranking her as an equal part of the United Kingdom, Virginia continued on in her own life, not selfish, but self-reliant.

CHAPTER VII

CAROLINA UNDER THE PROPRIETORS

ONE becomes so accustomed from his early lessons in geography to naming the Atlantic States from top to bottom of the map, that he instinctively thinks of North before South Carolina. And yet historically they for a long time constituted but the one colony of Carolina, governed from the one city of Charleston, about which was the fuller development. Although later settled than the other principal colonies, South Carolina has always preserved so marked an individuality as to be a study not less interesting than any of them. The courage, the high spirit, the independence, and the love of home which have made this little State remarkable have given it a fame far out of proportion to its present limits. Its beginnings, therefore, deserve special attention, for they throw light on what has distinguished the country from its settlement until the present.

Somewhat as Mr. Green correctly begins the study of English history on the shores of Frisia, whence the Anglo-Saxons came, for the beginnings of Carolina we must not turn to England as in the case of Virginia and Massachusetts, but to another quarter of the globe. The spirit of exploration and colonization of the days of Elizabeth and James led to the acquisition by England of islands and countries in many parts of the world. Thus came several places in the West Indies and the Caribbean Islands, and not the least famous of these was Barbadoes. This little island, containing hardly one hundred and sixty-six square miles, was known to the English from 1605, but it was not settled until 1625 under a patent of James I. creating Lord Leigh, afterward Earl of Marlborough, its proprietor. The year before, King James had granted to the Earl of Carlisle the twenty-two Caribbean Islands, including Barbadoes, although the patent did not pass the seal for three years. The conflict between these two grants continued a long time, and yet, nevertheless, the island became well peopled and prosperous. It was the first English colony to plant the sugar cane, cultivated by negroes brought from Africa, and the distance from England enabled its people to develop institutions of their own, built upon slavery, sugar cane, and a military system, all tending to create a spirit of independence. It had an Assembly, among whose early enactments was a slave code of severe but wholesome nature, and the Church of England and the parish system were fully adopted. During the civil disturbances it was neutral, and under the Commonwealth royalist. The Navigation Ordinance and later Act were mainly directed against this little community, which finally accepted the Commonwealth, but with practical independence. The Restoration brought no advantages to the faithful colony, for, in fact, the Navigation Act, forbidding foreign ships to trade with the colonies, was made more stringent. It is true that the dispute as to the two patents was quieted, but it was by imposing a tax of four and one-half per cent upon all produce to provide a fund to buy out the contestants, and with a proviso that after this was effected the proceeds of the tax should go to the royal treasury. There was some danger of overpopulation also, for about this time the island, hardly larger than the Isle of Wight, contained one hundred and thirty thousand people, of whom fifty thousand were whites. To its political difficulties were added disastrous hurricanes, and the result of it all was that not a few Barbadians were inclined to look for other homes, and some turned their eyes toward the continent of North America.

There, ever since the unfortunate fate of the French under Ribault and others, the territory between Virginia and St. Augustine had been a debatable land. The Spaniards extended their occupancy of the islands toward the north, kept in touch with the Indians of the mainland, and from time to time explored the coasts, with the primary object now of keeping off English intruders, for Spain's days of active advance were over, although she did not know it. In 1630 Charles had seen fit to make grants of all the region between thirty-one and thirty-six degrees, from the Atlantic westward to the South Sea, to Sir Robert Heath, the attorney-general, under the name of Carolana. This patent was not to be the one under which settlement was actually made, but, as a return to an earlier plan of colonization, and a precedent for one actually carried out, this instance of the proprietary charter deserves study. The Heath patent preceded that of Maryland to Lord Baltimore in 1632 and of Maine to Gorges in 1639, and so is really the first of those upon the mainland after Raleigh's.

America was not only a field of colonization of different races, but for different kinds of colonization by the same race. We have seen how the English founded Virginia by a patent to men prominent in the time of Queen Elizabeth and King James, and how this proved inadequate to the ends in view. It was found that a commercial company, where many stockholders risked comparatively little each, succeeded best; but this plan was not to prevail in the settling of all the great English colonies in America. In some cases the crown reverted to the old plan of a personal patent because of special conditions. It was really a reversion to a remote feudal past. Just as in earlier times an outpost had been established on the Rhine by the Carlovingians to protect their domains from the heathen Saxons and called the "Palatinate" because ruled by an officer of their palace; just as the Mark of Brandenburg was an outlying province designed to defend the march, or border, of Germany from the northeastern savages,—so, later, the Norman kings of England established the principalities or counties palatine of Chester, Lancaster, and Durham on the borders of Wales and Scotland to protect the boundaries. No more interesting spot of land exists than Durham, at once a palatinate and the seat of a bishop. The plan of such a grant was to clothe one man with great privileges, both governmental and territorial, giving him almost royal rights, so that he would be the better able to perform his duties as a watchman on the frontier. He coined money, he appointed his own officials, he held his own courts, and originally the writs and officials of the central government had no effect within his domain. But that was long ago, and in the time of Charles I. only Durham remained a palatine. No such privileges as the grant of Maryland had been conferred on any English subject since the Wars of the Roses. And yet, it seemed appropriate in colonization, and in particular presented advantages for any colony which might be placed between the well-established province of Virginia and her foes, whether of Indian or European origin. Only experience was to tell whether people emigrating so far from England and needing so much self-reliance to make a living and build up a country would be satisfied to take their law from a fellow subject and be cut off from the constitutional and commercial growth which might be attained by their kindred at home. One would hardly think that the matter of popular rights and the possibility of popular liberty were subjects which concerned the Stuarts, and yet the glorious, if unsuccessful, struggle of the Virginia Company had not been in vain. When Charles I. granted his charter of Carolana to Sir Robert Heath, there was an important limitation of the absolute powers conferred by the charters of Queen Elizabeth upon Raleigh and others; for it was provided that Heath should enact laws with the counsel, assent, and approbation of the major part of the freeholders of the province, whom as often as need require he should call together. It is true that this innovation was qualified by a right in the proprietor to make ordinances in emergencies, but as the colony developed, the general rights of the freeholders would in the nature of things become prominent. The proprietor was given the right to confer titles, provided they were not the same as were used in England. The Carolana patent was the first to name the famous line of thirty-one degrees and seems designed as a guess at the location of the river St. John's, on which was the Spanish post of San Mateo of famous memory. The claims of Heath descended in one way or another to Daniel Coxe, of New Jersey, but, somewhat as with Barbadoes, the patent was not to stand in the way of future grants. Nothing was done by Heath or his successors, and ultimately his claim was set aside by legal proceedings because of inaction.

Some Dissenters from Virginia made their way across the forests to Albemarle in 1633, thus constituting the first settlement in Carolina, although it was not to be embraced in the first charter. This was really an overflow from Virginia, on the waters consecrated by the sufferings and death of Raleigh's colonists, and will therefore always be looked at with tenderness. They were largely Quakers and others who were unwelcome in the Old Dominion, somewhat similar to the emigration not long after from Massachusetts to Connecticut and Rhode Island. Nothing further was done under the Commonwealth, but in 1660 some people came from Massachusetts to Cape Fear River; their stay, however, was only temporary, and when they left they gave discouraging reports of the country. The real settlement of Carolina was to be from the south, with the older Albemarle as a loosely connected part. It is the fate of the territory which we call North Carolina not to have had an independent beginning. It maintained, however, a continuous existence, even having for much of the time a separate governor or deputy-governor, and reached a real importance in the next century. At that time it will be more convenient to take up the thread of its story again.

We have arrived at an important epoch in colonization. The old personal way of looking at history makes us fix our attention too much upon the court intrigues of the time. With little in his personality to attract, beyond a species of wit and selfish good nature, the age of Charles II. represented a colonizing spirit unequalled since Elizabeth and her successor. The fevered energy which in Cromwell's day assumed a military shape was with the Restoration diverted into new channels; but the energy remained and produced memorable results, much as the restlessness of the Elizabethan epoch produced the colonization of James's time. Under the Commonwealth, Jamaica had been captured from Spain, and now it was made a royal colony, while its smaller neighbor Barbadoes two years later received similar institutions. Not content with remodelling these distant colonies, Charles took advantage of civil distress among the Dutch to seize in 1664 Manhattan, their greatest American colony, and turn it over to his brother James, the Duke of York, to become the more famous New York; and in other seas and under other skies similar energy, often untempered by scruples, was also shown. It was, therefore, only a part of the onward movement, when Charles II., regardless of the claims of Spain, undertook by his patent, or charter, as he called it, of March 24, 1663, to give to eight of his warm friends, or "cousins and counsellors," the province henceforward called Carolina upon the annual payment of twenty marks and a quarter of all its gold and silver. The boundaries were almost the same as in the disregarded patent to Heath, extending to the river St. Mathias, within thirty-one degrees, although two years later they were extended on the south even to twenty-nine degrees and on the north to thirty-six degrees thirty seconds, thus going far beyond St. John's and even including St. Augustine and bloody Matanzas. This was worse than bad taste, for it was not only insulting Spain, but turning over the country to private proprietors who probably could not, and who certainly did not, make good the claim against the Spaniard. The result was to awaken the hostility of Spain and vastly increase the difficulty of settling the country.

The eight proprietors were prominent men. We may mention first the Earl of Clarendon, who was the companion in exile of Charles; and it was his daughters Mary and Anne who, after the expulsion of James II., were queens of England. Next comes the Duke of Albemarle, George Monk, the famous general who effected the Restoration. He did not hesitate to act as admiral also, and on one occasion gave at sea the rather military command for his ship to "wheel to the left." William, Earl Craven, was another, noted during the civil wars, and, although aged, he was to survive the other proprietors. John, Lord Berkeley, had likewise seen active service in the Civil War and was in exile under the Commonwealth. While Anthony Ashley Cooper, Lord Ashley, had been a turncoat in politics and was later to lose the confidence of royalty and die an exile, for the present he was in high favor, and became Chancellor of England and Earl of Shaftesbury. From the navy was Sir George Carteret, the famous officer who, as Governor of Jersey, received Charles and Clarendon when fugitives, and who commanded Elizabeth Castle there, the last fortress to lower the Stuart flag; and that was done only on the express command of the king. An important member was Sir John Colleton, who had not only been active in the Civil War in England, but was among those who held Barbadoes for the king, and with others there rewarded by the empty honor of baronetage. He was now to take an active interest in directing people from the island to the continent. The remaining lord proprietor was no other than Sir William Berkeley, a brother of Lord Berkeley and better known as Governor of Virginia. Such were the lord proprietors of Carolina. There was much to hope from their influence and energy,—and possibly there was much to fear from their number and the fact that each had more important affairs at home.

They were to have, use, and enjoy their territory in as ample a manner as any bishop of Durham had held, used, or enjoyed his county palatine, and could make laws with the approbation of the freemen, whom the lord proprietors should from time to time assemble in such manner and form as to them should seem best. The province of Carolina was to be of his majesty's allegiance, and its people the denizens and lieges of the kingdom. The proprietors and colonists could trade with the natives and were to transport goods without hindrance except export customs and dues, and could bring into his majesty's dominions certain articles, which never became important, without paying any duty for seven years, and from his majesty's dominions could export free all necessary tools. The proprietors could establish ports and impose customs; they could build forts and towns and appoint governors and magistrates; could grant charters for incorporation, erect markets, and hold courts baron. They could wage war, and could impose martial law in case of rebellion. They were given the right to build churches and chapels according to the ecclesiastical laws of England, and enjoy the patronage thereof; and they received full liberty and authority to grant indulgences and dispensations to those who really in their judgment and for conscience' sake could not conform to the liturgies and ceremonies of the Church of England. Finally, they could also confer upon inhabitants of the province titles of honor different from those used in England.

The proprietors constituted the Quakers who remained at Albemarle adjoining Virginia into a county of that name, and sent a commission to Sir William Berkeley as its governor. The uneasiness in Barbadoes caused exploration to be undertaken from that island before any regular effort was made from England. Barbadians made a proposition through Sir John Colleton, but, without waiting, they sent out Captain Hilton in the *Adventurer* in the fall of 1663 to explore. This he did well, although nothing came of it. In 1664 Sir John Yeamans, under a contract with the proprietors, undertook a colony from Barbadoes to Carolina, and to plant what was to be known as the County of Clarendon, of which he would be governor. He was compelled to return from Cape Fear, where a settlement was made; but he sent Sandford to explore to the southward, who at Edisto, on one of the islands, took formal possession of the whole country by turf and twig. Sandford made the acquaintance of caciques and other Indians, and effected quite a thorough exploration of the coast, being particularly pleased with Port Royal, and he it was who renamed Kiawha River the Ashley. Little or nothing was seen of the Spaniards, whose forward movement in colonization had ceased. Sandford finally returned to the Barbadian colony on Cape Fear River, where some authorities have it that Sir John Yeamans remained as governor, ruling like a father. However, the colony went to pieces toward the close of the year 1667, the people going to Albemarle and elsewhere, and leaving the actual settlement of Carolina to other hands.

Meanwhile, in England, the proprietors had effectually got rid of the claim of Sir Robert Heath by their second patent, 1665. Peace came between England and Spain two years later, and the lord proprietors set about the double duty of providing colonists and laws for them. The private secretary of Ashley at the time was the philosopher John Locke, and he was appointed to draw Fundamental Constitutions for the new colony. Locke set to work with zeal and produced a remarkable document. It aimed at an elaborate system of government, with a feudal nobility of landgraves and caciques, an impracticable subdivision of the country into counties, signiories, baronies, precincts, and the like, and was more remarkable as the effort of a philosophical but impractical mind than for any real influence it had upon the development of the country. Even the proprietors from the beginning recognized this, and not only changed their form from time to time, until we have five or more editions, but expressly provided Provisional Laws under which the colonists should act until the time was ripe for putting in force the Fundamental Constitutions.

The other undertaking of the proprietors was to send over colonists. Carolina had so far been settled, even apart from Raleigh's experiment, principally toward the north, and it required the publication of Sandford's *Relation*, which gave special prominence to Port Royal, to attract the attention of the authorities toward the south. The proprietors signed an agreement by which each contributed £500,—worth four or five times that amount in present currency,—with the further agreement for £200 each annually for the next four years. With this money they purchased three ships,—the *Carolina*, the *Port Royal*, and the *Albemarle*,—and loaded them with stores and people. Joseph West was put in general command until arrival at Barbadoes, where Sir John Yeamans was given authority to appoint a permanent governor. Sir John accompanied the expedition from that place, but finally returned, appointing William Sayle, a Puritan of Bermuda, as governor. The expedition stopped at Sewee Bay and then went to Port Royal, where the first election by freemen was held of five men to be of the council, and we learn that for some reason one William Owen contested the result unsuccessfully. After sundry adventures as they coasted along, including buying pork, washing clothes, and losing to hostile Spaniards some of those sent ashore, they arrived at Kiawha, and landed on what is called Albemarle Point, on the Ashley. Here they built intrenchments and began to lay out a town, thus beginning what is known as Old Charles Town. The site was low, being little more than a marsh, in modern times found available only for manufacturing purposes. It is difficult to see what was the attraction, but, nevertheless, there they ran streets, built a fort, and a settlement came into being. Even the proprietors in England apprehended that the location would probably become unhealthful, and soon directed a change.

Across the Ashley, between it and the Wando, now renamed Cooper River, was a long peninsula or point, itself marshy and intersected by bayous in part, but on the Cooper side high above the tide. It had been already granted out to individuals, but they surrendered enough of their land to afford the site for what we call Charleston, then for some time called New Charles Town. The old settlement was not formally abandoned, but from 1672 to 1679 migration thence became more and more general. The new place was laid out in streets running north and south and then at right angles, bounded north and south by small creeks, where the present Market and Water Streets are found. Wharves were constructed in front, and fortifications, gradually made stronger and stronger, surrounded the settlement to the rear. From the beginning, a lot at the corner of Broad and Meeting Streets was reserved for a church, of course Anglican, and the quaint characteristics of Charleston architecture gradually developed. No buildings now go back to the earliest period, but in no American city do old colonial characteristics more strongly appear. And this was so because the city was for so long practically the whole colony. Almost inaccessible to Indian attack itself, the colonists extended inland from its fortifications only by degrees. First, plantations and homes gathered on each side of the long, shaded road traversing the centre of the peninsula, until finally there were settlers on the other side of the Wando, such as the influential colony at Goose Creek, and those at other points gradually won by war or treaty from the Indians. The savages in the immediate neighborhood were friendly, and there was no great difficulty in obtaining grants of land for what was almost humorously expressed as a valuable piece of cloth and beads, and for similar desirable considerations. One of these documents even acquired from the Edistos and others all the interior to the Appalachian Mountains, regardless of the fact that the grantors belonged on the sea and that the Cherokees claimed and controlled the greater part of what was described.

The proprietors were not dilatory in sending colonists, and in one way or another the population gradually grew; so that while in 1671 there were some four hundred whites, besides a few slaves, about 1680 the people numbered twelve hundred, and this was doubled in the next five years. They were principally English, Scotch, or Irish, although there was some aversion for a long time to admitting "such dangerous people as papist Irishmen." The very year that Charles Town was fully settled, there were negotiations for the coming of some Huguenots. It is possible that others were in Carolina already, but the persecutions in France at this time, culminating in 1685 in the Revocation of the Edict of Nantes by Louis XIV., caused a general emigration of that industrious portion of the people, and it was not unnatural that some of them looked with favor to the country where their great leader Coligny a hundred years before had planted a colony. This disposition was aided by the efforts of the English government, instigated by influential proprietors, so that first and last there were several immigrations of the Huguenots. They naturally settled near each other, selecting for this purpose the east branch of Cooper River, which became known as the Orange Quarter, and afterward the parish of St. Denis, while other Huguenots subsequently occupied the more distant region about Santee River. The British colonists, strange to say, regarded these with some suspicion, and their position became a matter of politics. The Dissenters and Barbadians in the neighborhood of Goose Creek opposed their being recognized as citizens, and gradually they affiliated with the Anglicans. The church at Santee was already English, but the Huguenots after a while made it practically their own, even adopting the English liturgy. In town there was also what was known as the Huguenot church, erected about 1687, possibly the oldest French church in Carolina. It has certainly survived all the others, retaining its own forms and services to the present day.

Town life exercised much greater influence in Carolina than in the other colonies, and there was early an attempt to found another city than Charlestown. In 1682 there was a movement to colonize about Port Royal, the old Santa Helena, a number of Scots, themselves sufferers under oppression at home; and Lord Cardross came the next year and founded Stuarttown, having a population variously stated as from ten families up. This settlement was to be measurably independent of Charlestown, and is an instance of the lack of consideration on the part of the proprietors. It seemed as if Port Royal was to be always the test point. The Spaniards had always claimed it, and if they had been sleeping heretofore they now awoke and hardly permitted the Scots to become well settled. The approaching attack was foreseen and attempts were made to get cannon from Charlestown, but in vain. In 1686, the enemy came in three galleys, one hundred white men accompanied by Indians and negroes, whom the few already at the new colony were unable to oppose. Of the Scots, some were killed, others taken prisoners, and the settlement plundered and blotted out; for although the Spaniards were no longer able to occupy the beautiful bay themselves, they were determined to prevent the English from doing so. And yet, in this instance they all but went too far. The people of Charlestown had lent no assistance to the incoming Scots, but at least they were roused to vengeance and prepared a formidable expedition to attack St. Augustine. A disavowal, however, was received from the governor of that place; the authorities in Carolina accepted it, and the colonists had to yield reluctantly to a policy dictated by supposed interests of the proprietors in England.

The Huguenots had been invited on the supposition that they would introduce the manufacture of silk and other French industries, but such result did not follow. The first hopes in the early colonies had been to find mines of gold and silver, and even in Carolina some venturesome travellers found ore in the northwestern mountains; but the Board of Trade justly laid little stress upon mines. We remember that Virginia became important only after the discovery of tobacco, and that it was this plant which gave a great impetus to slavery, and now Carolina was to have a somewhat similar experience. From a time which was early, but uncertain, rice was known about Charlestown, although it is a matter of some doubt who introduced it. The ordinary story of the bag of rice obtained by Landgrave Smith from a brigantine from Madagascar calling in 1693 is not now relied upon, for we know that it was tried many years earlier. At all events, when introduced it was found to be prolific in the cypress swamps, where the white man could not live but the negro flourished, and the economic result was that slavery became as important for Carolina as it had been for Barbadoes. Furs and skins were early obtained from the Indians by trade, and by 1710 Carolinians are heard of seven hundred miles in the interior. Thus peltries, rice, and some silk were exported to England, while meat, vegetables, hides, staves, and the like were sent to Barbadoes and the West Indies. Commerce so increased that as early as 1680 sixteen sail at one time were counted in the port.

The Fundamental Constitutions or varying Temporary Laws, which really took the place of other legislation, provided for a governor, council, and parliament, or assembly as it came to be called. There were constant disputes as to the initiative in legislation, and everything was subject to approval of the palatine court, the assembled proprietors in England. It was not long before the popular Assembly realized its importance, for everything done in a new country appeals to its inhabitants, and people become restive under laws reaching them from a distance, made under different circumstances. The first governor was Sir John Yeamans, but the first actually in Charlestown was William Sayle, who died in 1670. Joseph West followed him, to be removed by the proprietors in two years, and to succeed Yeamans again after two years more. Then came several short terms, among them that of West again, and two terms by Joseph Morton, until James Colleton was appointed by the proprietors in 1686. He it was that prevented the invasion of Florida and by a number of other acts made himself unpopular and caused the first of the many revolutions of Carolina. He was driven out in the year 1690 and succeeded by that able, if unscrupulous, politician, Philip Sothell, a proprietor who showed a rather antiquated certificate of his right to office; for he had been captured by Algerines and was a long time on the way. The proprietors had been wavering in regard to the Fundamental Constitutions, and now showed their weakness in disowning the new governor and yet permitting him to retain his authority. Revolutions were the order of the day. The English Revolution of 1688 had made William and Mary sovereigns at home, and the governors representing the too absolute James II. had trouble in all the colonies. Sothell had himself been driven out of Albemarle, but made a very good governor in Charlestown. Despite jealousy of the French and Swiss, he succeeded in enforcing the citizenship of these colonists, who were filling Craven County and the Santee country. Sothell also secured the passage of the first code concerned with negro slaves, modelled upon that of Barbadoes, but an improvement thereupon. Ludwell, who had succeeded Sothell in Albemarle, now succeeded him at Charlestown.

The country was now beginning to fill up with settlers. Craven County extended to Sewee Bay, thus including the Santee settlement, while Berkeley embraced the country from Sewee to the Edisto, and beyond that lay Colleton. Under Ludwell the beginning was made of the settlement at Savannah Town, the place afterward known as Fort Moore, high up on Savannah River and convenient for trade with the Indians. Berkeley, although it was the most thickly settled, had no more delegates in the colonial parliament than Colleton, while Craven was given six, although its population was even less and part of it French, and over this was much dispute. The Assembly seems to have united in what is sometimes called a Bill of Rights, signed by the speaker, defining the points of difference between the colonists and the proprietors. Some of these related to the fact that the proprietors did not all unite in their instructions, and others were as to fees and courts, the representation, and perhaps most particularly to the rule that no measure became a law until the consent was obtained of the proprietors.

John Archdale, from Albemarle, was appointed governor by the proprietors in 1694, being a Dissenter like his immediate predecessors, Smith and Blake. Although a Quaker, he found no difficulty in accepting the title of landgrave and becoming one of the proprietors by an attempted purchase of Sir William Berkeley's share. He made a very acceptable governor, but his term was short and it was under his successors that political questions became acute. There was a standing difference between the Assembly and the proprietors as to the Fundamental Constitutions, which were fundamentally altered so often as to fall into disrespect. Never having been adopted by the consent of the freemen, as required in the charter, and being in their very nature not the temporary laws which that instrument allowed the proprietors to enact, they became the crux of Carolina politics and the means of educating the colonists in political thought and discussion. From the beginning the people were strict constructionists, relying upon the charter as being more fundamental than the Constitutions. The proprietors at first ingeniously required colonists before or on arrival to agree to support these laws, but this was naturally considered an evasion of the charter itself.

The board of proprietors soon went to pieces from death, minority, and non-residence; and at the time of the English Revolution, of the original number only Craven was living. Colleton had been the first to die, and after a while his share was represented by the guardian of his grandson; Clarendon had died in exile in 1764, his share going to Sothell; Albemarle had died even earlier, and his share was long in litigation. Sir John Berkeley did not pay up his assessments and early lost interest, and so on his death in 1682 the proprietors appropriated his share. Shaftesbury intrigued with Monmouth, and, after being confined in the Tower, died in 1683 in Amsterdam. Carteret died in 1679, and his grandson now represented him. Sir William Berkeley had died two years earlier, and the controversy over his interest was not settled until after the end of the proprietorship. Such an incoherent board, non-resident, and ignorant of actual conditions, could hardly be expected to contend successfully with the active and growing colony across the sea, and yet with the conservatism inherent in Englishmen the colonists long permitted affairs to drift in their old course. The struggle over the Fundamental Constitutions was, however, practically ended in the time of Governor Nathaniel Johnston in 1702; and although this abandonment was due to weakness on the part of the proprietors, it was really the means of prolonging their power in Carolina.

Other questions took its place, for the colony made considerable progress in every way. Regular courts had been instituted, the first chief justice being Edmund Bohun in 1698; the celebrated Nicholas Trott, who had been of unsavory reputation as Governor of Providence, was the first attorney-general, and he succeeded four years later to a long and famous term as chief justice. The year before, it had been necessary to create a court of admiralty on account of the growth of the port and the prevalence of piracy. The same famous year 1698 saw the establishment of the first free public library in America and also of a foreign post office at Charlestown, and next year told the very different tale of a yellow fever epidemic and a disastrous hurricane.

Church affairs were the chief domestic question at the beginning of the new century, at which time there is some doubt whether the Anglicans or the Dissenters were the more numerous in the province. The charter had declared the Church of England to be the established church of Carolina, and the provision for toleration was expressed in terms which seemed to make it only optional with the proprietors. The report of one of the earliest ministers from Charlestown indicated great laxity in morals, but it may be that the picture was overdrawn. The ministers had always been active, sometimes too much so, mixing up also in political matters, and with the accession of Queen Anne in England a burst of Toryism and ecclesiastical reaction set in, reaching even the colony of Carolina. It was in its religious features aided by the foundation about the same time of the Society for the Propagation of the Gospel in Foreign Parts. As a result of it all, in 1704 an Assembly, whose election was not above doubt, adopted an act to require members to conform to the religious worship of the Church of England; and it was quickly passed, signed, and approved, despite great outcry in the house and in the colony. It provided also for the building of six churches; and in 1706 the colony was divided into ten parishes, Charlestown being St. Philip's, and the others in Berkeley County were Christ Church, St. Thomas's, St. John's, St. James's, St. Andrew's, and in Orange Quarter the French parish of St. Denis. In Colleton County were St. Paul's and St. Bartholemew's, and in Craven the French church of St. James's Santee. Most of these names and certainly the spirit of the whole legislation were borrowed from Barbadoes, but one innovation, an important one, was that the pastors were to be chosen by election of the people instead of being presented by a bishop or the proprietors. There was no bishop in America, but in some accidental way the Bishop of London had gradually become looked up to as the head of the American Church. His jurisdiction, however, was denied in Maryland and the West Indies, in Jamaica the governor being the head of the Church. The Church acts also provided a lay board for the control and removal of improper pastors, a provision afterward disapproved in England, but it seemed to be wise as providing some method of discipline for the Church in America.

The Indian policy of the Carolinians was more peaceable than that of Virginia. The original idea of the proprietors had been to appropriate such land as they wanted, conquering the Indians as they went, but Shaftesbury is given credit for the plan by which land was bought as needed. This course was generally pursued, and there was comparatively little friction with the natives. The first serious conflict grew out of civil commotion among the whites themselves, for the little settlement of Albemarle, far removed from the influence of Charlestown and the oversight of the proprietors, was often subject to civil strife. John Lawson, the famous explorer, was in 1711 engaged in surveying for a Swiss colony from Berne, under an arrangement made in Europe by the proprietors, and Baron de Graffenried was with him on Neuse River at the time of one of the factional struggles, this time between Moseley and Pollock. Unfortunately, the land was claimed by the Tuscarora Indians, a brave and powerful tribe, and they were led to believe that the Swiss were trying to expel them. As a result they seized Lawson and the baron, killing the former by piercing him with pine splinters and setting them on fire, and soon began massacring in the Albemarle district. A special messenger was hurried to Charlestown for assistance, which was promptly sent under Colonel Barnwell, who took with him militia, two hundred and eighteen Cherokees, and some Creeks, Catawbas, and Yamasis. They came up with the enemy at an Indian fort in January, 1712, and were only prevented from exterminating them by the presence of white captives with the savages. As it was, over three hundred Indians were killed, and then, after making what he supposed was a binding treaty, Barnwell, himself wounded, returned to Charlestown. Unfortunately, for some cause or other, the Tuscaroras almost immediately resumed war; and another expedition was undertaken next year, this time under Colonel James Moore, son of the governor. The troops consisted of forty white men and eight hundred Indians, and Fort Nahucke was taken and many hostiles slain or captured. The blow was so great that the Tuscaroras as a whole abandoned the country, going north to become the sixth nation of the Iroquois confederacy.

The Cape Fear settlements had ceased to exist, but besides New Berne there was after 1715 a kind of capital at Edenton for what was already called North Carolina. The explorations of Lederer as well as of the unfortunate Lawson had led to better knowledge of the interior, and there was only lacking a political recognition of the difference of the two Carolinas, with better organization of the lands won from the Indians on the rivers discharging north of Cape Fear, to induce immigration.

As if to show the unity of Carolinian history, the people about Charlestown soon suffered an invasion similar to that of North Carolina. The Yamasis had been friendly to the English, having been their allies in the Spanish war and even in the Tuscarora expeditions, but their contiguity to the whites led to encroachment and misunderstanding, and at last some of their chiefs renewed the old intimacy at St. Augustine. Theirs was the fatal country which had seen the failure of the Huguenots and the wiping out of the Cardross colony, and now the project to settle the town of Beaufort again aroused the hostility of the Spaniards. They worked upon the jealousy of the lowland Indians, while the whole of the up-country tribes at this time became alienated, due to the advance of the French from Mobile and their building Fort Toulouse high on the headwaters of the Alabama. In 1715 there was an alliance formed between the Yamasis, Cherokees, and others, its influence extending even to Cape Fear River, designed for the complete extermination of the English. Beginning at Pocotaligo, the massacre extended through Colleton, Goose Creek, and even to the Santee. Governor Craven implored assistance from the proprietors, but, better yet, with the Assembly took active steps to save the colony. And it was well he did, for the proprietors took only interest enough to meet in London and declare that they had no money to expend, and that the colony must rely upon assistance from the royal government. The Board of Trade was to take the hint and ask the quashing of the charter, but in the meantime the pressing matter was war against the Indians. Moore, Barnwell, and Mackay were active leaders, and six hundred whites and four hundred negroes were enrolled in companies. North Carolina promptly sent assistance, and soldiers came from Virginia, but under the humiliating terms of payment for them by South Carolina. However, Craven finally succeeded in driving out the Indians, and sent Chicken and Moore across the Savannah at Fort Moore to follow the savages through the Cherokee country even to the Hiwassee. Four hundred whites had been killed and much property lost, besides £10,000 in debts to the traders, but the full respect of the Indians had been earned and no war in future was ever to assume such proportions. The Yamasis, forced out of Carolina, were welcomed at St. Augustine with bells and salutes. Their lands were now finally seized by the British.

The commerce of Charlestown had been steadily growing. From sixty-eight vessels entered in the year 1706, there were one hundred and twenty-one after the treaty of Utrecht closed the war with France, increasing two years later to one hundred and sixty-two. The city walls being found in the way, they were demolished. When peace was conquered from the Yamasis, the parish system of Barbadoes was adopted and provision made for somewhat decentralizing the government and electing representatives in the country precincts. This did not mean any extension of ecclesiastical rights, but was merely an adoption for political purposes of the parish divisions of the country. It was to be disapproved by the proprietors and to become another ground of complaint, but for the present a more absorbing matter of interest was found in the pirates infesting the high seas. During the French war there had been privateers and other vessels exercising war rights, and with the close of hostilities this same energy was continued piratically until it was said that there were fifteen hundred men on the coasts, their operations extending from Newfoundland to South America. Eight hundred were at Providence, which became, as it were, their capital, and when Great Britain drove them thence they only transferred their operations to the landlocked waters of North

Carolina. There have been slurs from early times as to the complicity of the Carolinians with these enemies of the human race, but they seem undeserved. In fact, the acts of the pirates seriously injured the commerce of the province, and Governor Daniel was energetic in opposing them; in 1717 a number were captured, tried, and executed. His successor, Robert Johnson, was even more active; he asked the proprietors for armed vessels to protect the Carolina commerce, saying that "hardly a ship goes to sea but falls into the hands of the pirates." But all to no effect.

Possibly the most celebrated of these desperadoes were Blackbeard Teatch and Stede Bonnet. Colonel Rhett was sent out with two sloops, and attacked the *Royal James* under the command of Bonnet in Cape Fear River. For five hours they bombarded each other, but the rising flood gave Rhett the advantage, and the pirates surrendered. The surrender did not protect them from trial. Nicholas Trott was judge of the vice-admiralty court, and his charge to the grand jury, with all its roughness, contains much good law. The pirates were duly convicted and executed. The governor himself had experiences similar to Rhett's and shortly afterward captured other pirates, and finally the piracy was broken up. Teatch, *alias* Blackbeard, had been killed in an expedition sent by Spotswood of Virginia, Bonnet had been executed at Charlestown, and the hardly less noted Worley was killed in battle with Governor Johnson. At last, after Carolina had as usual worked out her own salvation, the lords of the admiralty, in 1719, sent one or more men-of-war to guard the harbor.

This year was to be more famous in another way. The rule of the proprietors had degenerated into the arbitrary action of a small clique, usually represented by a secretary or other subordinate, deaf to agents sent by the colonists and even to those sent by their loyal governors. They listened only to the counsel of the unscrupulous Trott, whose advice was as bad as his morals. Johnson approved acts for the benefit of the colony, only to find them abrogated in England

and himself reproved for consenting to them. Thus the legislation as to parishes, the sale of the Yamasi lands, Indian trade, sinking fund, and duties was disapproved. A new Assembly was called; and if the proprietors were obstinate, the colonists were determined. They had issued £80,000 of paper money to pay for their expeditions, had suffered greatly in mind, body, and estate, and were now thwarted by proprietors as arbitrary as they were weak. Of all the colonies, Carolina was from her antecedents the least likely to submit. The Assembly, resolving itself into a convention, on the model of that which deposed James II. of England, renounced the authority of the proprietors and appealed to the king to take them under his protection as a royal colony. They requested Johnson to act as governor under the new state of affairs, but he refused, saying that he held his commission only from the proprietors, and he even called out the militia—only to find that almost to a man they adhered to the convention. The colony had effected a peaceful revolution, and a revolution which was approved in England. The king granted the prayer of Carolina, and the rule of the proprietors was at an end.

We have thus traced the origin of Carolina in the older colony in Barbadoes and followed its development along the three independent settlements on the mainland. The two Cape Fear colonizations of New Englanders and Barbadians early became extinct, while the Quakers of Albemarle were to become independent. The typical Carolina of the earlier times was that which was founded at Charlestown, and gradually expanding from it toward the interior became what we now know as South Carolina. When the proprietors were overthrown, Carolina, like Virginia, became a royal province, the form which British colonization had now definitely assumed.

CHAPTER VIII

BRITISH INSTITUTIONS

BRITISH colonization had begun in Virginia under governmental sanction and had next secured a foothold on Massachusetts Bay under more or less independent auspices. From these two centres colonization had gradually widened, by expansion of the original settlements themselves and by subsequent grants in England, until in the south was a series of settlements making up the provinces of Virginia, Maryland, and the Carolinas, and in the north those of Massachusetts, Rhode Island, and Connecticut, each homogeneous in many respects. These groups had been separated from each other by Dutch and Swedish colonies on Hudson River and adjoining districts, until during a war with Holland these also were seized and held by the British. With the founding of Pennsylvania the chain was complete. It it true that Georgia was yet to come, to finish the list; but, as we shall see, Georgia was founded later under special circumstances. So that the present is an appropriate time to pause and gather up the threads of development of the country and see wherein the different colonies, particularly toward the south, agreed and wherein they differed in their growing institutions.

The essential fact in Anglo-Saxon civilization from the institutional side is local self-government, and from the individual side, corporate activity. In no other quarter of the globe, at least in modern times, has there been such a survival or development of local governmental institutions;

and yet, strange as the conjunction may appear, in no other quarter of the globe has there been such associated activity, assuming in our own day the forms of legal corporations and what are called "trusts." The two tendencies, after all, grow from the same root, that is, individual rather than State energy. The freer a man is, the more jealous he is of supervision. This may go to an extreme and produce a kind of anarchy. Fortunately, the Anglo-Saxons have stopped halfway, and, while they will have no more government than is necessary for the general security of the commonwealth, internal and external, the energy which in other communities causes the State to take the initiative in business as well as government here assumes the form of association of citizens themselves for all business purposes. We see this in England in the schemes of colonization which we have discussed. While, relative to the colonists, the overlordship of Raleigh, the Virginia Company, or the Carolina proprietors might be as bad as the absolute rule of a monarch, it was not the government of England itself that sent out the colonies, but individuals or associations who undertook this just as they undertook any other form of business. So when it came to the new colonies themselves, the settlers or their descendants, as they grew in wealth and lost personal touch with the mother country, developed the same self-consciousness and the same desire to be rid of all superfluous government. And in this they were to be aided by the terms of the several charters or patents, differing in form, but essentially agreeing in the one important declaration found in the Virginia charter of 1609, that the settlers should have all the rights that Englishmen had at home. This was the foundation and palladium of American liberty.

Taking up first the governmental institutions, we find that Blackstone perceived clearly enough a distinction between the forms of colonization. He distinguishes these as follows: "With respect to their interior polity, our colonies are properly of three sorts. 1. Provincial establishments, the constitutions of which depend on the respective commissions issued by the crown to the governors, and the instructions which usually accompany those commissions; under the authority of which provincial assemblies are constituted, with the power of making local ordinances, not repugnant to the laws of England. 2. Proprietary governments, granted out by the crown to individuals, in the nature of feudatory principalities, with all the inferior regalities, and subordinate powers of legislation, which formerly belonged to the owners of counties-palatine; yet still with these express conditions, that the ends for which the grant was made be substantially pursued, and that nothing be attempted which may derogate from the sovereignty of the mother-country. 3. Charter governments, in the nature of civil corporations, with the power of making bye-laws for their own interior regulations, not contrary to the laws of England; and with such rights and authorities as are specially given them in their several charters of incorporation."

We have seen that the first attempts at colonization under Raleigh and others were under patents granted by the crown alone, conferring proconsular or even greater powers upon the patentees. Raleigh, however, was not successful, and the same kind of effort was then made under a body corporate as patentee instead of an individual. This, the first plan of the Virginia Company, hardly succeeded any better, and the form of the patent gave way to that of a charter, which allowed the settlers themselves more rights and therefore more interest in the government. It would seem, then, as if the patent was the initial form of colonization and that, in point of fact, although it was not successful, the three kinds which did succeed, given by Blackstone, grew out of it.

We may fairly say that the form which was first really successful in America was the corporate, by which the Virginia Company, composed of nobles, merchants, and guilds, and managed by energetic men, gathered into one treasury the contributions of many and established the settlements on the James. In some respects the Company was a proprietor, but it so happened that the proprietor, being corporate and its business directed by broad-minded and liberty-loving men, provided a free government and voluntarily called into existence the first General Assembly upon American soil. This corporate proprietor could have acted otherwise and built up the same kind of State as the individual proprietors; but fortunately it did not, and this fairly entitles it to be classed as a special form of colonization. Its legitimate results were not reached in Virginia, on account of the dissolution of the Company, but they appeared in New England when the corporation itself emigrated to America, taking its charter and rights with it.

Making up a second class, therefore, were the proprietary governments proper, of which Maryland was the first successful representative and, with Pennsylvania, the most lasting. Carolina exhibits a peculiar example, in what may be called "associated proprietors." The Carolina form had all the disadvantages and none of the advantages of a proprietary government.

The third and last species of colony was what Blackstone calls the royal or provincial establishment. This proved to be the best adapted to the colonies after they had attained some growth, but it is characteristic of Elizabeth and the Stuarts that what would seem the most obvious way of planting a State was never tried at the beginning of these enterprises. The fact was that the king was perfectly willing to give away land that he did not own, and to encourage in any way that did not cost him anything the efforts of individuals and corporations to increase his power and revenue beyond the seas. It was all an experiment; besides, the kings were much absorbed in eastern politics. It was the old story of Columbus and Ferdinand over again. But when the scene changed, when population was firmly seated and new dominions actually existed in America, royalty became interested. With the Virginia Company it assumed the shape of a fear that subjects were not properly cared for in the wilds of America, and so the king put an end to the Company; and in Carolina the king recognized the revolution by which the colonists put an end to the proprietary government. In both instances, the legislative assembly which had grown up was recognized and the principal change actually made was that the governor and the council who advised him were appointed directly by the king or those representing him. This was somewhat on the model of what was found at home, for the colonists inherited the English genius for political development. At home the lower house was elected by the people who were eligible as electors, while the upper house was composed of the nobility created by the king or by his predecessors. There were differences, and among them that the American upper house was not hereditary, because there was outside of Carolina no nobility in America; and the difference made for freedom. Another difference, and a great one, was that in England there was, strictly speaking, no veto by the executive. It existed in theory and partially in practice for a long time, but in reality the only veto was by the creation of new lords to sit in the upper house and overcome an adverse majority. In America, from the nature of the case, the king through the governor had a full veto on the popular legislature. If the colonies were to be dependencies of Great Britain, this was a necessity, for there must be a higher authority somewhere. A misfortune of the case was that the governor had to report to England, which took a long time, and thus the veto power was out of touch with popular needs. Otherwise there would have been little complaint as to this element. A more troublesome question was to grow up as to who should exercise the needful supervision over the colonies.

We are so accustomed to that development of government in England in which all business is transacted by ministers whose office is dependent upon the confidence of Parliament, that we are apt to overlook the fact that the body which concerned itself with colonial affairs was not at first responsible to Parliament; for this responsibility of ministers was not in the seventeenth century so clearly defined, and the Privy Council, which actually exercised the supervision, was a body of advisers selected by the king without regard to Parliament. We will recall that it was this council which acted for King James as to the Virginia Company, and it always represented rather the will of the monarch than of the Parliament.

The regulation of colonial affairs takes us back to one of the English institutions which has now practically disappeared and yet at one time was the greatest of them all. The *Aula Regis*, or, as it was also called, the *Curia Regis*, of Norman times was that assembly of notables about the king from which has developed gradually the independent courts of common law and chancery and, with additions from the commonalty, even the Parliament itself. There was still left after these changes a large residuum of power, exercised by this same body of advisers under the name of the Privy Council. Their authority varied with the power of the king. After the Wars of the Roses had all but extinguished the old feudal nobility, the Tudors were able to reconstitute the council of new men, and thus Cromwell, Walsingham, and others were able to direct the foreign policy of the kingdom. In the earlier days there had been no colonies, and it was quite prophetic that under Henry VII. the little Channel Islands, Jersey and Guernsey, came within the direct jurisdiction of the Privy Council. This was natural, for the council had been the origin of the several institutions developed as occasion required, and heretofore there had been no occasion for any supervision of colonization. The patents granted the earlier discoverers passed through the council, and the importance of that under which Virginia was actually settled was such as to presage a separate Privy Council for such affairs. This was not realized, and the Privy Council itself supervised colonial matters so far as there was room for supervision under later charters. After the abolition of the Virginia Company and the growth of other plantations, there came about the appointment, in 1634, of a commission or committee of the Privy Council for making laws and orders for the government of English colonies. This reflected the king's will, and the same system, under the name of Special Commissioners, was adopted by Parliament in 1643, Pym, Cromwell, Vane, and Saye and Sele being of the number.

The colonial system of the seventeenth century was founded upon the idea of trade and commerce to be carried on for the special benefit of the mother country, so that it is not surprising that at the Restoration the oversight of the colonies was placed under what was called the Council of Trade and Plantations, a branch of the Privy Council with some outside additions. Of it John Locke was secretary. This continued until 1674, when its business was turned over to a committee of the Privy Council, nineteen in number.

Thus colonial affairs during the formative period were conducted essentially by the Privy Council, which under the Tudors and Stuarts meant the king, acting through this body, but exercising his own will so far as he chose. After the English Revolution the responsibility of ministers to Parliament was more firmly fixed, and it was not long before a change was necessary also in colonial matters, so that in 1696 there was instituted what was called the Board of Trade, consisting of officers of State and others. This board was connected more with the ministry than with the Privy Council as such, which gradually, almost unobservedly, led up to the interference of Parliament, to whom it was responsible, with colonial affairs. The Board of Trade was suppressed by what was called Burke's Act in 1782—but that carries us beyond our present scope.

As long as the people in the colonies felt that they could legislate subject to a veto, reasonably and promptly exercised, friction could be adjusted. When this supervision was assumed by Parliament, however, it seemed to be a different matter. The first effort which need concern us for bringing up colonial matters in Parliament was that of the friends of Sandys, which we have already mentioned.

In that instance Parliament would have acted, if at all, on the side of liberty, but, in point of fact, it did not intervene because of the message of the king practically forbidding action. The colonies were hardly important enough before the French wars to attract much attention, and so far as anything was done the colonists felt it to be more in the nature of an aid than an injury, their immediate local concerns not being touched except by their own legislatures. Thus they were not much concerned even when the statute 7 and 8 William III., c. 22, declared "that all laws, bye-laws, usages, and customs, which shall be in practice in any of the plantations, repugnant to any law made or to be made in this kingdom relative to said plantations, shall be utterly void and of none effect." The real interference by Parliament did not come until after the decline of the Privy Council.

The American colonists felt and desired their connection with the mother country to be rather through the king than through the Parliament, rather with the royal councillors than with the ministers representing the British people, thus presenting the anomaly that the distant settlers were more in touch with the monarchical than with the popular element of the constitution, and this willingly. The explanation is easy and lies in the fact that they thought of the king as their own king and not so much as the sovereign of Great Britain. Instinctively, but none the less truly, they were beginning to feel that not only Virginia but the other colonies were integral parts of the British Empire.

The evident tendency of all forms of colonial government was toward the royal colony, with local legislature and a governor representing the king, and on American soil just as previously on British began the struggle between the people and the crown, between liberty and prerogative. At home, politics had been softened, in that the conflict in case of divergence was between Parliament and a cabinet of ministers instead of with the king himself. In this way loyalty was not disturbed, although the conflict for liberty was none the less intense. In America, somewhat the same conditions prevailed, in that the local legislature representing the people came in conflict with the removable governor instead of with the monarch himself. There was the very acute difference that in England the cabinet fell on an adverse vote, while in America the governor could absolutely disregard a hostile majority, and, in fact, dissolve the Assembly, while nothing could effect his standing except some form of appeal to the home government. The Assembly, or rather the lower house, truly represented the people, although to modern notions the franchise was rather restricted. We have grown accustomed to manhood suffrage, each man having a vote, but this has not long prevailed, and was not the British theory in the seventeenth century. Even in the nineteenth, as advanced a thinker as John Stuart Mill was to declare that man's right was not to make his government, but to be governed well. The theory and practice in colonial days was that one must have property, must be a freeholder, before he was fit to be an elector. What these qualifications actually were in Virginia and in Carolina at particular times we have to some extent seen. Both colonies united in prescribing property qualifications, and the tendency, somewhat stronger in Carolina than in Virginia, was toward requiring also connection with the Church of England.

Taxation was effected by acts or resolves of the Assembly, generally upon recommendation of the governor and council, although we find the Assembly often declining to pass the bills requested, and sometimes passing others which were not acceptable to the executive. It would be unreasonable to expect descendants of the men who had been fighting out at home the battle of the right of the people to prescribe what should be taken from the public treasury to do other than continue the fight in America when proper occasion arose. And it arose frequently. The salaries and fees of officials were constantly a ground of complaint, and the home government did wisely in paying these from sales or rents of land or from customs, where feasible. With the short-sightedness peculiar to democracies, the expenses of forts and military preparations against the Indians were a source of irritation. When the time came for action the people were willing enough to enroll themselves and march against the enemy, but they disliked the expenses of military preparations and expeditions whose necessity they could not or would not always see, particularly if it were another colony that was in danger. There was, therefore, ample opportunity for difference between the executive and the Assembly over appropriation bills, and American colonists had almost from the beginning a training in politics superior to their friends at home.

Among the institutions brought by the colonists to Virginia, none was greater and none exercised a more lasting influence than law. It was the boast of Coke and was to be the dream of Blackstone that the English common law was something *sui generis*, that it was not unlike Minerva, who sprang full-armed from the head of Jupiter. More modern research traces its origin to Germanic customs, but finds it largely modified by Norman and civil law. This is even true of its dearest institution, the jury system. The early kings and the text writers systematized the law, giving it much of its present form and not a little of its present substance. Just as it came into being to suit the special needs of the English people, developing with their growth and in the hands of able jurists expanding to meet their increasing commerce, so it was not unfit to cope with new conditions in America. The Virginians brought it with them when they came, and moulded it to suit their new environment. And yet, it was not the whole system that emigrated. It was universally recognized that much of the machinery and some of the principles which prevailed in semifeudal England were unsuited to the conditions of the New World. Precisely where the line ran was hard to determine.

We can never be too grateful to James I. for the requirement in the Virginia charter—if indeed he was the author of that feature—that tenures were to be in socage and not military. It prevented the creation of a feudal nobility in America, then dying out at home. Charles II. authorized it in Carolina, it is true, but titles were even there to be different from those in England and were too fantastic to last. An American nobility could not from the nature of the case have been permanent. As to titles, the Indian right extinguished by war or purchase, the land was patented to individuals either for money or service. The usual form of sale in the beginning was by livery of seizin, consisting in the symbolical delivery of the land by handing over a clod of earth and a twig from a tree on the territory conveyed. We have seen an explorer taking possession of the Carolina coast by twig and turf, and with variations the practice long remained common. A house was sometimes delivered by taking hold of the door latch, as to this day vendors frequently turn over the key. As the estates grew larger and patents called for lands at a distance, such symbolical delivery became unmeaning or impossible and gave way to written deeds. Another instance of the common law was the survival of primogeniture, by which the oldest child received the larger portion of, if not all, his father's estate. This tended to sustain even in the new country the aristocratic feeling which was to outlast the colonial period. Domestic relations generally were transplanted almost unchanged. Just as the villein, a man whose labor was annexed to the soil, was rising to the condition of the serf, in America the servants of whom in earlier records we read so much were only the apprentices that had become usual in the mother country. The apprenticeship was generally for a period of four years. Had the evolution gone on unchecked we should have had in the South a free peasantry, for at the expiration of his term the apprentice or indented servant became a free man, with certain privileges and property to begin life for himself. But the peculiar conditions of Virginia and Carolina led to the introduction of negro slavery, and until toward the end of the seventeenth century it was, except in Carolina, uncertain whether slavery or free labor would prevail.

Of the earliest of all institutions in England, the village community, we find little trace in the Southern colonies. We have been taught by Sir Henry Maine that this was an Aryan institution, and then by Seebohm that so far as England was concerned it came in with the Romans, while later inquiries seem to show that it is of primeval origin and extends to all races of man. However this may be, it reproduced itself under a special form in the New England township, and one naturally seeks for it also in the South. In Virginia the early divisions were hundreds, in Maryland, manors, and it is very likely that these were village communities under the form surviving in England; but under the conditions in Virginia they were unable to develop. Scattered settlements left to themselves would doubtless have instinctively worked out something of the kind; but it was rather the settlers who were scattered than the settlements, and the necessity for supervision by the Company, both as to supplies and as to defence, led to a centralization of government which extinguished these local units. It is true the hundreds expanded, but it was an expansion which made them cease to be hundreds. They lost their individuality in the greater unit called the county, which became coterminous with the parish and politically the electoral unit of the State. There was a promise of local development along the older line in Berkeley and other specially chartered settlements. Indeed the privileges of one were objected to in the first Virginia Assembly. But these were blotted out by the massacre and other causes, and the typical Virginian unit or subdivision was the county, due largely to the plantation system. The same was true in Carolina, although there it was perhaps an adoption from Barbadoes rather than altogether a local growth. So that the anomaly is presented of the old Saxon kingdoms degenerating into shires or counties at home, and in America of the primeval hundreds developing into counties. Both at home and in the colonies, however, the result was the same. The county became the political unit.

The age of Elizabeth was in almost every respect the new birth of the English people. It was so in commerce, for it was then that English shipping opened the way to markets all over the world. It was so in religion, for it was then that the national church created by Henry VIII. became established and the germs of the Puritan movement came into being. It was so in politics, for then were the first effective assertions of popular as against royal right. It was so intellectually, for Shakespeare and his contemporaries made a new literature, to which we have since only added. And, although it is hardly realized, the same was true of the English language itself. Up to that time Latin had been the language of culture, when not only the impulse of literature, not only the translation of the Bible, but the discoveries and settlements by Englishmen all around the globe placed them in environments which caused the need for a more expansive speech. English in the time of Henry VIII. was insular and restricted; English in the time of Elizabeth and James began to be what it has become, a world language, fitted for all the exigencies and affairs of mankind. Some beginnings of this we can trace in America. The colonists at first applied their home names to the plants and animals of the New World, sometimes with curious results. Thus the bison was called a buffalo, the puma a lion or a tiger, while several different birds were nightingales. The strangeness of a fowl found in America caused the English at home to associate it with Turkey, from which they named it, somewhat as the French were to call it a *coq d'Inde*—Indian cock. "Muskrat" is really a native word, sometimes spelled "muscat." "Maize" was named "wheat," and as that was "corn" in England, we call it "Indian corn" to this day. To its blossoms the colonists gave the names "silk" and "tassel," and for its envelope we have in Virginia "shuck" and in New England "husk." For some things even the expanding English tongue had no analogy, and Indian words had to be adopted. Thus a form of corn bread was "pone," from a James River word, while "hominy," "succotash," "persimmon" and other words are Indian either in their present form or are some variation from it. "Hickory" is part of a native name, as "squash" and "wampum" are of others, while "chinquapin" is but an easier pronunciation of "chechinquamen." These are but specimens, for the same kind of addition and variation went on in all the life and business of the cosmopolitan Englishman.

And yet, with all the needs of the new day, we find local dialects of England translated to America and becoming what across the water are now forgetfully thought of as Americanisms. A great deal of the modern slang was once good English, and in corners of this broad land much that passed current in the old country in the seventeenth century is still preserved in local expressions. "Kotched" and "kiver" are instances in point, and it is sad to think that even "jag" goes back so far. "Tote" is sometimes spoken of as local English, although it survives among the negroes only, while of African words "buckra," which is now out of use, and "juba" are thought to be almost the only survivals. The tendency of the negro to substitute "d" for "th," as in "dat" for "that," is said to be common in Surrey even now. Curious it would be to recall the many proverbs of that day still current among us; and Ann Cotton, in describing Bacon's Rebellion, shows that cards were not unusual, for she speaks of occurrences which put Bacon and his friends to their "trumps." To pursue this further, as into the subjects of superstitions and folklore, would take us too far afield.

It would be interesting to trace the general mental development of the colonists. To do this, one would have to know exactly what they brought over with them, and study its gradual growth and variation due to the new surroundings. Unfortunately, this is impossible. It is difficult to find out the intellectual condition of England at the time, and practically impossible to find out what the colonists did with it. They were too busy with their own new problems to record much of anything except births and deaths and make up official reports when necessary. Material is lacking in both the old and the new country, and especially in the new.

And yet, it does not require a profound study to realize that when Jamestown was settled, and for almost a century afterward despite the reaction after the Commonwealth, the principal intellectual interest of Englishmen, as of all the rest of Europe, was in religion, or, perhaps more properly speaking, in theology. The Bible had been translated into English several times since Wyclif's day, but what was known as the King James version made the English language, and English thought as well. The movement culminating in the Puritans affected a vast number who never became Puritans in name. Generally, it was realized that the greatest thing in this world was man's relation to the other world; and toward civil magistrates there was profound reverence, not only because of their power, but because they were regarded as ordained of God. God himself was thought of as a despot, ruling and disposing all things for his own glory. Man's chief end was to glorify and enjoy him, and that enjoyment consisted largely in applying Old Testament and primeval rules of conduct to modern and Christian times, and especially in making other people conform their conduct, and their thoughts also so far as they could be got at, to one's own standard.

Religion in the Southern colonies perhaps did not assume quite so rigid a form as in England. The same causes which made the hundreds lose their value as units to the county made the parishes equally extensive, and in so doing they lost in intensity. A parson could not successfully minister to people scattered over so large a space, and as education declined among the people it must be confessed that it declined also among the preachers. Sunday became in Virginia more a day of idleness, and perhaps of amusement, than of religious observance. And yet this tendency, so thoroughly human, was partially checked by the coming of the Cavaliers. They brought with them an almost equal reverence for king and Church, and among them came many dispossessed parsons from England. This event gave the highest tone to society and to religion in Virginia, and from that time, the time of such men as James Blair, may be dated more of a forward movement in the Virginia Church. In Carolina there was, after the time of the first ministers, considerable complaint, but some of it probably unjust. Both the culture and the religion of Charlestown, although imperfect, were of a higher grade than the more rural communities further north. A State Church, and such was that in both colonies, is apt to settle down to the administration of rites to its members, providing its clergy with comfortable surroundings, and to be more disturbed over heresy than morals. It is not in this manner that religion is built up in a new country, and often the authorities at home were to blame for not appreciating better the situation in America. The people were not irreligious, but exposure to a rough life, the inconveniences and often impossibility of attending regular church services, the danger from savages, combined to make people indifferent to the externals of religion, and sometimes the effects went even deeper. But, on the whole, toward the end of the century affairs assumed a better position, both socially and religiously.

In other branches than theology, the England of that day was hardly emancipated from mediæval thought. Copernicus and Kepler had lived and died in vain so far as concerned Englishmen of much of the seventeenth century. Astrology was still firmly believed, and the influence of the moon on agriculture was not then held by the vulgar alone. Harvey had discovered the circulation of the blood, but Paracelsus was for much of the century the higher authority. The humors of the body were the basis of medical treatment, and bezoar stone and dittany were among the most famous remedies. Botany was only gradually to build up at home and in the colonies a real pharmacopœia.

Shakespeare had written many of his best plays before Jamestown was conceived, and he died while tobacco was coming to the rescue of Virginia; but his fame was not to reach the colonies for several generations. Even in England he was not at first generally known. The Puritan movement threw a slur upon dramatic art, and it required a Milton to rescue even poetry from the charge of being an accomplishment only. Such was the feeling in England and it would be even truer of the colonies. The Bible was the chief literature of the day, and sermons were a close second. Only religious books were frequently used, such as those on the practice of piety and versions of the Psalms. American libraries were small in size and few in number, and it is only toward the end of the century that a copy of Shakespeare is mentioned in a Virginia inventory. Face to face with all the beauties in the new continent, we yet find little love of nature and her moods. She appealed more to the practical side and fears of settlers. To John Smith the great forest was "uncouth." The seas were thought of in their stormy aspect, and the woods as something to be cut down with toil. Man was in America to do something, not to write, and after the early books descriptive of the country we find little or no literature. George Sandys's translation of the *Metamorphoses* stands almost alone.

This was not the cause which checked literary effort in England. There Latin was still not only the polite language of the day, but the language of science and art. In America there was little knowledge of Latin after the first generation of colonists died out. The schools in England had been those attached to the destroyed monasteries, and it was with difficulty that more modern foundations took up their work. Grammar schools were also Latin schools at home, but this was not so much the case in Virginia and Carolina. The school development of which we read in New England toward the middle of the century did not obtain in the South, because the population was more scattered. Children could not go twenty or thirty miles by river or through dangerous forests, and the result was that the better classes employed teachers of their own, while the lower classes, so far as they existed, had none at all. Many of the indented servants brought over were educated men and they were quite generally used as tutors, somewhat recalling the old Roman days when the philosopher or the author, not to say stenographer, might be a white slave. So that, on the whole, after a generation there came a decline in education, as is shown by the entries in the parish and other public records.

Thus we have reviewed to some extent the British institutions in America. The primary foundations of all society are the State, the Family, and the Church, and we have now considered these and their incidents. So land, labor, capital, production, and distribution need not further detain us, except that it will be interesting to notice some divergences from British economic models. Negro slavery was one, but it assumed importance later than the first century of colonization. At least two subjects closely associated with what we now deem essentially British character, however, are from the beginning remarkable by their absence. One of these is manufacturing, and yet it would be misleading to think of this industrial development as even British in the seventeenth century; for at the time of the settlement of America this industry had not developed at home. It was not until the middle of the next century that the industrial revolution effected by machinery and steam made England the manufacturing country of the world. So that it is not wonderful that the Virginians and Carolinians did not develop something which their conditions did not call for and a tendency to which they can hardly be said to have brought with them.

But why did not the shipping industry flourish in the descendants of those who explored the world under Raleigh and Drake, and whose own immigration was its fruit? The indented coast of Greece made that the maritime nation of Classic times, and it is strange that Chesapeake Bay and the many admirable harbors of the Atlantic did not create a seafaring population. The New Englander developed this English tendency better than his Southern brother. It is probable that the sparse settlement of the country had something to do with it, for there was much local shipping about James River. It is probable that the distances between the colonies prevented the growth of a true coasting marine. And yet, the foreign carrying trade was largely developed, particularly at Charlestown. The tobacco and rice of the two colonies, together with the furs and peltries of the Indian trade, gave rise to a large business, carried on mainly in ships owned abroad. Charlestown seemed even a rival to the recently acquired Dutch port of New York.

The growth of Charlestown modified the rural tendency of the South in several ways, for the Carolinian plantations were more compact and the planters spent what time could be spared in what became a cultivated community. Charlestown developed into a considerable city, wealthy and influential, to such an extent that, as at Rome, elections and public affairs for the whole colony were transacted in the town. An aristocratic population grew up, unlike any other in America. There even came to be a modification of the distinctive Southern type of home. The warmth of the climate, the lowness of the soil, made the long summers oppressive, and an essential part of the Charlestown house was the front piazza or gallery, always faced to catch the southern breeze. To such an extent was this carried that in course of time not only did the family deem the piazza the most important part of the house, but, however the streets ran, the houses faced south, and on north and south avenues were entered by a door at one end of the piazza. This modification would not be so much needed in the country, and there as in Virginia the original type was a house with a porch or piazza in front opening into the hall, inherited with its traditions from England, and on each side of this were the various rooms. In Virginia and Carolina the house had both hall and porch, but perhaps we may think of the

Virginian porch as an outdoor annex of the hall, and of the Carolinian hall as somewhat an indoor extension of the piazza. The archetype of both styles may to this day be seen throughout the South in log cabins, with gallery in front outside and rooms within on each side of an open central hall; but in time the hall would be closed and entered through the door from the front gallery, another story added, and architectural improvements made. The result was the majestic Southern mansion, of which many examples still survive from colonial days.

The presence of the central hall probably dictated the building of the chimneys at the end of the house instead of in the centre, and the location of the chimney has been made the text of a very interesting study of life in the South as contrasted with the North. While at the South the cool hall was the central attraction, in New England the great fireplace was in the centre of the building so as the better to warm the house, as was the more necessary in so inhospitable a climate, while the piazza became a mere entrance porch. And yet the more inhospitable without, the more the people were driven to home comforts, and thus induced to live closer together and build up villages and towns, while in the South the influences were centrifugal, with tendencies toward less crowded quarters and more outdoor life.

England had now founded or acquired in America a number of colonies, which were gradually developing along lines which were to determine their future. What that might be, no one could tell, and, in fact, the colonists at least hardly cared, and did not speculate. Communication even within the limits of one colony was difficult. Each plantation was in a measure independent of the others. Except so far as the Carolinians met in Charlestown, the principal gatherings throughout the Southern colonies were at religious and political meetings. There thus grew up a local patriotism in each province. What might happen in Virginia affected Carolina very little, and what happened in Carolina

Captain John Smith. *From the copperplate by John Davies, in possession of the Historical Society of Pennsylvania.*

might be almost unknown in Virginia. Maryland and Virginia had more interests in common, and to some extent they drew together, as did the New England colonies. On the whole, the development was that of isolated settlements, having little interest in each other. The population steadily grew, as is apt to be the case in colonial and frontier settlements, and was increased from time to time by immigration from the old country. As a rule, there was growing up in each colony a remarkably homogeneous population. Had there been any such diverse immigration as we find in our day, it is questionable whether an American type of any sort could have developed. Fortunate it was that continental nations abroad were absorbed in their own affairs and in their own wars, and did not to any great extent send a surplus population over the Atlantic. In this way the settlements were permitted to have a strong and healthy individualistic growth and become able in course of time to assimilate what was to come to them from other countries.

The colonies extended in an irregular half-moon from Massachusetts on the north to the Carolinas on the south. They not only fronted the Atlantic, but their principal development was on the seacoast. Nevertheless, they were gradually extending back into the interior, and in course of time were to reach the Alleghanies and their continuations, and, in Pennsylvania and New York, to follow the river courses even beyond these mountain barriers; but for the time now under consideration the tidewater was the seat of population and of industry. The lack of cohesion among their Indian enemies tended to increase their mutual independence. Had it been necessary to combine against a common Indian foe, the sentiment of nationality would have had an earlier growth. But Carolina had to fight only its own Indians, Virginia hers, and Massachusetts her own, and single-handed each was able to prevail.

It is true there were germs which tended ultimately toward greater unity. There was the sentiment of loyalty to the British Crown, originally strong among those who came from England and kept up in their children by commercial and intellectual intercourse with the old home. Their governors came from England, their books, their clothing, and furniture, and oftentimes even bricks and household utensils. There was everywhere and always a sentiment of attachment to the mother country. This was to some extent reinforced by the feeling that, after all, they were her outposts in a New World, that to her they must look for salvation in the future as in the past against the savages of the interior. If the different colonies seldom applied to each other for assistance against the Indians, each one of them did look for help to England. The old feeling, so prominent in the settlement of Virginia, of hostility to the Spaniards had in a sense migrated to Carolina; for the Spanish terror was but past history to Virginia of the eighteenth century, although an ever pressing dread to the Carolinians. The new power arising in the Mississippi valley was likewise to interest the Carolinians more than other southern colonists, although the French wars were to affect New England more than any other part of America. Whether in Massachusetts or in Carolina, the feeling that a conflict with the French meant one with the greatest power in Europe led to a curious mingling of self-assertion and dependence,—assertion against the French in America, and dependence upon the British government in Europe.

The general result of the growth of institutions in America, particularly in the South, was a feeling of self-reliance, which assumed the form of political unrest and military activity. Like most other instances of local self-government well developed, it showed a lack of cohesion. It developed individuals first, the colony second, a nation not at all. It was a system strong in peace, but weak in war, especially a war requiring more than local action. For the net result of British colonization was rather a series of settlements on the Atlantic coast than a systematic occupation and plantation of America.

CHAPTER IX

LA SALLE FOUNDS LOUISIANA

MAZARIN, the guardian of Louis XIV., grandson of Henry IV., was not an unworthy successor of Richelieu, but he lacked the commanding presence and influence of the old cardinal. The Great Condé, Turenne, and the nobles submitted with impatience to his rule, and in 1648–1649, despite the éclat of effecting the Peace of Westphalia, there broke out the insurrection of the Fronde, at first headed by the Parlement of Paris, seeking reforms in the government, and when this was appeased there was a subsequent outbreak lasting four years longer, engineered largely by De Retz and other conspirators. In the course of this, Mazarin had to retire from Paris, and the young king and the queen-mother suffered such privations as to make a deep impression upon Louis. Young as he was, it all had a determining effect upon his character, for it persuaded him of the need of keeping the Parlement in subjection and of establishing over against the nobles and the people a strong royal government. The contemporary rebellion in England, culminating in the execution of Charles I., and the teaching of Mazarin united to confirm his resolution; and, boy as he was, to this period we can date the policy he afterward pursued of making the French monarchy absolute, of recognizing at home, abroad, and in the colonies no will but his own. He attained his majority at the sedate age of fourteen, and the only effect was a more mature dependence upon Mazarin. While his general education was perhaps neglected, he was taught to be a soldier and given manners worthy of a king, while Mazarin inculcated the necessity of being powerful at home and of obtaining for France a scientific frontier. Only four years after his nominal majority came the famous incident of his lecturing the Parlement, hunting whip in hand; and with the death of the cardinal in 1661, Louis quietly but with determination assumed the reins of power, announcing that he would be his own prime minister. He had inherited efficient officials, and in Colbert especially had one of the first rank, and it may be said that to Colbert France owed all that was best in the reign of Louis XIV. It is true that Louvois was an admirable minister of war, and aided greatly in the reorganization of the French army under Condé and Turenne which made it largely infantry and in all respects the finest in the world; but it was Colbert who reorganized the State and supplied the means by which wars were carried on, and, better yet, instituted a commercial and colonial policy by which war was almost unnecessary. In the years preceding Colbert's death in 1683, the reign of Louis XIV. was seen at its best. Before that year came the encouragement of manufactures, the placing of the finances of the kingdom in the state which was the wonder of the world, the extension of commerce and the upbuilding of a navy, and the adoption of a definite and far-reaching colonial policy covering the world from India to America. Heretofore over half of the taxes had been absorbed, legitimately or illegitimately, before reaching the royal treasury, while from the time of Colbert all were received after light costs of collection. From an annual deficit of millions, there was an annual surplus of millions of livres. While not prime minister, while not even foreign minister, the policy advocated by him prevailed to a large extent during his lifetime, and this was to keep up the relations established by Henry IV. and continued by Richelieu to maintain alliance with the Protestant princes of Europe against the Catholic Houses of Austria and Spain.

There gradually developed also the old ambition of Mazarin to have as the French eastern boundary the river Rhine; and with the exercise of good judgment this could have been attained, if there had not been added the wish to make the Scheldt the French boundary on the northeast. That was a different matter. As to the Rhine, there was only the loose Empire to contend with, divided against itself and half looking to Louis as protector. In the other case, there was not only the declining power of Spain to reckon with, but the jealousy, commercial and military, of the rising Dutch. It was essential that Vauban be able to fortify a strong frontier to the east and northeast; but Colbert, unlike Louvois, held that statesmanship dictated going ahead slowly, and Louis vacillated in the matter. His first great war was against the Spanish Netherlands upon the conclusion of the Peace of Breda, and then one with Holland, during which the Dutch cut their dikes; and in 1678 the Peace of Nimeguen ended what was in a sense the first act of the drama, leaving France the most formidable power in Europe, and free now to influence other continents.

By the end of the seventeenth century the French had established a sure footing in North America. It was no longer by Huguenots, exiles rather than colonists, that settlement was attempted. The royal government itself moved in the matter, and, the year after the foundation of Jamestown, Quebec was built, itself younger than Acadia. It is true that for a long time Quebec was simply a little place whose mountain perch was essential to its defence from surrounding Indians, but it was nevertheless a true settlement and the starting point for French influence in what was to become Canada. Montreal followed, and explorers, missionaries, and voyageurs gradually pushed up the St. Lawrence to the Great Lakes. By the time of Colbert, French power was well established in Canada and on the north coasts; while in the West Indies, among others, Martinique and Guadaloupe were theirs, and buccaneers had paved the way for French colonization of a part of Santo Domingo. In Africa, the French power was felt in Senegal and across the continent in Madagascar, while in India there were French factories at Surat and Masulipatam. All of these were only beginnings, but they were the beginnings of true colonization. Colbert had become *controleur général*, and a little later minister of marine, commerce, and the colonies, and he saw to it that colonial taxation was light and that the immigrants were aided. Colbert, more than anyone, realized the importance of colonies. He saw that much of the commerce of the world was to be upon the western seas and that a strong navy was a necessity for France, and therefore made or improved five great ports, providing suitable arsenals, shipyards, and the like. On the Mediterranean was Toulon, on the channel Dunkirk and Havre, while Brest and Rochefort looked out upon the Atlantic. In 1672, France had only sixty vessels of the line and forty frigates, carrying sixty thousand sailors. Nine years later, the navy included one hundred and ninety-eight war vessels, carrying one hundred and sixty thousand men, and by 1690 it amounted to seven hundred and sixty men-of-war. Great naval commanders were also forthcoming, and from then date Tourville, Jean Bart, Duquesne, and others; for neither Holland nor England was to remain mistress of the seas, and some of the French admirals were perhaps as great as the world had ever seen. Schools of instruction were founded at Rochefort, Brest, Dieppe, and Toulon, to which the principal families of the coast, including some from the colonies, were invited to send their sons to learn to be officers. Thus three Le Moyne children came from Canada, one being Pierre, afterward known as Sieur d'Iberville; they spent four or five years in these schools and upon war vessels in actual service. What battles they were in we do not know, but it was the time of the Sicilian war, in which the famous Dutch admiral, De Ruyter, was killed, the time when Tourville won Beachy Head over the British, lost La Hogue, and then next year won Lagos, and when Jean Bart was as successful as he was daring. Colonial sailors might meet foreigners like the Italian Henri de Tonty, proud to lose an arm for their adopted country, and even students in seacoast towns would, like La Salle, hear and see what would fire them to explore unknown wilds. To us absolutism means the deadening of all ambition, and yet the age of Louis can only be understood in Europe and America by realizing the contrary. The will of the king was supreme, but the absolute monarch evoked absolute devotion on the part of a brave and adventurous nation. Man's chief end was to glorify the king. His glory was the inspiration of his people. By the Rhine and on the Indian Ocean, in Hudson Bay and on the Mississippi, the honor of Louis le Grand nerved the arm and called into play all that was best in Frenchmen. Belief in something akin to fatalism had not long since inspired the Puritans on the battlefield and in the council, and zeal for an earthly ruler hardly less absolute than Deity created the epoch of Louis XIV. It was more than love of an army for its general, for the generals were but his servants. It was more than admiration for a ruler, for the actual rulers were his ministers. The king was the State,—"L'état c'est moi,"—but he was king by Divine right, and, all in all, was idolized until the feeling of the French was akin to adoration.

In England we have seen that the Virginia Company had long since been dissolved, but the East India and other corporations still showed active life, as they did in Holland. It is not surprising, therefore, that Colbert also should look to the development of his colonies by means of corporations. We find, in 1664, the formation of a privileged East India Company, although Pondicherry was not to come for a decade and the French interests in that quarter were small; and in the same year came the West India Company, to take in charge Canada and the islands. This latter, however, was unsuccessful, and ten years later America was placed under the direct administration of Colbert as minister of marine. A more lasting institution was the Company of the West, whose zenith was yet to come. Thus it was that French colonization in America was part of a world movement. Our field is limited to the west, but it is not amiss to remember that this was only a part of the colonial enterprise of the age of Louis XIV. In the east the contest of France was to be mainly with the Dutch, while in the west it was ultimately with the English; but for the time being, now that Spain was less powerful, it seemed as if the interior of America was open to the first comer; and that the time would soon come when Quebec would be a name almost as familiar as Antwerp, and the as yet unknown Mississippi even eclipse the Rhine. For De Soto and Menendez we must now read French names, and study minds and men who could make plans greater even than those absorbing the attention of the cabinets of Europe.

To such an extent did Canada embody French plans, that with the neighboring coasts it received the name of New France. A few facts of its history are necessary to our story, because out of Canada and its interests sprang the French enterprises in the interior. Just as in France Richelieu had instituted *intendants* in all the provinces to look after finance, so in Canada, from the time it ceased to be a mission, we find the government conducted by a governor representing more especially the military side, and an *intendant* who was at the head of finance, justice, and commerce. In the earlier settlements of France and Spain we have not seen this distinction, and it was due to the reforms of Richelieu. Well as it worked in France, where the *intendants* superseded the older nobility and had the real administration of affairs, it was a division not suitable to the new conditions of America. If the people were not to be taken into account, the proprietary or palatine form which we have noticed in English enterprises was the best. One man could better govern than two, and yet it is characteristic of the jealousy of the king that as in France he employed spies on everyone, in the colonies he divided what should have been one strong central power into two, in order that they might be checks and spies on each other.

One of the earlier *intendants*, Jean Baptiste Talon, was a man after Colbert's own heart. He was not content with developing the settlements along St. Lawrence River, but looked forward to the future. France, it is true, had some tropical islands, but the occupation of the coast by Spain and England after the unfortunate events about Fort Caroline had forced her to colonize in a bleaker climate. On account of the fisheries, Acadia and Newfoundland were their own excuse; but the river St. Lawrence did not pass through a country of mines or agriculture, and was not worth much in itself. The inhospitable climate led Talon to urge the acquisition from the Dutch and English of the Hudson valley and its commodious harbor, so as to have a more southern outlet for the commerce which came to the St. Lawrence. This was found impossible, but Talon's plan for a southern port was, all unconsciously to himself and to his contemporaries, to be carried out further to the west and in a different way. The daring Jesuits had long since pressed forward among the Iroquois and all but made a new Paraguay among the Hurons in the triangle between their lake and Lake Erie. Further yet had they gone and founded missions for the salvation of the western savages: at Sault Ste. Marie, where Lake Superior discharges its water through rapids and falls, and St. Ignace at Michilimackinac, not far away, overlooking the outlet of Lake Michigan; and even beyond, missions were located at different times at the extreme west end of Superior, on its southern bank, and on the waters tributary to the western shore of Michigan. In such schools were brought up Joliet the trader and Marquette the priest; but providing lonely chapels for the conversion of souls was not the object of the French government. The missionaries were explorers, but political and commercial influence must follow them if France was to gain any advantage from their labors.

Voyageurs, whether religious or secular, must give place to others, and other interests came.

The fur trade, especially in beaver skins, had now grown from casual and small beginnings until it was an organization of which the State took cognizance; and at certain seasons of the year canoes of peltries swarmed down the lakes to the St. Lawrence, the natives carrying their freight around the great falls of Niagara or through Georgian Bay across to the waters of the Ottawa, to float them to Montreal and Quebec. Emissaries among the various Indian tribes bought peltries or themselves hunted and brought furs down the lakes and river, so that the explorer gave way to the trader, voyageurs to the *coureurs de bois*, of whom possibly the greatest was Tonty's cousin, Daniel Greysolon Du Lhut. Firearms and liquor constituted a large part of the consideration paid the Indians, with the result of changing their barbarism into a semi-civilization which had few of the virtues and most of the vices of the French. To drink became their consuming desire, and it was necessary for the government to forbid traders from going among the Indians, so that commerce in Canada could be under proper police supervision. This restriction upon trade was evaded, and priest, governor, and *intendant* at different times not only winked at its infraction, but themselves shared in the profits of the illicit fur trade. Gradually the missions became military outposts, and in 1671 came the *prise de possession* by Deaumont de Saint-Lusson, when, raising a clod of earth at Michilimackinac before natives and followers like Le Sueur, he claimed the whole country tributary to the Great Lakes for Louis XIV. Empty claim it was in some respects, for the Jesuits had been driven from among the Iroquois, and the Five Nations had almost exterminated the Hurons in the "reductions" of the new Paraguay and forced them headlong westward. Not only did the Five Nations by their savage wars make themselves feared and at this time the masters of all tribes near the Great Lakes, but they were the most formidable foes of Canada, whose governors contended with them in war and raid, and welcomed peace when it could be obtained.

Thus the all-lake route to the west was long impassable, and, instead of using Lake Erie, the fur trade had to come through Lake Huron and the Ottawa portage down to the St. Lawrence. And yet, the other lakes were now becoming commercialized, a back country for Canada, and explorers must go further to find anything new. Rumors had come through the western missions of the great river which we now call the Mississippi, and it was discovered by Marquette and Joliet shortly after Talon returned to France and the energetic Frontenac came as governor. It is sometimes claimed that a Colonel Wood had been on a branch of the river almost twenty years before, and one Captain Bolton on the Mississippi itself in 1670; but, if so, they have been less fortunate than the Frenchmen in their chroniclers. It would seem that La Salle, a young man from Rouen, educated among the Jesuits and come to America with zeal to discover something, passed down Ohio River to the falls where Louisville now stands and possibly to the Mississippi itself; at all events, he secured the confidence of Frontenac and was with him when the governor in 1673 built a fort named for himself on Lake Erie with the intention of controlling a part of the fur trade. With the nice dispute whether this was done for the benefit of the colony or for that of the governor we are not concerned, nor with the accusation that the Jesuits opposed it because it would divert some of the trade from the old Ottawa route, by which the missions profited. More important is it that next year La Salle carried back to Colbert a letter from Frontenac highly recommending him, and acquired through the great minister the grant of the fort and the signiory around it, and three years later was there in command, having among his Récollet priests Louis Hennepin, of famous memory. La Salle was soon again in France, and with the minister planned exploration and colonization of the interior country tributary to the great river, then known as the Colbert. Marquette and Joliet had descended far enough to be satisfied that it emptied into the Gulf of Mexico, and La Salle was to go to the mouth and verify this. Then in the prime of his power was the Prince de Conti, not yet in the debauched old age by which he is generally remembered, and from the Italian wars of the king the prince had brought with him to Paris an Italian who was to be no unworthy second to La Salle,—Henri de Tonty, whose ingenious father had invented the scheme of insurance now called by his name. The prince at this time took a deep interest in the widening field of colonization opening up to France, and recommended this Italian to La Salle, who, even on the voyage across the Atlantic, found that the fact that Tonty had lost an arm by the explosion of a grenade in Sicily did not impair the singular force and usefulness of the man. La Salle was to accomplish the greater work, but it would have been almost impossible without his lieutenant, the beauty and vitality of whose life and character made him the Bayard of colonization.

The wealth of his relatives enabled La Salle to reconstruct his fort of stone, but it was to be less a resting place than a point of departure for his future life. The Iroquois pacified, he built the beginnings of Fort Niagara, and above the falls constructed the first home-built boat of the upper lakes. This *Griffin* was to carry him further, and in 1679 his party ascended the lakes, passing St. Ignace at Michilimackinac, and, loading her for a return voyage, La Salle, through the St. Joseph and its portage, reached the Illinois. The next year saw the building of Fort Crèvecœur, on Illinois River. The *Griffin* had been sent back with furs from Michilimackinac, but perished on the way, and La Salle returned overland to Fort Frontenac only to learn the loss of the ship from France bringing him supplies. As if the archer thrice must strike, the Iroquois, jealous of the fur trade and of his growing influence on the lakes, in a rapid expedition dispersed and destroyed the Illinois who had gathered around La Salle's camp, and drove off even Tonty and his men. Father Hennepin had been sent by La Salle to explore the upper Mississippi, and this he did with some success, and named the Falls of St. Anthony for the Paduan saint. Years afterward he was to disgrace the gray gown and cord of St. Francis by claiming also to have descended to the mouth of the river, but this was after the death of La Salle.

It required much exertion, money, and courage to gather his resources again, but this La Salle did, and in 1681 all was ready to his satisfaction for the descent of Mississippi River to its mouth. His original plan before the loss of the *Griffin* had been to make the voyage in a large boat so as to bring back buffalo hides acquired in trade, and thus pay the expenses of the expedition; but he now resolved to go on in canoes. His party embraced in all fifty-four people, of whom eighteen were French and the rest Indians, some of these being Abnakis and others who had been vanquished in contest with the New England settlers and had found their way to Crèvecœur. All went down the Illinois, and on February 6th entered the broad Colbert, or Mississippi. Descending, they saw the muddy Missouri, later the Ohio, and toward the end of the month built a stockade fort on the Third Chickasaw Bluff, naming it Prudhomme for a hunter who was temporarily lost. As they rowed southward spring became more and more apparent and the beauties of nature began to appeal to them. Although ever and anon they saw Indians, generally they were well received. In March they were with the Kappas, or Quapaws, near the mouth of Arkansas River, and found there not only corn and beans, but peaches and domestic fowl, turkeys and tame bustards,—opening up an interesting question as to the origin of the fowl. Gravier, in 1700, saw numerous cocks and hens among the Houmas, who did not eat them. The stock of the Bayogoulas was said to have come from a shipwreck, but off Mobile Bay in 1685 La Salle was himself to take aboard Indians who already had "moutons, cochons, poules, coqs d'Inde, et vaches." Marquette had years before seen guns among the Akanseas, as among the Chickasaws also, indicating trade with Mexico or Carolina. Here La Salle proceeded to take possession of the country in the name of the king by erecting a cross bearing the arms of France, the priest Membré intoned a hymn, and the men shouted "Vive le Roy!" Then, continuing their journey, they visited the great town of the Taensas, or Tensaws, in which were large square buildings of adobe, crowned by a dome of canes, one of them for the chief, and another the temple of the Sun. Somewhat similar were the customs of the Natches, whom they also visited, and where they also erected a cross with the French arms.

And thus they went on down the stream, seeing or hearing of various tribes, passing Red River and sundry bayous, until on the 6th of April they came to the three passes by which the Mississippi discharged. La Salle examined the western, Tonty the middle, and D'Autray the other. Soon the water under the boats changed to brine, the breeze itself smelt salt, and then they saw before them the Gulf of Mexico—so long sought and dreamed of, now at last a reality. After some exploration came La Salle's magnificent *prise de possession.*

In many respects it was the grandest event since the landing of Columbus, grand even in its simplicity. At some place, now lost, above where the passes separate, dry and not subject to inundation, they landed and prepared a column and cross. On the column they painted the arms of France, with the inscription: *Louis le Grand, Roy de France et de Navarre, règne le 9e Avril 1682.* Everyone being under arms, they chanted the *Te Deum*, *Exaudiat*, the *Domine salvum fac regem*, and then, after salvoes of musketry and shouts of "Vive le Roy!" La Salle erected the column, and at its foot, according to the official report, made the following address:

"On the part of the high, powerful, invincible, and victorious Prince, Louis le Grand, by the grace of God king of France and Navarre, fourteenth of the name, to-day the 9th of April, 1682, by virtue of the commission of his Majesty which I hold in my hand open to the inspection of all whom it may concern, I have taken and in the name of his Majesty and his successors I do take possession of this country of Louisiana, its seas, harbors, ports, bays, the straits adjacent, and all nations, peoples, provinces, cities, towns, villages, mines, mining rights, fisheries, rivers, and streams within the bounds of said Louisiana, from the mouth [embouchure] of the great River St. Louis from the east, otherwise called Ohio, Olighinsipou, or Chukagoua, and this by consent of the Chaouesnons, Chicachas, and other peoples who live there with whom we have made alliance, and also for the length of the River Colbert or the Mississippi and streams which discharge into it from its origin beyond the country of the Sioux or Nadouesioux, and with their consent and that of the Ototantas, Islinois, Matsigamea, Akansas, Natchez, and Koroas, who are the largest nations which dwell there with whom we have made alliance by ourselves or people for us, to its mouth in the sea or gulf of Mexico about the twenty-seventh degree, to the embouchure of [the river of] Palms, upon the assurance which we have had from all these nations that we are the first Europeans who have descended or ascended the said River Colbert. I protest against all those who may undertake to seize all or any of said countries, bays, and lands above specified to the prejudice of the right of his Majesty so acquired with the consent of the above named nations, of which and of all which should be done I call to witness those who hear me, and I demand the certificate of the notary present to serve for confirmation."

Thereupon everybody shouted "Vive le Roy!" and discharged musketry, and La Salle placed in the ground, at the foot of the tree to which was attached the cross, a lead plaque, engraved on the one side with the arms of France and this inscription in Latin: *Ludovicus Magnus regnat nono Aprilis*

1682; and on the other: *Robertus Cavelier, cum domino de Tonty, legato, R.P. Zenobio Membre, Recollecto, et viginti Gallis, primus hoc flumen, inde ab Ilineorum pago enavigavit, ejusque ostium fecit pervium nono Aprilis anni 1682.* Quite characteristic of the time was it that he should add that his majesty, as elder son of the Church, never acquired land for his crown without making it his principal care to establish there the Christian religion, and in evidence of this La Salle erected a cross, before which those assembled chanted the *Vexilla* and the *Domine salvum fac regem*, finishing the ceremony with shouts of "Vive le Roy!" To the *procès verbal* made by Jacques de la Metairie, notary of Fort Frontenac, were signed twelve names besides that of the notary, and among them were those of De La Salle, the Récollet Zenobe, Henri de Tonty, and Nicolas de La Salle.

It will be observed that La Salle says little as to the Ohio and gives no eastern boundary on the Gulf. A chart later made or used by him, however, makes a branch of the Mississippi empty into what we call Mobile Bay; and the almost contemporary map of Franquelin indicates the boundaries as extending on the coast from the Rio Grande to Mobile, beyond which in both directions lay the Spanish possessions, and in the interior includes the whole Mississippi basin, extending to the summits of the mountains on the east and west, and on the north bounded by the watershed separating the Great Lakes from the Mississippi. The domain thus acquired was more valuable than all Canada, and the subsequent history of Louisiana was one long effort to turn La Salle's challenge into reality,—Spain and England to the contrary notwithstanding.

It seems to have been La Salle's original plan to sail to Santo Domingo or elsewhere, but, coming in canoes and not the larger vessel planned, nothing was left except to ascend the river to the Illinois again. This they slowly did, and, realizing that the destiny of the great valley was not to be necessarily the same as that of Canada, with which for the present, nevertheless, it must be connected, La Salle

A
TRVE RE
lation of ſuch occur-

rences and accidents of noateas
hath hapned in Virginia ſince the firſt
planting of that Collony, which is now
reſident in the South part thereof, till
the laſt returne from
thence.

Written by a Gentleman of the ſaid Collony, to a worſhipfull
friend of his in England.

LONDON
Printed for *Iohn Tappe*, and are to bee ſolde at the Grey-
hound in Paules-Church-yard, by *W.W.*
1608

Title-page of John Smith's earliest work on Virginia, printed in London in 1608. *From the very rare original in the New York Public Library, Lenox Branch.*

erected on Starved Rock, overhanging Illinois River, a more permanent fortification than the palisades of Crèvecœur. To it he gave the name St. Louis, and then endeavored by negotiations to make it the centre of French influence on the Mississippi. Indeed, about it soon gathered thousands of the Illinois and neighboring Indians, including the Shawanoes, or Shawnees, from the lower Tennessee and Cumberland Rivers; and he even sought to attract the Chickasaws, who were so long to hold the key to the history of Louisiana. The Illinois were agricultural, raising especially corn and squash, unlike the Sioux beyond the Mississippi. La Salle, possibly having in mind the "reductions" of his enemies the Jesuits, wished gradually to make all the Indians agricultural, and thus about Fort St. Louis were the beginnings of civilization in the great valley and of the harvests of the Illinois region, so important ever since. The next year brought only disaster, for Le Fèvre de La Barre succeeded Frontenac and did all he could to belittle La Salle's achievement, interrupt his trade, and draw off his followers. Worse yet, Colbert was dead, and Seignelay, the son who succeeded him, was not to take the same interest in colonial affairs. Even the king was convinced by La Barre that the great discovery was useless, and La Salle found it necessary to repair to France. There, however, such was his energy that everything succeeded to his wish. Louis changed his mind as to the value of the discovery, remembering that Colbert had thought a port on the Gulf necessary for his glory and the commerce of France. La Salle did not fail to point out that the English were in danger of hemming in the existing French settlements as in a vise between their establishments on Hudson Bay and in New England, and his remedy would be a countermove by which the great Mississippi valley should become French and the English in their turn confined between the mountains and the ocean. To do this a fort was needed about sixty leagues above the mouth of the Mississippi, and La Salle had the address to suggest also that by Red River, which he called the Seignelay, he could conduct an expedition westwardly and strike rich Mexican mines like Santa Barbara in New Biscay. There was a short war in progress at the time with Spain, and La Salle may have counted on peace as relieving him from this part of the plan, although he may not have known that it was impracticable because the wilds of Texas intervened; but it may have had its effect on the king and his ministers.

As with the king, so with France. Great interest was excited in the proposed expedition to the Gulf of Mexico. A Spanish decree in the time of Philip II. attempted to close the Gulf to all foreigners, but it was now the time of Louis XIV. and not of Philip. The French proposed to override the claims of Spain, and prepared a fleet of four vessels at La Rochelle. It was in 1684, the year before the Revocation of the Edict of Nantes was to banish from France so many of her best and most industrious citizens, but it was not the wish of the king to make this a colony of Huguenots. If any went along, it was not because they were wanted, and yet the people who were gathered up from the streets for colonization might far better have been of the industrious Reformed. It is sometimes hinted that the commander of the expedition, Beaujeu, was a friend of those persistent enemies of La Salle, the Jesuits; at all events, it was the misfortune of the explorer now as so often to fall out with superiors and inferiors alike. Intent upon his own plans and ambitions, he expected all to obey and none to share his counsels.

The expedition sailed and, after touching at Santo Domingo to refresh the many sick, proceeded to the Gulf. One vessel was unfortunately captured by the Spaniards, and thus La Salle lost what was in it and could only expect opposition now that his plans were known. The 6th of January, 1685, the fleet probably passed the mouth of the Mississippi, but, from misjudging the currents, thought they were much further to the east, and so continued on their way, until Beaujeu claimed that the supplies of the ships threatened to run short and insisted upon returning. Making a virtue of necessity, La Salle and his colonists went ashore at what we now call Matagorda Bay. Minet, the engineer, seems to have returned with Beaujeu and made a map which has survived, showing exploration after leaving La Salle, thus proving that the pretence was false as to shortness of provisions.

In a sense the colony planted on what we now know as Texan soil is beyond our scope, and yet it was in Louisiana and, as La Salle thought, near a western effluent of the Mississippi. There was one series of misfortunes from the start. In landing, the vessel *Aimable* was wrecked, and in exploring not long after the *Belle*, given him by the king himself, was also lost; and worst of all, they soon found that, so far from being near the Mississippi, they were in an inhospitable wilderness far to the west, separated from it by many a weary league and by almost impassable rivers. This, of course, settled the matter with La Salle. His desire was not to plant a feeble French colony, doubtless ultimately to share the fate of Fort Caroline. If he was not near the Mississippi, it was necessary to move the colony there.

This, too, was impossible, and after a year, seeing never a sail except some Spanish ships, which fortunately did not see them, he undertook to go with a few men overland to the Illinois for aid, just as he had gone, on the wreck of the *Griffin*, to Canada from the Illinois. With him went Joutel, an old retainer of the family, besides La Salle's brother,—Cavelier the priest,—and others. After interminable sufferings some of the men became mutinous, and at last, on March 19, 1687, near the bank of Trinity River, La Salle was murdered from an ambuscade. Several of his friends were killed at the same time, and the murderers took charge of everything. The priest and Joutel were compelled to go along, but after a while the assassins fell out among themselves, and Joutel and Cavelier managed to make their way to the Arkansas, where they found some Frenchmen. These the faithful Tonty had left when, in 1686, he heard of La Salle's trouble and went to the Gulf. He had explored for miles in each direction along the coast, and left a letter with the Indians on the Mississippi for La Salle—a letter to have so strange a future. From the Arkansas, with this assistance, the wanderers made their way to Fort St. Louis, and thence by Canada to France, concealing La Salle's death for various unworthy motives until they reached the court.

With the death of the leader the government seemed to think it useless to make any attempt to relieve the colony, and the rest is soon told. The anxious Spaniards had not been able to find Fort St. Louis of Texas from the sea, and it was not until 1689 that an expedition by land under Alonzo de Leon, guided in part by a French deserter, came upon the site of La Salle's settlement. They found it wrecked, the buildings and palisades dismantled, and the only trace of human beings consisted of bones, some with long hair, evidently of women. Not strong at best, they had fallen victims to attacks of the Indians and perished almost as completely as Raleigh's colony at Roanoke.

The second settlement of the French in the more southern parts of North America had failed as completely as the first. It had not needed a Menendez to finish the story. It seemed as if the fatality which had accompanied Spanish endeavors to find and utilize the Mississippi had fallen, like the fateful shirt of Nessus, upon their successors. It was to need no decree of the French king similar to that of Philip to keep his subjects from further exploration of what Joutel calls the "fatal river." France had entered upon a different career from that which had seemed hers when Colbert was at the helm; and as Virginia was to Elizabeth, and Caroline to Charles IX., so was Louisiana to Louis XIV.,—named for the sovereign, but a name of sadness and not of inspiration. *Stat nominis umbra.*

CHAPTER X

IBERVILLE AND MOBILE

Louis seemed to have forgotten Louisiana. It was certainly not the chief object of his diplomacy and conflict. His personal rule was from Mazarin's death in 1661 until his own in 1715, and it is sharply divided into two parts by the Revocation of the Edict of Nantes. In the earlier period while Holland and England were contending for the mastery of the seas, Louis became the predominant power upon the continent; for his minister Colbert had succeeded to the centralizing policy of the cardinals, developed the internal resources of France, and for the first time turned the attention of the country to the ocean also. France during this period waged two wars with Holland, her old protégé, the first ending on the formation of the Triple Alliance to prevent the further annexation of Flanders and adjacent provinces; the other in revenge for that check, and closed by the Peace of Nimeguen.

Thus the object of the first part of his reign had been to increase the resources of France at home and to give her an adequate frontier toward the Rhine and the Scheldt, but from the death of his great minister Louis's tendencies went further. France being already developed, economically speaking, and there being immediately opposed no enemy worthy of the French army, Louis was disposed to abandon the traditional moderate attitude. By attacking Holland he ceased to be the protector of the Protestant States, and by the Revocation of the Edict of Nantes in 1685 he compelled the Huguenots either to apostatize or to leave the country. Many of them chose the latter course, and in their new homes in Germany and England helped to build up the manufactures and contribute to the political growth which in course of time were to deprive France of the supremacy which she held in Europe. Louis now aimed to make France wholly Catholic at home and to pose in international politics as the head of Catholic Europe. He felt that he was greater than Richelieu and could abandon the policy inaugurated by Henry IV.

During the second part of his reign Louis was still intent on extending the boundary of France to the Rhine, and by "reunions" or annexations based on old claims gradually succeeded, even during peace. For the Empire had no cohesion, and Germany was but a geographical term. Thus for a time such was the spell which he had woven that it seemed possible Louis's plan of aggrandizement to the east might succeed. The effects at home might come more slowly, but in disowning and even attacking the Protestant States he at once brought against himself coalitions and leaders who could adopt and make their own the strategy and tactics of the French. A common danger at last led to putting aside political and even religious jealousies, and several German princes, the year following the Revocation, united in a league at Augsburg embracing both Protestant and Catholic States; and after Louis attacked Germany came the Grand Alliance, which in effect added England and Holland to the older coalition. Turenne and Condé were dead, while the war with Holland had brought to the front William of Orange, who realized that eternal vigilance against France was the price of safety for his country. He was not a successful general, but he was a wise and persevering statesman; and when the Revolution of 1688 placed him on the British throne, the army and navy of the two leading commercial nations were at his disposal. He had to encounter jealousies, and sometimes could hardly hold his subjects under command, but the cause appealed to them in the long run and William proved the most formidable foe of Louis XIV. If Louis was the leading figure of Catholic Europe, he had created a leading figure for Protestant Europe. If he had made France a religious unit, it was at the sacrifice of commercial diversity and the banishment of many of his best subjects perforce to aid the enemy. His earlier years had taught him the advantages of political unity, but, intoxicated with success, he had translated politics into religion also. It was to require all the resources of France to sustain him in the struggle which he had unnecessarily invoked, and this at a time when flatterers and second-rate men were succeeding to the ministers and generals whom he had inherited.

A new feature, if only an incidental one, was that the colonies of France and England were now for the first time brought into the active sphere of European war. Louis had rejected a proposition of colonial neutrality, and Port Royal was taken and retaken; while of special importance, at least to us, were the daring expeditions of the French against the English forts on Hudson Bay. In one of these the Canadian Iberville performed herculean feats and became the idol of the northern French. He likewise subdued Newfoundland from Pemaquid, but an attack upon New England went no further than the plan. The hardy Canadians, despite their smaller number, were of greater assistance to their sovereign than the English colonists to theirs, for to these, except in New England and New York, the war was almost in name only.

Louis felt that he could not gain further headway for the present, and in 1697 offered such concessions that negotiations for peace were begun, which, after dragging wearily along, ended in the Peace of Ryswick, which brought a truce of five years; for all parties were looking forward to the struggle which must come over the Spanish succession upon the death of the childless Charles II. In Europe Louis gained much, although far less than he wished, while in

America there was a mutual restitution of all countries, islands, forts, and colonies, wheresoever situated, captured during the war, and commissioners were appointed to carry out this arrangement.

Peace was restored in Europe by the treaty of Ryswick, and the importance of colonies demonstrated by the war that led to it; heed was at last paid to memorials and papers relating to Louisiana. The old claims of Spain had not been mentioned one way or the other in the treaty, and it was on the discovery and actual settlement of La Salle that France was to rest her rights. Even the old plan was recalled for a harbor on the Gulf of Mexico from which the Mississippi valley could be settled and communication maintained with France.

A map of 1699, dedicated to William III. of Great Britain, was made by the Récollet Hennepin, and shows the knowledge or guesses of the day. The Great River is there depicted as the Meschasypy, and to the east, entirely distinct from that stream, is the large harbor of Spirito Sancto, with Chicagua as the name of Mobile River. Virginia, New Netherlands, and New England fill up the coast until we reach New France, or Canada, while in the other direction we find on the Gulf of Mexico the province of New Spain. No tribes are shown near Chicagua River, except the Cosa far to the northeast near some mountains, although many are placed on the lower Mississippi.

The curiosity of the French was now directed to the Mississippi region. Rémonville visited America, and in 1697 wrote a full memorial, urging colonization of the region about the Great River despite La Salle's failure. La Salle's plan became a French aspiration. The Mississippi valley was to be part of New France, which as Canada should front the Atlantic on the north, as Louisiana, face the Gulf of Mexico on the south, and constitute an empire worthy even of the Grand Monarque. Forts along the Great Lakes and rivers would protect the trading posts, serve as strategic and diplomatic centres for French influence among the Indian tribes, and thus hem in the English colonies between the mountains and the sea.

At the time of La Salle's death in Texas several of the Montreal family of Le Moyne, who were to carry on his work, were winning laurels to the north. Charles Le Moyne had emigrated from Dieppe in 1641, and in Canada gradually climbed the ladder of fame and fortune. He was soldier, interpreter, *garde magasin*, *procureur général*, and, as proprietor of an estate, died Sieur de Longueuil; but his real title to fame was as the father of twelve children, of whom three sons died in the wars with England and all became well known. The oldest son, Charles, succeeded to the signiory, and was as a father to the youngest, Jean Baptiste, Sieur de Bienville; while among the others were Iberville, Châteauguay, Serigny, and Saint-Hélène. Iberville was perhaps the most noted of these sailor brothers, especially for a combat near Fort Nelson in 1694, where his vessel, the *Pelican*, contended with three English, capturing one and putting the other two to flight. In this battle Bienville commanded a battery.

Iberville had throughout his life heretofore been thrown in opposition to the English in America. It seemed to him on one side of the line, as it did afterward to Franklin on the other, that there could be no security for either so long as the opposing country retained a foothold in America. Iberville pointed out to his government that not only were the French fewer in number than the English, twenty thousand as against two hundred thousand, but that the English had the choice of territory. For although in Europe England was further north than France, in America the English occupied the south Atlantic coast, while the French were confined to Acadia, the St. Lawrence, and the frozen North. He therefore advocated the following up of La Salle's plan,—the occupation by France of the north shore of the Gulf of Mexico and the Mississippi valley. The French expected that mines would be found and that, in any event, peltries and timber would furnish considerable profit, and that in course of time agriculture might become important.

In estimating Iberville's work we must remember that every step was opposed by Frenchmen. The Canadian authorities were hostile to the establishment of Louisiana because they thought it would draw to the Gulf much of the commerce of the upper Mississippi, particularly in beavers, which passed through the Great Lakes and the St. Lawrence. So Iberville found himself at odds even with his own kinspeople in Montreal; and Ducasse, Governor of Santo Domingo, opposed the new colony on the idea that it would lessen the importance of his own. On the other hand, far-seeing men advocated its establishment. Henri de Tonty, as far back as 1694, when Iberville's thoughts were confined to Hudson Bay, had prepared to continue the enterprise of La Salle in order to prevent the adventurous English from doing the same thing, and Rémonville, a friend of La Salle, but a little later proposed the formation of a company to colonize Louisiana. The minister of the marine and colonies had been Louis de Phelypeaux, Comte de Pontchartrain, until in 1699 he was succeeded by his son Jérôme, at first called Maurepas, but also known as Pontchartrain. In some respects not unworthy successors of Colbert and Seignelay, they became personally interested and sought out survivors of the earlier attempt and collected all the literature of the subject. And none too soon, for it was reported that the renegade Hennepin had interested William in the Mississippi, and that, as an English company was organizing under the patronage of that king, France, if she would hold the territory, must take possession first.

The correspondence between Iberville, the minister of the marine, and Begon, intendant at Rochefort, shows intense interest on the part of all three, resulting in the careful equipment of an expedition consisting of the *Badine*, of forty guns, commanded by Iberville himself, and the *Marin*, of thirty, under command of the Comte de Surgères, with several smaller boats to carry supplies, and a large vessel of war to meet them in the West Indies.

This expedition was for France almost what that of Columbus was for Spain. In tropical America she owned a part of Santo Domingo and a few other islands; on the continent in temperate zones, nothing,—and Iberville sailed from Brest to change all that. He stopped at Santo Domingo, where the Marquis de Châteaumorant joined them with the *François*, of fifty cannon; and for pilot they took on an old buccaneer named Laurent de Graff, and with him made good progress toward their destination.

While affairs in Europe had been shaping themselves toward recolonization of Louisiana, matters had not stood still in America. Canadian opposition was active against the Mississippi movement. Tonty had been checked in every way possible at his Fort St. Louis, which had lately been abolished and himself confined to the Mississippi region. No use was made of the great river except for the fur trade, but in its upper reaches even the Sioux had now come within the sphere of French influence, and Le Sueur, a kinsman of the Le Moynes, had built up considerable commerce among them. The interest of the Church had increased. The Jesuits as usual were anxious to press forward into the new regions, and Father Gravier, stationed among the Indians at Kaskaskia, made the earliest permanent settlement in the upper valley; but the advance of French control was not to be through the Jesuits. Bishop Laval had, or assumed, jurisdiction over the Roman Church in Canada and preferred to foster the affairs of the Church through the Seminary of Quebec, an offshoot of a similar institution at Rouen, and independent of the great orders. We soon find several stations occupied by the Seminarians on the Mississippi. Saint-Cosme was placed among the Tamaroas, near the modern St. Louis, and afterward among the Natches; Foucaut, on the Arkansas; Montigny, among the Natches; and the most interesting of them all, Davion, went to the Tonikas on the lower Mississippi. Their success was hardly encouraging, and yet they labored faithfully on. Davion kept his sacred relics in the trunk of a tree, and built a chapel on a rock at the foot of a large cross—*Roche à Davion*. His influence was great, and he is said on one occasion to have fearlessly destroyed the gods of the Yazoos.

On the Gulf itself were very different settlers. The Spaniards had finally discovered the ruins of La Salle's colony, and apprehension of further efforts led them in 1696 to send Don Andres de Arriola with a force to occupy the Bay of Santa Maria, known to us as Pensacola, already explored three years before by Don Andres de Pes. The post so established comprised fortifications at the west end of Santa Rosa Island and on the mainland opposite, which were not extensive, and consisted as usual of palisades. The location forbade any permanent colonization. The soil was sandy, and without the use of fertilizers, then almost unknown, could produce little in the way of fruits or vegetables, even had the Spaniards been able to overcome their aversion to manual labor. This post was designed to hold the northern coast of the Gulf, for there was still no recognition of any French right to Louisiana.

Knowing little or nothing of these Spanish settlements, the fleet of Iberville arrived near the land of Florida in the last days of January, 1700, when the presence of masts behind the island led him to discover the Spaniards already in possession of the harbor of Pensacola. Despite remonstrance, Iberville continued on his way and on January 31st cast anchor off Mobile Point, and made a careful examination of the entrance which was to become so familiar. From the skulls, bones, and kitchen utensils found on a long island vis-à-vis it was named Massacre Island, and, when permitted by breaks in the stormy weather, Iberville made his way over to the mainland and examined the bay. The flora and other features of the district were carefully noted, and after taking on wood and grass he sailed to seek the Mississippi. On the way he visited and named the chain of islands forming a landlocked passage to the west along the coast, and had friendly intercourse with the Indians of Biloxi. The mouth of the great river he found on March 2d, after much trouble and no little danger, for it was hidden by sandbanks, reeds, and logs like a palisade. La Salle could not see it from the Gulf, but Iberville was as fortunate here as in everything else.

Iberville went upstream in boats as far as the territory of the Houmas, and returned to his ships by Bayou Manchac and the lakes, which with some policy were called for Maurepas and Pontchartrain. Bienville, however, went back by the main stream, and, promising a hatchet, persuaded the Indians to produce the letter which Tonty had written La Salle fourteen years before. This left no doubt that the river was the Mississippi, and further explorations convinced them that Hennepin had never been on it below the Ohio.

The result was that, while Bienville was to maintain a fort at a comparatively dry place some leagues above the mouth, Iberville decided that the swift, tortuous stream did not admit of sail navigation or its marshy banks of habitation. A site for his colonial enterprise must therefore be found on the seashore further east.

On a bluff behind the Louisville and Nashville Railroad bridge at Ocean Springs, once called Biloxi, under beautiful oaks commanding a peaceful prospect over the water, there are still dug up hatchets, cannonballs, and even iron shoes of tent or flag poles, and there, beyond doubt, was the site of Fort de Maurepas. Iberville slept on the spot which he selected, and there supervised the erection of his fort of four bastions, two of stockade and two of logs, guarded by twelve cannon and apparently surrounded by a palisade. There was no town laid out, for this was intended only as a temporary settlement, of whose vicinity a map drawn by F. Joussette for this occasion is still preserved in the archives of the Marine at Paris, showing the gulf and shore, with soundings and islands. The Pascagoulas, Capinans, Chichachas, Passacolas, and Biloxis came to smoke the calumet, and, all being now set in order, Iberville sailed for France to report his success and obtain instructions and supplies.

He had instructed Bienville to explore the Mississippi and its tributaries so as to become better acquainted with the country. While returning in a rowboat to the river mouth from one of these expeditions, Bienville was surprised to meet a vessel which turned out to be English, under the command of Captain Bar. So the threat of English colonization was not an idle one, for he had come under the auspices of his government, bringing a colony of Huguenots to settle on the river. Bienville, with a diplomacy which history has pardoned, assured Bar that they were not on the Mississippi at all, but on a stream already occupied by the French, and that Bar must go further west; and the unsuspecting Briton turned around at what has ever since been called the English Turn. Bienville had some intercourse with the proposed colonists, and found them anxious to settle even under French authorization, and forwarded their requests to the home government. What became of Bar we do not know, but the French government dryly replied to the suggestion of the Huguenots, that the king had not made France Catholic in order to have his colonies heretic.

These explorations of the Le Moynes made them acquainted with many of their future neighbors. The lowest large tribe, the Houmas, were at the portage via Bayou St. Jean to the lakes, and above, nearly opposite to the place where Bayou Manchac branched off to Lake Pontchartrain, was another bayou going to the west, named from the Chetimachas upon it, and later known as the Fork [La Fourche]. Yet higher, opposite the mouth of Red River, were the Tonikas; and a little above them, also on the east side, was that remarkable race, the Natches. The Yazoos came next on their river, and the Akanseas on the west bank of the Mississippi completed in that direction what was to become Louisiana. There were smaller tribes, such as the Tchaouachas below the Houmas, the Chapitoulas, Colapissas,

Bayogoulas, and Coroas not far above, and of these the Taensas, near the Tonikas, were the most interesting.

Sauvole, governor of Fort Maurepas at Biloxi on the Gulf, also gave time to examining and sounding the coast, and discovered a harbor at the east end of Massacre Island, while from the Mobile Indians was learned the fertility of their river country. Nor did the French lack white visitors. Davion and Montigny came from their posts, and Tonty with peltries from the Arkansas, and later, diplomat as he was, we find him at Biloxi bringing chiefs of the Choctaw and Chickasaw nations. Gravier also passed through, and there were *coureurs de bois* from the upper Mississippi to sell skins and help to consume the scanty supplies.

Less welcome were Spaniards from Pensacola, whose governor came early to protest against the new settlement. The French received him courteously and entertained him well, but declined to acknowledge any right on the part of Spain. It so happened that these Spaniards came to grief, for they were wrecked on their return voyage and had to make their way back to Biloxi to ask aid. This was promptly given, and the incident closed.

Interest in America was at its height in France, and plans to complete the reduction of the great valley were pushed forward. Iberville's reports aroused the interest of science and the zeal of commerce, and encouraged the government to greater exertions. The Mississippi was surely rediscovered and open to French enterprise. Iberville recommended also the acquisition of Pensacola, and the court tried to obtain it; but despite the fact that a grandson of Louis XIV. had mounted the throne and the two peoples were united against Europe for the right of the peninsula to choose its own sovereign, the Spanish Junta declined to cede the port. There might, indeed, be no longer any Pyrenees, as Louis declared, but there was still a Mexican Gulf, the sacred gift of popes to Spain.

It was anent this negotiation that we first appreciate the statesmanlike grasp of Iberville. The Canadian sailor was in these southern seas and lands beyond local ties and interests. His memorial furnished the material of Pontchartrain's diplomacy, and in it Iberville told the future as in an unsealed book. The claim of Spain to monopoly, he showed, was without basis, and, worse than that, would soon be disputed by that Protestant country whose rulers recognized no papal gifts, whose pioneers on the American seaboard were increasing at a rate that would soon take them across the mountains to contend for the valleys of the Mississippi and its tributaries. In less than a hundred years, said this prophet, the English, unless opposed by growth and persistence like their own, would occupy the whole of America.

Some point near the mouth of Mobile River would serve Iberville's purpose as colonial headquarters even better than the Natches site first thought of, for it would be near enough to Pensacola to keep an eye on the Spaniards, near enough to the Mississippi to be the port for the valley trade, which could come through Bayou Manchac, the lakes and the sound behind sheltering islands to Mobile Bay, and with a fort on the Mississippi delta could guard the great river. Then also, with its easy river communication to the northwest and northeast, it gave means of influence among the Indians, and even access over the mountains, in case of war, to the English colonies of Carolina and Virginia.

It appears that Iberville selected the new site after exploration before his return to Europe, and, when he came back, his plans were all made and ready for execution. The daring fighter was transformed into a practical colonizer. We find him insisting on Spanish sheep instead of French, which he deemed inferior, a stallion to improve the American breed, which if native must have been of Spanish extraction, for the Indians originally had no horses, and on taking only such things and people as were essential to the development of the country. No one realized better than he the sturdiness necessary for pioneers. He wanted no dependents, for the weakness of French colonies, he said, lay in sending the poor and giving them no start.

He called at Santo Domingo, refitted his vessels, and took on horses, cattle, and swine. The climate of the tropics was beginning to tell upon the hardy Canadian, and yet, although sick in bed at Pensacola, Iberville, amid protests of the Spanish authorities, arranged the details for placing his colony upon what was intended to be its permanent site. He directed that Fort Maurepas should be abandoned and everything brought by way of Massacre Island to a point on Mobile River seventeen leagues from the island, at the second bluff. The actual removal was under the supervision of Bienville, and probably the middle or last part of January, 1702, saw the foundation of Fort Louis. It was of logs, "piece upon piece," sixty *toises*, or fathoms, square, with four bastions thirty feet long, six guns at each corner advanced in semicircle. Within were four buildings,—chapel, *gouvernement*, and officer's quarters, *magasin*, and *corps de garde*, and in the centre a parade forty-five *toises* square. The barracks for the privates and Canadians were outside, one hundred and fifty paces to the left upstream on the bank, and on the bluff was a powder magazine twenty-four feet square by ten deep, which was filled for a time by the heavy rains. Next month Iberville was able to come himself, and under his eye were laid out the streets of the city. This Fort Louis—named for the king and not, as the others, for the saint—was nevertheless called by the people Mobile from the beginning.

The same problems confronted the French that had to be overcome by the English on the Atlantic coast. The colony had to be considered in relation to the natives and to the hostile Spaniards; its government and soldiers must be attended to; and if it was to be anything more than a local post, not only had immigration to be induced, but employments found for the inhabitants which would produce a surplus for export. As to the Spaniards, there was, beyond protests, little to fear, for this was a royal colony and the courts of Spain and France were now too closely allied to admit of conflict. More trouble might come in future from the English to the northeast, and, therefore, proper treaties must be entered into with the Indians. The Mobilians, near whom the colony was placed, are supposed to have been survivors of the town destroyed by De Soto not many miles above, although the five clay figures of man, woman, child, bear, and owl found on an island may not have been the work of the Spaniards of that day, as Iberville supposed. Although their dialect is said to have been the trade jargon from the Mississippi to the Atlantic, thus pointing back to a more powerful past, the Mobilians now were not numerous nor were they the predominant tribe in this part of the country. The river upon which Fort Louis stood was formed a few miles above by the junction of two great streams coming from far in the interior, their headwaters rising in the foothills of the great Appalachian range. The one from the northeast was by the French called River of the Alibamons, from the lowest member of the Creek confederacy on its banks, the uppermost town of which was the Cosa known to us from Tristan de Luna not less than from De Soto. The river coming from the northwest was generally known among the French as that of the Chichachas [Chickasaws], from the great tribe which flourished between its upper waters and the Mississippi, and below this tribe, nearer the coast, were the Chactas, known to us as Choctaws, possibly the largest of the southern tribes.

La Salle had been impressed by the Chickasaws, and Iberville now sent the veteran Tonty to call them to a conference at Fort Louis. On March 23d, he returned with seven chiefs and principal men of the Chickasaws, besides four Choctaw chiefs. Iberville made them presents of ammunition, guns, hatchets, knives, beads, and the like, and took occasion at once to exhort them to peace among themselves and enmity against the English, who, he declared, aimed at making slaves of all natives. He announced his influence among the Illinois, who would now cease to make war upon them, and furthermore promised to establish a trading station where they could obtain everything they wanted in exchange for skins of beef, deer, and bear. The talk was satisfactory and peace was arranged. A French boy, Saint-Michel, was sent back with the Chickasaws to learn the language, and the trading station was arranged on the river between the two tribes, not far from where a post was ever afterward to remain.

Iberville had now accomplished his object, and returned to France to make a report. With an insight foreign to his predecessors of whatever nationality, his first step had been not only to conciliate the natives, but to begin a policy designed to hold them to the French interests and unite them against his enemies. He would attract the Indians by means of river trade. The English could bring their wares only by painful overland journeys across the Alleghanies, while the French would command the Gulf rivers, in particular the Mississippi, with its many tributaries. Iberville would have four grand posts besides the capital at Mobile, and would distribute them judiciously. One he founded low on the Mississippi, another should be among the Arkansas, a third on the Ouabache, as the French called the lower Ohio, and the fourth on the Missouri. Perhaps we may say that he thus foresaw the necessity for New Orleans, Memphis, Louisville, and St. Louis, although he did not select their sites. A lake city like Chicago would in his division of territory belong to the St. Lawrence rather than to the Mississippi basin, and therefore not enter into his plans. Mobile was the key without which the others were worthless, and from Mobile there could be communication by horse with even the furthest of these in fifteen days. At each he would have a sergeant and corporal, with at least ten soldiers as a nucleus for a colony, and the principal industry would be tanning buffalo hides and deerskins for shipment to France. His plans went even further, and contemplated the resettlement of great tribes so as to put them nearer his river commerce and influence. The total Indian population that should be tributary to the French amounted, as he figured it, to twenty-three thousand eight hundred and fifty families. Of the tribes, the most populous were the Sioux of four thousand, the Panis [Pawnees] of two thousand, the Chactas of four thousand, the Chichachas of two thousand, the Conchaques [Appalachicolas] of two thousand families, the Illinois and Tamaroas estimated at eight hundred, the Missouris at fifteen hundred, the Quicapous [Kickapoos] and Mascoutens at four hundred and fifty, and the Miamis at five hundred families. These Iberville would move like men upon a chessboard in his game with the English.

The first tribal change he contemplated was to induce the Indians in the mountains west of Maryland, Carolina, and Virginia to settle nearer Mobile, doubtless on the waters we now call the Tennessee and Coosa, so as to substitute French for English influence. Next was to make the Ouabache [Ohio] of use to France. More than one hundred and twenty leagues long, it had not an Indian on its banks, and there he would settle the Illinois and have them bring to this river highway the buffalo skins of their chase. With the Illinois, the French would have one thousand armed men in case of need, and their old grounds would then be occupied by the more distant Mascoutens and Kickapoos, who were heretofore given to beaver hunting, and who would supply four hundred and fifty friendly warriors more. There were as many Miamis, who sold beavers at Chicagou, and by their giving up that trade for buffalo and deer hunting about the Illinois there would be saved the expense of a fort. The Sioux, also devoted to beavers, were useless where they were, as were the Mahas and other populous tribes between the Missouri and the Mississippi, and they should be placed on Monigona [Des Moines] River. The Akanseas had abandoned their former habitat, and on their river he would place the Kansas, Missouris, and Crevas. Like the Mahas, they did not use firearms, nor had they heretofore traded with Europeans. Up that river were the Mantons, and among them he would settle the Panis. All these hunted the buffalo, and were often at war with the Spaniards of New Mexico and their Indian allies. He admits that some of these changes would injure the beaver trade of Canada, but only to give it an easier outlet down the Mississippi.

The expense of this readjustment, says Iberville, would not exceed twelve thousand livres for moving all these twelve thousand Indians, and part could even be met with knick-knacks. In four or five years, he estimated, there could be built up a trade of sixty to eighty thousand buffalo hides, and more than one hundred and fifty thousand deer and other skins, which would bring in France more than two million five hundred thousand livres per annum. Each skin would yield four or five pounds of good wool, which brought twenty sous, and two pounds of hair at ten sous. Besides this, one would get each year more than two hundred thousand livres of other peltry, such as bears, wolves, wildcats, foxes, and martens, whose customs duties would bring the king annually more than two hundred and fifty thousand livres. There would also be the products of numerous lead mines, while silver could be found near New Mexico, and copper too was abundant. But, no doubt, Iberville dwelt even more fondly on another result of these proposed changes. Not to mention tribes further west, he could count on twelve thousand good warriors to invade Maryland, Virginia, and Carolina as a part of his plan to check, if not to annihilate, the English colonies, and in this way there would be no need of many French soldiers except as officers. In short, he aimed less at interior colonization on a great scale than at building up a native empire subject to France, like that which the French were already beginning in India. How far the government would adopt this comprehensive scheme remains to be seen. At least here was a definite plan proposed by a man who could carry it out if anyone could.

Transpositions of Indians on a smaller scale did occur, and soon we find above Fort Louis the two obscure settlements of Tchaouachas and Chaouanons, names sometimes spelled differently. The former would seem to be one of the Alibamon tribes from up the river, attracted by trade or driven by civil war; the other, possibly a distant and wandering offshoot of the great Shawnee connection from the Kentucky region. And it was characteristic of the diplomacy of Bienville that, finding the Apalaches driven away from the east by the English, he gave them also as early as 1705 a new home on Mobile River. The power of this tribe was now broken, but the onslaught of the English had been due to their prominence. Bienville considered that all enemies of the English were friends of the French, and never had cause to regret his kindness to these fugitives, who always remained the most civilized of the neighbors of the colony, preserving their Spanish names and customs.

As to the white population, colonists under Iberville's supervision were brought from time to time, and the sight of women and children in the new town ceased to be unusual. There had been priests from the beginning, and Father Davion soon took up his abode permanently at the fort until a regular curé should be sent out by the Bishop of Quebec. Iberville visited the town now and then, but the War of the Spanish Succession, which broke out in the year Fort Louis was founded, drew him into other fields; and even in 1704, when he was to have come over, he had to seek relief from sickness at mineral springs. The *Pelican* therefore came without him, bringing live stock, food, and merchandise, besides a curé, artisans, seventy-five soldiers, and, best of all, under the charge of two gray nuns, twenty-three virtuous maidens, who were all married in less than a month, except one unusually coy and hard to please. She would have no man in the colony; somewhat later they all rebelled against corn bread and other Southern luxuries; and what is called the "Petticoat Insurrection" took up a good deal of the time and patience of the bachelor commandant. The curé was Henri Roulleaux de la Vente, missionary apostolic of the diocese of Bayeux; and on the

28th of September, Davion placed him in charge of the parochial church of Fort Louis by formal entrance, sprinkling holy water, kissing the high altar, touching the Mass book, visiting the most sacred sacrament of the altar, and ringing the bells, opposed by no one, all as recorded on the first page of the venerable records of Mobile, witnessed by Davion, Bienville, Boisbriant, and De La Salle. The colonists were distributed in eighty one-story thatched houses, and the census shows a number of cows, bulls, calves, kids, one hundred hogs, and four hundred chickens. Indian slaves there were, one belonging to the king, as did a bull and some oxen. Negroes did not come in for three years, and in number not until much later.

This was a fateful season, for the *Pelican* had touched at Santo Domingo, and from there brought what seems to have been the first visitation of yellow fever. Half her crew, thirty of the newly arrived soldiers, Father Dougé, and, worst of all, Henri de Tonty, died in that dreadful September. A setback it must have been in any event, but the loss of the gentle and heroic explorer was possibly the greatest blow that could have been given the colony. Bienville, in the absence of his brother, was in charge, but even his death would have been less deplorable on account of the experience and influence of the one-armed Italian. Where the cemetery was we do not know, but it must have been in the woods behind the little town; and there in an unknown grave they laid the remains of one of America's great men, with murmuring river and sobbing pines to keep his vigil. By a sad coincidence, it was soon the fate of Iberville to encounter the same disease. In 1706, with eleven vessels carrying three hundred men, he captured the British island of Nevis with its seventeen hundred soldiers and many people, and then sailed north to attack, no longer a plate *armada* from Mexico and Peru bound for Spain, but a merchant fleet from Virginia and Carolina to England. At Havana he was himself attacked by yellow fever, and death came on July 5th. His remains were placed in the parish church of St. Christopher, where for a while were also the bones of Columbus.

Thus doubly orphaned, the colony of Louisiana had to go forward under the leadership of young Bienville. He found himself unable to carry out the great transposition of Indians planned by his brother, and it is doubtful if anyone could have accomplished it in the face of the existing war. Bienville's policy was devoted to building up such trade as was possible with the Indians, and there seems to have been an honest endeavor to introduce agriculture; but cotton was unknown, and it seemed much easier to buy maize and provisions from the Indians than to raise them in quantity. Little garden patches there were, attached to houses, but they did not even suffice for local needs; and when supplies did not come from France, it was sometimes necessary to disperse at least the unmarried colonists among the friendly Indians—a measure of distress, it is true, but one of policy also. In the *Relation* of the contemporary Pénicaut we have charming accounts of such expeditions, in which the fiddle sometimes played a part, and love-making always, and which only drew the ties tighter together between the French and the natives. The church registers indicate many occupations, the military of course ranking first, while there were also locksmiths, armorers, and a number of tradesmen [*marchands*], carpenters, and cabinet-makers; almost every man was a hunter; several industries were at least planned, such as tar kilns, sawmills, and tanneries. The local name Fondlou is the creole rendering of Fond de l'Ours [bear ground], and even the site of the settlement is still known traditionally as Vieux Fort. There, yearning for beautiful France, and straining the eye to catch the first glimpse of boats from Dauphine Island, colonial life began and went on henceforth with all its lights and shadows.

Corresponding to Virginia Dare on the Atlantic coast, the first creole born in Louisiana was Jean François, son of Jean Le Camp, locksmith of the colony, and his wife, Magdelaine Robert; for in the church records the maiden name of the mother is always given. This is confirmed by a civil report recently found in the State records in France, that for some reason is particular to say he was the first male. There is a curious entry a number of years later that Robert Talon, master cabinetmaker, was then the "first creole of the colony," and the same office or title occurs afterward. It would seem therefore as if, not unnaturally, the fact became a mark of distinction, possibly the next oldest holding it in turn. There can be no reasonable doubt that Jean François Le Camp was the first child born to the French upon the soil of Louisiana, but what became of him afterward we do not know, although his father we can trace for a number of years.

The government was essentially military and from the beginning lacked every trace of representation of the people. The king's lieutenant or governor was at the head and was assisted by the *commissaire* or *ordonnateur*, who was in charge of the stores and apparently had some civil functions, and other officials, varying from time to time, but making up what was called the Superior Council. This was the court of first and last instance, although as the colony developed some of its functions became vested in lower officials. Unfortunately, it seemed that whenever a body of men, of whatever nationality, were sent to America to found a colony, they would, instead of uniting for the common good, fall out and waste the energies of the enterprise in quarrels over matters unimportant. Nicolas de La Salle, the commissary, quarrelled with Bienville, accusing him of wasting stores and favoring the Canadians, and the curé La Vente soon found himself also in opposition on account of Bienville's preference for Jesuits and told his grievances in letters to the government at home. On his side, Bienville did not mince words, and accused the curé of keeping shop like a Jew and stirring up the commissary against him. Between them they at last convinced Pontchartrain that there should be a change, and in 1708 the *Renommée* arrived with royal orders to that effect. De Muys would have been the new governor if he had not died at Havana, and Diron d'Artaguette succeeded La Salle. D'Artaguette remained friendly with Bienville, and henceforward affairs moved on more smoothly.

The strength and reputation of the settlement were shown by hostilities with the Indians to the east. There had earlier been warfare with the Alibamons on account of an inroad, and on the Mississippi the murder of a missionary had been avenged; but the most serious matter was a formidable alliance in this year between the Cheraquis [Cherokees], Abikas, Cadapouces [Catawbas], and Alibamons. This was significant and alarming in many ways, and it is impossible not to see in it the hand of the English trying to avenge the attack of the French and Spaniards upon Charlestown in 1706. In numbers the allied Indians amounted to four thousand warriors; but the French were put on their guard, and the expedition melted away with the destruction of the Mobilian cabins a few miles above the fort. And yet, such evidence of hostility boded ill for the future. The Cherokees inhabited the mountains northwest of Carolina and were in many respects the most formidable as well as interesting natives of the southeast. The Catawbas were only less to be feared because of their exhausting wars with the Iroquois, passing the Shenandoah Valley in raid and counter raid. The Abikas came from near the sacred town of Coosa; while the Alibamons were also members of the Creek confederacy, although originally possibly a distinct nation, preserving many independent traits and customs. It would appear, therefore, that at the beginning the French were more successful with the Indians to the northwest and on the Mississippi than with those lying toward the English settlements of the Atlantic coast. Here was a problem for the future.

This invasion in a sense showed the intimate connection of Europe and America, for it was a part of the War of the Spanish Succession, which may be said to constitute a third period in the reign of Louis XIV. In the first, France posed as of old as protector of the Protestant States of Europe, and thus gained territory for herself at the expense of the House of Austria. With the death of Colbert and the growing influence of Madame de Maintenon, especially from her secret marriage with the king, came the different policy of making France wholly Catholic, both at home and in her influence abroad, the principal effect of which was the war with Holland and England terminated by the Peace of Ryswick. A continuation, perhaps an intensification, of the same policy followed, but the peculiar circumstances of the time entitle the last part of the king's reign to be classed almost as a separate epoch. Just as Louis had been seeking through his late queen to claim provinces to the east and northeast, so now after her death he was led to take a deeper interest in Spain. It is true that on his accession he had renounced all pretensions to that throne arising through his wife, but when Charles II. died bequeathing it to the Duc d'Anjou, her grandson, Louis was prompt to accept the bequest. Unwelcome as this was to Europe, it is probable that Philip's claim would not have been seriously disputed had not Louis at the same time given way to sentiment at the deathbed of the exiled James II. and promised to support the claims of his son to the throne of England. This alarmed Great Britain, strengthened the hands of William of Orange, and resulted in a formidable European coalition. The old generals of Louis were gone, William himself soon died, but there came to the front Marlborough and Eugene. While the war was at first varying in its fortunes, in 1704 Louis suffered the disastrous defeat of Blenheim, Spain the loss of Gibraltar, and thenceforth the struggle of France was largely defensive. Louis was willing to make great concessions, but when required to wage war against his grandson he nobly refused, saying that if he must fight it would be against his enemies and not against his kindred.

The details of the admirable resistance of France, backed only by Spain, against the resources of Europe are of absorbing interest, but we can only take into account the consequences of the struggle. The war was carried on with energy until the whole country became almost a wilderness. Industries of all kinds were paralyzed, and the government racked its brains to discover new objects of taxation to meet the ever growing deficit. Few people of wealth were left, and the Crozats were rather exceptions than instances of riches, especially among merchants interested in maritime commerce.

The effect of all this on America can readily be imagined. The principal uses of fleets were not known or had been forgotten in France, and England was mistress of the ocean; so that even had the means existed at home, there was no way of regularly sending supplies and colonists, and Louisiana had to get along as best it could. Thus while Pontchartrain had selected what is called Twenty-seven Mile Bluff as the seat of the colony, when in 1710 this was overflowed by a freshet and the neighboring Indian farms drowned out which had supplied much of the maize consumed, Bienville needed no special instructions to remove his fort and city to the mouth of the river, where Mobile has ever since remained. On a bluff separated from the river by marshy land at ordinary tide was laid out a town, its front street called Royal along the stream, and two thoroughfares at right angles bearing the names Dauphin and Conti for the princes so well known in France. The fort, a little to the south and extending nearer to the river, was named Louis. Trees were spared or planted on its esplanade, and squares were laid off around it, ten fronting the river and two deep, while thirty more were projected through the pine woods behind for expansion of the capital of Louisiana.

The death of Iberville had defeated the execution of his grand plan for resettlement of the Indians, and the War of the Spanish Succession had prevented his brother from carrying out the more modest but more feasible policy of attaching them to the French by a trade which should upbuild the colony and attract immigrants from France. It is true, something had been done, for there were settlers along the Mobile waters and coast as far as Pascagoula, and French influence was known throughout the Mississippi valley. But agriculture had not flourished, although encouraged from home, and war had prevented much development of trade. The king felt compelled to make a different arrangement as to Louisiana, and Pontchartrain sought for several years to secure the formation of a company, at first of St. Malo merchants, who should take it over. At last, in 1712, with the Illinois struck from its boundaries, it was turned over to Antoine Crozat to exploit commercially for fifteen years, while for a more limited period the government should maintain forts and forces. Hostilities had ceased, although the Peace of Utrecht did not come until next year, and the future was brighter. Crozat naturally wished to change the whole system of management, and sent as governor La Mothe Cadillac, a man of experience, who almost the same year Mobile was founded had established Detroit, the better to control the lake traffic, now that the Iroquois gave less trouble. His present instructions were especially to seek for mines and to open trade with the Spanish possessions. In the former he was unsuccessful, although at one time he went far up in the northwest for the precious metals. Minerals there were, although not in quantity and location to attract attention. Nor did he neglect commerce. Something was done with Pensacola, but, despite the intimacy of the two courts, Spain remained unwilling to open her ports even to the French. At least three attempts were made in the direction of Mexico. Thus Louis de Saint-Denis, an adventurous character, at one time in command of the fort on the lower Mississippi, led a famous expedition up Red River for that purpose, and somewhat later he undertook a larger one by way of the Natchitoches, but won nothing for his principals. On another occasion we find Crozat sending a vessel under Durigouin to Vera Cruz on a similar mission; but all in vain. The Spaniards would not trade, and all such efforts had to be abandoned.

Mines were elusive, agriculture not a success, foreign commerce unattainable, but at least a good deal of exploring was done and some posts founded that were to mean much in future. In the very direction from which the great Indian peril had lately come, Crozat was in 1714 able to extend French influence. During jealousy of the Creeks toward the English, possibly growing out of the Yamasi and Tuscarora wars, application was made by the chief called the Emperor of the Creeks, asking the French to build a fort among them. Bienville or La Tour agreed to this, and Fort Toulouse, named for Crozat's birthplace or Louis's son, rose in the fork of Coosa and Tallapoosa Rivers, the centre of the district known to the colony as Aux Alibamons. There were two guns in each of the four bastions, and because of its location the fortress had a power far beyond its garrison and equipment. Situated almost at the head of navigation, among the foothills of the Alleghanies, it was to encourage French trade and block any military advance of the English around the mountains, and from this time Coxe, in his *Carolana*, dates the decrease of English influence among the Indians. In the same year an Englishman, Price Hughes, was captured on the Mississippi, and Bienville gave shelter and a home on Mobile River to the Taensas fleeing in one of the exterminating wars on the Mississippi. He also inflicted upon the Natches severe chastisement for robbing and murdering traders, and two years later the French built Fort Rosalie among them.

The death of Louis XIV. and the beginning of the Regency in 1715 made no change in Louisiana; but Cadillac spent so much of his time in complaining, that Crozat in 1717 replaced him by L'Épinay, rewarding Bienville with the much-coveted cross of the military order of St. Louis. There was local improvement in that the palisaded fort heretofore known as Fort Louis was rebuilt of brick destined to endure for centuries, and in honor of the great man who unfortunately no longer conducted the military affairs of France it was renamed Fort Condé. And yet, the year was a fatal one for Mobile. Vessels from France had always been required to transship their goods at the little port on Massacre Island, and naturally a village had grown up there, and a breastwork and palisaded fort commanded the approach. A public-spirited captain had even built a church, and Port Dauphin enjoyed a fame almost as great as the city on the mainland. There it was that L'Épinay had been welcomed by twenty-four Indian tribes, and when we are told that Grandville's house was worth sixteen thousand livres we are less surprised that a pirate from British Jamaica should be able to destroy property worth fifty thousand livres. And now, in one of those sudden storms not unknown on the Gulf, the sand from Pelican Island was washed into the channel, and the harbor of Massacre Island was a thing of the past; except for light-draught vessels, the port and the bay were bottled up. If this was not the last straw on Crozat's back, at all events, on August 23, 1717, the council in France at his request accepted a surrender of the colony. It had grown from four hundred inhabitants to seven hundred, and since the Peace of Utrecht had shown some vitality. But a success commercially it was not. What the regent would have done with it if left to his own resources it is hard to say; but a greater than the regent was abroad in France, and Louisiana was suddenly to leap into fame and favor.

CHAPTER XI

THE MISSISSIPPI BUBBLE

Out of the War of the Spanish Succession France had emerged with resources impaired; all lost save honor. The old ministers were gone, and yet the State had more need of such than ever to cure the economic distress caused by long wars and expensive establishments. The king himself when young had been famous for his amours, while the last years of his life had been devoted to Madame de Maintenon, his wife, and the rigid observance of all that the Church demanded. There was poverty in the provinces and enforced piety in the palace. As he was dying, Madame de Maintenon deserted his bedside for her foundation of St. Cyr; and when death came, the joy of the people could not be restrained. Such was the end of one who of all French sovereigns had played the greatest part in history! His successor was a little child, and the will named the Duc d'Orléans as regent; but a codicil made in the last few days of his life under the influence of Madame de Maintenon appointed his legitimated son, the Duc de Maine, tutor with such extensive powers as practically to put the regent at his mercy. The Parlement of Paris had in times past endeavored to uphold its own privileges, and incidentally the rights of the people, and now had as a law court the function of registering, perhaps we might say probating, the instrument left by Louis XIV. Before it the Duc d'Orléans succeeded in having the codicil rejected as obtained by undue influence, and he became regent with extensive powers.

This nephew of the late king was, according to his intimate friend Saint-Simon, of considerable ability, pleasing address, and some eloquence, and withal not only dissolute to the last degree, but an utter sceptic as to honesty in man and virtue in woman. His principal adviser was the Abbé Dubois, a man after his own heart; and while the regent's days were spent in application to State affairs, his evenings and nights were given up to debauchery in the Palais Royal, upon which no business of whatever importance was allowed to intrude. On the other hand, it is only fair to remember that his mistresses and his roués were not sharers of the secrets of State, that he kept out of foreign wars and complications as much as possible, even making an alliance with England, and cast about for some way of relieving the financial embarrassment of the treasury. Public bankruptcy was urged upon him, but he refused to take a step which would in his opinion ruin France before the world. He tried to economize with one hand, but was too easy-going to refuse pensions and gifts with the other. He could hardly be dissuaded by Saint-Simon from demolishing Marly in order to save expenses, while his other friend, John Law, had no difficulty in inducing him to buy for two million livres the great diamond secretly brought from India by a soldier, and which, named for the regent, is still the priceless jewel of France.

Before the time Dr. Samuel Johnson could say of the scenery of Scotland that the finest view a Scotchman ever enjoyed was the road to London, this John Law left his native Edinburgh to become distinguished in the southern capital until an affair of honor drove him abroad; for he had the misfortune to kill his man in a duel in London and the good fortune after sentence to escape from prison; and his strange previous history was to be eclipsed by that yet to come. Proficient in everything relating to mathematics, the Bank of England recently established attracted his attention, and during his exile upon the continent the even more famous institution at Amsterdam was studied closely. He thus became a master of finance, and, the truth to tell, not less a master in the art of gaming. Indeed, to his mind the two went together, for there was in both cases only the application of fixed rules; to him there was no element of chance in either. He worked out a scheme of national banking, which he tried to introduce in Scotland, but his canny countrymen did not take kindly to the idea that abundance of money makes the State wealthy. On applying to the Duke of Savoy, that prince suggested that he was not powerful enough to ruin himself, and that Law should go to France. Louis XIV. would not consider his plans, and the lieutenant of police drove him away because he knew too much of the game of faro, which he introduced. Nevertheless, Law, with his scientific gambling, managed to accumulate a fortune of sixteen hundred thousand livres, and this he took to Paris when his friend the Duc d'Orléans became regent, with a State debt to meet of two billions and a half. After some changes in plans, Law succeeded in getting the regent to issue letters patent on May 2, 1716, registered shortly afterward by Parlement, authorizing what was called the Banque Générale. It had a capital of six millions, divided into twelve hundred shares payable in four instalments, three of which were to be in State paper, and it had power to discount paper and issue notes payable in coin of the weight and value of the date of their issue. Thus the public paper found a use and was gradually absorbed, while the new banknotes had a stability heretofore unknown, with the result that the debt was reduced and confidence gradually restored. Next year the notes were made legal tender for taxes, and thus circulated all over France. There is no doubt that much good was effected, and if Law's institution had continued on this basis he would have been justly called the financial savior of the country.

The dissatisfaction of Crozat coincided in time with the rise of Law. How far the resignation of one was caused by the ambition of the other we do not know, but the acceptance of Crozat's surrender was contemporaneous with letters patent of August, 1717, authorizing the corporation called the Compagnie d'Occident, sometimes also the Compagnie des Indes Occidentales, to take over Louisiana. Crozat's right had been commercial; that of the Compagnie was of absolute sovereignty, political and commercial, over Louisiana, upon the sole condition of rendering fealty and homage to the king. The capital was one hundred million livres, divided into two hundred thousand shares, payable like the subscriptions to the bank. The progress of Law was not without opposition. Parlement was hostile to him, and at one time, but for the support of the regent, would have seized and hanged him in its own court; while the brothers Paris, with their new company called Anti-System, obtained a concession of the general taxes. But Law triumphed over all, and on January 1, 1719, his became the Royal Bank, the king guaranteeing the notes, and Law becoming director. He now had the opportunity of carrying into effect his theory as to banking, which was that while it is necessary to have a solid foundation for money this need not necessarily be specie. He perceived clearly enough that the bulk of business transactions were founded on credit, and conceived the idea of making the public credit the basis of money. The State with its taxes and powers was the source of all security, and why not make this confidence the foundation of the medium of exchange? The possibility of overissue of notes, particularly with such a superior as the extravagant regent, was one which might become a reality; but this did not, at least at first, appear to Law as a danger. The issue did attain to one hundred million livres, and branches of the bank were established in different large cities such as Lyon, La Rochelle, Tours, Orléans, and Amiens, where all payments above six hundred livres must be made in notes. Becoming a Catholic convert, Law was made *controleur général.*

The System continued to grow. In May, 1719, the company received the monopoly of commerce from Cape of Good Hope to the southern seas, with similar rights in

Madagascar, Bourbon, Isle de France, Sofola, the Red Sea, Persia, India, Siam, China, and Japan, including also the commerce of Senegal. Naturally, it became now the Compagnie des Indes, and increased its capital by fifty thousand shares more; and the increase of stock gave rise to the names of "mothers" for the original shares, "daughters" for the new, and in time we find also "granddaughters" for payment for the privilege of minting the State coin. Thus, step by step, Law in effect substituted his Compagnie, or System as it was called, for the financial officials of the State, and paper money had a vogue never known before or since. The colony of Louisiana, generally spoken of as the Mississippi, was the Mecca of all hopes, and was painted in colors which now only raise a smile. Gold was washed down by its rivers, while silver was too plentiful to be regarded, the air was balmy, the soil fruitful, and the Song of Solomon was but a prophecy of Louisiana. The *Arabian Nights* were outdone, for the dew overnight even congealed into diamonds. It was like the pictures of Virginia in Ben Jonson's time, but it was a picture sanctioned by the government. Fortunes were made in a day, and Rue Quincampoix and Place Vendôme were crowded with the wildest speculators.

The new era was accompanied by a new American administration, and on February 9, 1718, three ships arrived at Dauphine Island, bringing Pierre Duqué de Boisbriant as royal lieutenant commanding Mobile and Dauphine Island, and a commission dated September 20, 1717, for Bienville as governor representing the Compagnie d'Occident. The original reason for the colony had been the possible use of the great Mississippi, and the plan of the new governor was to make an establishment upon it which should help to justify the dreams of Law. Although he was opposed by the commissary Hubert, the closing of the port of Dauphine Island made some change necessary, and a compromise was effected by selecting what was spoken of as New Biloxi, on the western side of the bay originally settled by the

French. Nevertheless, Bienville examined the Mississippi and selected the site of a city which, in compliment to the regent, was named New Orleans. He established also a post at Natchitoches, on Red River, where he stationed Blondel, and recognized the importance of the Illinois region by sending Boisbriant there to build Fort Chartres. Bienville himself asked for a fief on Pearl River to bear his name, and got Horn Island instead in socage, and built a handsome house and garden just below Mobile on a height on the bay side. In France it was a time of extravagance, but this château on the water was as close as was allowable in America to Iberville's old plan for a Le Moyne *comté* which should embrace the upper shores of the bay.

Military fiefs were not to flourish in Louisiana, although they were common enough in Canada, but lands were granted out in extensive tracts to *concessionnaires* who agreed to people them. The Compagnie itself undertook to bring inhabitants, and was not very particular as to whom it obtained. As colonists did not rapidly offer themselves, hospitals and jails were resorted to, and scenes not unusual when the Huguenots were harried out of the country were reënacted now. Many a man and woman was carried away unwillingly. Spite played its part, and a whisper in the right quarter rid one of an incongenial wife or husband, or put folks who would not die out of the way of hungry heirs. Manon Lescaut may never have come to Louisiana, but many a one of other name but similar character found there a grave; for if the Compagnie was indifferent as to how it secured colonists, it was even more so as to what became of them. Huddled together before leaving France, without proper food and attention on shore and at sea, they were dumped upon Dauphine Island and died by hundreds before reaching the concessions on the Mississippi or elsewhere, and of the remainder others fell victims to the climate. In March, 1719, the warship *Comte de Toulouse* brought a hundred, and a month later other vessels, under the Sieur de Serigny, brought more, besides soldiers and workmen. Law himself had an extensive grant upon the Arkansas, whither he sent industrious Germans, and the Mississippi, at least on the map, was now lined with grants, some of them inhabited. Thus, near Natchez, the Compagnie made concessions to Hubert, the royal commissary, or *commissaire ordonnateur*, and to a company of St. Malo merchants; at Natchitoches on Red River, to Bénard de La Harpe; at Tunicas, to Sainte-Reine; at Pointe Coupée, to De Meuse. The site of the town of Baton Rouge was conceded to Diron d'Artaguette; the right bank of the Mississippi, opposite Bayou Manchac, to Paris Duvernay; the Tchoupitoulas lands, to De Muys; the Houmas, to the Marquis d'Ancenis; the Cannes Brulées, to the Marquis d'Artagnac; the opposite bank of the river, to De Guiche, De La Houssaye, and De La Houpe; the Bay of St. Louis, to Mme. de Mezières; and Pascagoula Bay, to Mme. de Chaumont. Grants on Yazoo River were made to a private company composed of Le Blanc, secretary of state, the Comte de Belleville, the Marquis d'Auleck, and Le Blond, who later was commander-in-chief of the engineers of the province.

Almost contemporaneously with Law's Compagnie came the real establishment of negro slavery. There had been some few negroes before, and we know that from the beginning the French held Indian slaves, in this only copying the example of the Indians themselves. The Church records early name a number of "Schittimacha," as well as some Natchitoches, Chichacha, Alibamon, Taensa, and even Padouca [Comanche] slaves. Many were enslaved in childhood to make them more tractable, but Indian slavery has never been successful. The example of the Spaniards in the West Indies affected the French of Louisiana, as it had the French of the islands and the English of Virginia one hundred years before, and in 1719 came the first cargo of Africans, two hundred and fifty in number, who from Dauphine Island were distributed among the concessions. This was but the beginning, and even three years later we read that the supply was still quite unequal to the demand.

There came a temporary interruption of exploitation, in the shape of a war with Spain. In the time of Louis XIV. such an event would not have been possible, and the friendliness of the two countries made it almost fratricidal even now. The cause was not important, for it was due to the ambition of Cardinal Alberoni, an Italian who had accompanied Philip's new queen into Spain and had been shrewd enough to gain complete control over the royal couple. Although of short continuance, the conflict had the effect of enabling Bienville and his brother Châteauguay to get together an army of eight hundred French and Indians at Mobile for a land attack on Pensacola, while Serigny sailed thither with four vessels. The place was invested on May 14th, and soon succumbed. Châteauguay was left in command with three hundred men, and the Spaniards were repatriated to Cuba. The governor there, however, seized the ships bringing the prisoners, and fitted out an expedition which speedily recovered Pensacola, captured Châteauguay, took him to Havana, and undertook to attack Mobile in return. A powerful fleet lay twelve days before Dauphine Island, but Louis Saint-Denis with his two hundred troops and Indians drove them off. A gunboat succeeded in entering the bay, and plundered a place on Mon Louis Island; but on the second attempt, Mobile Indians killed and captured a number of the invaders. The natives took them to Mobile, where they were clubbed to death.

Another act was now played in the drama, for Bienville and Saint-Denis by land and Champmeslin by sea reinvested respectively the large fort on the mainland and the little one on the point of Santa Rosa Island, and captured them again, hanging forty deserters whom they found. The French flag continued to wave over the little Spanish town during the rest of the war; but this was only a short time, for peace was made in the next year, when Pensacola was restored and the prisoners were released on both sides.

The forward movement which Law had instituted went on. Concessions increased, more people came, some to die and some to live; figs, oranges, and other fruits were introduced, and agriculture began to play some part in the life of the colony. But the master spirit was no more. In February, 1720, disenchantment began at Paris, and a panic was threatened. The price of the shares in the Compagnie fell. Forced measures for the circulation of notes were necessary, becoming more and more stringent, and soon it seemed necessary even to interdict the hoarding of gold and silver, and then of diamonds and precious stones, so as to leave no other standard of value than notes. The union of the bank and the Company of the Indies did not improve affairs. Uneasiness finally gave way to indignation, and the general control of the finances was taken away from Law. Next, the bank was abolished and the Compagnie was deprived of taxes, of public collections, and of the monopoly of tobacco which it had held, and henceforth remained exclusively commercial. Such was the end of the bubble, which all but ruined the country. In the month of December, 1720, Law, after having been protected by guards, found it necessary to leave France, taking only two thousand livres. He remained for a time near Brussels, in expectation of a recall which never came, and then spent the last nine years of his adventurous life in Venice. There he died in almost complete poverty.

The Compagnie des Indes moved on, actually disowning Law, and gradually meeting with some success. The population of Louisiana increased to such an extent that the Compagnie, which was the sole buyer and seller, fixed prices of imports and exports. The standard was the figure controlling at Mobile and Dauphine Island, to which was added five per cent for goods delivered at New Orleans, ten per cent for those at the Natches, thirteen per cent at the Yazoos, twenty per cent at Natchitoches, and fifty per cent at the Illinois and on the Missouri; while the Compagnie bought colonial produce at its own warehouses in Mobile, Ship Island, New Orleans, and the new capital at Biloxi. Or, at another time, in New Orleans,

Biloxi, and Mobile the profit was to be fifty per cent upon the cost in France; at the Natches and the Yazoos, where was a new establishment named Fort Claude, at seventy per cent; while at the Arkansas it was to be double the cost, although the Alibamon post, far up in the interior, was placed on an equality with Mobile on the Gulf because of the competition arising from the British colonies to the east. Thus early did the law of international competition appear in America. France, following, perhaps unconsciously, the precedent of Spain and England long before, forbade the cultivation of anything which could compete with her own products, and thus the vine, hemp, flax, and some other things were prohibited. Rice, however, and tobacco were encouraged, and in course of time cotton came into notice, although the difficulty of removing the seed prevented it from becoming of the same importance as the other crops. Upon the request of the local council the Compagnie had issued copper sous, of which many are still found in the Gulf country, showing on the one side a double L crossed and on the other the words *Colonies Françoises*, with the date, generally 1721, and the mint mark, frequently of La Rochelle. Law's money does not figure in Louisiana finance to any great extent, for pistoles and dollars were generally used, their value being fixed by decrees, which unfortunately showed great variation and were just grounds of complaint. In the sales of the Compagnie it was arranged that slaves should be sold for six hundred and sixty livres each, on three years' credit, payable in equal instalments, sometimes in tobacco and sometimes in rice,—thus, showing, as in Virginia and Carolina, how naturally a standard of value passes into a medium of exchange in the absence of the precious metals. Ultimately the Compagnie issued bonds or notes, which constituted a large part of the currency.

The growth of Louisiana had now become such that it was advisable to divide the country into districts for better government, each under a commandant and judge, from whom an appeal lay to the Superior Council at Biloxi.

These nine departments were Biloxi, Mobile, Alibamons, New Orleans, Natchez, Yazoo, Natchitoches, Arkansas, and Illinois, having in all a white population of five thousand four hundred and twenty, besides six hundred negroes, though the Compagnie had transported up to May, 1721, seven thousand and twenty people. The expense of administering this new country with its scattered population was very great, amounting at this time almost to five hundred thousand livres, and somewhat later it was calculated that the cost of each inhabitant was the extravagant sum of one hundred and fifty thousand livres. Only three years later, we are told by La Harpe that the white population had diminished to seventeen hundred, while the blacks had risen in number to thirty-three hundred, and of domestic animals in the latter year we find eleven hundred cows and three hundred bulls, but only two hundred horses, one hundred sheep, besides sundry other animals, including goats, hogs, and fowls. The importance attached to horses and horned animals is attested by a law punishing with death their killing or maiming, and one had to obtain lawful permission to slay even his own animal, under a penalty of three hundred livres. It may be there is some mistake about La Harpe's numbers, for immigration almost ceased for a while after 1721, and yet ten years later we know the white population amounted to five thousand people. The government had made a decree forbidding the further importation of convicts and vagabonds, but it is uncertain how far this was carried out. Even in the year of the decree, while three hundred colonists arrived for the Chaumont concession at Pascagoula, eighty girls from La Salpêtrière, a house of correction in Paris, were sent over as wives for the colonists.

Of life at New Biloxi, of the interregnum between Mobile and New Orleans, we have a desultory but interesting memorial in the journal of Sieur Bouquès, secretary of the council, relating to the year 1722. The troubles of the Compagnie in France were fully reflected at the provincial capital, where people suffered greatly from lack of provisions and other necessaries, and on the arrival of the *Profond* and other relief ships they chanted a *Te Deum*. Nevertheless, they did not fail in military ceremonies. They blessed the flags, appointed officers at the head of the troops, fired salutes, and Bienville from time to time gave a state dinner or supper. Indians would come to a council or to bring scalps, Canadians descended with furs or news, and a buccaneer ship called from time to time. The news would be of what was happening at Natchitoches, at the Illinois, or on the Mississippi, and commonly related to inroads of the Indians or to what the Spaniards were doing. Possibly the occurrence that happened oftenest was desertion. At one time some twenty-two soldiers, sailors, and inhabitants made off with a *chaloupe* to go to the Spanish possessions to the east. At another, even a Swiss company, instead of going up to New Orleans to work on the public improvements, forced the captain of a *traversier* to put to sea, declaring that they had had enough of misery. Later, three *forçats* [convicts] stole a pirogue and left for parts unknown. This was the time when the short war with Spain was terminated, and Wachop and Spinola came with their suite from Vera Cruz to bear a letter from the Marquis de Balero. French officers received them on the seashore and conducted them to Bienville's house, where troops were under arms. The letter related to the double alliance between France and Spain through the marriage of the king with the Infanta and that of the Prince of Asturias with Mlle. de Montpensier, and the delivery of Pensacola back to the Spaniards in the condition it was first captured. La Tour, as lieutenant-general of the colony, gave the visitors and the French officers a magnificent dinner, as did De L'Orme, the *directeur ordonnateur*. Nor were these compliments confined to the officers, for there were public rejoicings, including a *Te Deum* for all in the chapel, *feux de joie*, and artillery salutes from the fort, responded to by all vessels in the harbor. We are told that from the beginning of the year until the last of August the Church registers recorded eleven marriages, twelve children baptized, and fifteen deaths,—showing a balance on the wrong side; but life at Fort Louis, as was the name of the post, was now coming to an end. La Tour sounded the river mouth and went to New Orleans to superintend the public works, and all improvements stopped at Biloxi. The vessels in port were used for the evacuation, and everything was taken up to the new capital. There the first interest seemed to be in experiments with indigo and with rice, both of which were to play so great a part in colonial life, for the Compagnie desired interest in plantations to supersede that in the Indian trade, and explorations for copper and silver up the Mississippi were set on foot. At the same time, the harvests of the Illinois attracted attention and it was noted that a mine of coal was in use.

One of the greatest acts of Bienville was the foundation of New Orleans, his selection of a site prevailing over the preference of the officials of the Compagnie for Bayou Manchac as higher and offering a bayou as well as the longer river route to the Gulf. The place he chose was where the river and the lakes were closest together, requiring only a short portage between the Mississippi and Bayou St. John, although low and subject to overflow, which happened several times, and made it necessary to ditch the streets on each side. As the water to some extent remained, every block was an island, and within it each lot was similarly ditched, presenting from above, if one had been able to get the view, the curious spectacle of a town even more aquatic than Venice. The front on the river was eleven squares, the depth six, each lot being sixty feet by about one hundred and twenty. The streets were named from the nobility of that day, as Chartres for the son of the regent, Maine and Toulouse for the illegitimate sons of Louis XIV. by Mme. de Montespan, of whom the latter was efficient in the naval administration. Bourbon recalls the royal family, and Conti, Royale, and Dauphine other famous names, as at Mobile.

We possess several plans of New Orleans in its first stages. A picture purporting to date from 1719, two years after its foundation, shows the lake, or bend, which has given it the name of the Crescent City, and at its apex are several long houses. The legend says that the quarters of the bourgeois are surrounded by water during three months of the year, although it also notes that there is a levee in front and a ditch behind the town. The plan in Du Mont shows the *place d'armes* by the river, faced by the parochial church of St. Louis, flanked by the Capuchin quarters and a guard-house. Above the town are a powder house and a mill, while below are a brickyard, a convent of the Ursulines, the Hôtel Dieu, and several mills on a stream, and back of all Bayou St. John wanders in numerous curves through the forest. This plan also shows a levee, as does a plan in Le Page du Pratz, on the bend in the river which is not apparent in Du Mont. The other buildings are much the same, including in the block above the *place* the *intendance*, *conseil*, and *caserne*, while opposite the *place* are a *caserne* and *magasins*. The indications of private residences on all these plans are scanty, and we evidently have the city in its infancy. There could not yet have been much of a levee, and the indication of the Ursulines betrays a later touching up. In 1719 La Tour was instructed to see if the location was suitable, and three years later streets were cut through. Previously, according to Pauger, there were only some barracks in the forest.

Such was the beginning of New Orleans. After the removal of the government thither in 1722 it grew faster, and during Bienville's second term became a town of some importance. The low houses, at first of wood and afterward of brick, separated by narrow, unpaved streets, ill lighted, reproduced in America the French town of the eighteenth century. The population was a mixed one, consisting of the middle class as well as the refuse of France, together with some of its best families. Withal it was a gay place, laughter and song were often heard, and apart from the deaths caused before acclimatization the mortality was small, for the habits of the people were simple and healthful. They did not take life too strenuously in the long summer months, and the second generation learned to think of Louisiana as home.

The negroes, owing to their increasing number, began to be a subject of uneasiness. It would seem as if at this time they outnumbered the whites, if La Harpe be correct, and the council through the governor enacted a code taken largely from the royal laws in force in Santo Domingo. Its name of Black Code has been misleading as to the contents, for it was not so much black in its provisions as in its subject—that is, it related mainly to the negroes. The intolerance of Louis XIV. was reflected in the two articles decreeing that Jews should be expelled from the colony and prohibiting the exercise of every form of worship except the Catholic; but the code goes on to compel masters to give religious instruction to the slaves, and thus only five years after the real introduction of negroes disposed of a difficulty which long troubled the English on the Atlantic. To effect this more readily, negroes placed under the direction of anyone except a Catholic were to be confiscated, and to aid observance of Sundays and holidays, slaves made to work on these days should also be confiscated. Intermarriage of whites with blacks was prohibited, all priests were forbidden to solemnize such alliances, and concubinage was placed under severe penalties. The negroes, bond and free, were permitted to marry with permission of the master interested, the children following the status and ownership of the mother, and Christian slaves were to be buried in consecrated ground. Slaves were forbidden to carry weapons and to gather in assemblies, under pretext of weddings or other cause. Their clothing, subsistence, and protection were provided for, masters to be punished if this article (twenty) of the code was not observed, and slave families were not to be broken up by voluntary sales. Manumission was permitted and was equivalent to an act of naturalization, although the powers of freedom thus granted were restricted and freedmen were commanded to show the profoundest respect to their former owners. Masters were responsible for what negroes did by their command or in the line of their business. The crimes of slaves were particularly set out and were punished corporally, as by whipping and branding in some cases, or ears were to be cut off, the prisoner hamstrung, and in extreme cases death inflicted. We find also provisions as to runaways, their capture and punishment, and, in fact, few cases were left unprovided for.

As to government, the Canadian system, by which the governor and the *intendant* were naturally spies on each other, had been in effect adopted in Louisiana from the beginning. The governor had military command, while civil affairs were placed under an official whose title varied from time to time, but whose duty of keeping watch and reporting the acts of the governor remained the same. Even at Fort Louis, when there was but one settlement, the commissary was to do this, and under the Compagnie Hubert and others did the same. The quarrel sometimes was acute, and the capital found itself placarded with pasquinades, which occasionally led to duels. This, of course, could not continue, and at last Bienville had the mortification of finding himself summoned to France to answer charges. This he did with dignity, but unsuccessfully, and he saw Périer in 1726 appointed in his stead, and Châteauguay and other relatives retired. De la Chaise and Périer were thus able to begin their administration with new assistants.

A letter of the time described Louisiana at the beginning of this régime as a country without religion, without justice, without discipline, without order, and without police, so that it was fortunate that the year 1727 marked the coming of the Ursuline nuns and the Jesuits. The Ursulines took charge of the recently established Charity Hospital in New Orleans, and were given a plantation south of the city, although their town residence was built on Rue Condé, where they lived for a century. The Jesuits were placed

Indian village of Pomeiooc, in Virginia. *From the copperplate by Theodore de Bry, after the drawing by John White in Hakluyt's "True Pictures."*

on the other side, in a plantation somewhat above what has become Canal Street, but they were not the controlling religious force of the colony. The Seminarians of Quebec had long since relinquished Louisiana, and the Compagnie, by contract with the ecclesiastical authorities, now recognized the colony as divided into three districts, of which the Mississippi shore up to the Illinois was the domain of the Capuchins, the Mobile waters were under the Carmelites, while the Jesuits received the Ouabache and the Illinois country, with the right of a settlement in New Orleans without jurisdiction. The boundaries were not strictly observed, for the Jesuit Beaudouin later lived among the Choctaws, and reported misdeeds of Indians and French commandants, and was in turn charged with misconduct. Even in New Orleans conflicts of religious jurisdiction occurred.

Périer marked the beginning of his government by erecting a much-needed levee in front of New Orleans, eighteen hundred yards long, and on its summit eighteen feet across, while it was continued in smaller proportions eighteen miles above and below the city. He planned also a canal from the rear of the town to Bayou St. John, but this water communication with the lakes was not to be carried out until Spanish times.

Outside of New Orleans and Mobile, the most considerable settlements of Louisiana were those at Natchitoches, Natchez, and about the Arkansas. As the former on Red River was to keep an eye on the Spaniards, it will concern us later. The Akanseas, who had moved from the Ohio, were located on the Mississippi, rather than on the Arkansas, in three villages, of which that of the Quapaws seems to have been the best known. De Soto died and was buried not far away, and under the name of Akansea their settlement was the southernmost point of the voyage of Marquette and Joliet. It was there, we remember, that La Salle, in 1682, took solemn possession for the King of France and Membré planted the cross. Tonty in vain had asked for confirmation of La Salle's grant of it to him, and had guided Saint-Cosme thus far on his voyage down the Mississippi in 1699. A Jesuit had ministered at Tonty's Arkansas fort, and at the time of Iberville's first voyage the Minister of the Marine, at the request of the Superior of Foreign Missions, directed him to take with him a missionary to join those already among the Akanseas.

The river Arkansas is said to have had some exploration as early as Crozat's time, but, if so, nothing came of this, and its nature may be inferred from the fact that the mines on which the Mississippi Bubble was based were supposed to be in a mountainous country high up on this stream. Even the more modest plan of colonizing its mouth was not carried out properly. Law was to have settled on Arkansas River nine thousand Germans from the Palatinate, and Charlevoix pronounced the country second only to the Illinois in capacity for grain; but when he passed, the settlement was a ruin, although the Compagnie still had a magazine and clerk on the Mississippi somewhat higher up. In 1722 La Harpe made an elaborate exploration of the river, but under many inconveniences. One hundred colonists in that year came via Ship Island under the direction of M. Élias, and required thirty bateaux to take all their goods and effects. De La Boulaye was directed to move from the Yazoo country and build a fort on Arkansas River.

The ultimate result of the Arkansas experiments was abandoned ruins there and the reëstablishment of the German colonists lower down the Mississippi at a place known from them as the German Coast. Only a post of thirty men was retained, to reach which required a trip of six weeks in the case of the Jesuit Du Poisson in 1727. He gives a graphic account of the trip in canoes at the time when the banks were overflowed and the current ran swift. He suffered many hardships, especially from mosquitoes. "The greatest torment," says Du Poisson, "in comparison with which all the rest would be but sport, which passes all belief, and has never been even imagined in France, still less actually experienced, is that of the mosquitoes, the cruel persecution of the mosquitoes. The plague of Egypt, I think, was not more cruel. This little insect has caused more swearing since the French have been in Mississippi, than had previously taken place in all the rest of the world." Further on, in his *baire* we recognize our own mosquito bar, and his *boucane* was the frame for quickly drying meat not uncommon still among us, and which gave the name to the unsettled buccaneers of the Gulf.

The Natches live in history on account of their native civilization and fire worship, described by Pénicaut, and because of their tragic extermination. Père Montigny was among them a short time, but labored unsuccessfully. Traders fared better, and Cadillac established a bureau there in 1713 under MM. de La Loire to counteract the English, who already traded even to the Mississippi. The Indians were friendly for a while, but at last murdered some French on the river, and Bienville in 1715 exacted redress. He seized chiefs, had the murderers punished, and even obtained a site for a fort. Pailloux, who had built the forts at Mobile and Toulouse, now erected Fort Rosalie, the first permanent settlement of the French in the Mississippi valley below Kaskaskia. Such was the origin of Natchez. The Indian tribe of this name was in many respects the most civilized and interesting in the whole southern country, and it was unfortunate that so arbitrary a man as Chopart should in Périer's time be in control of relations with them. He took a notion that a certain hill, occupied by their village of White Apple, should receive a French settlement, and acted with a high hand. The result was that the Natches apparently yielded, but, gaining a respite, employed their time in concocting a great conspiracy, embracing the Choctaws and many other tribes. The tradition is that a friendly Indian woman revealed the plot, and by abstracting some sticks from the bundle which indicated the days precipitated a conflict, so that the Natches acted almost alone. Two hundred and fifty men were killed in the ensuing massacre, and many women and children taken prisoners, while terror spread throughout all the French settlements, not excepting New Orleans and Mobile. Fortunately, the Choctaws took no active part, and the colony was enabled to rally from the blow. Périer promptly enough got together a small army, embracing Choctaws also, and proceeded against the enemy, while the Indians on the other side used some artillery, captured with Fort Rosalie, and served them. The French were finally successful, and the Natches were dispersed, the main body to the bayou country to the west, others taking refuge with the Chickasaws. A second expedition was undertaken against those in the west and that body also broken up. The captured were sold into slavery in the French West Indies, among them the squaw who had given notice of the intended massacre. The war reflected little credit upon the French, and the extremes to which they went only exasperated the Natches, who far and near cut off parties and attacked settlements. Negroes had served against the Natches, fighting bravely, and one method now adopted by the Indians to harm the whites was by stirring up a black insurrection. It was fortunately discovered in time, and Samba, the chief, a negro of the tribe of Banbara, was broken on a wheel with several companions. It seems that these Banbaras intended to kill the whites and keep all other negroes than their own nation as slaves, electing a king or other leader from time to time.

Finally, matters quieted down, and the chief concern was as to home affairs. In the first place, the authorities at home at last perceived that prostitutes and abandoned women would make poor mothers for a growing colony, and sent over twenty-three girls of good raising and irreproachable character, each provided with a trousseau in a trunk, or *cassette*. They naturally were in great demand and married without difficulty. They were called "*cassette* girls," and have a high place in local history, although it is not necessarily true, as is sometimes said, that their descendants were the aristocrats of the colony. There was another question as to women, but this time it was as to Indian wives. The law of Paris being that of the whole colony, the question of the property of Frenchmen who had married Indians often came up. La Vente had favored such marriages, and the Church soon found it a matter of necessity to recognize what were called *mariages naturels*. In any event, the widow had half of the succession; and if there was no child, all the property went to the wife or her heirs, in preference to the French heirs of the husband. But the Indian widows ran away and debts were not paid, and so there was just ground of complaint. The Superior Council met the difficulty by decreeing that there should be a tutor or curator to keep the property together, paying one-third of the revenue to the widow so long as she remained in a civilized community.

The Compagnie after the Natches war seems to have lost heart. It had expended twenty million livres, and its obligations were more than it could meet. So in 1731 it surrendered its charter and property, the latter worth two hundred and sixty-three thousand livres, mainly in slaves, and its debts, being quite largely in paper money, called *billets de caisse*, and the government resumed the colony. Whatever else may be said about the Compagnie, it had increased the population from five hundred whites to five thousand and from twenty negroes to twenty-five hundred, had developed agriculture quite extensively, although there were still not infrequent famines, and had made important settlements at Natchez, Tchoupitoulas, Cannes Brulées, Bâton Rouge, Manchac, and Pointe Coupée, besides more distant towns of which we have spoken. Exploration had increased knowledge of the country, and the Ohio, Missouri, Arkansas, and Red Rivers, besides the Mississippi, Alabama, Tombigbee, and Mobile, were the seats of trade and to some extent of settlement, and the coast was claimed from Matagorda Bay to the Perdido; for the increase of French settlements caused even the Spaniards to concede that Louisiana extended beyond Mobile Bay to the east.

One cannot help but compare the ending of the two great colonizing companies of North America, that of England and that of France. The Virginia Company had the longer life by a few years, and its success was more striking, for its colony was self-sustaining when the State attacked the charter. In fact, it was this success that drew down the hostility of the king and made him wish to resume its powers. The Compagnie d'Occident, on the other hand, met no royal opposition. The French court was only too willing to continue its commercial privileges, even though they embraced somewhat of sovereignty also. Its surrender was voluntary and because the enterprise was too great for its means. It had found no agricultural product which made the colony independent, and it had established no representative government which would give the people self-reliance. The commercial monopoly which was the foundation of most companies was more burdensome in Louisiana than in Virginia on this account. The English Company found its child growing almost too large for tutelage, and rejoiced in it; the French Compagnie, after spending much time and money, was still a paternal despotism which reaped no commensurate returns. In each instance the powers of the company were surrendered to the crown, the future only could tell with what result.

CHAPTER XII

THE ILLINOIS COUNTRY

TO THE French the district on both sides of Mississippi River above the junction of the Ohio was known as the Illinois, from the large tribe of Indians that Marquette and La Salle found on the river which aided their descent to the south. Marquette long hoped and prayed to be a missionary among them, and the more secular La Salle founded Crèvecœur on its banks, as afterward Fort St. Louis on a great rock overhanging the stream. Henri de Tonty, called the Iron Hand, succeeded La Salle in possession of the fort, but the jealousy of the Canadian authorities ultimately secured orders from France which caused its abandonment and placed Tonty upon the Mississippi. The Iron Hand afterward joined Iberville in the south, and for a while the Illinois region, although remaining French, was without other French representatives than the Jesuits of Kaskaskia and the *coureurs de bois*.

There was long a contention as to whether the region properly belonged to Canada or to Louisiana. Iberville's claim, following La Salle's, was that Louisiana embraced everything draining into the Mississippi, and at first this was sustained by the home authorities, although when the king came to make his grant to Crozat he embraced in it the river St. Louis, or Mississippi, from the sea only as far as the Illinois,—thus annexing the Illinois to Canada. The Mississippi, or St. Philippe, and the Ouabache, with their tributaries, remained parts of Louisiana, whose boundaries the king reserved the right to extend if he saw fit, which, however, was not done until the time of the Compagnie d'Occident. For our purposes we may consider the Illinois as a unit, despite these changes.

To modern minds, Illinois embraces the country between the Ohio and the lower part of Lake Michigan on the one hand, and between the Mississippi and the Wabash Rivers on the other, and this has always been the heart of the district. The lake posts at Sault Ste. Marie, Michilimackinac, and even Fort St. Joseph and the several missions and posts on the western side of Lake Michigan and on Lake Superior, were subject to the authorities of Canada. The Illinois district embraced in a sense the Missouri banks, and it extended south of the Ohio for a varying distance. Thus the mines of the Merameg, or Meramec, on the little river below the present St. Louis, were within its limits, as was Vincennes in what is now Indiana. It is true that at the beginning these several districts had different origins and different histories, but finally we shall see them converging into one system.

The beginnings of every country depend upon water communication. It requires means, skill, and peace to construct roads, none of which are common in primitive times, while boats in one shape or other have been known ever since the dawn of history. There must be an interchange of products to create wealth, and this means the institution of government in some shape to afford police protection. The region about Paris, the nucleus of France, owed much of its development to the interlacing of its streams with those of Flanders; and the use of portages, thus old at home, was to play a great part also in New France. If Louisiana and Canada were to be one country, even if they were to be only connected, there must be means of going from the waters tributary to the St. Lawrence and the lakes to those tributary to the Ohio and the Mississippi. Such portages were numerous from Presqu'Île, the modern Erie, around the lakes to that which created Chicago and that by Illinois River, the favorites of the Indians and the French. Not a few of the portages then used have given place to canals, and some of them are represented by railroads, but the old method and its sites, once so common and of so far-reaching utility, have passed even from the map.

The earliest discoverers of these carrying places were, of course, the *coureurs de bois* and the missionaries, behind whom soon followed the fur traders. One of the greatest of the *coureurs* was Du Lhut, sometimes spelled "Duluth," who has given his name to the modern city. His operations were largely about Lake Superior, and he even crossed the Mississippi; in fact, he was for a time in the country of the Sioux, then called the Nadowessioux, where he desired to make an establishment from which to explore toward the Pacific, or the Vermilion Sea. The king disapproved such far-reaching aspirations, and Du Lhut restricted his research to nearer regions.

Le Sueur had come over to Canada in 1683, and went by way of Lake Superior and Wisconsin River to the Sioux, and six years later was with Nicolas Perrot in his explorations, and at some time discovered Minnesota River, which he called the St. Pierre. One account says that in 1693 he was sent by Cadillac, Governor of Detroit, to the Sioux, while La Harpe has it that in this year he built a fort on an island in the upper Mississippi by order of Frontenac, effected a peace between the Chippewas and the Sioux, and descended with the chief of each nation on a visit to Montreal, thus bringing them under French control. In 1697, while in France, he received a short-lived permission to open mines, but in the interval before coming with Iberville he was in captivity with the English, and in his absence his Mississippi fort was abandoned.

Pierre Le Sueur was therefore a fit man to explore the northwest, and by royal permission ascended the Mississippi to the Sioux country in April, 1700, in a *chaloupe* with twenty-five men. On the way they found an English trader among the Akanseas, who gave the French some supplies and saluted their flag, although travelling under passport of the Governor of Carolina by way of the Ohio [Ouabache] River. They found Père Davion among the Tonikas, speak of seeing Montigny, passed Écores à Margot, Écores à Prudhomme, the Arkansas, Ohio, Illinois, Missouri, and the bluffs near where St. Louis now stands, and met Frenchmen on the way. The expedition received a warm welcome among the Illinois, somewhat below the mouth of the Missouri, from a settlement of thirty of Le Sueur's old acquaintances, among them Berger, Bouteville, Saint-Cosme, and two Jesuits. The Illinois River Le Sueur notes as the route to Canada via the Chicago country from the south, and the Ouisconsin with another portage to Lake Michigan as the way from Canada for traders among the Sioux [Scioux]. Higher was the fort named for Perrot, and near it an islet on which traders wintered. They were stopped by the falls of St. Anthony, and turned up the St. Pierre and its branch Green [Blue] River, to build their Fort L'Huilier, named for that one of the farmers-general who had assayed the copper which Le Sueur had taken to France.

Le Sueur had numerous talks with the Sioux, and himself returned, although the expedition wintered at the fort in what is now Minnesota. He brought back one thousand three hundred pounds of green earth, which he took to France, but it led to no settlement and the troops were soon withdrawn. The green earth, whose nature is not mentioned, was highly esteemed in France, for the supply from Germany was running short. Le Sueur was the constant cause of fear and suspicion to the company and the authorities of Canada, who accused him of engaging in the beaver trade. In October of this year we find his wife coming from Montreal to show Callières a letter from the home government allowing his associates to send to the Sioux the goods which had already been two years at Montreal. But the governor thought that two hundred guns had no proper connection with such trade, and made her exchange them for other goods. We know that Le Sueur took his family to Mobile, where they were long prominent, and that there he applied for the position of judge, with the salary of five hundred escus. Pontchartrain refused his request, but told Iberville the king would pay Le Sueur when he was travelling on official business among the Sioux and Illinois. He is said to have died on the way thither from France.

Pénicaut's "Arkansaw traveller" came from Carolina by way of Ohio River, and the French early explored this region. La Salle had been in doubt whether the Ohio, also called St. Louis or Chicagou River, emptied into Bay St. Esprit, and Iberville at first suspected the same thing when he heard of English from St. George's threatening the west by way of the Ouabache. Le Sueur had already pointed out this danger years before. Iberville recommended in the same letter of July, 1701, that Juchereau de Saint-Denis, of Montreal, a different man from Louis of Texas fame, be granted a land concession at the mouth of the Ouabache; for with eight or ten men Juchereau could establish tanneries and stop the beaver trade between the *coureurs de bois* and the English colonies. Tonty desired the place and a whole company to guard it, but Iberville's preference prevailed, the more readily, perhaps, because Juchereau was in Paris to plead for himself. Juchereau left Michilimackinac for his new post in the fall of 1703, to the joy of Iberville, who had heard with much misgivings rumors of an establishment of English from Carolina or Maryland at the junction of the Ohio and the Ouabache. He pressed frequently for a fuller exploration of the Ohio, which name at first was confined to the river above the Wabash junction. So far as Saint-Denis was concerned, however, the experiment was short-lived, for in September of next year we find Bienville desirous of bringing down his Canadians to Mobile on account of the death of Juchereau in the preceding year.

In 1710 Rémonville even advised that Detroit be abandoned and the inhabitants go to Mobile or some be settled where the Ouabache empties into the Mississippi, on account of the copper and lead and because hunting was good there. But this was not done, and indeed next year it was alleged that the Miamis and Mascoutens of that region avoided the French at Mobile because of injuries received at Detroit. Charlevoix found no settlement when he passed, although Law instructed Duvergier that one of the principal objects of the Compagnie was to locate troops upon the Ouabache to keep out the English and establish a tannery there. Late maps show that the French actually had a fort at the mouth and a stockade on the Ohio where the Wabash empties.

Cadillac had explored up the Mississippi to find minerals, and reports of lead and copper were so persistent, together with the unquestionable productiveness of the soil, that one of the first acts of the Compagnie, within whose territory it was comprised, was to send Pierre Duqué Boisbriant in 1718 as commandant at the Illinois, which on account of the distance from Mobile was equivalent to making him a semi-independent governor of the north. It needed two years to build Fort Chartres on the Mississippi, sixteen miles above the Indian village of Kaskaskia, the early seat of Jesuit missions. The fort was made of palisades, and within it and its bastions were barracks and commandant's house, besides storehouse and hall for the Compagnie. The name, like that of the New Orleans street, was given in compliment to the son of the regent. Among the early arrivals was Renault, who, from being a banker in Paris, had become director-general of the mines, and now brought with him two hundred and fifty miners and soldiers, besides blacks from Santo Domingo. When Charlevoix passed next year he found the country beginning to build up between the fort and Kaskaskia. In the village at the gates the Jesuits erected the church of Ste. Anne, whose records are still preserved; and, curiously enough, the book destined for use in this distant wilderness begins with a decree of Louis XV. in 1716 regulating church etiquette, showing how the governor-general, *intendant*, commander of troops, and others should march in procession and be seated in church,—reminding us somewhat of the state held by the first governors of Virginia. The civil official, corresponding to the *intendant* in Canada and *commissaire* in Louisiana, was La Loire des Ursins, principal director of the Compagnie, and these with one other formed the provincial council which made grants of land and dispensed justice. It is said that a large tract patented to Renault near Fort Chartres until lately remained marked upon maps as his property.

When Boisbriant succeeded Bienville at New Orleans, he gave place to Desliettes in the Illinois, who made way for Saint-Ange de Belle Rive, and Pierre d'Artaguette, younger brother of the D'Artaguette of Mobile, was in turn appointed commandant for bravery in the Natches war. His tragic end came in the first Chickasaw expedition, whither he took many of his garrison, a company of volunteers, almost all the Kaskaskias, besides Illinois, Miamis, and even Iroquois. Vincennes also accompanied him from his post on the Wabash. On account of delays, Bienville did not meet him promptly, and then it was that D'Artaguette, Vincennes, the Jesuit Sénat, and a younger Saint-Ange were taken prisoners and burned at the stake. The remainder of the troops returned to the Illinois without meeting the French from the south. During the second Chickasaw expedition the Illinois was also represented by Frenchmen and natives, troops came also from Canada, and warriors from many tribes between it and the Illinois.

Thus it would seem that the earlier troubles with the Fox and other Indians had ceased, for agriculture flourished and the Illinois became the granary of lower Louisiana. Other settlements grew up, such as Prairie du Rocher and St. Philippe, all looking to Fort Chartres and its church of Ste. Anne as their head. The old village community reappeared under its French form of house lots, commons, and fields, which to some extent have left their impress until now. Thus it is said that Prairie du Rocher still derives revenue from commons dating back to French time. The paternal nature of the government is shown in the reasons given here as elsewhere in Louisiana for some of the grants. Thus, a young man receives land because he is the first creole of Illinois to marry, while another gets a tract for each of his seven children.

Bertel was long in command; and after he left, Makarty came with new companies of troops and rebuilt Fort Chartres of stone, at a total cost of a million crowns. The quarries may still be seen across the little lake, but the finer stone of the gateways and buildings came from over the Mississippi. A description given of the fort, of a later date, but no doubt applicable to the middle of the century also, shows it with an arched gateway fifteen feet in height, while above was a cut-stone platform reached by steps with a balustrade. The walls of the fortress were eighteen feet high, and in each of the four bastions were forty-eight loopholes, eight embrasures, and a sentry box. In the interior the two-story warehouse was ninety feet long by thirty feet wide, and there were besides a guardhouse large enough to have two rooms above for chapel and similar uses, and a governor's house eighty-four feet long by thirty-two wide, boasting iron gates, stone porch, coachhouse, and a well, all of stone. Within also were a house for the *intendant*, also of stone and iron, two barracks one hundred and twenty-eight feet long, a magazine thirty-eight feet long and thirteen high, a bakehouse with two ovens and a well, a prison of four cells with iron doors, and a large relief gate. This extensive fortress enclosed an area of four acres, and was probably in some respects the most formidable held by the French king in Louisiana; for those at New Orleans were smaller, and the older Fort Condé at Mobile was only of brick.

While the government of Canada extended to the watershed between the lakes and the streams flowing south, on account of the portages there was need for a complete understanding between the military authorities of the lakes and those of the rivers. It will be recalled that the French thought of the Wabash as the principal river and of the Ohio above their confluence as a branch and not the main stream. This was due in part to the falls and to the fact that the Ouabache with its portage to Lake Erie was one of the great lines of communication between the Mississippi region and Canada. There is said to have been a Jesuit mission about the site of Vincennes as early as 1702, but it is not quite clear as to when military possession was taken. In 1725 Boisbriant was advocating the establishment of a post upon the Ouabache, although he said it did not seem as if this would be done before the English acted. However, the Compagnie took the hint and instructed him to write to Vincennes at the Miamis on the subject, and take steps through all officers reporting to the Canadian government to protect the post which the Compagnie was establishing and keep the English from penetrating toward the river. The letter of the Compagnie to Governor Périer next year also showed that it was fully alive to the situation. It recognized that besides the Ouabache there was the Ohio, having its source among the Iroquois, and the rivers of the Chaouanons and the Casquenamboux (probably the Tennessee and the Cumberland), taking their rise toward the Virginia, all of which would be under the control of the fort upon the Ouabache. Boisbriant, however, had to write that lack of supplies prevented him from sending to establish the post, and that he believed it necessary to give the command to Vincennes, who was very active among the Miamis. Vincennes himself reported an establishment by the English high up on the Ohio, and was sent to investigate. If found true, a fort was to be established near the confluence of the Ouabache and the Casquenamboux. To attract Vincennes to the colony of Louisiana, Périer was to inform him that the Compagnie would give him an annual "gratification" of three hundred livres in addition to his pay as lieutenant.

This led to the establishment of Fort Vincennes, which with its town and the posts at Ouatenon and Miami further north contained several hundred people.

The Missouri region also was always a source of interest. The discoloration of the Mississippi by this fierce, muddy stream was noticed by Pénicaut, Le Sueur, and Rémonville, as well as later by Charlevoix, who pronounced their junction the finest confluence in the world. Upon it lived the Missouris, and higher were the Kansas [Cansez] and Pawnees [Panis], besides a dozen other nations; while beyond its mountain source was believed to be a river running west to the Pacific. *Coureurs de bois* early penetrated to the banks of the Missouri, and in 1704 Canadians were there as well as on the Ohio, one Laurain being especially named. Four years later Nicolas de La Salle, who with all his faults at least was energetic, advocated a systematic exploration, because of "pieces to be found there, which slaves from the nations on that river call iron, of the same color and quality as piastres." He says *coureurs* had ascended three to four hundred leagues without finding the source.

In 1709, Mandeville describes the hair and wool of the innumerable buffaloes [*bœufs et vaches*] on the Missouri, and hopes were entertained of taming them to draw plows, and afterward we find Hubert advocating an expedition to discover mines, as well as the river leading to the western sea; but we do not learn that it was undertaken, unless by Bourgmont, who had then been several years among the Missouris. Even as late as 1718, Sieur Presle writes from Dauphine Island that he hears from savages that small men with oblique eyes, wearing clothes and boots, live on a lake six hundred leagues beyond the Panis, that they had gold and rubies, and were, of course, supposed to be Chinese.

Now came the turn of the Compagnie d'Occident to explore the neighboring river Merameg for lead and silver. They spent much money, and sent De Lochon, a Spaniard named Anthony, and royal miners under Renaudière; but none of them knew much of the business, and they realized

Thomas, Lord Culpepper. Patentee of Virginia and governor for life.
From the painting in possession of the Virginia Historical Society.

little. Charlevoix suspected that even the company's director, Renault, would fail as well; but, at least if the story told him by chiefs was true, the Spaniards were alive to the danger of interference, for about 1718 they had marched with the view of driving the French even from the Illinois. They defeated some of the Octotatas high up on Missouri River, but finally, while drunk, were ambushed at the third village. A Catalan pistol, a worthless pair of Spanish shoes, an ointment, and a breviary were the spoils of which Charlevoix learned. Du Tisné in 1719 ascended the Missouri and has much to say of the Osages, Panis, and other Indians; he planted the French flag among the Panis, but he did not reach the Padoucas and had to return to the Illinois. Bourgmont was sent to establish a post on Missouri River about that time, upon his undertaking to make peace among all nations between Louisiana and New Mexico, assure a safe passage for travellers, protect the Illinois mines from Spanish enterprise, and open up a trade for the French. The scheme attracted even the regent, and Bienville was instructed to assist.

Almost contemporaneously came the expedition of the genial Charlevoix, commissioned to find means for the discovery of the Pacific. His first attempt was in 1724 from Michilimackinac, and later he wished to ascend the Missouri and make an establishment among the Sioux, from which he was dissuaded. He also offered to conduct among the Sioux the missionaries sent to that nation. An establishment among the Sioux presenting difficulties, Charlevoix returned to the project to discover the western sea by means of the Missouri. The Jesuits went among the Sioux, but Charlevoix never discovered the Pacific, and, instead, the French established Fort Beauharnois on Lake Pepin, named for an official in Canada who was to be the ancestor of Napoleon's predecessor with Josephine. There were different commandants at this post to protect the business of the Sioux company, among them being Linctot and Saint-Pierre, and the beaver trade was considerably aided in this way; but the inconstant savages turned against the French in 1736, and the next year the post was abandoned.

Exploration to the west did not cease with this misfortune, for La Vérendrye pursued the quest and reached at least the vicinity of the Rocky Mountains about 1744, for which he seems to have been made chevalier of the order of Saint Louis. After his death, Saint-Pierre, also a chevalier, was charged with this discovery, but the war with the English caused his recall to the east.

It will thus be seen that the history of the Illinois region has hardly a unity, either of time or place. It originated in the *coureurs* and the Jesuits, and from the time of the Compagnie centres about one place, but Fort Chartres was not the capital in the north in the sense that Mobile or New Orleans was the capital in the south. The Missouri district was more or less independent, as was the Ouabache. The northern settlements were rather several communities in the making than a single colony made up of several parts. And yet, what concerned one affected the others. They all looked to Fort Chartres and were all proud of it as the best-constructed fortress in Louisiana; for this it was, despite the original idea of the Compagnie that there was no need of a formidable post so far in the interior, although even at that time the Illinois produced greater returns in proportion to its expense than any other part of Louisiana. Primarily, the value of the Illinois at first was in the portages between Canada and Louisiana, and to these it always owed much. Then the fertility of its soil and to some extent the reliability of its crops made it even more esteemed by the people of southern Louisiana, where in some places the soil was less rich and in others was somewhat subject to storm and inundation. Gradually other values opened up, and the mines of lead and copper gave great promise for the future, when the country should be better developed and transportation easier. Last, but not least, the Illinois found much of its importance in the trade and communication it commanded with other regions than Canada by means of the great rivers from the west and the east. The Pacific was never discovered from the Missouri, but the Rocky Mountains were, and one had at least to be on his guard against the Spaniards or the Indians who might become influenced by the Spaniards. This fear was lessened as France and Spain themselves grew closer together, so that ultimately the chief value and the chief weakness of the Illinois was in its outlook toward the east, toward the sources of the great rivers rising in the mountains behind Pennsylvania, Virginia, and Carolina.

CHAPTER XIII

LOUISIANA UNDER ROYAL GOVERNORS

Our inquiries have led us far from the scene of Iberville's settlement. We have traced the abortive work of La Salle to his death, the voyage of Iberville and its results at Biloxi, and studied the history of the capital at Mobile on its two sites. Thus far we know the country as a royal colony, at first promising, and then after the death of Iberville making little progress on account of the great War of the Spanish Succession at home. After the second Mobile was built, we saw the colony turned over to Crozat, and noticed that during this time other posts were founded and considerable exploration made. Then came the brilliant promise of John Law's scheme; and in the course of his operations New Orleans was built and the Mississippi made the centre of the efforts of the Compagnie. This led us to consider the Illinois country, and we shall likewise find traces of this period in other parts of vast Louisiana.

For the present we come back to the heart of the province,—New Orleans, the capital, and the neighboring districts which were connected so closely with it. The later French régime we shall find divided into three periods, which may be named according to the governors,—Bienville, Vaudreuil, and Kerlerec. The time, as a whole, might be called one of stagnation. The forward movement of the Compagnie had ceased, and the royal government was too much involved on the continent of Europe to have money available for the use of Louisiana. And yet, this is true only to us looking back upon the completed term, for the rule of Bienville, and of Vaudreuil too, presented hopeful signs.

Upon Bienville's return to begin his third term [1733–1742] he found universal distress. In one of his reports he speaks of the people as reduced to eating the seeds of reeds, but this must be hyperbole. And yet, the situation was bad enough. Of the many concessions and settlements of the Compagnie, some were abandoned and all were depressed. Agriculture, it is true, had at last taken hold, but in the uneasiness caused by the raids of the Natches and their friends no one far from the forts could be certain of his life, much less of gathering the fruits of his labor. For this reason, one of the first things to be attended to was some action relative to the Chickasaws, who had been actively antagonistic. Several years were consumed in preparation, and a formidable but unsuccessful expedition made its way up the Tombecbé [Tombigbee] in 1736; and a second, of doubtful result, operated by way of the Mississippi five years later. So that during Bienville's troubled third term Louisiana was full of military preparations, which yet did not increase greatly the feeling of security of her people.

On the civil side there was also difficulty. The Compagnie had issued paper money, which had become the circulating medium of the country, and now in 1735 the government, despite the opposition of Bienville and Commissary Salmon, undertook to replace the paper by card notes [*billets de carte*], supposed to offer greater security, inasmuch as France was greater than the Compagnie. In course of time, however, there was as great depreciation in the king's money as there had been in that of the Compagnie, coin being worth three for one; so that after a lapse of ten years another substitution was made, this time of drafts on the French treasury. As only one hundred livres in drafts were allowed for two hundred and fifty livres of paper, and the drafts themselves were at a discount, it seemed to make little difference to the colonists whose name was signed to the paper making up the circulating medium, whether it was that of King Stork or King Log, Law or Louis. Bienville became discouraged and asked to be relieved when he faced not only military disaster on the frontier but general bankruptcy even in the capital. The expenses of the Chickasaw war, from 1737, amounted to over one million livres, while the ordinary budget for this time was upward of three hundred thousand. Even the current expenses were not met by the products of the colony. In September, 1740, came a disastrous hurricane, the effect of which was worst perhaps at Mobile; but it ravaged all the coast, although it spared New Orleans. It blew down houses, destroyed magazines and provisions, drowned cattle, and caused universal distress. Part of Dauphine Island was washed away, and it is even said that a cannon, a four-pounder, standing near the guardhouse, was blown away eighteen feet. A second hurricane followed a week later in that fatal September, with the result that all provisions became scarce, flour absolutely wanting, and great distress prevailed.

The next governor of Louisiana was the Marquis de Vaudreuil [1743–1753], the son of a governor-general of Canada, and himself a distinguished man, of fine bearing, and a good administrator. Perhaps even better yet, he had influence at court. This boded well for the future of the colony, and, in point of fact, before many years he succeeded in having sent to Louisiana more soldiers than had ever been there before; for during his term the king directed that there should be maintained thirty-seven companies of fifty men, and permission was given to discharge soldiers from time to time on condition of settling in the colony. All immigrants were to be supplied with corn, rice, and necessary agricultural implements, and somewhat similar inducements were offered to mechanics desiring to locate in the towns. All concessions were to be close to each other, and the building of villages was encouraged. The soldiers in New Orleans were for the most part lodged in the barracks which had been erected on each side of the *place d'armes*, or public square. Contentment increased, and this, together with the dignity of Vaudreuil's court at New Orleans, made his term of office notable.

The policy of the French in relation to the Indians will be studied in another place, but the effect on the whites themselves was so marked that it will be well to recall that not only were the Chickasaws ill-disposed and never really subdued, but that the progress of the British traders coincided with the decline of French efforts in the west, and even among the Choctaws there was great dissatisfaction. This was due very largely to the parsimony of the home government in the way of presents for the savages, for it had been the custom from the beginning to hold an annual congress and make extensive gifts of supplies and goods to the Choctaws to keep them in good humor. This was perhaps more in the nature of a subsidy than a tribute, but at least the natives had come to expect it as a matter of course; and when it failed, as happened a number of times under the later governors, they became restless. They even frankly said that the English furnished them better goods, and that they would have to turn to the east despite their affection for the French. The result was that this, the largest of all the Southern tribes, extending from Alabama River to the Mississippi, not far from the coast, became alienated, and marauding parties made life and property insecure almost everywhere beyond the limits of the several posts. It was worse than a blow to French prestige; it was a threat to the dominion of the French in their own territories. Hence D'Arensbourg, in command at the German posts with a force of upward of a hundred men, could not subdue a few Indians who were active there. Some hunters were killed even in the vicinity of New Orleans, and a detachment sent to capture the marauders was put to flight by warwhoops. This throws a side light upon the difficulties encountered by the governors, who were almost unanimous in complaining of the nature of the troops sent from France. Bienville inveighed against their small size, some being four feet and a half tall, and declared their vices were equalled only by their cowardice. Périer said they usually fled at the first flash of an Indian gun, and that negroes were far better soldiers, except that they were too valuable to be used thus; and a French officer of the time mourned that there was less of the French temperament in Louisiana than anywhere else. It would seem as if the refuse of France was sent to Louisiana as troops, and the picture is only relieved by the bravery shown by the creoles themselves.

Vaudreuil was active in allaying the alarm which he found to be prevalent, and, by 1750, of thirty-two Choctaw towns only two were left to the English party, and Grand-Pré from Tombecbé effected a treaty which not only drove out the English and allied the Choctaws against the Chickasaws but gave special favors to the French. It was in consequence of these disturbances that the forces in Louisiana were raised to the respectable strength of two thousand men.

A census has been preserved from the year 1745, at which date the Choctaw disturbance was at its height, which shows that the male white population, exclusive of the troops, amounted only to between three thousand and thirty-five hundred people, and the blacks of both sexes to some two thousand—a decrease since the time of the Compagnie, for when it had relinquished its claim the country had a population of five thousand. The distribution of the people is interesting. Thus, New Orleans is given as having eight hundred whites and three hundred blacks, with one hundred whites at the German Coast, and two hundred at Pointe Coupée not far above, while the slaves at each of these last places doubled the number of the masters. To the east Mobile is named as having one hundred and fifty whites, besides two hundred blacks, and Pascagoula only ten whites to sixty slaves, while Biloxi is too insignificant to mention at all. To the west we find at

Natchitoches sixty white people and the surprising number of two hundred blacks. Proceeding up the Mississippi, we find at the Natchez only eight whites and fifteen negroes; at the Arkansas, twelve whites and ten blacks; while at the Illinois there were three hundred whites as against six hundred blacks; and up the Missouri, as many as two hundred whites, although there were only ten negroes. This shows that the greatest number of slaves was on the Mississippi plantations above New Orleans, while in the two towns, Mobile and New Orleans, the proportion between the races was reversed. At the capital, the negroes were somewhat less than half the number of the white men, while at Mobile slaves were in excess. On the frontier one would expect proportionately fewer slaves on account of the unsettled conditions necessarily prevailing, and this we find to be the case on the Missouri, while it is otherwise at Natchitoches, which may have been due to traffic, legal or illegal, with the Spaniards, and possibly also to captured runaways. This statistical study is defective in that the whites mentioned were only the men, while the blacks included both sexes. We can fairly include at least as many more for women and children, and in almost any other country it would be fair to make their number double or even treble that of the men, but the figures preserved do not allow us to give the proportion of women and children in the different settlements. We can only conjecture that there were more in the older places than on the frontier.

It was in this year that Lenormant succeeded Salmon as royal commissary, and between him and the governor there was soon the usual state of war. Vaudreuil complained that the commissary starved the troops and deprived the settlements of provisions, which was bad enough, and did not furnish presents and merchandise for the Indians, which prevented the governor from paying for scalps and remunerating the friendly tribes.

On account of the prevalence of war in Europe, Vaudreuil thought that fortifications should be constructed below New Orleans and the entrance to the river better cared for. These things would seem to go almost without saying, for Louisiana meant the Mississippi, and the Mississippi could not be useful unless guarded against the enemy in time of war and its mouth kept open at all times. La Salle had designed a fort somewhere on the lower river, and one of the first acts of Iberville in taking up La Salle's mantle was to build one which lasted for some time. Even before the closing of the port at Dauphine Island, the Compagnie had ordered boats to ascend the river to the Illinois as well as to the Natches, and instructions were not infrequent to captains of vessels as well as to officials of the colony to take soundings on the bar and note the depth, course, and rapidity of the Mississippi; and before any town was planned, Hubert urged the necessity of digging or destroying the bars, for the approaches to the river were formidable and its bends made it difficult to establish a port. There were some fifteen feet on the first bar and only eleven on the second, and to increase the depth Hubert urged the use of drags in fair weather. The Compagnie gave instructions to La Tour as chief engineer and Pauger and others as assistants, not only to explore the coasts, but to seek means to render the Mississippi navigable, among other things by putting buoys or marks at the entrance. Bienville sent boats through the channel even while New Biloxi was the capital, and Pauger established the proposed buoy, or *balise*, from which the adjacent island received its name, and upon his report Bienville wrote to the minister of marine that he was assured of a port for vessels of the third class. Charlevoix, he adds, had descended the river and was charmed. Vessels drawing not over thirteen feet entered at full sail without touching, and Bienville did not think it would be difficult to render the pass navigable for much larger ships, the bottom being soft mud. He had in 1722 sent two boats [*flûtes*] of three hundred and four hundred tons, which had entered under full sail, and next year he could write that the water was deeper.

He writes he was then establishing batteries and lodging for a garrison to protect the entrance. The people gave the entrance a bad name, even saying that it was easier to pass an elephant through the eye of a needle, and La Tour and Pauger had actually to force the captain of the *Aventurier* to enter the river. It was true that they ran aground, but they got off and could report that the pass was getting deeper. In 1723 Pauger reported that where there had been only thirteen feet of water before the island of the Balize, there were then sixteen or seventeen, and he urged that some one of the other passes be closed so that the current thus increased would carry away this bar.

Something, of course, was done afterward, but not a great deal until Bienville, seeing the necessity of a structure of some sort to protect the mouth of the river, had, in 1741, made a contract with Dubreuil to erect fortifications at the Balize at the cost of almost three hundred thousand livres. Subsequent opinion favored forts higher up the stream, as it was almost impossible to find a foundation near the Gulf. The engineer Deverges thought fortifications could be built there, while Lenormant favored Plaquemine Turn, but Vaudreuil selected the English Turn fifteen miles from New Orleans. He was led to this opinion by the fact that the change of direction of the river at this point deprived ascending ships of the wind which had brought them up. Even since Bienville's day the river had formed for itself a new channel near the Balize, and thus considerable work was necessary to make the pass defensible. The planters furnished negroes, and something was effected; but it would seem that the quarrels between the governor and the commissary prevented much that might have been. But at least the Balize was improved, for, according to the governor, the fort already there was a place of dépôt for commerce with the Spaniards and a point from which the coast could be watched.

The principal matter of interest during this period of Louisiana's history is to be found in the capital itself. Its males, we have learned, numbered about eight hundred, which would mean a total population of double or treble, and in addition to this there were two hundred soldiers and three hundred slaves. Most of the houses were still of wood, although brick was already being used either by itself or to fill up wooden frames. There was still one cargo of prospective wives to be brought from France in 1751, sixty in number, but immigration had practically ceased and the country was to find its development, such as it was, in the natural increase of the creoles. No change was made in the plan of the city, and it was gradually growing along the line of that made at its foundation. Everything centred about the *place d'armes* on the river, to the right and left of which were barracks, while fronting it were government buildings. In the squares beyond, between the high-sounding streets, dwelt the creoles, who loved this country as home, and the officials, who thought of it as a place where they could put money in their purse in one way or another and then go back to France. Behind the city came the district known as Gentilly, a local corruption of the famous Chantilly where the old race of Condé lived in princely magnificence.

Agriculture flourished despite the many drawbacks. Of old were indigo and from 1740 some cotton, and in 1751 ships bringing soldiers brought from Hispaniola sugar cane and negroes used to its culture, the gift of the Jesuits of the island to those of Louisiana. It was planted above Canal Street, but did not flourish, and it was not for almost half a century that Louisiana really acquired one of her most famous crops. Another of the best-known products was wax from the candleberry tree, *myrica cerifera*, which grew abundantly. We have already seen it used on the Atlantic coast, and here Vaudreuil was authorized to purchase the whole crop for the king at ten to twelve livres per pound. It was prepared by placing the berry coated with wax in hot water, then the wax came off and was skimmed for use. Among the producers, Dubreuil is said to have made six thousand pounds weight. It was a valuable crop, because it furnished the only light used by the colonists, and it was also exported. There were the standard crops of maize and vegetables, although the growth of the Illinois district led to the importation of supplies from that region, and after the hurricane of 1740 famine was prevented by flour from up the river. The boats from the Illinois came down in the late fall and returned in January, exchanging grain and the like for goods imported from France.

The commerce of the province was of some importance, and this was due to a wise if belated provision as to duties. It was, of course, still held that a colony was valuable only for what the mother country could get out of it, and that not only must its products be shipped home, but that these should pay duty to the government for the privilege of being taken there, and, further, that articles imported into the colony should likewise pay duty. This we have found to be the doctrine everywhere, as also the corollary that trade should be carried on only with the mother country and in her bottoms. In 1732, and thus shortly after the surrender of its charter by the Compagnie, the wise provision had been made that for ten years goods imported into the colony or exported thence to France should be exempt from duty. In 1741 it was found that the ordinance had worked well and, moreover, the distressed condition of the colony after the hurricane made it almost imperative to renew the provision for ten years, and in 1751 a similar extension was made. Thus free trade between Louisiana and France became practically a part of the policy of the country.

The intellectual and moral condition of the colony could hardly have ranked very high, although we know that even La Salle's Texan colonists had many books. Education was largely in the hands of the Church, and when an attempt was made to found a college the home authorities decided that Louisiana was not sufficiently important to make that proper. It would hardly, therefore, be expected that in Louisiana, any more than in the earlier English colonies, there would be found much in the way of native literature, although in one or two respects perhaps Louisiana has the advantage. For, the government being absolute, fuller and more frequent reports were made of the events in the colony. For another reason also we have more in the nature of memoirs than might be anticipated. The very fact that officers came to Louisiana without the intention of settling, while it helped the colony less than if they had come to live, as was the case on the Atlantic, led them to take a great interest in what they saw and frequently to write back to friends in France some of their experiences. And this is as true of the later as of the earlier times, so that we have in the way of accounts of travel a number of journals, letters, and even formal books, which sometimes purport to be actual histories. So that while we have little or nothing of the nature of what is sometimes called pure literature, a great deal has survived of what is actually of greater value for the understanding of the country.

The letters and reports of La Salle, of Iberville, and of the *ordonnateurs* are numerous, and many have been collected in Margry's monumental volumes, while some not in the printed works of Margry may be found in the manuscript collections of Magne and Margry made for the State of Louisiana and still preserved. The French have always been good *raconteurs*, and the personal element, perhaps shown in angry and spiteful tales upon each other, adds a zest to these papers, even where only abstracts are preserved. Papers from the ecclesiastical side of colonial life would be equally valuable, and it is a loss to us that the Jesuits did not have a stronger hold in Louisiana, for the *Jesuit Relations*, even with the additional letters found by Mr. Thwaites, contain little relating to the lower colony. This we have seen was not their province, and yet a letter of Gravier in praise of Bienville's government and Du Poisson's description of the mosquitoes on the Mississippi make us long for more such literature. We do have the *Relation of the Voyage of the*

Ursulines, containing letters of Marie Madeleine Hachard to her father, and one would not willingly let this charming account lapse into oblivion. And yet, possibly, the private works of the time are if anything more interesting, because they were generally written without bias or at least without the constraint sometimes felt by those in official position. Thus the journal or relation of Pénicaut is charming, and as a rule reliable, as we have had occasion to notice in the earlier years of Louisiana. It was written with the object of securing a pension, and records that he was even then one of the *concessionnaires* upon the Mississippi. One feels a distinct loss when this "literary ship carpenter" returned to France for treatment of his eyes; but, in a different way, his place is almost immediately supplied by pleasant old Father Charlevoix, whose observations in Louisiana appear in several forms. He wrote an *Histoire* of New France, and to it is sometimes appended his *Journal of a Voyage* made by royal order from Quebec to New Orleans. The journal consists of letters to the Duchess of Lesdiguierres, and imparts a great deal of information in a rambling sort of way. Thus, although he playfully reproaches the people for speaking of New Orleans as a female while the original Orléans in France was of another sex, he was pleased with the place and gives us many entertaining views of it and other posts. While Charlevoix confines himself almost exclusively to Mississippi River, what is generally quoted as the *Journal Historique* treats also of the western explorations. This has been attributed to Bénard de La Harpe, because of a memorial of his going with it, although Margry ascribes it to Beaurain, the royal geographer. It purports to be drawn from the memoirs of Iberville and Bienville as well as from those of Le Sueur, and much material seems to be furnished by La Harpe himself. A companion of La Harpe seems to have been Dumont de Montigny, who was at the Yazoo post and involved in the Natches war. He is the author of *Mémoires Historiques*, gives much information, and never spoils a good story in the telling.

Robert Cavelier, Sieur de la Salle. *From the engra·ving by Henri Waltner.*

When we remember his dealings with rattlesnakes twenty-two feet long and frogs of thirty-two pounds, we may consider ourselves fortunate that he survived to relate so much. If Dumont is to be considered as a realist, his contemporary, Le Page du Pratz, is an idealist, for he has theories as to many things in his *Histoire de la Louisiane*, based upon his sixteen years in the colony ending in 1734. The book is remarkable for the number of the plates and maps which are found in some editions, no less than forty-two in number, and which have proved of great value to all subsequent students of the period.

Among the last writers was Bossu, captain in the French marines, whose *Nouveaux Voyages* is made up of letters back to France, giving his adventures in America. From New Orleans he was sent to Fort Toulouse, and, after a disagreement there as to rank, up to Fort Tombecbé in charge of a convoy, and he was also in the Illinois. His description of Indian customs and of his own adventures is happy and interesting. He has an alligator story which somewhat rivals Dumont's, for on the banks of the Tombecbé, while he was wrapped up in the corner of the tent, an alligator, smelling a fish which Bossu had at his feet, dragged him and it off toward the river. Bossu thought the Devil had him, but managed to escape, glad to lose only the fish. He was a great partisan, and in his love for friends and hatred of enemies would have rejoiced good old Dr. Samuel Johnson, for he does not spare the derelictions of officials in the colony.

Such were the principal writers of Louisiana. We know that there were more, for Le Page quotes the manuscript memoirs of Saint-Denis and others, and there has recently been discovered a journal of Bouquès for the period of the second Biloxi experiment, full of interest for that time, although it has no broad outlook and possesses small literary merit. The works referred to are real Louisiana literature, although none of them were printed there and possibly some were put in their final shape in France; for they were written about Louisiana and by people who lived in the colony, and give us not only our clearest impressions of the country itself, but of the creoles and travellers who were within its borders from Iberville's time down to that of Kerlerec. Some books, however, were published at New Orleans, and one of the late acts of the colonial government was to confer the monopoly of printing them on M. Braud.

The quarrels in the civil government were reflected in the Church also. When Louisiana had been divided into three ecclesiastical districts, it will be remembered the lower Mississippi had been given to the Capuchins, and they attended faithfully to such administration as they found possible under the circumstances. The Jesuits had been confined to the Illinois district, but to this they had never been able to reconcile themselves. It seemed to them that every frontier and all newly settled colonies were theirs by right. So they obtained the privilege of having a Superior at New Orleans. This priest secured his own appointment as vicar-general, and took advantage of the trustfulness of the Capuchins. The result was that for years there was a constant struggle between the two orders, which, in fact, was not terminated until France expelled the Jesuits in 1764, when their colonial property was confiscated and sold.

Thus lower Louisiana drifted along, hardly flourishing at best, but finding amusement and employment for the natural *esprit* of Frenchmen in the quarrels between the governor and the commissary, between the Capuchin and the Jesuit, as well as in war and trade with the Indians. Agriculture was growing, commerce at last really favored, and if France could supply more encouragement, or at least could keep out of European wars, Louisiana might yet become not unworthy of the dreams of La Salle and Iberville. The energy of Vaudreuil was recognized, although at the expense of Louisiana, by his promotion to be Governor-general of Canada, and he departed with the regrets of all. They loved to compare him to Louis XIV., and the counterpart of the Grand Monarque to them was the Grand Marquis.

And although his departure was a loss, his successor was not unequal to the place. Kerlerec came in 1753, and took active charge of his post. Almost his first business was to study the Indian question and hold a congress at Mobile with the Choctaws, with whom he was favorably impressed. The necessity for counteracting the wiles and the trade of the English appealed to him at once, and he promised all they could ask, while, on the other hand, the chiefs were so much pleased with him that they voted him the "Father of the Choctaws."

Despite all drawbacks, the French had good leaders, understood the Indians, knew the routes of the great valley, and could make up for their lack of numbers by alertness and mobility.

CHAPTER XIV

FRANCO–SPANISH RELATIONS

At the beginning of our story we found Spain the dominant nation in Europe and America. Her infantry was the terror of the world, her fleet of the ocean, and her possessions embraced the fairest provinces of both continents. We have seen how from the defeat of the Armada her power was checked, and later how her wealth could hardly maintain her in a doubtful supremacy. When less able monarchs ruled, her position became impaired, although it was a gradual process and for several generations not realized even by her neighbors. With the extinction of the direct line and the great War of the Spanish Succession, it became evident that the hegemony had passed to France, and from that country came Philip, the new monarch, although it would be a mistake to think of Spain as ever becoming in effect a province of France. The France of Louis XIV. fully realized her own leadership in Europe, but she also realized the pride and the importance still of her ally on the south. The war came about immediately from the family alliance of the two countries; but this itself had been founded on community of religion, feeling, and interest. Spain under Charles V. had great possessions in Italy, the original Latin country, and in the Netherlands, essentially Teutonic. As long as France felt herself bound in by the Spaniards on both sides as in a vise, fear of the future and true patriotism united her able kings and gradually coalescing nationality in a struggle against Spain. It was not so much a contest for leadership as for existence. When the decline of the Spanish power began, caused by pressure without and stagnation within, the French fear was removed and gave way to a sense of community of origin and interest. Unconsciously the line was drawn again as it had been under the Roman emperors between Latin and Teuton, a line which even to the present has never been obliterated. The result of the Succession War was gratifying to the Spaniard, although Italy and the Netherlands passed to Austria. His fatherland was preserved intact and the feeling of race affinity with the other great Latin power of Europe was intensified, so that the later Family Compact of the crowns of France and Spain was but the royal seal on the popular feeling. The *entente* of the two nations was to last for a long time, despite temporary breaks, and it was both more and less than an alliance of the two governments. While there was a sympathetic union, based on blood and somewhat on institutions, it left the two nations independent, each developing its own policy in its own way, but ready to help the other by diplomacy if not by arms. In America their territories adjoined. Spain had finally recognized the fact that France owned the Mississippi valley, although the boundaries between their colonies were not always certain. On the west, Louisiana and New Spain afforded points for negotiation, and the boundary shifted backward and forward with the alternate energy of the two governments.

At first blush it seems strange that the French should have in mind so much the Spaniards, far distant to the west. This may have been due in part to imperfect knowledge of southwestern geography, and yet in some respects it was perfectly natural. Cabeza de Vaca, with some survivors of Narvaez's expedition, had in the sixteenth century crossed the continent, and his report was such that Coronado sent some of these with other men to explore the country as far as the Zuñi, or Cibola, and in 1540 came the celebrated expedition of Coronado himself, when a number of missions were established. Toward the end of the century Oñate did much toward colonizing the district now known as New Mexico, and mining was rapidly developed. There was an interruption on account of the revolt of the Indians, who had been almost reduced to slavery, but after that the mining industry and population gradually increased, and Santa Fé became a famous place. The Spaniards thus controlled the passes between the Atlantic and the Pacific where the Rio Bravo [Grande] cuts through the Rocky Mountains, and claimed not only all toward the Pacific, but indefinitely toward the east. They came as near as the facts permitted to Menendez's ambition to possess the passage from the Gulf to the Pacific. The sources of Canadian and Arkansas Rivers were not far away, and branches of the Missouri headed a few days' march further north; so that through the wandering Indian tribes, such as the Comanches and even the Sioux, the French would learn of the presence of the Spaniards, and the Spaniards would learn of the growing power of the French. This led to a fuller occupation of the Texas plains by the Spaniards, while, on the other hand, it led the French to push as far up Red and Arkansas Rivers as they could to anticipate their rivals. Louisiana was to be confined to the region east of the Rocky Mountains, and in the south the Spaniards were to hold to Sabine River; but for a long time this was open to question on both sides, and each nation tried to push its borders as far forward as possible before the other developed strength. The crucial points, therefore, might be the Red, Arkansas, and even the Missouri basins, and, as it turned out, on the first was the main tug of war.

Gravier in 1700 said the French already talk much of Red River, and Pénicaut on his return from Minnesota heard of an expedition of Bienville and Saint-Denis up what was then called the Marne to learn the eastern limit of New Mexico, the old Spanish colony, as well as to see if there were any mines. They went as far as the Nassitoches [Natchitoches] and the Cadodaquious, and found no mines; but at least they found no Spaniards, although legend placed the death of De Soto at the mouth of Red River and they learned that Spaniards sometimes came thus far. High water interfered, and fuller exploration was left for Saint-Denis some years later.

Louis de Saint-Denis was a lieutenant at the first fort guarding the Mississippi until it was abandoned, when he settled in Mobile, and soon, not receiving his pay, moved to Biloxi. In 1711 he seems to have been at New Mobile, for on the interesting plan of that date lately discovered he is assigned a regular city lot on the tree-shaded parade, immediately facing the palisaded fort. His peculiar talents were well known, and when by letters patent Louisiana was leased to Crozat, and La Mothe Cadillac from Detroit succeeded Bienville as governor, a new field was opened to Saint-Denis.

La Salle, in his argument to the French government for establishing Louisiana, represented that it would be within striking distance of the Mexican mines, but we have seen that he lived to find between the Mississippi and Mexico a vast region of which he had not dreamed. In his day the Spaniards had made no settlement in the district north of the Rio Grande, and it may be doubted whether they had really explored it except along the coast. But this was within their Florida, or at least New Filipinas, and his settlement at Matagorda Bay was the first indication of conflicting boundaries. La Salle was murdered early in 1687, and, despite attempts of the Spaniards from Mexico to find it, his colony lived on for possibly two years longer, when it was exterminated by the Indians. Those of this part of the country were apparently a loose confederacy generally called Tejas, or Texas, while further to the west were the Apaches and Comanches. After ascertaining the extinction of La Salle's colony, the Spaniards undertook several expeditions under Captain Alonzo de Leon, accompanied by Franciscan padres. They found several of La Salle's Frenchmen living among the Indians, and in 1690 established the mission of San Francisco de los Tejas to the east of Trinity River and possibly not far from the scene of La Salle's death. This lasted only three years, and although these *entradas* gave the country the name of Texas there was little or nothing of real colonization beyond the mission of San Juan Bautista near the Rio Grande in 1700, although different padres were at sundry times among the Asinais and other tribes to the northeast. One of the padres in 1711 invited Cadillac to help to establish a mission, and Louis de Saint-Denis was sent at the head of an expedition to open communication. It is possible he had been even to the Rio Grande before, and, at all events, now took goods of ten thousand livres in value for sale in Mexico. He left his goods at Natchitoches village, and spent some time trading among the Asinais. After reporting to Cadillac at Natchez, Saint-Denis went further and reached the mission of San Juan Bautista or the neighboring *presidio* on the Rio Grande where Diego Ramon—in French "Raimond"—was in command. Ramon received instructions to send Saint-Denis to Mexico, and the result was that a younger Ramon was ordered to establish missions as far north as the Tejas Indians. Pénicaut's account dwells largely on the romantic attachment and marriage of Saint-Denis to the daughter of Ramon, and omits the important fact that he returned with the Spaniards and was in their pay. The details are obscure. The Spaniards by Saint-Denis's advice desired to place the boundary at the Mississippi, while in a letter to Cadillac he suggested placing it at the Rio Grande. It looks as if Saint-Denis faced both ways, and the net result of his action was that the Spaniards occupied the country up to the valley of Sabine River.

La Harpe founded a French post among the Nassonites above Natchitoches and in 1719 engaged in a cordial correspondence with Padre Margil, superior of the Spanish missions, and it seems that a clandestine trade was the result.

There were six of these Texas missions, the furthest to the east being at the Adaes, founded about 1717. The map of this year of the *oydor* of the royal treasury of Mexico, based on explorations at the instance of the viceroy, shows the coast and the interior from Vera Cruz around to Pensacola. With the perspective natural to a Mexican, the Rio Grande appears in great detail from Santa Fé near its sources in the mountains down to the Gulf, while the Mississippi is shown as rather a small stream, hardly longer, although wider, than Trinity River, upon which is a *presidio* of the Tejas. Natchitoches does not appear, and, indeed, while four or five settlements seem to be indicated, two of these are on the Bay of Espiritu Santo and they have no names. A French fort is indicated on the Mississippi below the St. Jean, but the nearest of the French posts with a name is Mobile. The Texan rivers are given elaborately, but the natural inference from the map is that, whatever might be planned, the only place actually occupied north of the Rio Grande at this time was the *presidio* of the Tejas.

Saint-Denis afterward undertook another expedition, with Canadian associates named Graveline, De Léry, De La Fresnière, Beaulieu frères, and Derbanne, who carried forty-three thousand two hundred livres of goods for trade via Natchitoches. Don Martin de Alarcon,—in French "Alarcomme,"—captain-general and governor of the province of Texas, arrested Saint-Denis and confiscated the goods, and his companions turned back; but he finally obtained release for himself and property, sold it privately to advantage, and returned to Dauphine Island in March, 1719.

The net result was that commerce between the Spaniards and the French was not authorized, but to some extent was carried on in secret between Natchitoches and the adjacent Spanish missions. The short war between France and Spain (1719), when Pensacola was captured, led to the abandonment of the Texas frontier, but whatever demonstration there was by Blondel at Natchitoches was apologized for at the dictation of La Harpe, and the missions were restored.

Indeed, Aguayo in 1721 built the new fort of Pilar among the Adaes, as well as restored the *presidio* of Tejas. The French protested against Forts Pilar and Bahia, but Saint-Denis, who was now in command at Natchitoches, took no active steps in the matter.

The *entente* between France and Spain prevented any further conflict on the Texas border. In 1735 the French moved their fort of Natchitoches from an island in the river to the mainland and thus nearer to Pilar, which provoked some discussion; and in the same way, as late as 1756, the Spaniards established a new *presidio* at Orcoquisac on Trinity River, against which the French in their turn protested. Nothing came of either protest, both were to some extent for the sake of form, and there is no reason to doubt that the frontier military remained on good terms and that trade was quietly carried on between the two posts all the time.

We find the Natchitoches question complicated with that of the Spanish boundary on the coast, where the French claim dated from La Salle's settlement on Matagorda or St. Bernard's Bay. As early as 1707 the French court had ordered stakes [*poteaux*] planted, with the royal arms affixed, at the eastern and western limits of Louisiana. When the king ceded the province to the Compagnie, it was with the power of making forts, and they determined to establish one at the Bay of St. Bernard. Bienville accordingly in 1721 made La Harpe commandant of the proposed post, and sent him with twenty soldiers to set up the royal arms and build a fort to repel attack. Simars de Belle Isle had been wrecked there in the *Maréchal d'Estrées*, and showed the way. La Harpe returned with a glowing report, but as the Indians were hostile Bienville abandoned the idea of making so distant a settlement at a time when men and ships were needed nearer home. But it resulted in confining the boundary forever to the Sabine, for the active Aguayo appeared in the same year and established the *presidio* of La Bahia on the site of La Salle's Fort St. Louis. Earlier, the Spaniards had burned the old French settlement, and Aguayo's action not only fixed the Spanish occupation in this direction, but kept open what was esteemed the best port at that time known on the coast of Texas.

On the other side, there was the boundary with Florida. At the beginning, of course, Spain had not recognized that there was any Louisiana at all, and even while the temporary settlement still existed at Biloxi the Spanish governor from Pensacola had come and made due protest. A trace of the dispute still survives in the name of one of the outlets of the Alabama-Tombigbee system, for Spanish River apparently marks the western claim of Florida. French occupancy of both shores of Mobile Bay, and gradually of all tributary streams, however, made the Perdido the final boundary, and it was near here that Bienville established a boundary post or pillar marking the east line of Louisiana about the time that he did so at St. Bernard's Bay on the west.

The history of Pensacola was different from that of almost every other post with which we have been concerned. All these were in the nature of mother cities from which other colonies went out, gradually developing into quasi-States or else, failing to obtain a foothold, disappearing, and in their abandonment involving the community of their origin. We have found it difficult to account perfectly for the origin of Pensacola. The later Spanish tradition was that Tristan de Luna was the first settler, and certainly Tristan's short-lived experiment was somewhere between Mobile and Pensacola Bays, but it was ephemeral, valuable only as giving the Spaniards a little advantage in time over the French settlers on the Atlantic. Don Andres de Pes was there in 1693, and added the title of the Mexican viceroy, Galvez, to the name of Santa Maria, and perhaps he colonized and fortified it, as the Spanish claimed. The French speak of its being first occupied only a few months before Iberville passed, but the Spanish are unanimous in dating its settlement at least back to Arriola, in 1696. Whenever founded, it remained only a fort, with no town about it worthy of the name. Gardens were hardly known, and but for a little trade and exchange with the French at Mobile the place could hardly have continued at all. At one time Governor Guzman spent four days at Mobile, and some years later he was a witness at a baptism there, attesting the register with a bold hand as Dom Joseph. Pénicaut tells us that on one such occasion Guzman was received with salutes and entertained in great state. He was godfather at a christening, and distributed money as largess with a generous hand. Prisoners were released in his honor, and at his departure he was speeded by salutes. During the war with Spain we saw that Pensacola was captured twice by the French, Châteauguay being left there by the latter and afterward captured by the Spaniards. On the restoration of peace it came again under the Spanish flag, and was never afterward disturbed by the French. The place cannot be said to have flourished greatly under the Spanish, and always remained an outlying post, holding the country perhaps, but at no time the centre of a growing district. Its nearest neighbor was Appalachee, over a hundred miles to the east, from which a longer road went overland to St. Augustine.

At one time it seemed as if the Spaniards at Pensacola might become merely an *enclave* in a larger Louisiana, for in the old reports and maps we often find a notice of the French at St. Joseph's Bay, as we also find the English as settled in the same neighborhood. The two items may refer to the same thing, as there are indications that the French in question were Protestant refugees brought from England, and so being in one sense English and French at the same time. This note of an English settlement is found on a map made or used by La Salle himself; and even Iberville, in discussing the report of the projected English colony on the Espiritu Santo, declares that it was the river known to us as the Appalachicola. There is some uncertainty as to how far this settlement was carried out, and, at all events, if made it was not lasting. In 1718 the French did establish there a fort and colony, but this was temporary also, and next year we find the Spaniards in possession under Baraona. In fact, after the acknowledgment of the French right to colonize Louisiana there was, with the exception of the Pensacola war, little or no friction between the French and Spaniards in America.

The *rapprochement* between the French and the Spanish in Europe, we have seen, was due to similarity of origin and institutions. In the same way the colonial systems of the two were not unlike. Neither was a conscious imitation of the other, but both were founded on the double idea that the colonies were designed not to develop independent communities, but as outposts to hold territory for the mother country, and that the plan upon which they were to be administered was by military officials sent from home either with definite instructions under which to rule, or with autocratic powers of government. There was no intention of founding a popular State, as had been the case with Virginia. In fact, there was no popular condition known in France or in Spain, and it would be expecting too much to think that the stream could rise higher than its source. Really it rose much lower than its source, for the rulers at home at least had custom, law, and old institutions upon which to build, while the provincial administrators had to do the best they could in a strange country, with enemies both red and white, and hampered by the neglect or the inability of their superiors at home. At the same time, there were reasons for this which we are apt to overlook in thinking only of the American side of colonization. The home country would send out an expedition well equipped in every respect, or, at least, so far as could be determined at home by orders and powers for full equipment, and yet directions might not be carried out, or a war might break out and sever communications, or storms wreck vessels, and disease carry off men. So that the best-laid plans would fail of execution from causes beyond the foresight or control of even the most absolute monarch. We have seen the same thing time and again happen to the colonies of Great Britain, and that they only gradually worked out their own salvation. With the Latin communities there was even less success, and one of the causes of this was that absolute governments kept the people subjects rather than citizens, with no desire for better institutions, because ignorant that they were possible. The French and Spaniards have been conquerors rather than colonizers, and their form of colonial administration was largely along military lines even as regards their own people. Thus the Spanish commandant was both civil and military governor, with almost absolute powers, although nominally the civil *ciudad* was different from the military *presidio.* For although the *ciudad* had a municipal council [*ayuntamiento*], practically the colonists found all legislation made to hand at home without their initiative. They were not expected to legislate, but to obey, and, as happens with almost every unused function, they soon forgot the use of what was denied them. At the same time, human nature is not completely submissive in any clime or under any institution. The pride of the Spaniard will bow to the king, but not to his fellow officers. The loquacious Frenchman will seemingly carry out royal orders, but will report any defects of his fellow officials. So habitual was this even at home that suspicion became erected into a system. From Richelieu's time the old system of territorial aristocracy found itself gradually supplanted by a bureaucracy instituted in the name of the king, and the chief of these new officials were the *intendants* of the various provinces. There coexisted the noble, perhaps nominally the king's lieutenant, but the *intendant* was really the man in the saddle, actually managing everything and reporting on even the nobility. The same plan was carried out in the new colonies, which sprang up at this time. What had some justification in the condition of affairs in France and in the king's desire to build up a centralized government at the expense of the old nobles was without excuse in the colonies; for both colonial *intendant* and governor were mere officials of the king, and their differences resulted in anything but centralization. As Louis XIV. grew older, however, his system of espionage grew more perfect, and the plan was continued under his less able but not less suspicious successors. If it grew to such a point in France, it was only a fuller development of what had long prevailed under the absolute government of Spain, and gradually the colonial administrations on the north shore of the Gulf became almost identical. The governor had charge of the military, and the *ordonnateur*, or *intendant*, of supplies, and, under the Spanish, more particularly of lands; and in endeavoring to report the doings of each other they were almost always in opposition. This to a large extent prevented advance of the colonies.

Another fact strikes us in the study of the Latin settlements. Among the English we have found a constantly increasing immigration. In Virginia at first those that died outnumbered those surviving, and yet the tide still kept up until finally there was a self-supporting community. Measurably, the same thing is true of the other English colonies, but with the French we find that few came except at the beginning, and the rate of increase was smaller among those who did come than on the Atlantic. Even more marked was this among the Spaniards of Florida, although a comparison in this regard is unfair. We must remember that Mexico was the centre of Spanish influence in North America, and that Texas and Florida were remote outposts rather than established colonies. There was, after Menendez's time, little attempt by the Spaniards to colonize Florida, as it was looked upon more as a military establishment, increasing gradually, to be sure, but rather by natural growth than immigration. This was not true of Louisiana, for that was intended as a main French colony, on which blood and money were expended and toward which people were freely sent. But we are met at this point with the striking ethnological fact that the rate of increase among these Latin races was already smaller than among the

Jean Baptiste Le Moyne de Bienville,
Governor of Louisiana.

Pierre Le Moyne d'Iberville,
Founder of Louisiana.

From Margy's "Découvertes et Établissements des Francais," in the New York Public Library, Lenox Branch.

Teutonic. This we have only lately begun to appreciate, but its beginnings go back to the time of Louis XIV. The French race then expanded rapidly all over the world, but its weakness was soon apparent. The birth rate was smaller and France could spare few emigrants in proportion to that warren across the English Channel. In energy the comparison would be perhaps in favor of the French, but whether from overcivilization or other causes the increase of the French both at home and abroad was less than that of their Teutonic rivals. The important effect of this upon the history of the world was not foreseen, for even the fact was not then known.

As things stood, England and France were face to face in America, and the result could not be guessed. The stronger centralization of the Latin institutions enabled them to handle whatever armed population they had with greater ease and greater effect than the slow, more independent English. Even the *coureurs* among the woods could be sent backward and forward better than the English hunters. The only need on the Latin side was leaders, for the training and intuition of the people made them good soldiers. Such a system, whatever its defects, was one that was strong in time of war, and war was more than a possibility.

CHAPTER XV

THE ANGLO-SPANISH BORDER

THE time had come when the Spanish settlements of Florida were to have a trial of strength with the British of Carolina. Hostility there had always been, for we have found repeated instances of it; but this was at the foundation of the British settlements, and now they had grown as strong as St. Augustine and were able to take care of themselves even without assistance from England. There was no longer the question of wiping out an isolated French fort as in Ribault's time, or even of cutting off a sickly Virginia post. The English had become well established, and Spanish maps which had the names of Santa Maria Bay for the Chesapeake and Chicora for the adjacent country had to recognize the existence of the province of "Vyrgynea" and line the watercourses with English instead of Spanish names. Even Santa Helena was no longer the centre of active civilization. It was still the principal place in what Spain called the province of Orysta, but the Spaniards retired as Carolina extended in this direction, and when Lord Cardross established his Stuarttown there is little record of Spanish inhabitants.

Neither Spain nor England held the commanding position which they had once occupied, but they were the leading powers in America, and in 1670 found it necessary to make a treaty as to their possessions there. The phraseology was not so definite as the Spanish interpretation. The seventh article recognized possessions as they then existed, each power agreeing not to claim further and not to trade with the ports of the other. To the Spaniards this meant the latitude of thirty-three degrees as the line between the opposing colonizations. The charter boundary of Carolina had once been the line of twenty-nine, although it was even more nominal than the Spanish claim to the north. The Carolinians had never sought to make it effective, and practically considered the boundary as St. John's River, at about thirty-one degrees. The Spaniards, however, were more insistent on their claim and ever ready to resent encroachments below the line of thirty-three. So that the question of *uti possidetis* in 1670 was bound to give trouble. Thus when Lord Cardross established his Scots at Port Royal, an expedition from St. Augustine in 1686 exterminated them with a completeness recalling the time of Menendez. The Carolinians had to content themselves with a lame apology from St. Augustine, because the Catholic leaning of James II. made him loath to risk a breach with Spain. The privilege of furnishing the Spanish colonies with slaves under the *asiento* had not yet come to England, and it was not until the Peace of Utrecht that she even obtained the right to send one ship annually; but there was large profit in this traffic in human beings, and it influenced diplomacy even after the accession of William of Orange.

It is not quite clear to what extent Guale and Orysta were actually occupied at the end of the seventeenth century. Certainly there was little beyond a few settlements on the coast or on the islands and an occasional mission among the Indians of the interior. At the same time, it is entirely wrong to think of the Spanish claim as nominal and based only on the work of early explorers like De Ayllon. Maps and accounts existed of De Soto's journey, and Pardo's exploration had been somewhat also in the line of settlement far into the interior. Mines were still worked in the mountains of what are now Georgia and Carolina, and intercourse held with the natives from the Apalaches on the Gulf to the Cherokees and neighboring nations at the head of the Atlantic rivers. The time had passed, if indeed it ever existed to the extent often stated, when the Spaniards made of the Indians beasts of burden. More civilizing influences had been at work, and the self-sacrificing priests of the different orders had never wholly ceased their labors. Their missions were more extensive than those of the French to the west, and added to *presidio* and *ciudad* a third form of settlement. At the same time, the very adoption of a parallel of latitude as a boundary showed how little was really known of America and how little was made of it in Europe. Such a parallel cut the Gulf rivers off from their sources, and this was even more striking in the case of those emptying into the Atlantic. The real boundary of Atlantic settlements should be to the northwest, where the mountains separated the headwaters of their streams from those flowing toward the Ohio and Mississippi.

The province or district of Guale had a later history than Orysta. The principal Spanish settlement was on the island of San Simon, and this was, so to speak, the capital of the province, and the northernmost was the island of Sapala, or Sapelo, whose inhabitants retired with those of Santa Helena to San Simon. We are told that Santa Cruz, near the southern boundary of Guale, remained occupied by Spaniards and Timuqua Indians until the beginning of the eighteenth century, and that the same was true of Santa Maria and San Pedro, thus indicating the claim and occupancy of both mainland and island off the coast up to that time.

During the latter part of the seventeenth century we recall that the English and Spanish courts drew closer together, both on account of the religious proclivities of the Stuarts and because of French assaults upon the Low Countries, in which both Spain and England had interests. All this was changed by the War of the Spanish Succession, which began upon the death of the Spanish Charles II. and his devise of Spain to Philip V. Almost all the rest of Europe armed to keep the grandson of Louis XIV. off the peninsular throne, and the brilliant contest was to last until the Peace of Utrecht in 1713. The aim of this Grand Alliance was to partition the outlying portions of the Spanish empire, and Spain and France fought vigorously against dismemberment. It behooved Carolina to look to her southern frontier.

Even before the declaration of war in Europe the Carolinians and the Spaniards of Florida were in open conflict. The Spaniards moved first and led nine hundred Apalaches to the invasion of Carolina; the English, however, had the address to set on the Creeks as the enemy passed through their country, and the invaders were crushed at Flint River.

War was inevitable anyhow, but it would seem as if this Indian expedition determined the Carolinians to act promptly. Governor Moore induced the Assembly to vote £2,000, and six hundred militia, and a number of Indians were to constitute an invading force. They rendezvoused at Port Royal in September, 1702, and thence embarked in ten vessels. Some under Colonel Daniel proceeded by land and by way of St. John's River took St. Augustine from the rear, which they sacked without opposition because the inhabitants had retired to the fort of San Marcos. As agreed, Governor Moore's fleet entered the harbor, and the Carolinians laid siege to the castle. The cannon of the attacking force were of too small calibre, and Moore had to send to Jamaica for mortars and bombs, at first by some inefficient vessel and afterward by Colonel Daniel himself; but two small Spanish vessels came before the English brought their guns, and Moore incontinently raised the siege. He burned the town, and indeed vessels of his own fleet, and retired by land to Charlestown with slaves and church plate—and a debt of £6,000. When Daniel returned from Jamaica with cannon all was over, and he with difficulty escaped capture by the Spaniards.

Sir Nathaniel Johnson was appointed governor instead of Moore, whose failure had made him unpopular, but the ex-governor remained influential, and soon another force, a thousand Indians and fifty English, invaded Florida. This time the Carolinians did not go to St. Augustine, but laid waste the Spanish possessions far and near. Possibly the most extensive raid was that against the Apalaches in revenge for their invasion a few years before, and hardly anything was left of this once flourishing country beyond smoking ruins and fleeing inhabitants. Moore destroyed at least eight towns, and returned with the usual booty of church plate and slaves. Some of the fugitives from the Apalache country, we may recall, fled as far as Mobile, where they were warmly received by Bienville and given a location near his new fort, and they named their new home St. Louis, like their old. Others went to St. Augustine, and in course of time many went back to their old homes, but the glory of the nation that had been the first fruits of Spanish civilization and had made so great an impress upon the geography of America was gone forever.

It was soon seen, however, that invasion was not the rôle of the English alone. After three years of recuperation the Spaniards, in conjunction with the French, with whom they were then in alliance, prepared an expedition. It is not clear to what extent aid came from Louisiana, but we may be sure that Bienville would not be slow to help on the cause if possible. At all events, in August, 1706, a privateer suddenly brought the news to the Carolinians that a French and Spanish fleet was on the way to attack them. Charlestown itself was almost desolated by yellow fever, but the governor defied the foe that moved upon him from the landside, and repulsed attacks upon the adjacent islands. As for the threatened danger from the marine force, the Carolinians, who have never waited to be attacked, sent out a fleet under Colonel Rhett against the Latin foe. One vessel was captured with two hundred men; as for the rest, they had earlier sailed away, not stopping to exchange fire. Charlestown had repulsed the first of the three naval attacks known in her history.

It sounds incredible that a fleet of French and Spaniards should cross the ocean to attack an enemy, and flee without a blow before a militia squadron. Unfortunately, we have not the story of the other side to correct that of the victors; but, at all events, the contest was decided in favor of the English, and Carolina was free from invasion once more. Yet the contest was indecisive, for the Carolinians could not capture the fort of San Marcos any more than the Spaniards could take Charlestown. We find from the first year of the war Spaniards retiring from the sea islands toward St. Augustine. Even San Simon was abandoned, and in 1706 the English found the way open to build a tower and place artillery on San Pedro, while on the adjacent island of Ballenas they established a small fort of posts and boards. They had reoccupied Port Royal and on it built a fort named St. George, whose importance and influence even among the interior tribes is shown by the report which early reached Bienville that emissaries from it were crossing the mountains and descending the streams leading into the Ohio. How much of truth there may have been in this we cannot say, but it is a tribute to the sagacity of the English as well as of the French that such explorations, whether for trade or war, could have been planned and feared. It is possible that we have an echo of all this in the invasion, in 1708, of the Mobile territory by four thousand Indians from the northeast. We are told that the Cheraquis [Cherokees], Abikas, and Cadapouces [Catawbas] formed an alliance with the Alibamons and descended to attack Fort Louis, while we have already seen that, as with many another Indian invasion, the warriors could not be held together long enough to do anything effective.

There is little to record from this time as to the Anglo-Spanish border, except that it would seem that the short Triple Alliance War, in which for once the English and French were allied against Spain, brought as its results two fortifications on the Spanish border. We are told that the English of Carolina constructed a fort at the mouth of the river called Talace or Tamasa, which remained for ten years. This was probably the one built by Colonel Barnwell on the Altamaha, against which the Spaniards protested during the Charlestown boundary conference with Middleton in 1724. It was soon afterward burned, possibly at Spanish instigation. The history of this stockade is obscure, but the one established by the Spaniards at Appalachee is better known. We observed that when Moore raided this country he found it well inhabited and civilized, a part of his glory consisting in destroying churches and carrying off the plate. He mentions two forts by name, Ayaville and St. Louis, and describes Appalachee as the granary of Florida. After a while, many of the inhabitants returned to their older district, and the Spaniards in 1718, to protect them for the future, built at a considerable distance up St. Mark's River a fort known in later days only by its ruins. Later, twenty-five miles below, they constructed between the arms of the river, at the edge of the marshes nine miles from the sea, quite a formidable structure. It was designed to be of stone, and a bastion and curtains were finished of that material. The quarry was somewhat nearer the sea and protected by a castle, with a tower forty-five feet high of two or more stories, itself used as a landmark and watch tower and perhaps also as a lighthouse. Moore found white men, no doubt Spaniards, among the palisaded Apalache towns, for from the building of these forts a Spanish garrison was almost always maintained there. A road ran eastwardly to the Picolata on the St. John's and another westwardly to Pensacola, passing in both directions through friendly villages. The padres were at home among the Indians, whom they effectually civilized, but St. Mark's of Appalachee must have been lonesome enough for the troops. It was a lodge in one vast wilderness, with no other post short of Pensacola in the one direction or on the east coast of Florida in the other. But at least it served its purpose, and during the subsequent hostilities between the English and the Spanish we find little mentioned of invasions of Appalachee.

Somewhat later the English had influence enough to set the Talapouches on Pensacola, which certainly shows great influence to the west. The expedition was unsuccessful, however, because Périer, who was then Governor of Louisiana, informed the invaders that if they did not retire he would send the Choctaws against them. This was effectual, for the Talapouches were too far from their homes to continue a siege in the face of such an attack. They retired and Pensacola was saved.

For a time quiet reigned upon the Atlantic, but it was only a lull. It seemed as if there was an irrepressible conflict between the Teuton and the Latin. Just as Carolina had been interposed between Virginia and Florida and had borne the brunt of battle, the time was come when Carolina could shift the burden to other shoulders. There was to be a buffer between Charlestown and St. Augustine, to receive the shock of struggles yet to come.

CHAPTER XVI

GEORGIA, THE BUFFER COLONY

ENGLAND had changed greatly since the foundation of Carolina. In foreign relations, the wars with Louis XIV. had given her a commanding place in Europe, and the accession of the House of Hanover put an end to all reasonable chances of a Stuart restoration. An even greater change occurred in domestic affairs. Sir Robert Walpole was the first of the great commoners who governed the country in express reliance upon the House of Commons. From his time there was carried out in practice what had been the theoretical result of the English Revolution of 1688,—the king reigned and did not govern, and the ministry that conducted the government was only a committee of the dominant party in the lower house. Walpole has been called the first peace minister. He kept England out of foreign wars as much as possible, and aimed at lightening public burdens as far as circumstances would allow. During his long rule England developed wonderfully. Her successful wars had left her the mistress of the ocean, and the energy which had once gone to colonization now turned toward commerce and manufactures. She no longer shipped wool and other staples to be manufactured in the Low Countries so much as manufactured them herself. She no longer used Italian and Dutch bottoms to bring raw products and carry her goods abroad, for her seamen covered the ocean with merchant ships just as they had covered it for so many years with war vessels, and there was none, French, Spanish, or Dutch, to make them afraid.

It had been some time since the British established a colony on the North American mainland, but this was because the old colonies were themselves growing. In the year of the Triple Alliance against Spain, three years after the accession of George I., Sir Robert Mountgomery and others formed a scheme for planting one, to be named Azilia, in the southern part of Carolina. The prospectus, as usual in such cases, painted the country in glowing colors. It described the Golden Islands skirting the coast southwardly of the Carolinian settlements and the many beauties of the interior. The principal point dwelt upon in regard to the new colony was the method for protecting it from attack by Indians or other enemies. It was to be in the nature of an armed camp settled about the thirty-first and thirty-second degrees of latitude, and "thus in the same latitude with Palestine herself, that promised Canaan which was pointed out by God's own choice to bless the labors of a favorite people," and so not inappropriately we find the colonization designed to be somewhat as in Nehemiah's time, when the walls of Jerusalem were built by men with arms in hand. Thus we are told that "at the arrival therefore of the first men carried over, proper officers shall mark and cause to be entrenched a square of land, in just proportion to their number; on the outsides of this square, within the little bastions or redoubts of the entrenchment, they raise light timber dwellings, cutting down the trees which everywhere encompass them. The officers are quartered with the men whom they command, and the governor-in-chief is placed exactly in the centre. By these means the laboring people (being so disposed, as to be always watchful of an enemies' approach) are themselves within the eye of those set over them, and all together under the inspection of their principal.

"The redoubts may be near enough to defend each other with muskets, but field pieces and patareros will be planted upon each, kept charged with cartridge shot and pieces of old iron; within these redoubts are the common dwellings of the men who must defend them; between them runs a palisadoed bank and a ditch which will be scoured by the artillery. One man in each redoubt kept night and day upon the guard will give alarm upon each occasion to the others at their work. So they cultivate their lands, secure their cattle, and follow their business with great ease and safety. Exactly in the centre of the inmost square will be a fort, defended by large cannon, pointing every way and capable of making strong resistance in case some quarter of the outward lines should chance to be surprised by any sudden accident which yet with tolerable care would be impracticable."

An elaborate plan was attached representing the form of settling the districts or county divisions in this "Margravate of Azilia," showing a just square of twenty miles on each side, arranged somewhat like a checkerboard. On the outside are the fortifications guarded by cannon, and defended by men who in time of peace were to be employed in cultivating the lands of the margrave running around the plat next to the fortifications, being a strip a mile across. These people were to be hired in Great Britain or Ireland, taken over for a term of years, and given a life estate in the strip of land next within the margrave's and two miles in width, also running quite around the plat. Two great streets or roads run across from north to south and from east to west, meeting in a city in the centre, in the midst of which is the margrave's castle or fort. The city itself is four miles square, being encircled by a kind of park, and vis-à-vis the corners of the city are four great parks or forests, each four miles square, for herds of cattle, while all the rest of the land is divided by streets into one hundred and sixteen squares, each thus a mile on each side less the highways between. These were to be the estates of the gentry of the district, all of whom would thus have equal tracts, six hundred and forty acres each, and should therefore be emulous of outdoing each other in improvement.

All that materialized were the plan for sections of six hundred and forty acres and the movement to aid the distressed, and these not by Sir Robert Mountgomery; for, although extensively advertised, few or no colonists applied, and the plan remained one of those paper schemes not infrequent in colonization. Whether the war with Spain had anything to do with this or not we do not know, although it would seem an inappropriate time to colonize a district claimed by her; at all events, in three years the plan died a natural death. It seems incredible that any scheme should die for lack of encouragement at the epoch of the South Sea Bubble, the contemporary and in some sense offshoot of Law's great Mississippi Bubble. It may be that the attention of the British, and especially of the Scotch, was diverted from colonization by the disaster of Darien.

We are accustomed to date the Industrial Revolution, as it is sometimes called, from about the year 1760, when England had again been successful in war by sea and land and her released energies were about turning into the industrial channels which marked three successive years by the beginning of the Wedgwood potteries, the invention by Hargreaves of the spinning jenny, and by Watts of the steam engine. This, of course, was true, but it was in a sense only the consummation of an industrial movement begun not long after the Peace of Utrecht. These inventions came to fill a need, as inventions always come, and the need was caused by increase of population, of industry, and of commerce. The towns became larger, and Liverpool began to supersede the more southern ports of the kingdom. And yet old statutes remained almost the same. Not only did the poor laws press heavily, but imprisonment for debt was common, as it remained until the time of Charles Dickens.

Among the generals of James II. had been Theophilus Oglethorpe, and his son James Edward was ensign in the English army during the last years of the War of the Spanish Succession, despite the Jacobite leaning of the family. The young Englishman remained under Prince Eugene until the conclusion of the later war with Spain, and some years after became a member of the House of Commons for Haslemere in Surrey, which he represented for thirty-two years to come. Pope praised his strong benevolence of soul and it was certainly shown in his examination of the prisons, for it occurred to him that those who were there for debt could be paid out and transferred to the colonies, to make happy and useful citizens instead of expensive outcasts. In looking around he selected the southern part of Carolina as a territory suitable in itself for such a use and the more available because the Carolinians desired a colony between them and the Spaniards. Oglethorpe found other philanthropists like himself, and a petition to the Privy Council was favorably received and a royal charter issued June 9, 1732, in favor of Percival, Oglethorpe, and eighteen other trustees, who were constituted a body corporate for establishing the colony of Georgia in America. The land from the Savannah southwardly to Altamaha River, and from their heads westwardly to the South Sea was acquired. The scheme was strictly benevolent, and religious thought and worship were to be free to all except Romanists. The trustees were to administer affairs for twenty-one years, after which the crown would prescribe the government. The trustees adopted a seal, on one side of which were silkworms, with the motto: *Non sibi sed aliis.* Contributions were solicited, £10,000 granted by Parliament, and an account was opened with the Bank of England. Among other provisions, lands in the colony were to descend in tail-male, spirituous liquors were forbidden, and slavery was prohibited,—this last was the more remarkable, because based both upon moral and industrial reasons. Colonists came from the distressed classes, but only after investigation, and in the fall of the year Oglethorpe left England in the *Anne* with one hundred and thirty persons, representing thirty-five families, and made up of carpenters, bricklayers, farmers, and mechanics. They proceeded by way of Madeira, where they took on five tuns of wine, which in some way was not considered to come under the head of spirituous liquors. They arrived off Charlestown in the middle of January, 1733, whence the *Anne* was taken to Port Royal and the colonists to Beaufort. Meantime, Oglethorpe and William Bull of Carolina explored Savannah River and chose as the site of the new colony Yamacraw Bluff, rising forty feet above the river and fronting the water for nearly a mile. It was the first high ground found upon the stream, and selected for the same reason that had influenced the choice of Charlestown and of Mobile. The surroundings were good, despite marshes, and of especial value to the settlers was the neighboring Yamacraw village, for its chief, Tomochichi, took an interest in the colony from the beginning. Through Mary Musgrove, wife of a Carolina trader on this spot, Oglethorpe secured a cession of the lands he wished, and brought his people over in the first days of February. Unlike most colonies heretofore, Savannah was laid out as a city and not primarily as a fort. On the earliest plan a fort looks to the woodside, and a guardhouse appears with a battery of cannon before it on the bluff, but these are only incidentals, and the real interest of the plat is in the broad streets and squares, the stairs and landing places, crane and bell, the parsonage and plot of ground to build the church, the house for stores, guard, mill, and bake houses, and the draw-well for water; while in front of all, under five pine trees, we see Oglethorpe's tent, whence he could supervise the whole. The plan of Savannah seems to have been somewhat changed before long, for the first one above alluded to gives unbroken streets crossing at right angles, while the existing city has from time immemorial shown, almost alternating with business blocks, a checkerboard of small parks, crossed, it is true, by walks, but not intersected by the streets which come up to them. The object of this was healthfulness, although because it became a serious interruption to traffic the plan was not carried out in the modern extensions of the city. Each

James Edward Oglethorpe. *From the engraving by W. Greatback, after an original in possession of George Wymberly Jones.*

inhabitant was to receive fifty acres, and this consisted of the town lot, sixty by ninety feet, a garden lot of five acres adjoining the town, and a farm further out of forty-four acres and one hundred and forty-one poles; all such allotments have long since been absorbed and covered by lots and streets. It is curious to see thus surviving, all unknown to these philanthropists, the plan of the old village community, with its three divisions of lands.

The first thing every colony has had to consider was the attitude of the Indians. The Spaniards in this vicinity had carried off Indians, while the French had managed at Port Royal to retain their friendship in part. Tradition made a mound just outside of Savannah to be a tomb, where an Indian king was buried on the spot where he talked with Sir Walter Raleigh, for the Indians deemed the place of the conversation with that great good man to be holy ground,—although Sir Walter, as is generally believed, had not been in North America. Oglethorpe profited by the lessons of the past, particularly as they accorded with his own instincts, and he proceeded to conciliate the Indians. He ascertained who were the leading chiefs of the territory covered by the charter, and, with the assistance of Tomochichi, assembled them in a congress in May. On the 21st these Creeks ceded lands between the Savannah and the Altamaha from the ocean to the head of tidewater, including the islands from Tybee to St. Simon's except the three named Ossabaw, Sapelo, and St. Catherine's, which the Indians preferred to keep for hunting, fishing, and other purposes, clearly showing that no Spaniards remained on them. This treaty was recognized as valid, for the Yamacraws were an offshoot or dependency of the Creeks, and none of the other tribes claimed the territory; and the result was that the province of Georgia had less trouble in Indian affairs than any other colony,—and this due largely to the friendliness of Tomochichi.

Other colonists came from time to time, for soon £10,000 of the proceeds of land sales in the island of

St. Christopher was by the House of Commons turned over to the trustees toward defraying the charges of carrying and settling foreign Protestants. The trustees were thus enabled to extend their philanthropic plans so as to embrace people from the continent, and, just as South Carolina had become the home of Huguenots driven from France, Georgia became the home of Salzburgers, Lutherans expatriated from the Austrian Alps by religious persecution. They were neither fanatics nor beggars. They loved their old homes and clung to the mountains until it was clear, through many persecutions, official and private, that they must give up their religion or leave their country. They found a home temporarily in Germany, and now, after negotiations with the trustees of Georgia, they came, under Baron von Reck and their pastors Bolzius and Gronau, as British subjects to America. In March, 1734, the ship *Purisburg* brought seventy-eight of them to Savannah, where they were welcomed by cannon and huzzas, not to mention a very good dinner, so that "all were full of joy and praised God." Their agent had selected a site above Savannah, which they soon built up as Ebenezer, in the present county of Effingham; and next year fifty-seven more came over in the *Prince of Wales*, and others later. The soil was not fertile, for it was a pine barren, so that they afterward with Oglethorpe's consent built New Ebenezer on the main river. A number of Moravians also came over, under Spangenberg, and were settled between Ebenezer and Savannah. Although of a somewhat different faith, these foreign colonists became very friendly and both presented pictures of industry and even thrift not always shown elsewhere in Georgia. The Moravians came to convert the Indians, laboring with the zeal of that remarkable church, which has more missionaries abroad than pastors at home, all things to all men, and fearing neither the pole nor the tropics.

Oglethorpe now returned to England for conference with the trustees, and took with him Tomochichi and some others. The popular interest in the Indians advanced the objects of the trust, and the effect upon Tomochichi was such as to aid the colony very much after his return to America.

In order for Georgia to form a home for distressed Protestants, it was necessary not only to conciliate the Indians, as had been successfully done, but to fortify it against the Catholic Spanish, who had never abandoned their claim up to the thirty-third degree of north latitude. Parliament made a grant of £26,000 for the purpose of settling, fortifying, and defending the new colony, and the trustees caused an agent to recruit through the Highlands of Scotland, where he secured one hundred and thirty men, besides women and children, of good report and good fighting qualities. The wars of the Pretender had carried distress and persecution among the Scottish mountains, and were not yet over; so that the party were not loath to remove with their pastor, John McLeod of Skye. Oglethorpe placed them on the left bank of the Altamaha, where they built a little town which they called New Inverness, while the district in which it was situated was known as Darien. Their fort was named after King George, and it was connected by road with Fort Argyle on the right bank of Ogeechee River, which from the earliest days guarded the approach to Savannah from the west.

The early history of Georgia, therefore, is that of separate colonies sent over by the trustees to settle in different places north and south of Savannah. Vessels came from time to time, bringing additions to the different settlers, as in 1736 thirty-five Moravians under their bishop, David Nitschman, and many others. The coming of these was of special interest in that with them came the brothers Charles and John Wesley, who learned much that was spiritual on the voyage over, which subsequently was to have something to do with not only their own lives but with those of millions in England and America. In a different way, too, the bulk of this particular party contributed to the history of Georgia by laying out the new town of Frederica on the island of St. Simon's. Frederica was laid off with care and became the future residence of Oglethorpe, which was somewhat the cause of criticism. The main street was twenty-five yards wide, and on it each free inhabitant had a lot of sixty by ninety feet, although some who fronted the river had smaller lots. For temporary purposes palmetto booths were erected, and such vegetables planted as the season admitted. The houses were made of tabby, and thus were more substantial than those built of wood at Savannah. An embankment was built around and batteries placed to protect against enemies; and there was need for care in its erection, for it was to be the southern outpost against the Spanish. Well were its streets given martial names, for the short life of the town was essentially warlike.

It will be remembered that the colony of Carolina had prior to this entered into extensive relations with the Indian tribes. Not only the Cherokees and Catawbas to the north were visited by traders, but a well-known path led westwardly by Fort Moore across Savannah River to the Creeks and Uchees. Policy as well as commercial instinct early led the Georgians to build a settlement opposite Fort Moore, having its own stockaded fort, and in compliment to the Princess of Wales this was named Augusta. Here gathered traders from Savannah as well as Charlestown, and hundreds of caravans passing in both directions made it their stopping place. Two thousand ponies are said to have been on the road. Savannah had the advantage of river connection and Charlestown that of prestige, and between the rivalry of the two the Indian trade flourished and Augusta became a lively place. The prohibition against the sale of liquor was not strictly enforced, although it was impossible to evade so easily that against slavery. Plantations across the river in Carolina were cultivated by negroes, and for a long time the country about Augusta was unable to compete.

The value of Indian friendship and commerce was appreciated by no one more than Oglethorpe, and one of the most important services rendered by him to his infant colony was the long trip to meet the Creeks at Coweta on the further side of Chattahoochee River. This brought the Indians well within British influence and established better than ever before the power of the traders. It will be remembered that the French had in 1714 founded Fort Toulouse on the Coosa, and Law's Compagnie had designed the reconstruction of this outpost. Although the plan was never carried out, its importance in counteracting British influence in trade and war was never overlooked, and now growing out of Oglethorpe's treaty came a rival British fort.

It seems the irony of fate that a colony established to aid the distressed and so successful in its relations with the aborigines of the country must be involved in the European war over the succession to the throne of Austria. Spain as usual had resented encroachments upon her trade, and in England the popular outcry over outrages became irresistible. The alleged mutilation of an ear of the trader Jenkins wrought the people to fury. The declaration of war was greeted in England by peals of bells, upon which Walpole exclaimed that they were ringing their bells, but soon would be wringing their hands. At all events, war came and, while Frederick the Great was wresting Silesia from Austria, Oglethorpe was preparing to capture St. Augustine. In 1737 he had been made colonel and became commander-in-chief of all forces in South Carolina and Georgia, to be used for their joint advantage. He had to take an even deeper interest, for the trust was not flourishing financially, and he could only raise men and means by pledging his own property. Finally, he collected troops numbering about two thousand, with artillery, and in May, 1740, set sail for Florida. Jenkins's "ear" was bringing a storm down about the heads of the American Spaniards.

San Mateo had long since disappeared, and the furthest outpost of the Spaniards at this time was San Juan on the south side of the St. John's near its mouth, opposite the British fort of St. George nine miles away. The district about St. Augustine was a kind of peninsula, bounded north and west by the St. John's and east by the ocean, and St. Augustine, we recollect, was itself in a nest of waters. Coming in from the left was North or St. Mark's River, while from the south came the famous Matanzas, really an inlet from the sea and surrounding Anastasia Island. Immediately west of the town was San Sebastian Bayou, and little salt bayous through the marshes are to be found in all directions. Somewhat to the north was Fort Moosa and west on the St. John's was Picolata, two respectable forts, the last commanding the ford leading westwardly toward Appalachee. St. Augustine itself was protected by intrenchments and artillery, and Fort San Marcos had assumed its final form. It was the most impressive fortress of Florida and compared favorably with any south of Quebec. In the shape of a rough square, with bastions at the corners, and a lookout toward the entrance of the inlet, the fort had a parapet nine feet thick, and a casemated rampart twenty feet high, with a curtain sixty yards long, all guarded by fifty cannon, of which sixteen were brass and others were twenty-four pounders. There was a covered way also, although this was not completed.

Military operations from the north could be conducted in one of two ways. The depth of the St. John's was such that vessels could go up to Picolata and attack St. Augustine from the rear; in fact, Oglethorpe had previously captured Picolata and urged this plan upon the Carolinians as the best mode of operations. Another would be for his troops to march down the peninsula from San Juan and invest St. Augustine by land while the fleet attacked it from the sea.

It is difficult to make out the details of all movements of this campaign, or rather to understand their meaning. Oglethorpe certainly was indefatigable, and it may well be that he undertook too much himself, with the result that in the course of the season he fell sick of fever, and operations were not carried on properly. His biographers lay the blame largely on the delay of the South Carolina troops and their insubordination when they did come. On the other hand, an investigation by the Assembly of South Carolina claims that everybody was to blame except the South Carolinians. They say that Oglethorpe had no commissariat, that the fleet imagined difficulties which did not exist, and finally sailed off long before any danger of the stormy season. Possibly the truth lies between the two extremes.

Oglethorpe gave up his original plan of attacking by way of Picolata, and marched his troops by land from San Juan in order to keep in touch with the fleet. They seized a cattle pen and the so-called Fort Diego, and an accusation was made that its owner, the mulatto Don Diego Spinola, managed to obtain considerable influence over the English general. Fort Moosa was taken with little or no opposition and garrisoned, perhaps insufficiently, by men under Colonel Palmer, and the Carolinians under Vander Dussen were placed at Point Quartell at the mouth of the harbor. At the suggestion of the naval officers, Oglethorpe now transferred the bulk of his troops to Anastasia Island, and, unfortunately, Palmer's men disobeyed orders to remain outside the dismantled Fort Moosa and were massacred by the Indians. This enabled the Spaniards to communicate more freely now with the country. At his new post on the island, Oglethorpe threw up intrenchments and with cannon and mortars bombarded the town and fort. Little damage was done, and the bar of the channel prevented the larger ships from coming close enough to be of much service. The fort was repeatedly struck, but the soft stone closed over the balls without suffering damage. The marks of the bombardment remain until this day on the outer walls of Fort San Marcos. Even Vander Dussen was transferred to the island, and the blockade of the lower end of Matanzas River, the scene of Ribault's massacre, was abandoned or so relaxed that aid reached the town from Havana. Oglethorpe seems to have tried to keep the Indians under too great restraint, reproaching them as barbarous dogs for bringing a head of a hostile Indian and even objecting to their killing the cattle of the enemy.

Oglethorpe had passed over to the south side of St. John's River on May 9th. His troops landed on the island before the middle of June, and on the 29th bad weather obliged the men-of-war to put to sea. Upon this there was nothing to do except to raise the siege, and on the 4th of July this was accordingly done, although against the protest of Vander Dussen. On the 21st of July Oglethorpe crossed to Fort George and thence marched to Frederica. The Carolinians seem to have conducted a very creditable retreat, securing some things that Oglethorpe had overlooked.

Such was the end of the most formidable invasion the English ever undertook against Florida. Its issue was unfortunate and Oglethorpe was much criticised. It has been pointed out that during the rebellion of 1745 he exhibited a somewhat similar want of capacity and suffered a court martial, which, however, acquitted him. He was never given an important command, although he finally rose to the grade of general. His bravery and energy are unquestionable, but it is possible that he was not a great commander.

As in the case of Charlestown, the Spaniards waited long enough to recuperate, and then prepared a counter-expedition against Georgia. Oglethorpe was apprehensive enough to write to the Duke of Newcastle that all he could do if attacked was to die bravely in his majesty's service. The opportunity was presented, for in June, 1742, a fleet of fifty-one Spanish vessels, bearing almost five thousand troops, commanded by Monteano, appeared off St. Simon's. In resisting this invasion, Oglethorpe appeared to greater advantage, and certainly had greater success than in his attack upon St. Augustine. He had only six hundred and fifty men and a few small boats, but by strategy succeeded in less than a month in effecting a repulse which Whitefield declared could not be paralleled outside of the Old Testament. Frederica was saved and with it all Georgia. Although they never abandoned their claim to Orysta and

Guale, never again did the Spaniards attempt to drive the English out. As both sides had been unsuccessful in their invasions, the provisions of the Peace of Aix-la-Chapelle in 1748 for restitution of all captures had no effect in this quarter of the globe; but the peace relieved the colonies from the necessity of keeping up the forts to the south. Even Frederica soon fell into decay.

The most remarkable document of the day was by Patrick Tailfer, who, with companions, was compelled to leave the province, and then printed at Charlestown in 1741 a history of Georgia, representing the colony as mismanaged from the beginning. The book has been called "cool, poised, polite, and merciless," and, while probably not justifiable throughout, throws an interesting light upon the condition and views of some of the colonists. Oglethorpe himself retired from active administration in 1743 and returned to England, where he lived to a ripe old age, honored by all who knew him. Edmund Burke regarded him as the most extraordinary person of whom he had read, and Dr. Johnson admired him so much as to wish to write his life.

In the colony there had been some trouble due to the default of Causton, treasurer of Savannah. In the year of Tailfer's pamphlet, William Stephens, who had been secretary for the trustees, was appointed president of the county of Savannah, aided by four assistants, while about Augusta the peace was kept by Richard Kent, the conservator. After Oglethorpe left, the trustees extended the duty of the president and assistants of Savannah to the whole colony, which made the venerable William Stephens governor. He left an extensive journal, which details the history of the period with great minuteness.

The matters of chief interest henceforward were of domestic concern. The colony cannot really be said to have flourished for these first twenty years, and there were others besides Tailfer who laid part of the blame on the regulations as to slaves, liquor, and land tenure. The influence even of George Whitefield and James Habersham was thrown in favor of a change, for Whitefield became a convert in earnest to the view Hawkins had perhaps expressed to Queen Elizabeth half in jest, that removing negroes from barbarous Africa to Christian America was for their own good. The result of the agitation was that the trustees removed all three restrictions. Slaves were permitted and also the sale of liquor, while, instead of being held in tail-male, lands were permitted to be alienated without restriction. From this time Georgia began to assume her proper rank. It is true that the silkworms belied the motto on the seal, for their existence was more for themselves than for the benefit of the colony, despite efforts in the direction of silk culture. Nor did the wine and olive do much better. Hemp, flax, lumber, and cotton were hardly more than names, and up to the introduction of slavery the stores brought from England were perhaps the chief reliance of many of the people. Even money had been scarce and coin unknown, except copper. Henceforward, however, improvement was rapid.

It will be recalled that the brothers Wesley had been in Georgia, attracted in part by the desire to convert the Indians. They were able to effect little in this direction, but had their hands full with the whites. John had lived in Savannah and Charles in Frederica, and the fullest account of their lives and aims is in John Wesley's *Journal* of this time. In 1738 came the beginning of Methodism in London, and the Wesleys were soon at the head of the movement which not only created a new and increasing sect, but revived religion to a very large extent in the Church of England and among all other denominations. An even greater preacher than Wesley was George Whitefield, who at first acted with him, but afterward led a movement along more strictly Calvinistic lines. Whitefield followed Wesley to Georgia, and with a curious misapplication of energy devoted himself in 1740 to the establishment of Bethesda, an Orphan House in a colony where the population was sparse and children without means of support must have been few; in fact, Whitefield later tried to have his institution turned more into a school or college, although without much success. He returned several times to America, electrifying vast audiences, planning ever for his Orphan House. Thus Georgia in a way shared in the great missionary movement of the eighteenth century, as was not inappropriate for an enterprise whose trustees, like the old Virginia Company, regularly heard sermons. They believed that except God build the house they labor in vain that build it.

In 1751 Henry Parker became president on the retirement of Stephens, and his term is remarkable for the first Assembly of Georgia. It was composed of sixteen delegates, presided over by Francis Harris, and met at Savannah. It was a legislature not empowered to legislate, it is true, for the charter vested that right in the trustees alone, but its members did not fail to discuss and suggest measures which they deemed for the advantage of the colony, and these were considered and to some extent adopted by the trustees. Appropriately with the advent of a legislature came the end of the trust, for the trustees, who had borne the burden and the heat of the day for so long a time, all with philanthropic motives, now considered that the colony had advanced far enough to be turned over to the crown, and, although the twenty-one years' period limited by the charter had not yet arrived, they on June 23, 1752, surrendered the same. At this time the population consisted of two thousand three hundred and eighty-one whites, besides one thousand and thirty-six slaves, not including troops and some outlying settlers. To this had grown the little community begun from Yamacraw Bluff, and it would seem to have outlasted its external dangers.

And yet, this was not certain. The Latin nations had often shown powers of recuperation, and the more the Georgians extended toward the interior, the further traders carried their wares, the more powerful hold they might seek to have upon the Indians, the nearer they would draw to the French of Toulouse and Mobile, the more their future might become linked with the great valley across the mountains. French fleets might succeed where Spanish failed. Founded as a buffer colony, Georgia was still between hammer and anvil, the French on the west and the Spanish on the south, now closely united in their Family Compact.

CHAPTER XVII

ANGLO-FRENCH RIVALRY IN THE VALLEY

THE Peace of Utrecht ended the War of the Spanish Succession. Philip V. remained king, and yet, although the autonomy of the Spanish people was respected and their right to select their own rulers recognized, it was a dear-bought victory for Spain and her great ally. Spanish possessions outside of Spain itself were curtailed; France was shortened on the east and her colonial expansion checked. Worse still, the losses in America were not so serious as was the paralysis which came in all departments of the government. Louis XIV. was a great man, as one can see even in Saint-Simon's memoirs, but it was a greatness which showed itself only on occasions. He was given to favoritism, and toward the end of his life public and private misfortune tended to put him out of touch with his suffering people, or at least caused him to lose the initiative necessary to reform and rebuild his exhausted country. His death was none too soon, and the Duc d'Orléans as regent hardly had the power or ability to improve greatly the situation.

As for America, the delimitation of boundaries or of spheres of influence was not accurate; indeed, the interior of America at that time was itself very little known. The provisions of the treaty of Utrecht related mainly to Hudson Bay, Newfoundland, and Acadia, which were ceded by France to England, and nothing was said about the Great Lakes or the Mississippi valley. Whatever rights either country had there remained the same as before. It was only provided that "the subjects of France inhabiting Canada, and others, shall hereafter give no hindrance or molestation to the five nations or cantons of Indians, subject to the dominion of Great Britain, nor to the other natives of America, who are friends to the same. In like manner, the subjects of Great Britain shall behave themselves peaceably towards the Americans who are subjects or friends to France; and on both sides they shall enjoy full liberty of going and coming on account of trade. As also the natives of those countries shall, with the same liberty, resort, as they please, to the British and French colonies, for promoting trade on one side and the other, without any molestation or hindrance, either on the part of the British subjects or of the French. But it is to be exactly and distinctly settled by commissaries, who are, and ought to be, accounted the subjects and friends of Britain or of France."

With this very indefinite fifteenth article the two high contracting parties contented themselves. The important thing about the Peace of Utrecht was not so much what was written on paper as the relative conditions and outlook of France and England. France possessed the valleys of St. Lawrence and Mississippi Rivers, whose sources were not far apart and were closely connected by the interlacing portage systems. If the French should increase in numbers and influence and build up these valleys and make the Illinois and Ohio countries fully their own by settlements and commerce, the interior would be essentially French. On the other hand, the English were by geographical conditions confined between the Alleghany Mountains and the Atlantic Ocean, and, if they could be kept to this seaboard strip, British colonization would have to seek other quarters of the world; while if the British colonies grew and expanded across the mountains into the Ohio and Mississippi valleys more rapidly than the French, the link connecting Canada and Louisiana would be broken, and these two provinces would have to develop separately, if at all. If at all, because should British population and energy seize the Great Lakes and the Ohio valley, it would be questionable whether the mouths of the St. Lawrence and the Mississippi could remain in other hands. It is true that in Europe Holland lay at the mouth of the Rhine and yet had achieved and maintained her independence; but it is also true that when this was done Germany was disorganized and the stream itself a bone of contention with France. Neither one was willing to see the other possess it. Of course, the New World boundary question was not consciously in the minds of either French or English statesmen, for America was hardly of sufficient importance to be in the minds of either. To us, looking back, the successive steps are of more interest than to kings and generals to whom a fort in Flanders or a castle in Italy loomed so large in its nearness as to shut off countries across the ocean. It was a contest of national tendencies rather than of national intentions. The Mississippi valley was to become either a French colony or dependency, with or without connection with Canada, or it was to be a hinterland for the transmontane expansion of the British Atlantic colonies. This was the question set by Providence before the two races, and was to be worked out gradually. It was to be like the coming in of the tide, a progress, but with such flux and reflux of waves as to make the advance at any particular time almost imperceptible.

The question could be solved by war, but European diplomats thought too little of America for this to be worth while. It was left to settle itself, and this meant turning it over to the gradual growth of population and the hardly more conscious growth of trade. It is true that religion was sometimes thought to play a part. The Catholic colonists of Maryland, interposed between the Protestants of all shades north and south of them, were supposed to be favorable to the French, and their influence was dreaded the more especially because their country stretched far back into the interior and by means of the Potomac valley offered a fairly practicable means of communication between the ocean and the Ohio. The Jesuits were supposed to be active along this route, and yet, despite perhaps some individual cases, there was no reason to doubt the loyalty of the Catholics of Maryland to British interests.

We ordinarily think of the New Englander as the typical trader, and in the long run he had a great deal to say about the settlement of the Ohio and the Mississippi valleys. But here our prepossessions must be set aside. The New Englander was cut off from the Ohio by the New Yorker and the Pennsylvanian, who themselves were almost shut out from the great valley by the widely spreading ranges of the Alleghanies. Similarly, we do not ordinarily think of the Southerners as essentially commercial, and yet it was the Virginian and the Carolinian traders who first found passes through the Alleghanies to Tennessee, Cumberland, and Ohio Rivers, and by means of the Cherokees, Creeks, and Chickasaws checked French diplomacy and French development in the interior. The spectacular progress of Governor Spotswood to the mountain country of Virginia in 1716, when he stood upon the Blue Ridge and saw the beautiful Shenandoah Valley lying before him, untrodden save by wild beasts and by parties of the Tuscaroras and their foes, is justly thought of as a turning point in Virginian history. His eyes took seizin of that fair country to the west, and from that time the white man's longing for its undiscovered bourne became a passion. But the way had been blazed by English traders already. Bienville had early found them upon the Mississippi, and later they were only more numerous and influential. Even before the settlement of Georgia, Fort Moore was the place of assembly of Indians and the point of departure of traders. It was near the Lower Creeks, and it was with a just foresight that Bienville in 1714 seized upon a dispute between the English and the Creeks to build his outpost Fort Toulouse high up on the Alabama waters where the Coosa and the Tallapoosa, there hardly half a mile apart, drained fertile countries thickly settled by the Alibamons and allied tribes. From that

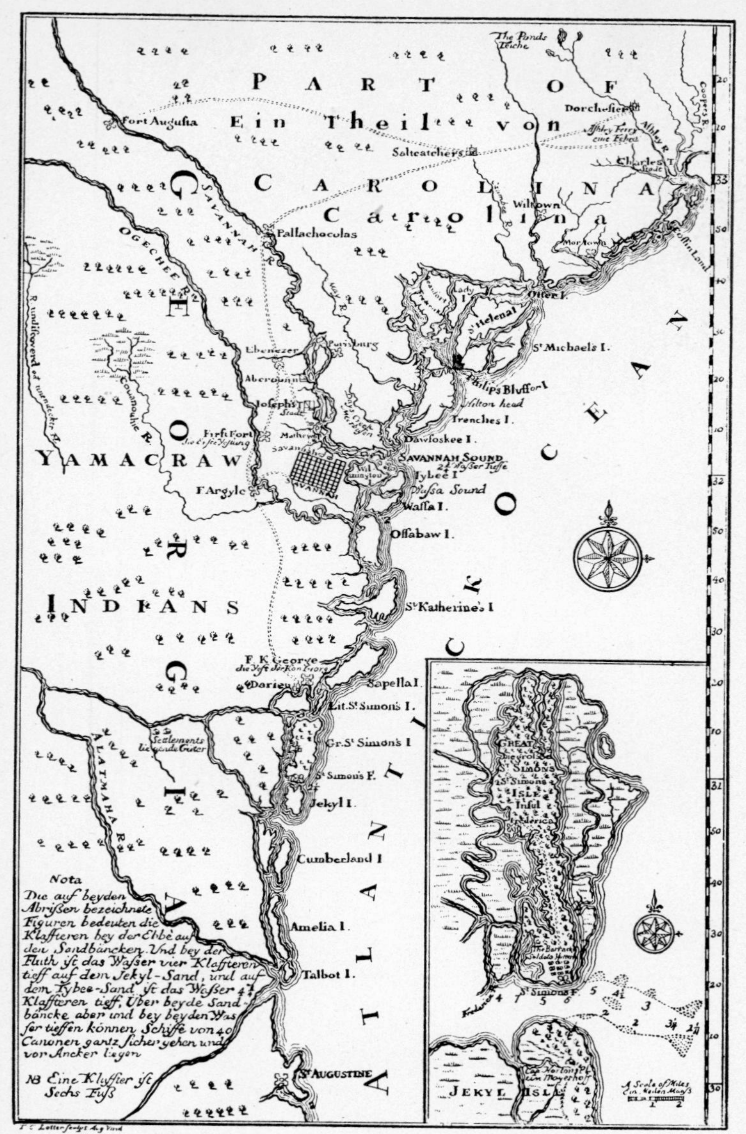

Early German map of the Carolinas and Georgia, engraved by T. C. Lotter, issued by Matthew Seutter at Augsburg in the early part of the eighteenth century. *From the original in the private collection of Julius F. Sachse, Esq*

time Adair, who was so long among the Chickasaws, dates the decline of British influence. Previously, the traders had come freely by Indian trails across country from Fort Moore and elsewhere to Coosa and other towns of the Creeks, and by the Tennessee to the Chickasaws and tribes of the west. This fort, Alabahma, as he calls it, interrupted the traffic and drove the traders to the more difficult hill country further north. To protect the new route and regain their influence the British built, hardly forty miles away, Fort Okfuske, and the rivalry of Toulouse and Okfuske has more than a local interest and importance. Thus it is that the rivalry of the French and English in the Mississippi valley, and more particularly at the headwaters of Ohio, Tennessee, and Alabama Rivers, was to decide the fate of the continent. We have noticed that it was in the southern part of the valley that this conflict was more intense, and it must not be forgotten also that it was all to the east of the Mississippi.

The Indian policies of the two nations were different. The French regarded the natives as subjects of their king, although on a lower plane of civilization and in a system of quasi-tutelage. The government sent or encouraged missionaries among the Indians, and trade was largely in the hands of the military commanders, although there were trading posts not strictly military. Gradually, the whole country, from the mountains to the Mississippi, from the lakes to the headwaters of the Gulf streams, was permeated by military or trading posts, all conducted by the French government or in some sense responsible to it, and in this way what was done was largely within the control and knowledge of the French authorities. It is true that from the beginning there were numerous *coureurs de bois*, who bought furs and other peltries from the Indians and brought them, mainly by canoe down the rivers, to New Orleans, Biloxi, or Mobile. These men were rather more than half-savages themselves. They married Indian women, or lived with them according to Indian customs, and were frequent thorns in the flesh of the Jesuits and other fathers, introducing liquor, and by their example counteracting the teaching of the missionaries. Nor were they much more amenable to the civil authority, and we have seen from time to time the attempts of the colonial governors to restrain them. But even they in a measure aided the French policy, for they supplied a bridge between civilization and savagery and showed that the French and Indian could pass insensibly one into the other. Unwittingly, they were a connecting link between the palace of Versailles and the wigwams of America.

In the priest was found another great factor for extending French influence. It would be an injustice to the Récollets, the missionaries of Quebec, and the Jesuits to think of them as aiming at the aggrandizement of France. As men, they shared the feelings of their countrymen, but most of them were missionaries in the true sense of the word, seeking the spiritual salvation of the natives, although to the extent that they made the savages familiar with French wares, language, and customs they forwarded the purposes of the French officials. And this counted for much, so that they may be fairly named as a part of the influence exerted by the French against the English.

The British traders, often Scotch, were men who carried goods, perhaps originally made in England, over the mountain ranges and portages from the Atlantic to the headwaters of the Ohio. Singly or in caravans, their jingling mules and pack-horses brought hatchets, firearms, beads, blankets, and whiskey to the waiting Indians, taking back in return furs, skins, and other native products. The essential difference between the two methods of trade was that the British traders were not government agents. There was not even general oversight on the part of the government in early times, and no cohesion between the different colonies in such matters. From 1746 we find Sir William Johnson acting in New York as colonial superintendent of Indian affairs. He was an Irishman who had come over to America to look after an estate on the borders of civilization and there gradually worked himself into the esteem of Indians and whites alike.

There was at the South no corresponding official, and yet in James Adair we have a man analogous to Johnson. He lived at one time in Charlestown, and Charlestown was to be for long not only the principal city in the Southern colonies but the chief seat of Indian trade to the west. In the earliest days there were traders from Virginia, but the relations of the Virginians with the Indians were generally hostile. We recollect that the Powhatans and other tribes in Virginia were practically extinguished, and that as early as 1713 a war with the Tuscaroras of North Carolina drove them north to become the sixth nation of the Iroquois. The great Indian tribes of the eighteenth century east of the Sioux and the Mississippi were, besides the Iroquois, the Cherokees in the Appalachian range, holding the passes and the headwaters of rivers flowing to the Mississippi and to the Atlantic; the Creeks to the southwest, forming the Muskhogee confederacy controlling the Alabama and its sources; the Chickasaws extending from the upper Tombigbee to the Yazoo; and the French-loving Choctaws nearer the Gulf. To these may be added the Catawbas east of the Cherokees, but they were gradually diminished by wars with the Iroquois and had ceased to play an important part. The field was thus left clear for the Carolinians, and Charlestown on the English side and Mobile on the French were the great claimants for the Indian trade. There was no supervision of the traders from Carolina before 1716, and even after the proprietors undertook the business themselves it was not exclusive. The route from Charlestown to the west divided, one branch going to the Creeks and the other to the Cherokees. Where the first crossed Savannah River was early built Fort Moore, and from the time of the Cherokee embassy to England a fort was planned for that tribe. James Adair, from 1735, among the Cherokees, and later among the Chickasaws, was by his personal influence supplying the lack of any fort. Oglethorpe founded Augusta opposite Fort Moore about this time, but it was not until much later that Fort Prince George was built at Keowee among the Cherokees.

On the French side, the *coureurs de bois* and traders coexisted among the natives, but on the British, while the traders lived among the natives, there were few wood rangers, for their hunters were of a later date and will be found generally to be hostile to the natives. The pioneers of the two civilizations were therefore principally the traders; and their rivalries, could they be traced, would be an interesting chapter in the development of America, especially the trans-Alleghany country. Little, however, can now be made out. The French had one or more trading stations or *magasins* about Muscle Shoals, where their commerce from Mobile and New Orleans met British competition from higher up the Tennessee. On or near the present site of Nashville a Frenchman named Charleville had a well-known station from at least 1714, while five years later we hear, on the other hand, of the English on the Wabash and even on the Illinois. The western Cherokees on the Little Tennessee were much influenced by the French, and at one time there was a French fort or station not far from Chota, the "beloved town." We do not learn of many traders of either nation in the country between the Cumberland and the Ohio, largely no doubt from the fact that there were few Indians there. It was a region claimed by the Cherokees from the south and the Iroquois from the north, but it was really more of a fighting and hunting ground than anything else. The great salt licks were the favorite resorts of buffaloes and other wild animals, and these grew and multiplied undisturbed save by occasional expeditions of the red men. The French at one period held Fort Assumption at Chickasaw Bluffs on the Mississippi, Paducah at the mouth of Cumberland River, and in 1734 they made an expedition to Big Bone Lick. The Shawnees have left traces in different parts of the country, but for a number of years prior to 1700 they were found about the lower Tennessee and Cumberland Rivers, whence Iberville wished to attract them to the Illinois. Warring with both the Cherokees and the Chickasaws, but friendly to the French, in the early part of the eighteenth century the Shawnees found their situation intolerable and gradually migrated to the Wabash and the Scioto. This was somewhat a blow to the French policy, for it left the Chickasaws less controlled and more subject to the English influence; but still, as a rule, the French could claim all streams running west of the mountains as draining their territory. It has been said that a spring named Herbert's, a half-mile above the source of Savannah River, ran into a tributary of the Tennessee and was thus French water; and a traveller from Carolina, leaving Broad River behind him, naturally named the similar stream he soon found running west the French Broad. To such extent had French influence proceeded that in 1734 the Carolina legislature memorialized the king to the effect that not only had the French built "Fort Thoulous" among the Upper Creeks and seduced other Indians with liberal presents, but they had even made the Cherokee nation insolent to British traders, and that circumstances called for building forts on the part of the British. And this, be it remembered, was after Governor Nicholson had in 1721 made a treaty with the chieftains of thirty-seven towns and appointed an agent to reside among the Creeks, and only four years after Sir Alexander Cumming had visited the Cherokees at Nequassee and taken six chiefs to England to do homage to the great king.

It is instructive to get together in a single view the principles of French colonization in the interior of America. France had the waterways of the St. Lawrence and the Mississippi, connected by the portages through the Wisconsin, the Illinois, and the Wabash Rivers, besides those further to the east controlled by the Iroquois. In rainy seasons it was actually possible to pass from the lakes to some of these streams without any portage at all, so little watershed was there between the two systems, thus realizing the idea of an old Spanish cartographer that both the St. Lawrence and the Mississippi took their rise in the Great Lakes. The St. Lawrence ran through rocky soil which was not the habitat of the maize, so that one would not expect the best results of colonization in that direction. The Mississippi valley, on the other hand, possessed fertile lands, and everywhere the maize flourished.

The French have ever been the best explorers of the globe. In America they blazed the way along which other nations followed, and the secrets of the interior wilderness were known to them long before the blundering English came. And yet, at the time of which we speak they had sent to Louisiana far fewer colonists, and these less productive, than had the British. France could not spare so many, or her people did not wish to leave for other homes, or both causes combined to keep down the number of her settlers. It would look as if instinctively the French aimed at organization, perhaps civilization, of the natives, among whom, on the whole, they had greater influence than their competitors. We have seen how Iberville counted on transplanting whole tribes to new situations near French forts, and organizing of them an empire. The missionaries aimed at gathering about their missions the natives, in families if not in tribes, and taught agriculture not less than the rudiments of religion, although less successfully than the Spanish padres. The French intermarried with the natives, while such a relation was not recognized by British law. Thus we find that the French themselves did not immigrate in great numbers, and they endeavored to make quasi-colonists of the Indians themselves. Up to this time it was not certain how the experiment would end. It was a question yet to be worked out, and even if the French could only utilize the warriors against the British they would command a strong force in time of war. On the other hand, while the British did not explore so well and so far, when they built a fort or a post it was not so much the means of influence among the natives as the foundation of a settlement, of homes for themselves. The test was now to come between the two methods of colonization.

Looking over this field of rivalry, we find that the French made good their hold on the Choctaws and Creeks mainly by peaceful methods. From the beginning the Choctaws, disturbed only for a short time by Adair, were friendly to them. While at the first there had been hostility on the part of the Alibamons, and in 1708 an invasion by the Indians from the northeast, this had been futile and the Creeks were brought firmly within the sphere of French influence by the erection of Fort Toulouse. The Chickasaws and the Cherokees were, and perhaps unavoidably, unfriendly to the French. It seemed to be an essential feature of Indian international relations that adjoining confederacies should be hostile. Naturally, therefore, whoever became the friend of the one could not well remain the friend of the other. Thus the Choctaws and Chickasaws were frequently at war, and if the French were allies of the Choctaws they could hardly be so with the Chickasaws. The Creeks and the Choctaws were also sometimes at war, but they occupied different river basins and conditions were not the same.

The Chickasaws were the thorn in the side of the French almost from the beginning, but particularly from the time that the Natches were driven from home and found a refuge among them. Resentment and English influence combined to prevent any real reconciliation. It is true the Chickasaws did by returning captives try to make their peace with the French, but Bienville not less than Périer was convinced that this warrior nation could only be conquered into friendliness. Bienville wrote home on his return to Louisiana in 1733 that "if we cannot gain over this nation it will be necessary to drive it away from the territory of the colony." As part of this policy he stirred up hostilities between the Choctaws and the Chickasaws, and while he refused to let D'Artaguette attack with one hundred French and the Choctaws from Mobile, he permitted Le Sueur with fewer French and more Choctaws to go on the warpath.

Adair had been so successful among the Chickasaws that he had been commissioned to open trade with the Choctaws also, and he tells us that he was able to do so through the circumstance that the chieftain of Quansheto, Red Shoe by translation, or "Shulashummashtabe" in Choctaw, had conceived an intense resentment against the French on account of the action of a soldier from Fort Tombecbé. This man had become over intimate with Red Shoe's wife, and the illicit connection was discovered by the husband. The result was that Red Shoe visited Adair by invitation, and was readily convinced of the advantages of alliance with the English. There followed a Choctaw civil war, and, of course, greater boldness on the part of the Chickasaws.

The Chickasaw country was that tract of land, never rising into mountains, which was yet the watershed between the Mississippi, the Tennessee, the Tombecbé, and the Yazoo Rivers, although practically inaccessible from any of these streams. The Chickasaws lived in villages made of houses covered with thatch and mud and surrounded with palisades, employed firearms, and were brave and daring. It was necessary to take every precaution against them, and Bienville spent the first three years of his second term in preparations. He obtained troops and supplies from France and ordered detachments from the Illinois, Natchitoches, and the Arkansas to advance from the Mississippi at Chickasaw Bluffs, while he took troops from New Orleans by the lakes over to Mobile, and with the military there was to advance up Tombecbé River. With the Illinois, young D'Artaguette was to bring Iroquois and Miami Indians, and thus the Chickasaws would be confronted by armies from the south, west, and north. Unfortunately, the gate to the east was left open, and it was from there that they received supplies from the English of Carolina. Bienville had been able to end the Choctaw civil war and had again attached Red Shoe to the French interests, so that it would seem as if all practicable precautions had been taken to make the enterprise a success.

Provisions were brought from New Orleans, artillery ordered from France, and troops from several posts. The plans were not thoroughly carried out, as cannon, for instance, did not arrive; but Bienville embarked at Mobile five hundred soldiers from Natchitoches, Natchez, and Mobile, a company of volunteers from New Orleans, another of unmarried colonists, and forty-five negroes under Simon, a free black, and they went up the Tombecbé in thirty large pirogues and as many flatboats in April, 1736.

Bienville's basis of supplies was what is now called Jones's Bluff, above the Black Warrior, where De Lusser built or strengthened Fort Tombecbé. There, after a trip of twenty-three days, a conference was held with the Choctaws, some, like influential Alabama Mingo, being loyal, and others, like Red Shoe, being more than doubtful. On the surface the situation was satisfactory, but it had been necessary to make a change of date, and Bienville sent word to D'Artaguette. Finally, on May 22d, the expedition reached the head of navigation, where they built Fort Oltibia, near a portage over to the Tennessee or Cherokee River. Nothing was heard of D'Artaguette, and Bienville, striking across country, reached Schiouafalay, where the Choctaws precipitated what is commonly called the battle of Ackia. To such an extent had the influence of the British extended over the Chickasaws through Adair and the mountain traders from Carolina, that now, in a time nominally of profound peace between England and France, the British flag, nevertheless, was flying from the stockades, and Englishmen were found to be aiding the Indians in their defence. The French advanced bravely, but the Choctaws did more howling than fighting. De Lusser was killed and Grondel rescued senseless, while the troops could not reach the palisades. The absence of the artillery made it sheer sacrifice to continue sending infantry against stockaded forts defended by such sharpshooters as the

Chickasaws and the English traders. After repeated attacks Bienville recognized his defeat, and retreated on the next day. The rains had impeded the boats coming up, and now the fall of the river almost left them stranded going down.

On reaching the coast Bienville learned that the disaster was greater than he thought, for D'Artaguette had been defeated even earlier, and with Vincennes, the Jesuit Sénat, and other prisoners, had been burned alive. Among the papers captured from them were despatches from Bienville, and thus it was that the Chickasaws learned the plans of the French and were able to complete their discomfiture.

It was necessary to retrieve this disaster, or French prestige among all southern Indians, if not in the whole Mississippi valley, was gone forever. The fleeing Iroquois, Miami, and Illinois savages spread the tale far and wide, and the disaffected among the Choctaws were more and more emboldened. The government agreed to a new expedition, but foolishly alienated Bienville by putting another in command over him. Still, he spent several years in preparations, and in 1740 another attack was made, this time by way of the Mississippi, which was better planned and better carried out. The Chickasaws retired on the approach of the French, although from a military point of view the expedition was hardly brilliant. But it impressed the savages and they sued for peace. Bienville thought it the wiser policy to accept their advances, and concluded with them what amounted to a truce of several years.

The Natches had to some extent been compelled to retire from among the Chickasaws, but friendliness was never restored or trade relations renewed between the French and the Chickasaws. They were, if anything, more confirmed in their attachment to the English. After Bienville left, even the Choctaws became divided again, despite Vaudreuil's great congress at Mobile, and there was a hostile expedition down the Mississippi of Choctaws and Muskhogees. The French not only thought of abandoning Fort Tombecbé, but found it prudent to erect a palisade in Mobile. The town must have shrunk a great deal, for in 1745 the male population outside of the garrison amounted to only one hundred and fifty and the negroes of both sexes to two hundred, and from this time dates the grant for agricultural purposes of some of the land which earlier had been in town lots. Red Shoe renewed his hostility, and three years later was killed by a Choctaw, rumor has it, for a reward offered by the French. Bossu tells us that the governor managed to end the revolt by cutting off supplies of ammunition from the friendly Choctaws until they forced the hostiles to peace.

Vaudreuil found himself able in 1752 to undertake an expedition against the Chickasaws, the third by the French, which was, like one of Bienville's, from Mobile and up the Tombecbé. In fact, it offered a curious parallel to that ill-fated first expedition, which terminated at Ackia. The canoe fleet proceeded up to Fort Tombecbé, where it remained for a short time, and then to what is now Cotton Gin Port, whence the troops marched across the country, and with the assistance of the Choctaws attacked the Chickasaw towns. Vaudreuil had the advantage of Bienville in artillery, and succeeded in destroying cabins and crops; but he met a defeat only less disastrous, and in retreating seems to have abandoned his artillery in the river on account of low water. He halted long enough at Tombecbé to enlarge and strengthen it and then returned to Mobile.

The Chickasaws were unconquerable, and their hostility to the French could not be appeased. They could be worn out by sheer attrition, but would not yield voluntarily. One cannot restrain admiration for a tribe gradually growing fewer in number before the increasing French, and who, unlike the oak, would neither bend nor break. The British hold upon the Appalachian Mountains and their southwestern foothills was unbroken. Forts Toulouse and Tombecbé remained a menace to their influence, and their traders had to use Tennessee River and the mountain paths near by; and yet, without a fort among the Chickasaws, by traders few in number, the English maintained this wedge of Indian tribes, extending westwardly from the mountains of Carolina almost to the Mississippi.

In the Kentucky region as elsewhere in the Ohio valley the mountains barred out the English settlers but not the English traders. In 1745 Vaudreuil writes to the French government that he has sent by the *Éléphant* three traders captured on the Mississippi, although we also learn afterward that the *Éléphant* was captured by the English themselves, and there were earlier and later instances of such trade invasions. Virginia, it is true, claimed all this country, because Maryland and Pennsylvania, unlike her, had definite western boundaries whose lines were perhaps uncertain but at least capable of being run, while we recollect that ever since La Salle's time all territory watered by streams tributary to the Mississippi was claimed by France as part of Louisiana. On neither side were the native inhabitants much considered. The French, however, had less difficulty, for they called the Indians their brothers, really with themselves subjects of the French king. We find treaties of alliance, but no cessions of territory to the French. Nor was any needed, for the French trader was either a royal officer or under official supervision, and the fort to protect French interests was not less a post for trade, welcomed by the natives.

The claim of the English to the Ohio valley as against the Indians was based upon treaties with the Iroquois, and that of the Iroquois upon conquest. The Five Nations had in many respects the most instructive history of the native tribes. They had learned that in union there was strength, and in one of their congresses with the British colonists they even exhorted their white brethren to a similar union, and this before confederation was planned by anyone. They claimed by conquest all the country east of Mississippi River from Hudson Bay to the Cherokees, themselves friendly to these northerners. The Catawbas they almost exterminated, and it was the Tuscaroras from the south who made up the sixth nation of the league. The justice of the claim is another matter, but for the present let us see how the English fell heir to it.

While the Canadians and the Iroquois were engaged in their long Thirty Years' War, the British were careful to cultivate and spur on the Long House. In 1684 and even in 1701, after the Iroquois had made peace with Canada, the British acquired their rights to different districts adjoining the northern settlements, and in 1726 yet other lands were thus obtained, "to be protected and defended by his Majesty to and for the use of the grantors and their heirs." In 1744, at Lancaster, the Six Nations were persuaded by means of whiskey and debauchery to recognize the king's right to "all lands that are or by his Majesty's appointments shall be within the colony of Virginia,"—which was a "walking purchase" putting to blush the original of the name. On this was based the grant by the government of five hundred thousand acres, to be principally located on the south side of Ohio River between the Monongahela and the Kanawha, by the Ohio Company, an association made up of Thomas Lee, Lawrence and Augustine Washington,—brothers of George Washington,—ten other Virginians, and a gentleman of London. Two hundred thousand acres were to be located at once and held for ten years free of rent if the company colonized there one hundred families within seven years and built a sufficient fort. In consummating this, Christopher Gist in 1750–1751 made his famous exploration from Colonel Cresap's house at the old town on Potomac River down the Ohio within fifteen miles of the falls and thence to Roanoke River in North Carolina.

It would seem as if the cessions by the Iroquois of these lands west of the Alleghanies violated on a great scale the principle as to conveyance by a party out of possession. The Iroquois had been much set back by the long war with Canada beginning in 1663, and the very fact of the cession of lands behind them showed that their activity now was more limited than their claims. On the other hand, while few Indians lived upon the banks of the Ohio, the upland was by no means a wilderness. What we call Kentucky, it is true, had few occupants, but it was the hunting ground for the Shawnees and tribes to the north. Not to mention those of the Illinois region, next west of the Alleghanies and thus about Muskingum River were the Delawares, who had retired from their ancient eastern seats; and there were gathered about the Scioto in the eighteenth century the Shawnees, those American Bedouins whose hand was heavy against the English. West of these, about the Miami Rivers, great and little, were the Miamis, or Twightwees, who extended over to the Wabash, and along Lake Erie were the Wyandots and other Canadian tribes. Altogether what makes up the States of Ohio and Indiana had a fairly large population of warlike Indians, far superior to the Illinois and other victims of French fire-water. These not only did not consent to the Iroquois cessions, but, on the contrary, did not acknowledge Iroquois supremacy in any shape, and the irritation of the Indians was readily taken advantage of by the French.

The rivalry of the French and the British in the Mississippi valley had reached a stage where dispute could only be settled by arms. The French held the banks of the Mississippi, and to some extent those of the Ohio, and were equally powerful upon the Great Lakes west of the Iroquois. The Gulf, too, was theirs or Spanish, but they had been unable by force or trade to come into control of the Chickasaws and Cherokees about the lower end of the Appalachian Mountains. The French *coureurs*, the French traders, and the French officials had their territory fairly in hand; and while the English were less organized, they were more numerous and seemed through their firm hold upon the Cherokees and Chickasaws to keep a great wedge between the Latins of the Gulf and of the Ohio valley. From a contest of traders it had come to be an almost incessant conflict of pioneers, if not of outposts. It needed but an outbreak in Europe to produce open war in the wilds of America.

CHAPTER XVIII

OPEN WAR

War has more often resulted from trade rivalry than from any other secular cause. It is true that in early eras uncivilized races projected themselves upon more cultivated but weaker countries, urged on by a desire to better their condition, or pushed by more savage races behind. Even in later times an expanding population has caused a powerful country to seize neighboring provinces. But the main cause of war, nevertheless, will be found in historic times to be the desire to secure a market or a vantage ground for trade. It is not necessary for this to be consciously in the minds of statesmen. Insult to the flag, real or fancied, injury to merchants, true or assumed, desire for territory better fitted for trade, commercial concessions to one power conflicting with those to another,—these and the like are the origin of most modern struggles. And so it was with France and England in the eighteenth century. At first, America had been drawn into European conflicts; now, it was to be at least in part the main object of war between the mother countries.

We have seen that the Mississippi valley was the field of commercial rivalry between the French and the English traders. This basin was bounded by the Alleghanies on the east, while the Great Lakes on the north and the Alabama-Tombigbee region and Florida on the south afforded access to and from it. Through the mountains also were different passes, used by the traders and passable to troops, while the Potomac, the Susquehanna, and particularly the Hudson and Mohawk Rivers were in the nature of gates through the Alleghanies to the headwaters of the Ohio. Thus the British colonies were not only hemmed in by the mountains, but could strike and be struck through these passes and gates in the rear, and, besides, were flanked by the Latin races in Canada and Florida. All this had been important in commercial rivalry in the past, and was yet to play a greater part in the armed conflict to follow.

The important points for trade were not necessarily the strategic points for war. The former must be among the Indian customers; the latter must be nearer the white enemy. Thus in the earlier days we find French forts along the rivers, as at Natchez, Tombecbé, the junction of the Ohio and the Mississippi, the junction of the Wabash and the Ohio, Fort Chartres, L'Huilier, Michilimackinac, and Detroit. In the period which we have now reached, a greater part was to be played by those at Niagara, Presqu'Île, the junction of the Alleghany and the Monongahela on the French side, and at Oswego, Cumberland, and Loudoun on the English; and it will be observed that most of these were in or near the Appalachian range or on the streams issuing from it.

What was in America called the French and Indian War and in Europe the Seven Years' War decided the contest, but it was not the only one in which the colonies were concerned. There had been previously three others. The first was spoken of in America as King William's War, being the American end of that in which Louis XIV. undertook to restore James II. after the English Revolution of 1688. This conflict had not decided results on this side of the ocean, the chief event being Frontenac's repulse of Admiral Phipp's attack on Quebec. The second was Queen Anne's War, corresponding to that of the Spanish Succession, waged mainly in the north and ended by the Peace of Utrecht, when England acquired Acadia and Newfoundland. The

Robert Dinwiddie, Governor of Virginia. *From a painting in possession of a member of the family.*

third contest was King George's War, beginning in 1744 and somewhat corresponding to the Austrian Succession. This again related mainly to the North, and among its achievements was the capture by the English colonists next year of Louisburg, which the French had built on Cape Breton Island to compensate for the loss of Acadia, and the unsuccessful attacks in the South on St. Augustine and Charlestown. So little yet did America weigh in the minds of English statesmen that Louisburg, the strategic point for the control of the St. Lawrence, was ceded back to France at the Peace of Aix-la-Chapelle, in 1748, in exchange for Madras, which the French had taken in India.

The French plan, dating back as far as La Salle and Iberville, was to develop Canada so as to embrace the St. Lawrence and Great Lake regions, and Louisiana to cover the Mississippi valley and north Gulf coast, and by portages and forts connect the two so as really to constitute one New France in America. Incidentally, this was to involve confining the British to the seaboard of the Atlantic if not to drive them out of America altogether, for France had taken up the burden of Spain, improving on it in that she would encircle the British from the rear instead of attacking from Florida to the south. The scheme was more promising because the French were better organizers than the Spanish, and in their hands it had the advantage that they interested and influenced the natives where the Spaniards had largely antagonized them. Spain had failed because of increasing weakness at home and the growing preponderance of the British at sea, the command of which was necessary. The French increased in Canada and Louisiana, almost unknown to the British, who stayed at home and developed their own colonies without thinking a great deal of what was going on across the mountains. The French had the inland, with almost complete water communication, but it was the longer line. The British had the coast, with the sea as a base, but were separated by distance and mountains, and even more by their local jealousies.

It is probable that the two nations would have gone on for a long time without clashing had it been simply a question of the Atlantic coast and the St. Lawrence and Mississippi countries. They were too far apart to affect each other very much. But it so happened that the French were not able to make themselves full masters of the lower lake region. The Mohawk River, rising near that system of lakes emptying into Ontario, and the old native warfare between the Iroquois of that region and their kinsmen the Hurons north of the St. Lawrence were unforeseen factors in the result. The early governors of Canada had felt compelled to take the part of the Hurons and had thus incurred the lasting enmity of the Iroquois,—the bravest, fiercest, and best organized of all the Indian leagues of the north. These, although mustering less than four thousand warriors, all but exterminated the Hurons, and extended their influence far to the south and down Ohio River even to the Mississippi, while their inroads and name were dreaded as far up the lakes as Michilimackinac. The French had tried to placate or to conquer them, and the devoted Jesuits had been martyrs in their country; but the Dutch and afterward the English secured their friendship, and French control was finally limited to the western tribe, the Senecas. The English built a post at Oswego in 1725, and the French followed the next year by a fort at Niagara. If the French could hold both sides of Lake Ontario and influence the Iroquois, their plan of developing the St. Lawrence and the lake region would be successful. If not, they would labor under difficulties which might be insurmountable.

Thus it was that where the two civilizations were closest together and where only the native league of the Iroquois was interposed between them there came the first clash. King George's War had settled the issue in favor of the English for the time being; but this arbitrament of arms was not necessarily final. It might be reversed, and, at all events, the French could develop the northern shore of the lower lakes and use these waters freely for communication with the west. There were portages everywhere, but curiously enough the course of the early explorers was the one afterward generally pursued. From Lake Erie there were portages over to Alleghany River on the east, and from near Detroit others to the Miami, leading also to the Ohio; but the pioneers had blazed the way for the great fur trade of the upper lakes, and the great highway remained still by way of the St. Joseph and the Chicago portages to the south end of Lake Michigan over into Illinois River. And yet the importance of the eastern routes from Lake Erie was never forgotten by the French, and when Virginians organized the Ohio Company the French were not slow to act. We can see now that they should have done so before, but even among pioneers the earliest established routes are apt to continue unless there is some good reason for a change, and the upper Ohio presented no attractions. It ran through a mountainous region, and, more than that, was peopled by few Indians. The Delawares and Shawnees were to become important again, but in early times the former had been conquered by the Iroquois, who called them women, and then had been driven west by the English, while the Shawnees were themselves comparatively late comers from what we now call Kentucky. In this way the French were not active in the upper Ohio valley until the English were making ready on their side to take possession. It was the conflict about Fort Du Quesne, rather than any question about the lake and Mississippi route, that finally decided the contest over America. The line was too long to be strong at all points, and it so happened that the British colonial advance was greatest at the place where the French defence was weakest, at what has been called the Portals of the Ohio Valley.

Heretofore the scene of the armed conflicts had been Canada and its approaches. Nothing had been thought of the Ohio or Mississippi valleys beyond some Indian fights on the Miami, and singularly modern is it to find the occasion of the greatest war of all in the claims of a land company. In consequence Céloron was sent from Canada in 1749, to take more formal possession of the whole Ohio valley, which he did by conferences with the Indians and by burying at important places leaden plates with the claim of France inscribed, as La Salle had done on the Mississippi. Better yet, they strengthened Niagara and built other forts and posts, as Sandusky in 1751, and a little later Presqu'Île, Le Bœuf, and Venango. Rumors of this induced Governor Dinwiddie to send young Washington to investigate, and on his report it was determined by Virginia to erect a fort also. Whether the junction of the Alleghany and the Monongahela was in Virginia or Pennsylvania was doubtful, but there the Virginia Assembly, in 1754, began its proposed post, and forthwith the French drove off the Virginians and finished it for themselves as the famous Fort Du Quesne. Washington led Virginia and North Carolina troops in this direction and defeated a body of French, but after throwing up Fort Necessity was himself attacked by a larger force and compelled to surrender on honorable terms. Fort Cumberland was erected to protect the western settlements of Maryland, and then came Braddock's attempt on Fort Du Quesne, resulting in his death. With this and the defeat of Dieskau at Lake George the war was on in earnest, although it was not until the next year that it was formally declared. Montcalm took charge in Canada, and Abercrombie and Loudoun proved unable to cope with him, so that the next two years were disastrous for the British.

A conference of southern governors, including Dobbs of North Carolina, Dinwiddie of Virginia, Denny of Pennsylvania, and Sharpe of Maryland, was held with the Earl of Loudoun at Philadelphia in March, 1757. It was proposed by Loudoun and agreed that the greater part of the troops should be employed to the northward and that the defence of the southern provinces should be left to a battalion of a thousand men and three independent companies of one hundred each in South Carolina, although the provinces should raise in addition enough to make up five thousand men. There being always danger of an attempt on South Carolina, there were to be raised for the defence of that province and Georgia two thousand men, including five companies of regular troops. Lord Loudoun was to supply provisions, and the transport was to be at the expense of the respective provinces. The troops were placed under command of Lieutenant-colonel Bouquet, a Swiss in the British service at Du Quesne, and the regulars were promptly taken by sea to Charlestown. Lyttleton, of South Carolina, was not present at the meeting, but coöperated in the plans.

The military reputation of Lord Loudoun has not been high, for his success was not great, but at least he made elaborate preparations during the French War and his name has been perpetuated in more than one fort and district. As a result of the conference of governors at Philadelphia, he sent Lieutenant-colonel Bouquet to the South with regulars, followed by troops from Virginia and other colonies. The object of this was to repel attack by the French fleet; for these vessels were heard from at different times, being now in the Gulf of Mexico, now at Cap François in Santo Domingo. They never did make an attack; but between them and the privateers the southern ports, and Charlestown in particular, were kept on the *qui vive*. A treaty effected by Governor Ellis with the Creeks west of the Georgia settlements rendered that frontier secure, although unfortunately this was not to prove true in the direction of Fort Loudoun over the mountains.

Charlestown, being the largest city, became the headquarters of Bouquet and thence he issued orders to the various forts, of which he named Johnson, Frederic, Moore, Prince George, and Loudoun as the principal, and his negotiations with the different governors and their assemblies are full of interest. Thus North Carolina was slow in furnishing her quota, and South Carolina for some time failed to provide barracks and furniture for the soldiers. Bouquet said that such things were managed better at the north, but he expressed his entire disgust with America as a whole, and declared that if he could once get out of it no consideration would make him return. In South Carolina the people he thought well to do, and yet, while they were pleased to have soldiers defend them, they made no difference between these and the negroes. On account of the exposure, troops, even the hardy Highlanders, who were well upon arrival soon became sick and unserviceable. He makes an exception in favor of Georgia, for Governor Ellis he declares to be indefatigable. It became even worse after Bouquet's departure, for we are then told that while previously "lawyers, justices, and the whole people had been eternally against the troops," now deserters were not only secreted but defended by mobs in Charlestown.

Bouquet was at Charlestown in charge of the Southern Department from June 15, 1757, to March of the next year, supervising troops in the field and the recruiting for the independent companies. As it took over a month to hear from Lord Loudoun, he was often thrown upon his own resources, and in despair for money to pay expenses. Not only did South Carolina lay a duty upon provisions imported for the military sent to defend the province, but among business men he found difficulty in negotiating bills on England for the payment of troops. Thus in October there was such demand for exchange for moving the indigo crop that military bills had to wait until spring. He says that one time he had to take money, but it is not clear whether this was in the nature of a forced loan or not.

A part of the anxiety of the British was caused by the Cherokees. We have seen how they were usually faithful, and, in fact, with the Chickasaws made up a wedge extending westwardly into what would otherwise have been French territory and so prevented communication between the Alabama-Tombigbee and the Ohio valleys. It was very desirable, therefore, that they should be kept in good humor. At some unknown time there had been a post or fort built by the French among them on the upper waters of what we call the Tennessee, but then known as Cherokee River, and after the fall of Fort Du Quesne a new fort named Massac, far down the Ohio, was the basis of French operations among the Indians. Yet the English approach from the east was more successful than the French from the west, and Fort Prince George had led in 1758 to building over the mountains near the Cherokee chief town a new fort, called for Lord Loudoun, which was to have an important influence and history. There was to be no attack on Charlestown, and the forts in their country kept the Cherokees quiet if not friendly. The stress of war was in another direction.

While Vaudreuil was doing his best to save Canada against great odds, his successor Kerlerec had trials enough of his own in Louisiana. Agriculture and industry had so far progressed that there was a fair export trade. The furs from the Northwest sought shipping at New Orleans, while cotton, indigo, tobacco, and timber were produced on a considerable scale throughout much of the province and some also went abroad. It is true that the inhabitants were easy-going, but many were industrious, and for some time the war was too far away to affect them seriously. The superiority of the British at sea finally had its result. They established a cruising station at Cape San Antonio off the west end of Cuba, whence they preyed on French commerce with such result that few vessels reached the ports of Louisiana. At last a ship was even stationed off the mouths of the Mississippi, and New Orleans was almost in a state of blockade. The effects of this were threefold; it not only cut off the supplies upon which the inhabitants still to a large extent depended, and prevented reports from reaching the home government and the local authorities from receiving instructions, but, even worse, no money or other presents could be given to the Choctaws, and they again became restless and threatening. Of money there was only the paper, which had reached the total of seven million livres. During 1757 Louisiana was practically isolated.

The inactivity of Kerlerec was thus unavoidable, and he was absolutely prevented from organizing and carrying out what had been the favorite plan of the French from the time of Iberville. For Kerlerec wished to unite the Indians, particularly the Choctaws and the Alibamons, whom he called the bulwarks of the colony, as well as all others of the Southwest, into a great confederacy and march at their head against the English, probably of Carolina. This would have made a great diversion and drawn off much of the military force opposed to Vaudreuil in Canada; for he says the Choctaws could supply four thousand warriors, the Alibamons three thousand, and the others in proportion. Next year Rochemore, the new *intendant*, managed to get through from France with supplies enough to keep the Indians quiet, but not enough to carry out any plan of invasion. And yet, Louisiana was not entirely idle during the war, for troops from the Illinois and from the lower province also participated in the operations about Fort Du Quesne upon the upper Ohio.

Louisiana was unfortunate in domestic affairs. The Compagnie had complained that the Indian trade prevented the growth of agriculture and that people tried to become rich by commerce with the natives. This had been suppressed, but the same desire for easy wealth broke out in another direction. The officials quarrelled among themselves, for even Rochemore was soon at almost swords' point with Kerlerec, but they seemed all to unite in one thing, to wit, the desire to make all they could out of their positions. A spirit of peculation prevailed from the time that Louisiana became again a royal province, and the reports of governors and *intendants* leave no doubt that it became a cancer eating out the life of the community. It was complained that the officers were addicted to trade and practically made slaves of their soldiers; that peculation became a system, even authorized by the governors provided they were allowed to share in it; that the military were dissolute; and that drunkenness, brawls, and duels ruined half the population.

If a quarter of this were true, the situation was deplorable. There was, moreover, little growth in the population itself. There were no immigrants, and, while the creoles increased somewhat, it is said that half the married women sent to Louisiana were between fifty and sixty years of age and had no children. It could have been with no regret that Kerlerec laid down the cares of office in 1763, when he was succeeded by D'Abbadie, but Rochemore's accusations, particularly that of spending ten millions in four years, lodged him in the Bastille.

Before this the end had come in America, where Pitt's policy was to attack the French in the north and strike at the heart of New France. Ticonderoga and Niagara were taken in 1759, followed by the death of Wolfe and Montcalm at the capture of Quebec. It had been part of the French plan, if Canada could not be held, to retreat to Louisiana. If this had been carried out and Montcalm or even Vaudreuil with disciplined troops had met the provincials of Georgia and Carolina up the Alabama or the British regulars and navy below New Orleans, another and possibly a different history might have been written for the Mississippi valley. But this was not to be. Vaudreuil was besieged at Montreal and finally forced to surrender the whole of Canada, including the fort on the Maumee and Ouatenon on the Wabash. The total population of Canada and Louisiana was ninety thousand, three-quarters of it being in Canada, as against a million and a half acknowledging British sovereignty. There could hardly be other than one result when the British became thoroughly aroused.

The surrender of Montreal marked the end of the war in America, but it was two years later before the diplomats could agree on what was the result of the world-wide struggle. The Treaty of Paris was not signed until February, 1763, and in the meantime affairs pursued their old course, although with great uncertainty as to what would be the outcome. The British gradually pushed their forces up the lakes and somewhat into the Ohio valley, endeavoring to secure the allegiance of the different tribes. This they found difficult on account of the hold of the French upon the savages.

With the close of hostilities the management of the Indians by the British was not tactful. From fear of results or overconfidence in their own power, they cut short the supplies, particularly of ammunition, to the savages, with the result of awakening distrust and resentment. Even this was measurably true of the Cherokees, urged on as they were by French soldiers and Indians from the Du Quesne region. Marauding parties began to appear on the frontiers, horses were stolen, and even scalps were taken. Demeré was in command at Fort Loudoun, and on his message to Governor Lyttleton the militia was mobilized. Occonostota and other chiefs went to Charlestown to adjust matters if possible, and were virtually made prisoners by the governor, who undertook an expedition to overawe the Cherokees. His troops, however, were ill disciplined, if not mutinous, and gradually melted away. A congress was held at Fort Prince George in December, the principal result being that Attakullakulla, or Little Carpenter, succeeded in securing the release of Occonostota and others. Lyttleton returned home with great glory from an expedition which had cost the province £25,000, and had hardly arrived in Charlestown and received instructions to proceed to Jamaica as its governor, when the storm which he had provoked burst in the Cherokee region. Occonostota enticed Coytomore, the commander, out of Fort Prince George and shot him, whereupon the garrison massacred the rest of the Indian hostages, and the result was to set the whole race in arms. The Abbeville district was laid waste by the Indians, followed shortly by a corresponding harrying of the Keowee valley by regulars under Colonel Montgomery, whose orders soon compelled him to sail to the north to take part in the closing events of the war.

This unfortunately left Fort Loudoun to its fate. Isolated as it was, it was invested by the Indians and starved out; so that Demeré and his two hundred men had to surrender in May, 1760, on condition of being permitted to retire to Carolina. As usual with them, the Indians did not keep the terms of the capitulation, and the next day surrounded and fired on the British, when Demeré, three officers, and twenty-three privates were killed and the rest were taken prisoners. Among the prisoners was Captain John Stuart, who seems to have come out with the Highlanders under Oglethorpe, under whom he had served against the Spaniards. He was now second in command at Fort Loudoun. Attakullakulla was much attached to Stuart, and with his rifle, clothes, and other things ransomed him from his captor. Having found some ammunition, the Indians determined to attack Fort Prince George, carrying with them cannon and cohorns, which they determined to make Stuart operate against his comrades. Attakullakulla thereupon secretly escaped with Stuart, travelling nine days and nights by the light of the sun and moon, until on Holston River they met a party sent by Colonel Byrd for the rescue of refugees from Fort Loudoun.

War being at last ended in the north, Lieutenant-colonel James Grant was spared to Charlestown, and with his Highlanders and provincials, in 1761, he marched to the Cherokee country, where he devastated the territory on all sides for thirty days. Finally, Attakullakulla succeeded in effecting a peace, but the kindly relations between the Cherokees and the English were never fully restored, and in the war of the Revolution they showed that they had not forgotten the invasions of Lyttleton and Grant. An even more significant feature of this campaign was the friction which arose between the regulars and the Carolina troops, for Thomas Middleton, commanding the latter, in some way considered himself slighted, and resented it. There came a discussion in the newspapers, and even a duel, but fortunately no one was injured.

At last the provisions of the Peace of Paris became known. They made Great Britain the foremost country of the globe as to colonies and trade. The dream of a New France in America ended at the same time as the dream of a French empire in India, and the mainland in the Orient and in the New World passed together from the French sceptre. In America the more fertile and better known half of Louisiana, that lying east of Mississippi River, and the more ancient dominion of Canada were ceded to England. Forts Chartres, Vincennes, Tombecbé, Mobile, and Toulouse have heretofore bulked large in our story because they marked the frontier in their several directions, but now they were swallowed up in one vast English empire. They ceased to guard the frontier, for that practically ceased to exist. It is true that an earlier treaty between the courts of Versailles and Madrid made another disposition of Louisiana west of the Mississippi and including New Orleans, but this remained secret for some time. For the present it seemed as if the eastern half of the valley was to become British and the western to remain French. But, in any event, Louisiana ceased to be a unit, and, in course of time, the very name was to be crowded down into a corner of the map. The creoles might remain, an infusion of other blood might bring them to the front, the future of the country might be even greater than the past. And yet, even if this should come to pass, it would not be the Louisiana named by La Salle, founded by Iberville, and built by Bienville and his successors.

CHAPTER XIX

COLONIAL LIFE ON THE ATLANTIC

PEACE brought great development to the English colonies, but the war can hardly be said to have retarded the growth of those at the South at any time. There was no attack from the sea, although that was anticipated, and the occasional ravages of the western borders appealed to the sympathies rather than the fears of the more numerous tidewater people. Even colonization in a sense continued, for immigrants still came from Europe and the old centres became themselves points of departure for new settlements. And this was as true of the oldest dominion as of the youngest, while running through them all was a constitutional growth, a *Zeitgeist*, which was preparing Virginians, Carolinians, and Georgians alike for something yet to come, when colonial growth, intellectual and political, had fitted them to assume their just place among the nations of the world. Consideration of their several situations will enable us to see better what they had in common.

In Virginia, with the accession of Queen Anne came the curious institution of titular governorships. The first was when the Earl of Orkney held the office for forty years while the duties were exercised by deputies of varying ability, as in 1710 by Alexander Spotswood, whose energy left marked impress upon the province. Up to his time there had not been the right of *habeas corpus*, and now that greatest of all civil remedies was brought to Virginia by this soldier, who had been wounded at Blenheim; and the colony was connected in another way with that victory, for Marlborough had sent the Virginian Colonel Parke to bear the news to the queen. Spotswood was well received, and the burgesses voted £2,000 to build a palace; but this cordiality did not last long, for when he wanted to fortify the frontier he could only get a bill passed for scouts. He at least managed to prevent the Virginia Indians from joining in the Tuscarora war, however, and when buccaneers came into Chesapeake Bay promptly sent out vessels to capture them. The combat with Blackbeard Teatch came on in his rendezvous in Pamlico Sound in true pirate fashion; for Blackbeard leaped upon the roundhouse of his sloop, tossed off a glass of liquor to the opposing masters, and imprecated damnation on him who should give quarter. But his bravado came to nothing, for his crew were killed, or captured to die on the gallows, and Blackbeard's head was brought back upon the bowsprit of the colonial craft.

Spotswood was in many respects the best executive Virginia had before the Revolution. He had an eye single to the public good, and, although he lectured and hectored everyone, from the burgesses down, who stood in the way of his plans, all respected him because they knew that he had no private object. He struggled with the vestries over the appointment of ministers, for they had become used to choosing their own pastors, and would even hear nothing of a Virginia bishop. There were not long afterward fifty parishes and one hundred and thirty pastors, and Spotswood had finally to abandon the unequal contest. More popular were his efforts in the way of developing industries. During her reign, Queen Anne sent over Germans from the harried Palatinate to make wine and iron, and they were placed at Germanna on the Rapidan, near which Spotswood had a house or castle. He took a deep interest in their labors. William Byrd visited him there and gives a delightful account of the trip, for, although it was a long way off from the capital, Spotswood was a fine host. He could tell good stories of campaigns under Marlborough, and even stand badinage over his recent surrender to the fair sex. Byrd thought him uxorious, but Spotswood said that whoever brought a poor gentlewoman into so solitary a place was under obligation to use her with all possible tenderness.

After he ceased to be governor, Spotswood's name became connected with that great civilizer, the post office. Up to the end of the preceding century letters had passed by private conveyance, and although Thomas Neale was authorized by the burgesses to establish post offices and receive threepence for the carriage of each letter addressed to a place not exceeding fourscore miles from the point where it was mailed, and there was a postmaster-general from a northern colony, we do not know what was done. When Spotswood became postmaster-general he arranged that post riders should be at Susquehanna River on Saturday nights to receive the Philadelphia mail, get back to Annapolis on Monday, by Wednesday be near Fredericksburg, and Saturday night at Williamsburg, where connection was made once a month for mails to Edenton. The time from the Susquehanna to Williamsburg was a week, an improvement over methods of transfer under earlier officials. One of Spotswood's appointees for Pennsylvania was Benjamin Franklin.

The postmaster-general had on the Chesapeake another home, which he called Temple Farm, and there he spent his last years, riding in his London chariot and dispensing hospitality. It may not have been so much of "an enchanted castle" as Byrd thought the other, but it was to have a famous history, at which perhaps its owner would have been aghast,—for many years afterward it witnessed the surrender of Cornwallis. Spotswood himself was to have commanded an expedition to the West Indies in 1740, but died just before embarking.

One of his successors in the governorship was William Gooch, who held the office twenty-two years, and his conciliatory attitude made him a favorite. It was during his time that the movement to the west became prominent, for the Episcopal population on the tidewater was now supplemented by a very different immigration, that of Dissenters. It was already evident that whatever might be the true western boundary under her charter, Virginia was to spread beyond even the headwaters of the James, and embrace the beautiful Shenandoah Valley. Heretofore immigrants had come from the ocean and settled mainly on the rivers; now there was to be a large influx from the more northern colonies, particularly Pennsylvania. The interior of that province had been developed from abroad until the real frontier was along the Susquehanna, and this region was filled with a very different class of people from the quiet Quakers of Philadelphia and the east. They were home-seeking Germans and Scotch-Irish, fresh from Europe, with no ambition to advance the boundaries of Pennsylvania.

The history of the Scotch-Irish takes us back to Cromwell's settlement and its results. In 1689 came the famous siege of Londonderry by James II., in which the Protestants of Ulster successfully drove back the Stuarts, and the same year was no less famous for the Act of Toleration. Unfortunately, although King William was in sympathy with the Dissenters, their position even in Ireland soon became intolerable. They had not only to see the Episcopal Church made the State establishment, and contribute themselves to its support, but in every way possible they found themselves incommoded and sometimes persecuted. This was the cause of the large emigration to America, which went first to Pennsylvania on account of the religious freedom established there by the Quakers. These colonists, however, soon found the border insecure because of the Indians and of the reluctance of the Quakers to take warlike protective measures.

In 1710 some adventurers had seen the valley of the Shenandoah from the top of the Blue Ridge, and six years later Governor Spotswood entered it and bivouacked along its river, which to him and his Knights of the Golden

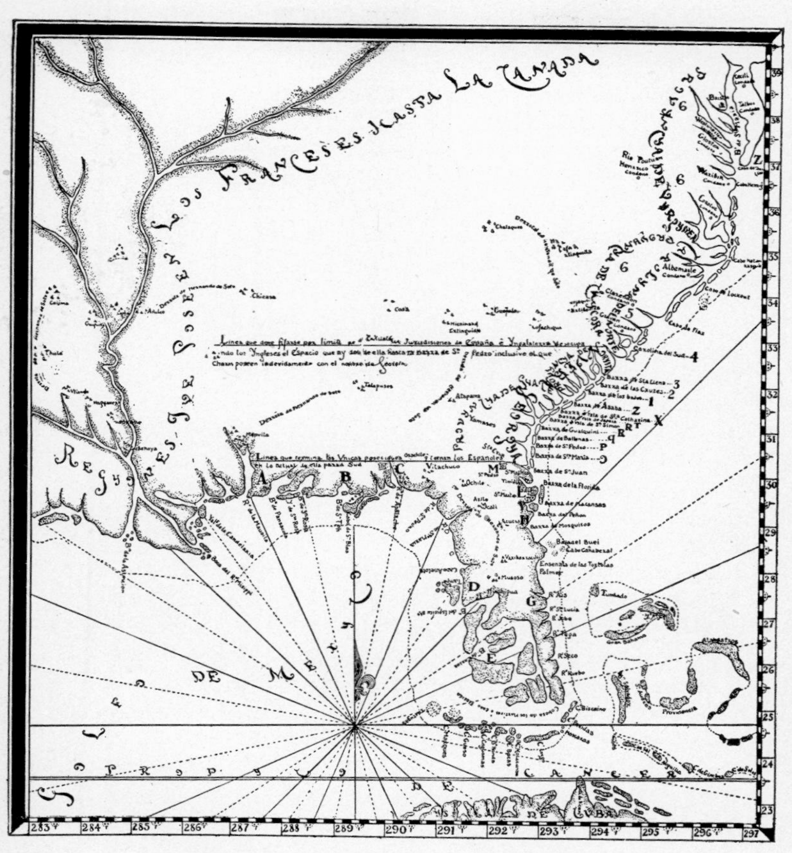

Possessions of the Spaniards and English in the South, *circa* 1742, according to the treaty of 1670. *Traced from the original, especially for this work, by D. Pedro Torres Lanzas, Chief of the Archives, from the hitherto unpublished original in the Archives of the Indies, Seville.*

Horseshoe was known as the Euphrates. This expedition was famous at the time for the variety and number of wines which were drunk in honor of the royal family and others, and famous to posterity for opening the way to the West; but the first settlers were the Germans and Scotch-Irish from the north.

The valley of the Shenandoah was claimed by Lord Fairfax in his grant of the Northern Neck, and he filed a caveat against settlements begun by Hite and others under a warrant of 1730. This brought on a lawsuit lasting for fifty years, and the result was that incoming immigrants found titles unsettled near the Potomac and so pressed on, past straggling Winchester, up the valley. Only some Germans remained and built Strasburg.

The valleys of western Virginia run approximately northeast and southwest, and although they are broken by a watershed from which the drainage is into New River, and thence through broken territory toward the Ohio, they communicate, and to pioneers there was no great difficulty in passing from the upper Shenandoah to where the headwaters run southwest to form the Tennessee and the Cumberland. So that, although a part of their history is only traditional, we early find settlers on the upper Shenandoah, and in 1738 the district was erected into the county of Augusta, named for the Princess of Wales. Caldwell the Pennsylvanian applied to Governor Gooch for leave to bring Dissenters, and they received a cordial welcome. All the benefits of the Toleration Act were promised, as there was then no doubt that this act applied to Virginia, and pastors were supplied from Pennsylvania by the Presbytery of Donegal. Presbyterianism had begun in another quarter, for its American birthplace was in eastern Virginia. As early as 1683 Francis Makemie was on the Eastern Shore, and in 1699, when Virginia adopted the Toleration Act, we find him qualifying and there exercising his ministry. But he had died in 1708, and his churches had all but passed away when the Scotch-Irish established his faith and doctrine in the valley, and Samuel Davies, Lewis, and others made the Presbytery of Hanover famous. To these immigrants their church was everything. As soon as a neighborhood had a handful of residents, a church and a preacher were wanted. Thus Anderson had been sent out by the Synod of Philadelphia even before 1740, when we find John Craig well established in the west. The church came even before the county organization, for it was not until 1745 that the governor appointed twenty-one justices of the peace, a sheriff, and other officers, for the vast county of Augusta, whose seat was in a couple of years to be Stanton, or Staunton, as it was afterward spelled. The western boundaries of this county were the western boundaries of the Old Dominion, but it was steadily filling up. It is said that from 1729 to 1750 no less than twelve thousand Scotch-Irish came each year from Ulster to America, and not a few of them found their way to these parts of Virginia. It can readily be understood, therefore, that not only was this an addition to the population, but one of such proportions as to threaten change to its nature.

It was a curious problem facing these Scotch-Irish. They were to be tolerated, to be sure, but in their part of Virginia there was no one to tolerate them, for they practically made up the community themselves. If there was to be a vestry, which was a legal necessity, they had to select the members from their own denomination. And this they did, and we find the vestries made up of good Presbyterians, performing the duties placed upon the parish representatives. How they reconciled this with their religious views we can readily imagine, for it was a matter of necessity, of predestination, so to speak. There had to be a vestry and there was no other way to constitute it except with Presbyterians. In one part of the county there were other immigrants, for there had been erected by Governor Gooch the manor of Beverley in favor of the son of the historian; and between the Scotch-Irish and the activity of agent Patton in bringing over Redemptioners the population increased rapidly.

There was no less need of courts than churches, for the Scotch-Irish will have their differences, and in this case it was not necessary to go to law before unbelievers. The judicial organization of Augusta is a fair sample of that of early Virginia counties. Each magistrate had a limited jurisdiction, thus bringing justice home to every neighborhood, and assembled together they made up the county court, whose jurisdiction, civil and criminal, was almost unlimited. There debts were collected, criminals punished, wills probated, road duties prescribed, and almost everything else done affecting the life, liberty, and pursuit of happiness of the people.

There came also to the valley Lord Fairfax, a very different kind of man from the Scotch-Irish. He was an English nobleman who was disappointed in love, and sailed to the New World to look after his property and forget his sorrows. He liked the country so much as to settle on his lands, where he built what he called Greenway Court. This was not the dignified mansion which he proposed, or like those lining the James, for it was only a long one-story building with low eaves, having an office adjacent which long survived, and the manor proper was never erected. Nevertheless, he lived in considerable state, and was famous for hunting and for hospitality. He is described as tall and gaunt, with defective eyesight, but a man of culture, for he was a contributor to the *Spectator*. There he remained until his death toward the end of the Revolution, and among his greatest claims to our gratitude was his employment of the young surveyor George Washington, who was thus given a knowledge of the western country and fitted by experience of its dangerous and warlike life to be promoted to a higher station.

The tidewater country had not lagged behind the valley section. The country of Powhatan and Opechancanough was now in counties and parishes, and at the heads of rivers where Bacon had raised his troops tobacco was king. The James was bordered with stately homes, and Brandon,

Westover, Shirley, and the like not only transferred to America the best features of English country life, but with the amenities peculiar to Virginia created the distinctive type which we call "colonial." Jamestown, it is true, declined, for after Bacon's destruction of the place it was never the same. The long brick State House was rebuilt, although not on the same scale, and was again burned near the close of the century. Although the church remained with its square tower, and the graves and old coats of arms recalled the past, an insular capital was inconvenient, and hygienic reasons also worked for Williamsburg. There the shaded college, built between the road to Jamestown and another to the west, was flanked on the one side by the mansion of Blair or later president, and on the other by the building supported by the Brafferton parish in England. All were of brick whose bond, showing a glazed checker pattern, betrayed a similar origin to that of Jamestown church. At the opposite end of Duke of Gloucester Street, likewise between two roads angling off to other settlements, was the provincial capitol, also of brick, the scene of political debate, warmed thus as well as by a new-fashioned three-story stove of 1700, donated by the inventor. Facing a green midway between college and capitol was the "palace" of the governor, near the quaint church and courthouse, and England, Scotland, Ireland, and Nassau Streets showed the patriotism of the people. The church held the Jamestown font from which Pocahontas was perhaps baptized, and near by was the provincial powder house soon to be equally famous.

Williamsburg was thus historical to the core and dear to all Virginians. It had a viceregal quality, but it never became a great city despite its ports toward York and James Rivers. It remained dignified, rather collegiate than urban, although the students and the Raleigh tavern enlivened it at times. And yet, although the Cohabitation Acts had brought only paper towns, the general prosperity of the period—for the eighteenth century was Virginia's golden age—had the effect of laying the foundation of real cities.

As early as 1728, William Byrd could speak of the seaport Norfolk as having most the air of a city of any place in the colony, and its St. Paul's churchyard goes back even to the preceding century. With seven thousand people at the end of the French wars, Norfolk retained its preëminence despite certain efforts of Byrd of Westover himself. He owned a place at the falls, which he called Shocco, and there about 1733 he had the surveyor Mayo lay off a town to be known as Richmond. It grew slowly, mainly along the river bank east of Shocco Creek, although in eight years there were enough people to justify the erection on its commanding height of St. John's Episcopal Church, soon to be made immortal by a Scotch-Irishman's appeal for liberty or death. Petersburg, too, owes its origin to Byrd, whose joke as to his cities in the air was unjust to himself.

His own library at Westover, the finest in America, consisted of four thousand volumes in English, French, Latin, Greek, and Hebrew, besides a few in German and Dutch. It shows a culture which must have had companionship, and inventories back even to the preceding century show many collections of hundreds of volumes. In general literature he had such authors and books as Shakespeare, Ben Jonson, Spenser, Chaucer, Dryden, *Hudibras*, *Gil Blas*, *Don Quixote*, and Molière; and in law there were Bracton, Glanvil, Coke, *Virginia Statutes*, and laws of other colonies, such as Jamaica and Barbadoes, besides the *Institutes* and *Corpus Juris*, and *Grotius on War and Peace*. In history he read Burnet, Clarendon, Commines, Raleigh's *History of the World*, Neal's *New England*, Beverley's *Virginia*, and had in manuscript that great historical source, *Records of the Virginia Company*. He was fond of travels too, and along with Purchas had the very different Hennepin and La Hontan. The department of theology shows Tillotson, Hall, South, A'Kempis, Prideaux; and in philosophy we find some volumes of Descartes, Locke, and Boyle. There were also Eliot's Indian Bible, and the *Monthly Mercury* from 1688 to 1742. These are only samples of the books, many in "the best editions" and "elegant bindings," contained in "twenty-three double presses of black walnut," and, moreover, there were "capital engravings" and many "philosophical instruments." On the whole, it would be a collection which would reflect credit on a student of to-day.

The writings of William Byrd are always interesting and instructive, often witty, even if with an occasional tinge of coarseness. They throw light upon him and upon the state of society in which he could move with ease, although they were not all published in his own day and so did not form a part of the printed literature of the era. Unfortunately, the same is true in all the Southern colonies. The literature consisted largely of controversial pamphlets, as by Blair and Garden, or for and against governors and political movements. This, of course, has all now lost its savor and hardly ranks high in a literary way, but it is quite characteristic of the Anglo-Saxons. It needed a Milton to write *Paradise Lost*, and yet much of his ability was acquired in political controversies. Nothing in Southern writings can compare with the *Areopagitica* in defence of public printing, but sometimes we find passages which remind us of the Junius who was yet to come. Neither pure literature nor economics were to flourish, but parliamentary debates, finding their counterpart in political pamphlets, were training Americans for the political struggles of the future. Men were too busy founding States to have time for fine writing.

The western line of the Northern Neck was surveyed by Byrd and others in the thirties, although not confirmed until 1745, and the growth of the Virginian commonwealth is indicated among other things by the necessity for running the dividing line with adjoining colonies. In this way commissioners were appointed by Virginia and North Carolina as early as 1710, and, 1728–1729, part was resurveyed on behalf of the two colonies. William Byrd was one of the Virginia commissioners and has left a history of the demarcation from the ocean, through the Dismal Swamp, west to the mountains. Twenty years later the line was run further by Frye and the father of Thomas Jefferson, and during the Revolution it was continued to Tennessee River.

Robert Dinwiddie succeeded Gooch, and it was his duty to conduct Virginia through the last French war. He was more successful than his predecessors in making the colony feel the need of action, for the Ohio valley was claimed by Virginia, and Céloron's *prise de possession* was resented as an invasion of her Augusta County. It was Dinwiddie who sent Washington to reconnoitre, and when Fort Du Quesne was finally captured and became Fort Pitt it was claimed by both Virginia and Pennsylvania as within their respective boundaries—a dispute settled only in 1779 in favor of Pennsylvania. The immigration into the western country was accentuated by the events of the war, for the families who fled from the French and Indians came southward. Virginia's activity had resulted in a debt of £400,000, but it had also resulted in a large accession of hardy and industrious people to her population.

Virginia's neighbor to the south did not occupy so commanding a position. North Carolina was the scene of Raleigh's experiment, and there was the first proprietary effort, and other settlements besides, but they were disconnected and temporary. We have seen that possibly the earliest settlers were those on the Chowan from Virginia, by whom the short-lived New England colony about Cape Fear was absorbed, and that this became the nucleus of North Carolina. The proprietors had got Berkeley to appoint a governor, and it was odd that his choice fell upon the William Drummond whom later he was so grimly glad to see. The normal state of the settlement has been spoken of as one of "tranquil anarchy,"—although the adjective may be doubted,—and on the occasion of one of the frequent rebellions Culpepper, when tried in England, was acquitted of high treason because this was impossible where there was no settled government. The Fundamental Constitutions were even more of a dead letter in what from 1691 was occasionally called North Carolina than in the southern colony, although as there was no revolution the proprietary rule lasted until 1729. The legislation which was enacted related principally to such things as exemptions from suit for debts contracted outside of the colony and to marriages by a declaration of mutual consent before the governor, indicating that the settlement was the resort of the needy if not of the wicked. The rebellion of Culpepper at the same time as that of Bacon in Virginia, and the rebellion of Cary later, were only extreme instances of the usual lack of government. An unfortunate result of the last was that it brought on the Tuscarora war, when the Swiss Baron de Graaffenriedt and many of the Palatines whom he had brought from Europe to colonize about New Berne were slaughtered before Barnwell and Moore forced the Indians into subjection. Byrd, in his account of the boundary line, does not spare his southern neighbors. He speaks of their felicity of having nothing to do, and says that Edenton enjoyed the evil preëminence of being the one capital in the world without any place of worship. This was more pithy than true, for her St. Paul's records show organization in 1701, and, although the building was moved, the church kept its identity. Edenton was incorporated in 1712, and Bath was a town six years earlier. Immigration of French Protestants settled on the Pamlico and on the Neuse, and of the Swiss and Germans who survived the massacre, tended to develop the interior, and at the surrender by the proprietors the population was upward of ten thousand. They had in Archdale, Hyde, and Eden fairly good governors, and of the royal colony Gabriel Johnson made a good executive for almost twenty years. This, of course, did not prevent his having the same trouble with the Assembly that was now becoming common elsewhere, for the salaries of officials were payable from quitrents which could not be collected without enabling statutes. Prorogation and dissolution were not uncommon and were equally unproductive.

There were originally the three counties of Albemarle, Bath, and Clarendon, and now the precincts of these were made into counties and the three original names disappear, and in time others were added to the westward. When the seven proprietors surrendered their rights, Lord Granville retained his share, and in 1744 it was set apart to him as a strip sixty-six miles wide, extending along the northern border from the Atlantic nominally to the Pacific. Practically, it did him very little good, although for years even after the Revolution he litigated over his rights. There were schools at New Berne and Edenton, the Legislature sometimes meeting in the former schoolhouse, but the act of 1754 to establish a public seminary failed for want of royal assent.

The population of North Carolina during the French war was upward of fifty thousand, for the Scotch-Irish immigration in the west by way of the Virginia valleys was great. From this time they exported tar, pitch, turpentine, staves, corn, and tobacco, besides skins and some other products, the tobacco amounting apparently to one hundred thousand hogsheads. Thus the colony had reached a somewhat stable condition and was making what have ever since been its main products. Its war governor was Arthur Dobbs, who came in 1754, and his very efficiency as he understood it brought him in conflict with the Assembly. They even insisted that the council had no proper part in the legislative functions. A fort on the Yadkin to protect the growing western frontier was named for him. He died in 1765, over eighty years old, and was succeeded by Tryon.

In South Carolina, on the other hand, the Proprietary Revolution was effectual from the proclamation of Governor James Moore, December 21, 1719. The royal fleet that arrived threatened to give some trouble, but, upon fully understanding the situation, abandoned all effort to reinstate the deposed Johnson. He himself afterward accepted the situation, and Francis Nicholson became the established governor. Instructions sent out at this time became in effect the charter of South Carolina, although until the purchase from the proprietors in 1729 the government was provisional.

They provided for legislation by the governor, council, and Assembly, which last should have the same rights as the House of Commons; the Anglican Church remained established under the jurisdiction of the Bishop of London, by whom, or by the governor, schools were to be licensed; and the Royal African Company was to be given special encouragement. The people were now happy and loyal, although Colonel Rhett could foresee that the revolt against the proprietors would be a precedent for setting up for themselves.

Internal affairs being arranged and Carolina now expanding in all directions, it was important to secure the frontier toward the Cherokees. The nation had become attached to the English trade, and yet the active competition of the French from Fort Toulouse and afterward from the Ohio valley gave great concern. To counteract this, in 1730, Sir Alexander Cumming was appointed agent to deal with them, and with traders and interpreters he undertook an expedition to Keowee, on the upper Savannah, where he met chiefs of the lower towns and then assembled at Nequassee a general congress of all the nation. He was completely successful, making Moytoy head chief, and bringing back with him a delegation to carry to King George their national crown or emblem of feathers, as well as scalps and the like. This was done, one of the Indians being young Attakullakulla, and a treaty was entered into at London putting the Cherokees under British protection, "brightening the chain of friendship which connected the breast of the king and that of their chiefs," and providing means for "keeping the trading paths clean of blood." What King George thought of the scalps we are not told, but all public men of Walpole's time understood well enough the value of presents, and the chiefs returned to their country much impressed. Peace was long preserved and the Cherokees became faithful allies.

On the other border, the Spaniards harbored runaway slaves, refusing to give them up from a desire to save their souls by converting them to Catholicism. This was bad enough, but it was found, or thought, that emissaries tampered with the negroes in their homes, and certainly in 1738 there was an insurrection, and murder and arson were rife about Stono River. The plot was discovered on a Sunday when the whites were at church, armed as usual, and prompt action resulted in its suppression while a number of the slaves were drinking and dancing at one of their fires. There were forty thousand slaves in the province, and the dread of a servile insurrection was great, for many of the negroes were fresh from Africa and were more savage than the Indians. The Assembly gave the number of negroes as three to one of the whites, and certainly they were always more numerous.

In Oglethorpe's war we saw a Carolina regiment, and afterward Governor Glen built Fort Prince George and aided Virginia in erecting Fort Loudoun among the Cherokees. These and Forts Frederica and Augusta were guarded by royal troops. The misplaced activity of Lyttleton, the next governor, insulted the Cherokees, and, despite the campaigns of the regular army under Montgomery, caused the massacre of Fort Loudoun. This war was ended only by the merciless invasion of the nation by Colonel Grant, under whom served such provincials as Laurens, Moultrie, Marion, Pickens, and other names shortly to become famous.

The growth of population in the Southern colonies in the eighteenth century was marked. It was no longer confined to natural increase, or even to continued immigration from the home country, although each of these had its share. Carolina from an early period had a large Huguenot element, and now Swiss and Germans, who were building up North Carolina, came through Charlestown also. Jean Pierre Purry, of Neufchâtel, late of the Compagnie des Indes, received the grant of twelve thousand acres from the proprietors on condition that he secure three hundred colonists, and he proceeded by publication to arouse interest in the project. Beginning in 1733 he brought several hundred Swiss, and in a year or two Purrysburg on the Savannah was quite a flourishing place. Unfortunately, the transfer from the Alps to these lowlands was too great a climatic change, and the settlement suffered so from malaria as to be almost broken up. Some Swiss, however, went in another direction, and about this time with Palatines settled what was named Orangeburg on the north Edisto. Many were for their ocean fare, say £5, sold for a period of several years, and from their working this out were known as Redemptioners. They were generally Lutherans, although their ministers affiliated indifferently with Presbyterians or Anglicans and preserved their German language and customs for a long time. Similar was the origin of Saxe Gotha, but less welcome and less lasting was another foreign addition—the hapless Acadians. Their story was sad and the policy barbarous which expatriated them and burned their homes to prevent their return; but when in 1755 over a thousand came to Charlestown in successive shiploads, their distress appealed little to the Carolinians, for they were French Romanists, enemies against whom the English colonies were in arms, and even the Huguenots looked askance at the exiles. The vestries were instructed to care for them as for other poor and bind them out to labor. The government had difficulty in making disposition of the forced immigrants, and on their side the fugitives could not feel any love for the land of their captivity. Nor were they always meek. Some committed robberies, and many attempted to escape by boats or through the woods. Ultimately most of them drifted away, and we shall meet them in Louisiana. Over eleven hundred had been imported into Virginia also, and these, after being cared for through the winter, were sent to England.

Other foreigners also came to South Carolina, as Germans to Hard Labor Creek, and French to New Bordeaux and New Rochelle, and thus in the sixties was settled the Abbeville district. But, as in Virginia and North Carolina, the principal increase in population was due to the invasion by the Scotch-Irish of the upper country. Their original seat was at the Waxhaws, where long continued the parent church, and thence they spread through the deserted Catawba region. They were to supersede the Cherokees after the massacre of Fort Loudoun and that of their own Calhouns had been avenged by Grant and peace arranged by Bull. By the decade following 1770 one-third of Carolina's population of sixty thousand was in these back districts, and this fact had unexpected results.

There had long been complaint of a judicial system which compelled all litigants to go to Charlestown. The chief justice and assistants sitting in criminal cases made up the court of general sessions, in civil, that of common pleas, and the governor and council constituted a chancery court as in other colonies. It is true that from the Proprietary Revolution there were local tribunals analogous to county courts, but the limited jurisdiction and the lack of sheriffs impaired their utility. With the growth of the interior, the old parish system became inadequate. The need became pressing, and in 1768 circuit courts were provided for Charlestown, Orangeburg, Camden, Ninety-Six, Cheraw, Georgetown, and Beaufort. There was a difficulty in that the office of provost marshal, or high sheriff, was held by a placeman in England, but it was obviated by buying him out, although this was not done in the similar cases of the attorney-general and the clerk. Various objections prevented the act, even when amended to suit the Board of Trade, from going into effect for some years, until the upper country was almost in rebellion, and only in 1773 were the courts actually opened.

Thus gradually the needs of the growing population were met, but outside of Charlestown no town came into being except, about 1733, Georgetown on the coast, and that remained small. The civil divisions were not uniform. On the coast were parishes, gradually increasing in number, taking care of the poor and managing elections, more powerful even than in Virginia. In the interior the Scotch-Irish might as there possibly have adopted the same system in time, and civil development gone on unimpeded, although this is not probable, as there was a large lowland Presbyterian population also, which was not the case in Virginia. The Presbyterians thus came to equal the Episcopalians, and with Garden passed away the time for the Church to be able to make a show of disciplining Whitefields. There was a township system, it is true, but it was artificial, and the name only indicated a division of land. As a civil unit the parish was not to prevail in the interior, although with the close of our period nothing had taken its place except election districts to a limited extent.

In all the colonies were political struggles, many of sociological interest as showing what a Teutonic people would do under new conditions, and some of historical importance as training the colonists for constitutional conflicts on a broader stage. Of peculiar value were those in South Carolina because of the insular origin of its people, and especially because, not having subsequent to their Proprietary Revolution any definite charter, they fought out the battle on general principles of British rights after a training of strict construction under the old Fundamental Constitutions. They established, and were probably the first to establish, several institutions which are now fundamental.

There was the standing dispute as to the extent of the royal prerogative as represented by the governor, and it was complicated by the fact that there were numerous and long interregnums when governors were not appointed or did not come over, and the office was filled by Carolinians as presidents of the council or lieutenant-governors. Thus Arthur Middleton acted from 1724 to 1729, Thomas Broughton, 1735–1737, William Bull, Sr., from 1738 to 1743, and William Bull, Jr., in 1760–1761, 1764–1766, 1768, 1769–1771, and 1773–1775. The Bulls were thus almost professional *ad interim* executives, and by their wisdom healed many breaches made by the royal governors. One result of it all was that the power of the people became fixed, for, although firm for all proper prerogatives, these temporary governors looked on the government with Carolinian eyes and feelings. A more novel struggle was that between the commons house and the council as to amendment of money bills. The lower body was expressly given the rights of the English House of Commons, and this carried with it the exclusive power of originating revenue acts. The council attempted, however, in 1735, to add an item of £2,100, and the house was at once up in arms. The dispute continued in one form or another for years, involving even the right of the council to act as an upper house at all. This was discussed along the rather technical line whether since the abolition of the Fundamental Constitutions and the nobility there could be any Carolinian equivalent of the English House of Lords. The advantage of an upper house as a check upon hasty legislation was not prominent in the minds of the writers and orators of the day. It was rather a drawn battle as to the power of amendment, for there was no common judge to decide, and the compromise was adopted of having the council's amendments offered on the floor of the house. The council went further, however, and insisted successfully that not only were they more than a body of advisers to the governor, but as they were an upper house it was "unparliamentary" for him to be present at their debates. This was assented to by Bull, and the only modification subsequent governors could obtain was the right to be present without participation in the proceedings. It was therefore settled that the Assembly was made up of two bodies, the commons house and the council, and that the governor's power in legislation was limited to a veto.

The independence of the judiciary was also early established, particularly by Chief Justice Wright, himself the son of the English chief justice who tried the Seven Bishops. Deeming certain land grants illegal, the commons house in 1733 had their messenger, or sergeant-at-arms, arrest the claimant and his surveyor. The chief justice released them on *habeas corpus*, and stood firm against resolutions of the commons as to their power to imprison whom they pleased—even the chief justice. They deprived him of his salary, demanded his suspension, and sought to pass an act to prevent suits against magistrates refusing the writ. But all in vain. Wright in Carolina was not less determined than Holt in England. The three departments of government were clearly differentiated, and this earlier than elsewhere in America.

The domestic history largely centres about Charlestown, and this fact gives Carolina a peculiar tone which is not found elsewhere, for it thus not only has many elements of urban life but urban life of a very high character. The relative importance of Charlestown in colonial times has not been fully appreciated.

It is usually thought that education was at a low ebb in South Carolina, while the reverse seems to be the fact. Even before 1710 a free school was attempted, and we often find mention of legacies to found them. In 1712 there was an act for the encouragement of learning, and next year one for a free school in Charlestown. Governor Nicholson helped provincial libraries and aided schools and schoolmasters all he could. A difficulty was found in the fact that the teachers were to a large extent ministers of the Church of England, who shortly after arrival had calls to churches, and this interfered a good deal with the continuity of education. We find, on the other hand, a great many societies, charitable and otherwise, and even those of a social nature frequently had a benevolent side to them. Thus the Winyaw Indigo Society originated in 1740 at Georgetown, and when later at a convivial meeting the president proposed a charity school for the poor, the members emptied their glasses as a way of saying "aye." The school is said for over one hundred years to have been the educational mainstay of the district from Charlestown to the North Carolina boundary. In the interior there was more difficulty as to schools, but it is to be remembered that with the Scotch-Irish education and religion went together. The ministers were themselves educated, and among their duties teaching was

The earliest portraits of Washington. *Showing an alleged preliminary study of head on the left and the corresponding portion from the finished painting made by C. W. Peale in 1772.*

prominent. From early in the eighteenth century there was not a parish in South Carolina where education could not be obtained.

In the same direction was the influence of the press. The beginning of printing in South Carolina, as in the other colonies, was probably in publishing the laws, and then came newspapers. These last were by no means the great unbound folio books of modern times, telling everything new and strange, true and false, and influencing if not controlling public policy. The colonial papers were generally called "gazettes," and were in many respects only official publications. The day of great newspapers had not come, and yet, in proportion to information and civilization, these weekly journals held no mean place. A *Gazette* began in South Carolina in 1731 which, after some struggles, became a regular weekly, and in 1736 we have the *Virginia Gazette*, and thirteen years later the *North Carolina Gazette*, published at New Berne and professing to give the latest advices, both foreign and domestic. A competitor of the first *Gazette* came in 1758 as the *South Carolina and American General Gazette*, its name shadowing a dim feeling of common American interests. In Georgia, too, we have the *Georgia Gazette*, undertaken by the public printer. Shortly before the great Revolution it is said that in all America there were thirty-five newspapers, of which fourteen were in New England, four in New York, nine in Pennsylvania, two in Virginia and North Carolina each, in South Carolina three, and in Georgia one. In proportion to the white population, South Carolina would therefore head the list, for there was in that colony one newspaper to every fifteen or twenty thousand white people; in Massachusetts, which heads the list in the North, there was one to every fifty thousand. At the present time such comparisons would be unfair, because of the immense circulation of journals outside of the State of publication, but such was not then the case, as a newspaper had few readers beyond the colony in which it was printed.

If the test were made in regard to libraries, this colony ranks high. While there was a library at Henrico in 1623, and the Rev. John Harvard left his books to the Wilderness Seminary somewhat later, these were collegiate rather than public institutions, and it is probable that the first library in America supported by the public as such was one at Charlestown from 1698. In 1697 Governor Nicholson, of Maryland, had recommended the support of one which Dr. Bray was endeavoring to found, but nothing was done then beyond a vote of thanks; while in South Carolina not only was a committee appointed to return thanks, but dressed skins were sent to England to the amount of £70 current money to pay for books bought and to be bought in London. This institution was in existence in 1712, and the acts of the legislature on the subject are probably the earliest library laws in America. It is not known how long this library existed, but an association formed in 1743 imported some books and soon had quite a collection. The organization assumed the name of the Charlestown Library Society, and after a long while this was duly incorporated. The governor for the time being was always president, except when politically unacceptable, as was the case with Boone. This corporation met with varying fortunes, but in one form or another has continued until the present, and its collections are invaluable.

The existence of a real city made South Carolina different from every other southern colony. The planters found it necessary to resort to town during the summer months on account of the malaria prevalent in the marshes in which the rice was cultivated, and not infrequently they were there also at one time or another during the winter. The advantages of the schools, libraries, and newspapers were thus generally diffused. Not only were goods imported from the home country, but British manners were preserved in Charlestown perhaps more than in any other place in the country. People even imported bricks, and after they began to manufacture their own they still called them English. In true English fashion, whether in town or country, the Carolinians, like the Virginians, were fond of horses, which at first probably came from the Spaniards of Florida, although, no doubt, afterward Virginia supplied them.

Racing has existed from the earliest times in Virginia, and a characteristic judgment entry of the York County court in 1674 declared that it was a sport only for gentlemen. They put a man in stocks there for letting his horse run out of the track so as to enable a confederate to win the race. The distances were so great that the use of horses was universal, and in the next century a traveller reported that in Virginia no one walked. Races were perhaps the favorite amusement both in Virginia and Carolina, and the prizes are often mentioned in court and other records. In 1734 there is notice in Charlestown of a race for a saddle and bridle, and the same is found also in Virginia. The native stock was much improved about 1740 by importing blooded animals from England, and the interest in the turf was correspondingly increased. In 1752 there was a great race on the Gloucester race ground between William Byrd the Third's Tryall and Selima, from Maryland, in which Selima won. One of the most famous horses in Carolina was Flimnap, which the royalists were to endeavor, although in vain, to capture during the Revolution.

Carolina had other amusements also, for before 1735 there was a theatre, which antedates the one in Philadelphia and was probably the earliest in the country. In course of time, we find on its boards many of Shakespeare's plays, besides *She Stoops to Conquer* and other familiar names. Concerts also date from an early year; Josiah Quincy furnishes quite an elaborate account of one given when he was in Charlestown. Social societies have been mentioned as giving rise to schools; they encouraged music, and aided the insane also. In 1735 there was an organization for mutual insurance against fire, and this is earlier than the one over which Franklin presided in Philadelphia.

Society was gay and, as it often centred about the colonial governors, was sometimes brilliant, for the governors held considerable state. Dancing was taught in "all the forms approved in London," and drinking prevailed, although there was no evidence that it was to excess. It is even said that madeira became fashionable in England from being recommended by army and navy officers who had served in the West Indies and about Charlestown.

Charlestown established a Chamber of Commerce in 1774, which is early for such an institution, but shipping had been extensive for a long time before that. Thus in 1749 when Governor Glen answered some inquiries of the Board of Trade, he reported that there had loaded at Charlestown on an average two hundred and twenty vessels annually for the preceding ten years. In one season the commerce of South Carolina was eleven times as large with Europe as with the northern provinces, three times as large with the West Indies as with the colonies on the mainland, and similar proportions generally prevailed. The exports amounted to about £160,000, being mainly of rice, of which but little went south of Cape Finisterre, although Walpole had secured an Act of Parliament permitting such export for the purpose of encouraging its cultivation. Even then, indigo was a great staple crop of the colonists. It came originally from Hindostan, but was in 1741 introduced into South Carolina by Eliza Lucas, afterward the wife of Charles Pinckney and the mother of celebrated men. Indigo seed was sent to her by her father from Antigua, of which place he was the governor, and it soon became a considerable crop. Even in 1747 one hundred and thirty-four thousand pounds were sent to England, and in consequence the next year a bounty of sixpence per pound was allowed for the American article. By 1765 the increase in rice and indigo had been such that there were cleared from Charlestown three hundred and sixty vessels, besides forty from Beaufort and twenty-four from Georgetown, carrying in all over one hundred and ten thousand barrels of rice, and almost five hundred and fifty thousand weight of indigo, and by that time over one-fifth of the rice went south of Cape Finisterre. A barrel containing over six hundred pounds was worth some fifty-five shillings per hundred. There was, moreover, still a considerable business done in peltries, for the period after the pacification of the Cherokees was a prosperous time for that trade. The whole nation was mapped out into thirteen ranges, with a trader for every one, and in 1747 we find exported from Charlestown two hundred weight of beaver skins, seven hundred and twenty hogsheads of deer skins, all worth perhaps $300,000. These three articles, rice, indigo, and peltries, made up by far the principal items of South Carolina's foreign trade. It was not found necessary to impose taxes upon real or personal property, all necessary funds being derived from a three per cent duty on imports and on deer skins exported. Of the whole trade of the American colonies, which amounted to £3,000,000, South Carolina contributed about one-sixth. The imports also were considerable, although Glen—the governor for whom the Church failed to pray—endeavored to restrain them on the idea that the colonists in buying laces, linens, tea, and other articles were indulging in too much luxury. However, as a result of commerce Charlestown had become a great port and by far the richest in the southern part of America. Its quaintly named streets were busy thoroughfares and on them were the State House, Armory, St. Michael's Church, and new Exchange, all built since 1752, besides probably one thousand five hundred houses, including six meeting houses. St. Michael's was a famous building with a steeple one hundred and ninety-two feet high, a landmark visible far out at sea. Charlestown was outgrowing her fortifications, and had a population of almost eleven thousand, in which the negroes slightly predominated. Quincy says that in grandeur the city surpassed all he ever saw or ever expected to see in America.

In some respects the history of Georgia is not unlike that of South Carolina, particularly from the time of the surrender by the trustees to the crown. Slavery had already been permitted, the sale of liquor legalized, and, perhaps the most important of all, titles had been simplified, so that there was little distinction between the eastern and western banks of Savannah River. Rice was cultivated in the marshes near the sea, indigo on the islands, and the Indian trade divided between Savannah and Charlestown. Indeed, the distinctive features of Georgia's origin became almost obliterated. With the surrender by the trustees there was no longer any organized effort to transport to America the distressed of England or the continent, and immigration was left to follow more natural lines. A new characteristic, however, took the place of the old ones which had been lost. While immigrants still arrived from abroad, there came into existence the new feature of immigration from the older colonies. As early as 1752 the Medway River region, in what is now Liberty County, was peopled by Congregationalists from South Carolina, who called their new settlement Dorchester from the name of their earlier ones in Carolina and Massachusetts. They proved to be a valuable addition to the Georgia population, and took the lead in the troubles to come with the mother country. Their church lasted until the American Civil War, and the town of Sunbury, which was afterward built as the port for this region, had on its beautiful site a brilliant if short existence. The Moravians left Georgia, for their refusal to bear arms against the Spaniards was misconstrued, and the Salzburgers also did not remain in their old seats. In course of time, they all became mixed with the rest of the population, and the descendants of these German Protestants gradually spread in all directions, carrying thrift and character everywhere they went. Their names under different orthography can be traced in other communities, for to this day many a family in the South goes back to these persecuted highlanders of Austria. Further up the Savannah, about and above Augusta, colonists from Virginia and North Carolina and Scotch-Irish from other quarters soon occupied the territory acquired by treaty from the Creeks, and began that advance to the northwest by which Georgia was to become far more than a seacoast settlement. This was indeed the line of growth of all the colonies. Settled at first on the coast, where they had to fight for existence against white enemies, they gradually extended into the interior, acquiring by war or treaty with the natives land which was gradually peopled by sub-immigration, by the back door, as it were, from the other colonies. Georgia's freedom from Indian wars was always remarkable, and at no time more so than when the sister province of South Carolina was convulsed by the Cherokee massacres about Forts Prince George and Loudoun. It is true that as a precaution Savannah was palisaded, but its defences were never tested.

After the surrender by the trustees, Georgia became a royal province, with governor, council, and commons house of assembly. The chief executive as captain-general controlled the military, as governor participated in legislation, and judicially he was chancellor, presided in the court of errors, probated wills, and the like. He affixed to documents the great seal of the province, its design still commemorating in wax the hope of the government that the colonists should cultivate silk. As Oglethorpe had preferred Frederica to Savannah, which he also founded, so Governor Reynolds endeavored to build a new capital at Hardwicke, on Ogeechee River, and the plan was favored also by his successor, the efficient Henry Ellis. It was not abandoned until the time of James Wright, son of the Carolina chief justice, the last royal governor. Savannah suffered by the scheme and did not assume its proper rank until Wright's final decision. In 1758 the colony was divided like South Carolina into parishes, eight in number, all on the sea or on rivers, and these were followed a few years later by four more. Christ Church included Savannah, St. Matthew's embraced Ebenezer, Augusta was within St. Paul's, St. John's held both Midway and Sunbury, and Darien and Frederica were in St. Andrew's and St. James's respectively. While some provision was made for churches, it was never thoroughly carried out, and the parishes were really civil divisions. They were very large, and as population increased were, during the Revolutionary War, subdivided into counties, many of which still remain.

Exports at the beginning of this period were hardly £30,000, and when the Revolution came they were almost seven times this amount; but it would be a mistake, of course, to think of Georgia any more than of the other colonies as progressing quietly. The fear of the French and the fear of the Spaniards was gone, because in both directions the English ruled the old regions which had caused so much alarm; but Georgia would not have been British if there had not been a dispute between the Assembly and the governor, although it did not assume so acute a phase as elsewhere. With the vast extension of British possessions by the Peace of Paris, it was appropriate that Georgia should be rounded out to the south, and her boundary was accordingly fixed by the famous proclamation of October 7, 1763, at St. Mary's River. This was as near as fairly practicable to the line of thirty-one degrees which at first bounded West Florida on the north, and on the west the colony claimed to Mississippi River. This was the proclamation which prohibited extension of the colonies over the mountains, but in that respect it did not affect Georgia, for she had no transmontane possessions. It led, in fact, to a more compact development, for the result was a general treaty of cession and of peace with the Creeks in the fort at Augusta in 1763, under the presidency of Governor Wright, attended by several Southern governors.

The sparseness of the population, the extent of the provinces, and the distance of the settlements from each other, tended to create and maintain in all the Southern colonies an interest and a love for their respective governments. Possibly nowhere was the particularistic feeling stronger, and pride and love for local institutions were to develop later into zeal for State rights. And yet, by a paradox, the Southern colonies had so much in common as to give them a real unity. This was due to several causes and it had important effects, the more so that it was all unrealized by the people themselves. It sprang up as naturally as the growth of the tree from hidden roots.

We have seen running through the texture of all history the four threads of Family, Church, State, and Industry, intermingling their strands until the full pattern of civilization is shown, but often traceable separately. The family relation presents no variations in the Southern colonies from those seen in the Northern or in the old country, but there are strong peculiarities in regard to the other elements.

Elaborate attempts have been made to trace the origin of American civil institutions to the old village community of the Aryan races, and to some extent this has succeeded. Thus Mr. Freeman finds it distinctly preserved on the civil side in the New England town meeting, while in Maryland it reappears in the feudal manors. But further south there is greater difficulty. The efforts to discover it in Virginia and Carolina are sometimes forced, for while the Anglo-Saxons took with them to this as to all other quarters of the globe the same love of local self-government, the extent of settlement and the social conditions were so different as to call for new forms. The colonists brought with them in each instance written charters and elaborate regulations based upon a civilization which had changed the old Aryan system almost beyond recognition, and these entered largely into the development of the new States. When it came to civil organization, while hundreds and towns were not unknown in Virginia, the official unit was the shire, copied largely from the corresponding division in England. Its limits had to be changed in order to cover enough people and plantations to be worth the expense and trouble of government by a lieutenant, sheriff, and county court; and yet, the very names given show the survival of the old English local feeling. Thus the shire containing Jamestown was called James City, and the names of a number of others repeat the word "city." There were few real cities in Virginia, and in the shires which contain no towns the county seat was frankly called the "courthouse," nothing more. Gradually the word "county" superseded "shire," but the thing remained the same, and this institution became as marked a peculiarity of Virginia as the town meeting did of New England.

Ecclesiastically, the same conditions did not obtain. The church was the Church of England, and the parish was, as in the mother country, the district under the control of one pastor. We have seen that the weakness of the Church was the size of its parishes, and yet they were not coterminous with the counties. Women and children made up then as always a large part of the congregation, and this necessitated a smaller district than the county. Not unnaturally, therefore, the vestry of the parish had control over many local concerns, for this necessity had been appreciated in England itself, where indeed the parish meeting was in a sense the old "Tun-moot," or village community acting as to worldly concerns, such as the poor and even sometimes as to elections. In Virginia there was imposed upon the vestry the further neighborhood duty of processioning lands at certain intervals so as to fix private boundaries. The administration of justice assumed a somewhat different local form, for beats assigned to the justices of the peace appointed by the central government had no necessary connection with parish limits. Just as convenience made the county larger than the parish, so the same reason made the beats smaller, and caused them to bear some relation to business interests; for the value of justice is in its promptness. Collectively, the justices made up the county court and had all forms of jurisdiction. They probated wills, attended to orphans and administration business, heard appeals from the local justices, and had considerable civil and criminal jurisdiction of their own. They were always subject to appeal to the general court at the capital. The necessity for circuit courts came later, and bears a striking parallel to the institution in the earlier ages of England of the justices in eyre for the same purpose of making justice more uniform throughout the State.

It would be a mistake to assume that what was true of Virginia was true in Carolina and Georgia too, and yet the preceding review is in its main features correct for them also. Carolina, we recall, owed its immediate institutions to Barbadoes, where the presence of slavery and the growth of the parish system created an almost distinct form of civilization. When the Fundamental Constitutions of Locke died their natural death, the development of Carolina was along the lines brought by the Barbadian settlers. The church became the unit of civil organization, and this was carried out with a thoroughness which cannot be equalled outside of the Latin colonies, where Church and State were almost the same. The population of Carolina being more compact, this form of government suited local conditions, and the town meeting of New England was more closely paralleled by the parish meetings of Carolina than by anything in Virginia. Elections were almost from the beginning definitely committed to the vestries, and the parish was frankly made the civil unit. Here again, in true Anglo-Saxon manner, the names and theory did not run on all fours with the facts, for the extent of the Carolina parish made it really equivalent to the Virginia county. In Georgia we find much the same state of affairs, due no doubt largely to the neighborhood of Carolina with its established institutions. It is true that in Carolina the administration of justice was long confined to the city of Charlestown, and this resulted in building up that city at the expense of rural interests. We have seen that this was not the fault of the Carolinians themselves, for they passed laws to remedy the evil and these were vetoed in England.

As if to make the question more complex, there came to modify the situation a large number of immigrants from the continent of Europe. The legal theory was that the discovery of particular regions in America gave England,

France, or Spain, as the case might be, the absolute right thereto, provided the claim was consummated by possession. At first the natives were practically an important factor, although theoretically to the public law of that day they counted for little. Now, after centuries of white invasion, the Indians had become a negligible quantity, and there was a tacit assent that where the English had settled there they should remain. When continental colonists came, as in the eighteenth century, they came to a British country. The incomers were numerous, but they came now as settlers and not as invaders. And yet measurably the same result was to follow as in the case of England itself. There Danes, Normans, nay, the Anglo-Saxons themselves, had entered, sword and spear in hand, and civilization was evolved from these different elements. In America, on the other hand, the new white invasion was peaceful. In England the different districts settled of old by the different peoples remained to some extent separate and had their own customs, although, in course of time, all this was modified by contact.

In America there was no such barrier between the newcomers and the older white inhabitants. The Germans or the French came indifferently to New York or Carolina, and although for the first generation on account of language they remained separate, a fact aided by their settlement in new and unoccupied localities, they soon yielded to their surroundings, and the second generation spoke the language as well as obeyed the laws of Queen Anne or King George. And yet, coming as they did, and often many at one time, these foreigners could not but influence the colonies in which they planted themselves. Possibly Virginia remained the most homogeneous, while in the Carolinas the French as well as the Germans became important enough to name districts and long preserve their own method of worship. It is true that all were of the Aryan stock and some time in their history had had forms of the village community; but that was long ago, and it came to the surface now only so far as suited the new surroundings. The instances mentioned in recounting the stories of the several colonies by no means exhaust the immigrations from France and Germany. The Revocation of the Edict of Nantes is said to have driven seven hundred thousand Huguenots abroad, besides causing the death of two hundred thousand more, and many of those who crossed the Channel to England continued further and crossed the ocean to New York, Virginia, and the Carolinas. The Thirty Years' War also and subsequent oppression almost depopulated the Palatinate on the Rhine. Its inhabitants were largely Lutherans or Calvinists, and often found a refuge not short of America. The same was true, we may remember, of the Salzburgers, and, indeed, the whole of beautiful Germany was but a battle ground for the rest of Europe, and the fatherland for centuries could offer no home to many of its loving children. It has been said that the history of the colonization of America is the history of the crimes of Europe, and, on the other hand, the story of the development of these colonies is that of assimilation by the English of foreign material, which in its turn modified the blood and institutions of the older colonists.

Possibly the greatest single immigration of this kind was that of the Scotch-Irish, whom we saw turned by the Alleghanies of Pennsylvania southwardly into Virginia, whence they spread to the Carolinas and even to Georgia. And yet it must not be supposed that all the Scotch-Irish who were in the Southern colonies came by way of the Virginia valley. No doubt the great majority journeyed by this route, but some also came direct from Ireland. Many Irish are mentioned from time to time as arriving at Charlestown and elsewhere, and they were almost invariably Presbyterians from the north of Ireland. Papists, as the Catholics were called, were not welcomed, and very few came before the Revolutionary War. Many Scotch-Irish settled in the lowlands of the South, but some ascended the rivers until they met their fellow countrymen coming down from the other colonies. They deserve special consideration because, possibly, they were the largest influence outside of the original English, and they were to play a part greater than any other immigrants in modifying the institutions which they found. In their own mountains and backwoods, with the gun in one hand and the axe in the other, they not only protected the tidewater colonies but built up new communities after their own manner. In course of time they did more than this, and the courtly Virginian on the James and the fiery Carolinian of Charlestown found that their old commonwealths had ceased to be wholly their own. The Scotch-Irish backwoodsman was religious, and adhered with the earnestness of his Covenanter ancestors to the form of worship which Knox had brought from Geneva and which had been endeared to him by centuries of strife and persecution. And the same strife and persecution which made that dear made him detest episcopacy and aristocracy in all their forms.

There was thus to arise not only the difference which will be caused by different occupations and surroundings between men of the seacoast and men of the interior, between lowlanders and highlanders, but also the differences, amounting almost to an antipathy, between men of varying religious beliefs. There was no longer the strife of Protestant and Catholic as in the times of Elizabeth and Philip, for the American communities were at least of one general race and, living under a representative government, could fight out the battle of different interests in the legislative chamber. These Presbyterian backwoodsmen of Virginia not only took advantage of the Act of Toleration which from the time of King William had become the law of Virginia also, but they even began to insist that "toleration" was a misnomer and that all creeds should stand equal before the law. To the battle between liberty and prerogative, between Parliament and the burgesses, was added that of the Scotch-Irish for religious liberty. It was not until later that George Mason was to carry this principle and Thomas Jefferson to write the bill which secured it, but any view of colonial times which ignores the struggle is imperfect. In Carolina there was less need for such an act, because on account of the composite character of its population religious freedom had long been practically carried out despite laws to the contrary. These Scotch-Irish came in such numbers as ultimately to affect the polity of America. They were to make toleration more than a name and in their own Jefferson inaugurate more than one kind of revolution. From them were to come Marshall, Henry, Paul Jones, and later the Jacksons, a Lincoln, and a Grant.

No small part in this movement was played by George Whitefield in his American tours. Differing from the Wesleys in his Calvinistic beliefs, caring nothing for the Episcopal forms which at first he did not discard, he shook the dry bones of ecclesiasticism and both revived religion and split the churches. He knew no North and no South, and from Boston to Georgia was equally at home. He was possibly the greatest preacher ever known, for it is said his hearers sometimes went insane, and, although of conciliatory temperament, the Word in his hands was like a sharp two-edged sword, piercing to the marrow, dividing even denominations asunder. The Old Side and New Side schools date from his teachings. The cast of his eyes does not seem to have diminished the charm of his personality, and it is curious that his domestic life, like that of his friend Wesley, was marred by marriage to a widow. We are gravely told by Whitefield's biographer that the death of his wife brought peace to his mind. His revivals affected even the Anglican establishment, and there was need, for Byrd tells us that the Virginians thought being members of the Established Church sufficient to sanctify very loose and profligate morals.

Thus grew the Southern colonies, the inhabitants of each intent upon his own commonwealth and yet all tending in the same direction, creating a sectional unity while building up separate States, forgetting the savages who had meant so much to their ancestors, and pressing onward to a new goal, they knew not what. There was still a Latin civilization facing them, there were yet to be problems connected with their relations to their own mother country. What the future held for them they could not tell, nor did they often stop to wonder. But perhaps they were building better than they knew.

On the whole, except for a while on the borders, the time of the last French war, as well as that just before and after, was one of prosperity. Politically something was won and much valuable experience gained, and agriculture and commerce were improved, although there was some uneasiness at the increase of slaves, enforced by the home government. City life came more to the front, especially in Carolina, and intellectual activity increased with education, newspapers, and discussion. The war itself brought a vast increase of population in the Scotch-Irish, who infused more religion and more sturdiness generally into colonial life. People even began to look westward to see if settlements were not possible beyond the mountains, and eastward to revise perhaps the relations with the mother country. If the period of original colonization of the coast had practically closed, that of colonial development had come.

John Page.
After the painting by Charles Willson Peale.

Edmund Pendleton.
After the painting now hanging in the State Library, Richmond.

Cyrus Griffin.
After the painting by Thomas Sully.

CHAPTER XX

THE FLORIDAS

THE changes called for by the Treaty of Paris were world-wide in their scope, and it was not for some time that the transfer of the Floridas and east Louisiana was effected. On August 7, 1763, Captain Wills, of the third battery of royal artillery, proceeded from Havana and received from the Spanish commandant possession of Pensacola, from which on the 3d of the next month every Spaniard sailed for Vera Cruz. In October a detachment of Highlanders reached Mobile, and the *procès verbal* of transfer was signed by De Velle and Fazende for France and Robert Farmar for Great Britain. The lilies were lowered, the red flag ascended to the music of bagpipes, and Bienville's fort was renamed Fort Charlotte for the young Queen of England. About the same time, St. Augustine was similarly occupied, and the British banner waved over the whole continent east of Mississippi River, except the New Orleans district.

The new possessions other than those immediately around the three towns named, and as many in the northwest, had few inhabitants except the Indian tribes; and the government, with true British indifference toward the past history of its provinces, proceeded as on a *tabula rasa*, and by proclamation of October 7th divided up the country on new lines. Of course, the old Atlantic colonies were not themselves disturbed, but their claims of extension westwardly received a rude shock. In the negotiations before the treaty

England had declined to adopt the French suggestion to create a neutral ground, or buffer country, to be reserved for the Indians between British and French possessions; but now it seemed good to carry out that idea and create an Indian zone embracing most of the Ohio valley, while the part of French Louisiana south of the parallel of thirty-one degrees and all Spanish Florida were thrown into hotchpotch and subdivided anew. Peninsular Florida, that is, the part lying east of Appalachicola River, was called East Florida, with its capital at St. Augustine; and all west of the Chattahoochee and the Appalachicola to the Mississippi was erected into a separate province called West Florida, with Pensacola for its capital.

The line of thirty-one degrees was soon found to be inappropriate, as it made continental Florida little more than a strip of seacoast, dependent, especially in the case of Mobile, upon rivers whose sources and main courses were far outside, among Indian tribes like the Choctaws, Creeks, and Chickasaws. Next year it was pushed up to thirty-two degrees twenty-eight minutes, and thus included the site of Natchez, which had been important in the past and for strategic reasons might become so again.

It may well be that the British government had no definite plan in view when it acquired the province, except to get at least two good ports on the Gulf of Mexico. Up to this time, the British possessions had been confined to the Atlantic coast, and the Treaty of Paris in effect exchanged the port of Havana for those of St. Augustine, Pensacola, and Mobile, besides affording the possibility of developing others. Intentionally or otherwise, this was one step in the expansion of British power over the globe and more particularly in America. With the acquisition of the valley of the St. Lawrence on the north and the peninsula of Florida with all ports west to Lake Borgne on the south, Great Britain had acquired a scientific frontier, or rather her possessions were so extended that there was no frontier except at Bayou Manchac.

Under the French in the Mobile part of West Florida, as under the Spaniards in Pensacola and the peninsula, the government had been practically military. So far as there was a civil or political side, it was carried on by the same persons under another title. This was not to be the case with the British, for George Johnstone came early on the scene as a civil governor. The military of West Florida was commanded until 1765 by Colonel William Taylor, and the post at Mobile consisted at first of the Twenty-second and Thirty-fourth Regiments. After Taylor came the famous Bouquet, whose administration would doubtless have been energetic and beneficial to the province had he not died shortly after his arrival. A pathetic feature is, according to the story, that while he was away on duty his fiancée, Miss Willing, of Philadelphia, married Mr. Francis, a wealthy Londoner, and that the soldier grieved himself to death. He was buried in a tomb of English gray brick on the shores of Pensacola Bay, but all memorial of this too faithful love has long since disappeared, possibly washed away by encroachments of the sea.

His successor was Frederick Haldimand, whose term was almost equally important for what he did and for what he preserved. Swiss by birth, he was, like his friend and fellow countryman Bouquet, an officer of note in the British service. A misfortune in the history of the Southern colonies is the lack of memoirs, letters, and diaries, so that it is a great thing to chance upon so methodical a man. He seems to have kept almost every paper written to him and copies of much of his own correspondence. This collection, very miscellaneous in character, but all the more valuable on that account, he left at his death to a nephew, who in turn bequeathed it to the British Museum. These documents present an attractive picture of his business ability. They cover almost every conceivable subject, from remarks on the relations of Spain and Great Britain, or the conflict between the military and civil authorities of West Florida, to the question of rum *vs.* sassafras beer for the soldiers, complaints of a widow about officers leaving her boarding-house without paying, or the planks, chickens, and eggs supplied by a French carpenter. When you add to this the fact that he was in debt considerably, and for family reasons active in trying to get commissions for nephews and friends, it may be imagined that he had his hands full,—as did also General Thomas Gage, at Boston, for he not only supervised Haldimand in Florida, but other commanders in different parts of America. Gage had to go to England in 1773, and Haldimand was promoted to take his place at New York until Gage returned to America two years later. Thus when the Boston Tea Party and other troubles came, Haldimand was in command, but, as it was thought inexpedient that a foreigner should be prominent in dealing with the colonists, he was sent to the West Indies. He was Governor of Canada for the ten years following 1778, and to Canadian interest in that fact we owe the existence in America of full copies of his papers.

At Mobile we have that very interesting character, Major Robert Farmar [or Farmer], of the Thirty-fourth Regiment. He was then forty-five years of age, and the picture of him by the contemporary Aubry is both valuable and piquant. "This governor of Mobile," writes he to the French government, "is an extraordinary man. As he knows that I speak English, he occasionally writes to me in verse. He speaks to me of Francis I. and Charles V. He compares Pontiak, an Indian chief, to Mithridates; he says that he goes to bed with Montesquieu. When there occur some petty difficulties between the inhabitants of New Orleans and Mobile, he quotes to me from the Magna Charta and the laws of Great Britain. It is said that the English ministry sent him to Mobile to get rid of him, because he was one of the hottest in the opposition. He pays me handsome compliments, which I duly return to him, and, upon the whole, he is a man of parts, but a dangerous neighbor, against whom it is well to be on one's guard."

The major was very active in entertaining the Indians in French fashion, although much against his will, in repairing dilapidated Fort Charlotte, and in securing military supplies. Farmar became quite attached to West Florida, and Mobile in particular, and managed to secure several grants of land, one being a place where the British had their statehouse or headquarters. On reaching Mobile he had complained that the real estate used by the government was claimed by private individuals, and it would seem that the lesson had not been lost on himself. Having a semi-independent command, he had large discretion in military affairs. He joined hands with Gage in opposition to Johnstone's claim of supremacy over the military, for the general distinctly instructed Taylor to recognize no such claim, and Farmar was among the nineteen officers at Mobile who signed the memorial against the governor which Gage forwarded to Lord Halifax at court. Johnstone heartily reciprocated Farmar's dislike and made charges of embezzlement, which, of course, led to a court martial. The charges were, specifically: "For sending flour belonging to the King to New Orleans, and selling or attempting to sell it there, by means of one Pallachio, a Jew. For selling the Fort of Tombeckbee to Mr. Terry, a merchant. For misapplication of ten thousand pounds said to be expended on Indian presents, and on the fortifications. For making a job of the Publick service, in the operation of the Iberville. For turning in a different channel the monies, which should have been expended on the Barracks, so that the officers and soldiers lived in a miserable condition. For insisting to charge five bitts p. barrel for lime, which could be made for three bitts, and dividing the profits with the Engineer. For desiring the Engineer to bear a man extraordinary upon the works at three shillings, P. Diem; and to charge a laboring negro belonging to him the Major at three shillings more, both which was done. For employing the King's boat to his own emolument, and dividing the profits with the sailors." The matter dragged on for some time on account of the difficulty of getting witnesses, and involved incidentally a court martial on charges preferred by Farmar against Lieutenant Pittman. It outlasted Johnstone's term and resulted in the full acquittal of Farmar.

On his arrival in Pensacola the governor was given a house in the fort as his residence, but this courtesy led to bad results, for Haldimand was to observe that it gave Johnstone the impression that he owned the fort, too. By decision of the attorney-general of the province, confirmed at Whitehall, the forts were declared to be subject to the governor's jurisdiction, but the military strenuously insisted that they themselves were not. The very opposite of the French system therefore developed; and instead of there being no distinction between civil and military governments, they were not only different but at odds, the civil department even claiming to be supreme and to have the direction of the other. The dispute was by no means courteously conducted. Everybody took sides one way or the other and the spirit of faction became rife, affecting all public and even private affairs.

Of the condition of West Florida at the time of the British occupation we may form some idea from that of Pensacola, the new capital, which then consisted of only forty thatched huts and some small barracks, all surrounded by a stockade of pine posts. Even as late as 1767, when some improvements had been made, Haldimand writes to Gage that the place was in a wretched state, the forts being decayed, the huts merely of bark and the palisades of wood, as were the hospital, storehouse, and everything else, which the least spark might destroy and which were at best entirely at the mercy of the Indians. The streets of the towns were narrow, as was the case in Mobile also, and the heat even in April great and the air stagnant, causing mortality. The water at Pensacola was a mere drain from the swamp and "when unadulterated was as bad as pure rum." There was confusion in the province caused by the quarrels of officials, but Haldimand was then trying to establish some method in public business, and appointing officers to carry on the public duties. He found Lieutenant Elias Durnford, the governor's engineer, a willing worker, but subject primarily to the orders of the civil branch and for a while not available for military purposes.

It was fitting that the capital of the province should present an attractive appearance, and the field was clear for reconstruction of the town according to Durnford's plan, which still prevails. This consisted in running streets north and south from the bay, the main avenue being named George [now Palafox], and one to the eastward Charlotte [Alcaniz]. The space between as far north as what is now Intendencia Street was reserved as a public park and on it was placed a star-shaped stockade fort, for some time the only defence of the town, and near it were barracks, storehouse, magazine, and other public buildings. As a military as well as sanitary measure Haldimand cut away much of the forest and undergrowth surrounding the town to the north, and converted what were swamps into meadows. Lots south of Garden Street were eighty by one hundred and seventy feet; north of this they were one hundred and ninety-two feet square, called arpent or garden lots, also private property, being numbered to conform to the smaller town lots, and used for cultivation by the respective owners. So that while the survey was English, the plan still preserved features frequent in the Spanish settlements and which recall the arrangements of the old village community. Durnford, without knowing it, was with his house and garden lots working on the same lines as the New England towns, whose origin goes back to Aryan or even more primeval times. George Street was extended by causeways or otherwise to an elevation known as Gage's Hill, now marked by the Confederate monument. Here Haldimand built a considerable fortress named Fort George, a part of which still remains around the Herron residence, and, as the safest place in the capital, within Fort George were the council chamber and the archive office. The city was not without good buildings. Bartram speaks of the governor's stone palace, with a dome, erected by the Spaniards, although this is somewhat doubtful. The largest business firm was that of Panton, Leslie and Company, whose senior member, William Panton, had a handsome house and garden on the bay. The warehouse still survives and the house foundations are visible.

The vicinity of the capital was not neglected. At Tartar Point, later the site of the United States Navy Yard, a battery and barracks were built, and it is an interesting though singular fact that the name of the point is almost the sole reminder of the British occupation. Similarly at Red Cliff, or Barrancas, were two batteries, one at the top and the other at the foot of the hill, with officers' quarters and soldiers' barracks in one structure, built in the nature of a block house. Near, was the powder magazine of the province, itself a survival of the old Spanish fort of San Carlos.

Thus Pensacola practically dates from the British occupation, but Mobile, far from being rebuilt at that time, became, by the exodus of many French, smaller than before, although it remained the largest town in the province. The centre was still the old fort, now renamed Charlotte, and the royal wharf leading out to fourteen feet of water is the only one shown in the plans. The town extended along the river bluff, the front street, still called Royal, running north and south from the fort. One block west was the government house adjoined by the bakehouse, and a block further was the long Indian house, the scene of treaties. Further north were the warehouse and hospital. All over the town were public parks. The principal residences were of brick, surrounding a courtyard, while those of the poorer class were made of cypress filled in with brick, plastered and whitewashed. It was a fair type of all the French towns in America, New Orleans being larger and Vincennes being smaller, but all were much alike. The houses were shaded by oaks and magnolias. The botanist Bartram travelled over the South at this period and was much pleased with the place, although he found many houses vacant and mouldering to earth. The Indian trade, he notes, was managed by the house of Swanson and McGillivray, who had made great improvements.

The principal change made by the British was in the way of improvement of trade, for the bulk of the inhabitants remained French as heretofore. For a while the British suffered greatly in health, according to Haldimand, on account of their own imprudence, and a summer resort had to be provided for the soldiers across the bay at Croftown. Gradually this difficulty was overcome, and the business of the port with Great Britain became considerable. By 1776 it paid upward of £4,000 annually in the custom house of London alone.

The work cut out for the British gradually developed along several lines. There was, of course, the matter of the old population of West Florida, Indian and Latin, and the problem of securing immigration. Development of agriculture and trade must be encouraged, and then again there was the fact that this country was valuable not only for itself but for its connection with Mississippi River, toward which routes by land or water must be opened. And lastly, there were to arise, although more slowly, the political questions connected with representation and government. Great Britain by this time knew how to colonize a virgin country; but in this instance there was an old, settled colony, of a Latin power, and on a small scale there was the same problem which was faced on the St. Lawrence.

First in immediate importance probably was the Indian question. We have studied the methods of the French and seen how the natives immediately adjacent became devoted to them, and that while they were dependent it was not the dependence of the Indians upon the Spaniards. There was, if anything, more danger of the French becoming Indianized than of the Indians becoming Gallicized, for their customs and habits were all respected and the natives had come to consider themselves as quasi-subjects of King Louis. With the British, on the other hand, the popular although perhaps not the official view was that the only good Indian was a dead Indian. The wars upon the James and elsewhere were almost incessant, and proceeded on the idea that there was natural enmity between the white and red races, and that the English were gradually to dispossess the Indians of their territory. There was no declaration to this effect, and yet the difference between the polished and insinuating Frenchman and the rough Briton was so marked that the Indians of the Southwest showed a tendency to leave their seats and retire across the Mississippi so as to remain with their old friends. The Alibamons, for instance, took this course, although for a while some of them remained on the east bank of the river near Bayou Manchac, and the Coosadas had camps for a little while on the lower Tombigbee. Even where they did not actually leave the country, a number of the small tribes whose names have become so familiar retired from the coast and were lost among the greater nations of the interior. Thus the Chattos, the Naniabas, and others joined the Choctaw tribe; and if the Taensas and Apalaches remained in part near Mobile River, they gradually thinned in numbers.

And yet, it would be a great mistake to think that the English had no Indian policy or that this policy was not a success. The contrary is true. Fort Toulouse and Fort Tombecbé, under its altered name of Fort York, were occupied, a garrison being maintained at the former, as much to watch the Indians, and perhaps foment their quarrels, as for any other reason. Toulouse never was much used, and Gage wrote that the expense of occupying Fort Tombecbé made it the dearest post on the continent. It was abandoned in the severe winter of 1768 and other means adopted to retain influence over the savages. Distributions of merchandise in the way of presents were regularly made, but in respect to trade there was quite a change from the French method, which had regarded it as a function of the government. It was still fully recognized that there was need for supervision, and the plan adopted was that of putting the traders under license and bond, which some thought worked successfully. While these measures kept the Indians more or less satisfied, there was need of some definite understanding under the altered conditions as to the acquisition of land. Where the white and the red man were equally subjects of the French king, this was hardly necessary; but from the British tendency to keep the races separate it seemed expedient to have a treaty basis. Thus came about the treaty of March 26, 1765, arranged and carried out by the influence of Superintendent John Stuart, of Fort Loudoun memory. This was more particularly with the Choctaws and the Chickasaws, but another at Pensacola, of almost the same time and embracing the Creeks also, pursued the same policy. The former was the more striking historically, because inaugurating for the Southwest the policy of the Atlantic colonies, continued by the American government after the Revolution, of extinguishing the Indian title. Practically the seacoast about Mobile and the lower river basin, particularly up the Tombigbee, was open to white occupation, but now there was a definite cession of this land with greater extent than heretofore actually occupied, constituting the first link in all chains of title.

The congress at which the treaty was made was attended by Governor Johnstone, Superintendent Stuart, and twenty-nine chiefs, and was probably held in the Indian house, which had just been repaired. Stuart's "talk" has been preserved by Hewat and is a model of firmness and tact, couched in the imagery dear to the natives.

A congress was held almost every year, although the military said the principal object was for the governor to make a show, and land cession was not the only subject of discussion, for there were questions as to traders, liquor, and murders by one side or the other. Stuart was efficient, and in influence in the southern department hardly inferior to Sir William Johnson in the northern. He had a deputy, Charles Stuart, located first at Mobile and then afterward at Pensacola, and various agents among the tribes, such as David Tait for the Creeks, and Alexander Cameron for the Cherokees. The department was subject to the military, although from 1768 the regulation of Indian affairs, including traders and supplies, was by direction of the home government left to the colonies, and the superintendent had control only of such matters as were of immediate negotiation between the king and the savages. There was almost constant trouble, the cause being principally the introduction of rum by the traders despite all regulations, and hardly second to this was the encroachment on Indian lands. As a result there were frequent murders of whites and sometimes of Indians, requiring diplomacy and satisfaction in their adjustment. The home government disapproved of fomenting quarrels among the tribes, but the military thought this the true policy, and as opportunity offered quietly indulged in it. There was ever fear that emissaries from the Northwest or traders and others from New Orleans would unite the southern Indians against the British, and so the authorities were not unwilling to see the restless Creeks involved in difficulties with the Choctaws, who were sometimes aided by the Chickasaws. There was war between them from 1766 until the summer of 1770, and it was renewed at intervals afterward. Haldimand and Stuart even thought the colonies owed their own exemption from Indian war, despite rather acute friction between the races, to the fact that the savages were thus too much taken up with their own quarrels.

The white population heretofore had been exclusively French or Spanish. From Mobile had gone out the families who settled New Orleans and the banks of the Mississippi; and now that the daughter settlements had grown and were, so far as could be seen, to remain French, it was not unnatural that many of the parent city should prefer to follow the old flag to the west. From the time of the British occupation, therefore, we find a partial emigration from Mobile and a complete exodus from Pensacola, the Spanish going to Mexico. The mass of people about Mobile remained French, and since the institution of negro slavery there had arisen a considerable mulatto population, who also spoke French and were even less apt to leave the old homes than their white congeners. Not only were these people in the towns, but also far up the rivers and in the interior. These quiet, thrifty creoles, both white and of mixed blood, did much to develop the country, and if they lacked the ambition and aggressiveness of the Anglo-Saxons they at least lived simpler lives and suffered less from disease. Even as late as 1771, when Romans descended the Tombigbee what few inhabitants he found bore French names.

When Spain sent Ulloa to take possession of her province of Louisiana, the dissatisfaction of the French at New Orleans was so general as to lead to a plan on the part of the British to induce them to come over in large numbers to Mobile. Haldimand, being a French Swiss himself, entered heartily into the scheme and did all he could to advance it. It is not certain what success it had. The French remain much attached to their native soil, and even in Acadia it took absolute force to make them move. Here, in point of fact, in some instances the movement was the other way. The British had succeeded in getting one Monberault, a French officer who had a pleasant home at Lisloy in the lower part of Charlotte County, to enlist in their Indian service; but Johnstone did not have the tact to keep on good terms with the new recruit, and as a result Monberault not only abandoned his place but left the province and became an officer in New Orleans under the King of Spain. Gage, it is true, calls him a dirty fellow, but then this was after Monberault had gone and Gage's views might have been biased.

The British have in tropical lands been content to adopt the French plan and rule subject races, but they have instinctively felt in all temperate zones that hold upon a country must be secured by colonization of their own race. West Florida was no exception. It was not long after Governor Johnstone's arrival in February, 1764, that he issued a glowing proclamation or circular painting the beauties and advantages of the country. Agriculture, timber, and trade with Central America were dwelt on, and analogies found to Tyre, Sidon, Carthage, Colchos, Palmyra, Amsterdam, Venice, and Genoa. "On the whole," we learn, "whether we regard the situation or the climate, West Florida bids fair to be the emporium as well as the most pleasant part of the New World."

There were from the beginning newcomers from Great Britain and the other colonies, besides a number of disbanded soldiers; and when friction arose between the parties known as Whigs and Tories on the Atlantic, there was a large immigration of the latter. In fact, how much is due to the British domination is not often appreciated. The country has been so long American that a great deal which is really British, dating back to this time, has been considered as American in origin. Many names of families, of plantations, and of natural objects can be traced to the British occupation of West Florida. As an inducement to settlement the colonial government was authorized to grant lands, without fee, to reduced officers of the last war and private soldiers disbanded in the province, as follows: a field officer might obtain five thousand acres, a captain three thousand, a subaltern or staff officer two thousand, a non-commissioned officer two hundred, and a private fifty acres. These grants were free of taxation for ten years, and only after that time subject to the same quitrents and conditions as other lands in the province; and many took advantage of the provision.

Besides the Indian trade and the promotion of immigration, there was the development of agriculture and all other natural resources for domestic consumption and foreign trade to occupy the British. They found that the products of the country about Mobile and Pensacola were insignificant.

Cotton was not unknown, but amounted to little. Indigo was cultivated with some success, while timber and lumber, which have become the two leading productions of the district, were as yet hardly touched. Hides were perhaps the principal export.

Trade with the Indians could use trails and rivers, but commerce with European and American centres called for good harbors and roads. So far as is known, the French had never made an accurate chart of the Bay of Mobile, nor had the Spaniards of Pensacola. There are numerous maps, but they usually give no soundings. Being the modern maritime nation of the world, England has always been quick to find harbors and necessarily to make soundings and charts, and such was now the case along the north coast of the Gulf, as is shown by the charts of Jeffreys and others. A special instance is found in the admiralty chart of Mobile Bay dating from 1771.

Later came a project of a road to the Natchez settlement, but it is uncertain how far it was actually carried out. The internal improvement of this part of the province was along another line. It early occurred to the provincial authorities that if Bayou Manchac, otherwise called Iberville River, could be made navigable, there would be an all-water route from Mobile Bay, under the shelter of the outlying islands of the sound, into Mississippi River, practically within British territory, instead of the longer way through the passes and the lower Mississippi under the cannon of the Spaniards. This plan was no new one, and even the old Compagnie had wished to utilize the Iberville. Until steam was applied to navigation, which was not to be for fifty years, rivers could not be used to the best advantage; but still a good deal was accomplished by bateaux or canoes in the old Indian fashion. Therefore, it seemed worth while trying to open what was called the Lake Route, especially as in March, 1764, when Major Loftus with four hundred troops attempted to ascend the Mississippi he was driven back by the Tonika Indians. For this reason in the summer of 1764 the British repaired Fort Rosalie on the commanding bluff of Natchez, renaming it Panmure, and stationed a garrison there; and in January, 1765, if not earlier, Colonel Taylor took steps toward clearing the river Iberville. In that month Lieutenant James Campbell, of the Thirty-fourth Regiment, received upward of £326 for this purpose, and next month the larger sum of £863 was paid to Dupard on the same account. In April, Pittman was at work there, but he contended that his predecessors had cut the drift logs up so near the Mississippi that they were carried by high water yet further into the Iberville and blocked it up. In connection with this work the Scots Fusiliers in the next year, by command of Governor Johnstone, built a fort on the site of the workmen's camp, and thus originated Fort Bute. Every summer the Iberville was dry, for its bed was then twelve or more feet above the Mississippi, and Strachan's plan for deepening it by drawing water from the Mississippi was hardly practicable in those days. Gage was never favorable to the Mississippi forts, and thought that the contraband trade of the French with the Choctaws could be better prevented by boats, although Haldimand was satisfied that forts had a good effect upon the Indians. There was ultimately much more smuggling by the British into Louisiana than by the French into Florida.

Of course, the building of forts by the British led to the building of forts by the Spanish, and soon opposite Bute and Panmure rose corresponding fortifications, confirming Gage's idea that such distant posts could not be held in the event of rupture with the Spaniards. Haldimand looked more into the future in suggesting a military colony at the Natchez, and a commandant there later declared it desirable to fix the site of a town near the fort. A settlement under military supervision was to be the ultimate solution. In 1765 or 1766 some adventurous North Carolinians came by sea and river and settled about Natchez and Bâton Rouge, and others emulating them pressed over the Alleghanies to the Mississippi country, and, exploring and

Joseph Habersham, of Georgia.

After the painting by Charles Willson Peale, in Independence Hall, Philadelphia.

Noble Wimberley Jones, of Georgia.

After the painting by John Wesley Jarvis, in Independence Hall, Philadelphia.

hunting, began the trade to New Orleans. By the irony of fate, on their overland return the adventurers were by the Choctaws robbed of all they had made. We find speculators even in 1767 discounting the future and securing warrants of survey for large tracts of land about Natchez. Thus the Earl of Eglinton, the Colonel Grant of the South Carolina Indian wars, got twenty thousand acres, and Samuel Hannay and associates five thousand. John McIntosh obtained five thousand contiguous to Fort Bute, George Johnstone ten thousand at Bâton Rouge, and Daniel Clark, afterward a famous name, showed his foresight by locating three thousand at Natchez, one thousand at the head of Lake Maurepas and five hundred more near Fort Bute.

Gage, in 1769, seems to have been glad to carry out the orders from England to abandon Mobile, Pensacola, and St. Mark's also, and to remove almost everything and everybody of military character. From three to six companies only were left to look after Mobile and Pensacola, and the rest were taken to St. Augustine, although some, especially those with artillery, were sent to Charlestown. The consternation in West Florida may well be imagined, and even the civil government suddenly discovered a warm attachment for the military. Every effort was used to procure the rescission of the order. The inhabitants of Pensacola petitioned vigorously against such abandonment of the "Emporium of the West," although Haldimand sarcastically attributed the anxiety there and at Mobile to a desire to make a hundred per cent or more out of the supplies they had to sell.

This flurry was not to last long, for by May next year Haldimand was back at Pensacola with instructions to distribute the troops between Mobile and Pensacola as before, for the English government was somewhat apprehensive that O'Reilly's Spanish troops were to be used against West Florida as well as the Louisiana insurgents, and for that reason restored its own. A guardship was also placed at Manchac.

During the withdrawal of the troops, one John Bradley received possession of Fort Panmure with the duty of keeping it in order and defensible. Even at this time some enthusiasts thought of Natchez as a terrestrial paradise, for the project of settling the Mississippi remained a favorite idea of the province, and in 1770 this began in earnest. It would seem that some eighteen families of immigrants with negroes settled down about Natchez, and Chester promptly applied for troops to protect them. Gage, of course, opposed it, and expressed astonishment that avidity for lands should make people scramble thither through the deserts. The necessity may be shown by a report to Haldimand in 1772 that the materials of Fort Bute had been destroyed and the writer turned out by the help of the Spanish officers; but this seems to stand unsupported. The jealousy of the Spaniards, however, might well be aroused, for Durnford reports that three hundred persons from Virginia and the Carolinas were then settled on the Mississippi and three or four hundred families were expected before the end of summer. As a result the posts at Natchez and Bute were ultimately repaired and some sort of government instituted on the Mississippi. Good order prevailed in the Natchez settlement, according to the surveyor Thomas Hutchins, and even the Indians were amicable, and a considerable immigration took place from New England under the distinguished General Lyman in 1775. Under a treaty with the Indians the boundaries of the Natchez district were marked off, and then development began in earnest. Colonel Putnam went to the Mississippi from New England with a company of adventurers, and returned charmed with the country in the neighborhood of the river Yazoo. In 1777 Bartram found at Fort Bute the large establishment of Swanson and Company, a branch of the great Indian trading firm of Swanson and McGillivray at Mobile, and writes of a wooden bridge over the narrow Iberville connecting Louisiana and West Florida, and commanded by the forts of both Spanish and British.

The public history of the province was not eventful, apart from quarrels of the civil and military authorities, but it is not without interest. Governor Johnstone had resigned in 1766, and Montfort Browne, the lieutenant-governor, proved more conciliatory to the military. Elliott, who succeeded, committed suicide, apparently just after his arrival at Pensacola. The influence of Haldimand then secured the appointment of Durnford as acting governor, and in the year 1770 Peter Chester came out to fill the office.

Chester made an excellent executive, as is shown by the fact that although involved in official controversy with both the army and the people he was a favorite with both. He remained in office throughout the rest of the British period. When Bartram visited Pensacola he met several members of the council and the governor also, for it happened that the "chariot" of his excellency passed returning from his farm a few miles off. The botanist was introduced and commended for his pursuits, the governor "nobly offering to bear his expenses."

As in the Atlantic colonies there were also a Council and an Assembly; the council, composed in part of other officials such as Terry, Blackwell, Livingston, Charles Stuart, Lorimer, and Durnford, made the land grants, superintended the Indians, regulated commerce, roads, pilots, elections, and, when they could, military posts. With the true British love of local self-government there were General Assemblies almost from the start. Thus we know of one in 1766, another in 1767, and so on, and ultimately the Assembly and the governor quarrelled quite as was the case in the east. The electoral boroughs or precincts varied from time to time, being at first Mobile and Pensacola with six members each, and Campbell Town with two, but in 1771 the writ was withheld from Campbell Town because it was almost deserted. From that time there was trouble, the origin of which is not quite clear. Chester explained it to the home government by saying that the people at Mobile did not want an Assembly at all for fear this would regulate the Indian trade and thus prevent their traders from selling rum to the Indians, and that the Mobile members seldom attended the Assembly anyhow. Whatever may be the truth of this, there was also dissatisfaction over the apportionment and term of the representatives. Thus in 1772 the freeholders of Mobile and Charlotte County elected eight representatives, but would not execute the required indenture except with a provision limiting the Assembly to one year, and so a special return of the writ had to be made to the council. Four of the six Pensacola representatives sympathized with the Mobilians and would not convene without their representatives, whereupon the governor prorogued the Assembly twice, hoping that the Mobile members would come; and when they did not, he dissolved it. The Earl of Dartmouth approved this action in the name of the king, and Chester was instructed to omit Mobile entirely from the next election writ. Chester prudently managed to get along without an Assembly until 1778, when militia and Indian bills had to be passed. Then four representatives were allotted to the districts of Natchez, Manchac, Mobile, and Pensacola, besides four more to Pensacola because it was the capital, but, as instructed, Mobile and Campbell Town were omitted. As a result the Assembly was "cantankerous," as Chester calls it, sat thirty-four days without passing the bills, and otherwise obstructed business in order to force reënfranchisement of the two places. They went so far as to present a memorial to the king's majesty in council, stating that Mobile was "by far the most important of any in the province, for its antiquity, commerce, and revenue of the crown." This was so thoroughly approved at Mobile that a paper was sent up by the principal inhabitants, thanking the speaker and members, and some of them the next year even signed a memorial to the king against the governor himself.

From this time we can think of the province of West Florida as made up of three distinct districts,—that of Pensacola the capital, that about Mobile, and a third on the

Mississippi from Natchez to Fort Bute. The first and the last were essentially British. The settlers were of British extraction, as were their customs and institutions in almost all respects, and nothing recalled the previous Spanish claims except an occasional name. Mobile and its district were predominantly French in blood; but many of the leading inhabitants were British, and even the natives were contented and prosperous under their new allegiance. Indeed, it is said an emissary bringing a copy of the Declaration of Independence from the North was imprisoned and the treasonable document confiscated. The settlements did not extend far into the interior. Alabama River still drained Indian territory throughout almost its whole extent, Fort Tombecbé was abandoned, and white settlers were few above McIntosh's Bluff. The coast was Anglo-French, but the long stretch between the Tombigbee and the Mississippi was occupied as of old by the Choctaws, whose nearest town toward Mobile was Yowanee, with a thriving trade. The north boundary was about the line of Vicksburg, Meridian, Montgomery, and Columbus, but practically all except the coast was occupied by Indians, more or less friendly, supervised from Mobile or Pensacola, and among whom McGillivray and Strothers from the one place and Panton, Leslie and Company from the other did a growing business.

Turning now to the province of East Florida, we come upon a much less animated scene. It would almost seem as if the *dolce far niente* spirit into which the inhabitants of Menendez's colony had sunk affected even their successors when the rivalry of the Briton and Spaniard ceased on the lower Atlantic. In fact, it is only by a stretch of words that East Florida was at first called a province at all, as then it practically consisted of only two real settlements,—St. Mark's at Appalachee on the Gulf, and St. Augustine with its dependencies on the Atlantic. St. Mark's was maintained for military purposes, in order to keep an eye on the Indians, and the garrison was generally hardly a score of men. St. Augustine was an interesting place, but of the existing remains other than the fort few date back even to this time. Narrow streets wound between adobe houses with projecting balconies and windows similar to those now there, and landing places for a small coastwise commerce took the place of the present sea wall. Across the inlet, Anastasia Island, with its salt marshes and low oak and palmetto growths, faced the town of that day, and on it the long quarries for the fossil called *coquina* were in use on both sides of the shell road. The site, the climate, the quaintness, were ever at St. Augustine, but under the British and long afterward the places of stately hotels and beautiful gardens of our time were still covered by sluggish bayous and occupied only by seaweed and waterfowl.

A transfer of sovereignty in those days had much more serious results to the inhabitants than in our own. Theoretically, private property was respected, but it was generally to the extent of permitting a sale within a few months, or taking the oath of allegiance to a new sovereign. This occurred about Mobile, and in the occupation of East Florida the conduct of Major Ogilvie is said to have been so oppressive that only five Spanish inhabitants remained in St. Augustine. It was the day of Scotch ascendency in England, as reflected in the name of Fort Bute to the west, and so James Grant was appointed governor. One of the most important things accomplished by the British was the building of highways, still known in part as king's roads. One was constructed in 1762 from St. Mary's River to St. Augustine by subscription, and many of the names indicate that at this time South Carolina families resided there. A bridge over the San Sebastian and the improvement of the Anastasia lighthouse date also from British times.

In 1766 about forty families came from the Bermudas to Mosquito Inlet to engage in shipbuilding, an industry which the live oaks of that neighborhood rendered promising, and shortly afterward near by was a more remarkable experiment. An association in London, with Dr. Andrew Turnbull at its head, brought next year from Smyrna, the Greek Islands, Minorca, and elsewhere, some fifteen hundred people and settled them under indentures which required them, in consideration of money expended for passage and support, to work for a fixed period, when they should receive allotments of land. The location was admirable, and much labor and money were spent in improvements, of which canals and ditches still remain, and indigo, sugar cane, and other products were successfully raised. When Haldimand was in St. Augustine, and retrenchment was the word, although he abandoned the posts of Matanzas and Picolette [Picolata] in that neighborhood, he retained Mosquito, or Mokeko. About 1769 there was discontent among the colonists as to their treatment, and a revolt grew out of some punishments inflicted on them; but the rebellion was repressed and several of the leaders convicted. Seven years later the dissatisfaction took the form of legal proceedings, carried on by the attorney-general Yonge, and resulted in a decree cancelling the indentures and releasing the colonists. They had been reduced by death to about six hundred, who now embraced the opportunity of leaving New Smyrna for St. Augustine; and lands were granted them in the northern part of the city, where their blood and complexion can still be traced.

Governor Grant was succeeded in 1771 by Lieutenant-governor Moultrie, and he in turn in 1774 by Patrick Tonyn, who issued a proclamation inviting the loyalists and other inhabitants of Georgia to Florida. Many accepted, and East Florida has, in fact, been called the Tory Paradise, so that we are not surprised that Adams and other American leaders were burned in effigy in St. Augustine. There were grants of land to English noblemen and also to others who actually established plantations, such as Mount Oswald on the Halifax, and Rollestown near Palatka, as well as at Beresford and Spring Garden. The new settlers brought with them their negroes, for slavery prevailed in both Floridas; but if the slaves in the eastern province were not better workmen than Haldimand represents them to be at Pensacola, the institution could not have been of much benefit to anyone except the negroes.

Haldimand, whether at Pensacola or St. Augustine, was head of the military department of the Floridas, and, in fact, seems to have been that of Jamaica also, if not of Bermuda too. It is interesting to see how closely united in this way the British possessions were. Troops came from Jamaica to Mobile, and deserters were sent from Florida to Grenada. The Taylor in command at St. Augustine is the one who was at Mobile, and the same difficulties between the military and the civil authorities prevailed in East Florida as in West.

However, we miss the friction between governor and assembly in East Florida, for there was no assembly there until 1781. Nevertheless, the province steadily grew, and at one time Haldimand thought it might equal West Florida in importance. British rule was a blessing in both and, despite all the troubles which have been noticed, there was no disposition in either province to join the revolt which about this time broke out on the Atlantic. The natives of French and Spanish blood were well enough satisfied with the unexpected measure of liberty acquired under the British, and among the British themselves the loyalists were so largely in the majority as to give tone to the whole society. The result was to be that the American Revolution was confined to the colonies early settled or occupied by the English from Massachusetts to Georgia, and was to make no impression upon the old Latin provinces of Canada and the Floridas. So far as could be foreseen, British colonization and influence were not only to be permanent in the lands on the St. Lawrence and the Gulf of Mexico, but were to have indefinite expansion in the future.

CHAPTER XXI

ACROSS THE ALLEGHANIES

Besides the growth upon the Atlantic and the assimilation of Canada and Florida, a new field was to open before the British. The interior of the country west of the Alleghanies had been by proclamation reserved for the use of the Indians, but not only were the old French settlements of Kaskaskia and Vincennes, the lake posts and other places, ready for future growth, but practically the land hunger of the Anglo-Saxons was to offer great obstacles to the preservation of such a buffer country. The Illinois, confined though it now was to the territory east of the Mississippi, the Ohio valley where had been so much of the late war, the interesting country extending from the Mississippi to the Cherokee mountains,—these were to have a story and a future greater than their past. The French were ready to surrender the posts, but the British had hardly been able to take possession of those along the lakes when they realized that a new danger had arisen. The Indian reservation had come too late to satisfy the savages, who were already in arms.

The French plan of indiscriminate presents had not commended itself to the frugal British authorities, and even the supply of ammunition was lessened. Sir William Johnson, it is true, was active and intelligent, but his influence was greatest among the Iroquois, and almost *nil* in the great western valleys; and while George Croghan was there indefatigable, he found himself hampered by lack of means. It was not the first or last time that the British when conquerors have not risen equal to their opportunities and responsibilities. Johnson bears witness to the "utter aversion of our people for them [the Indians] and the imprudence with which this was expressed."

As with most savage or barbarous races, American Indians would as a rule fight bravely, but only for a limited time and with lack of cohesion. Now suddenly came an instance to the contrary. It may or may not be that Pontiac saw the necessity for uniting the red men against the British now that the latter had become the victors in contest with the French; certainly others with him felt more or less clearly that they could no longer play off the French against the British, and that the British were the more ruthless. Probably the actual cause of the war was that the treaty nominally gave away the whole country to the Mississippi without taking into account the Indians at all, and that their supplies were lessened. Even of the Iroquois, the Senecas, the furthest tribe to the west, had become friendly with the French, and seem to have taken the lead in the early disturbances. The Shawnees and Miamis near the Ohio below Fort Pitt also became active factors, but finally the actual headship, strange to say, became vested in an Ottawa Indian near Detroit. It is said that, first and last, Pontiac had eighteen tribes under his command, and certain it is that his emissaries were active throughout the Ohio valley, and almost as far south as New Orleans, and the French traders throughout the valley, backed by at least a passive sympathy on the part of the military, urged on the Indians in every conceivable way. The longer English occupation was deferred, the more business there was for the French, and then no one could tell what would happen in the future. The progress of the natives in warfare was shown by their actually investing and besieging Detroit from May to November, 1763, and during that period they massacred the British garrison at Michilimackinac, and drove those of Green Bay and Fort Joseph toward the Atlantic. Open warfare would have been bad enough, but an Indian conflict meant treachery, assassination, scalping of men, women, and children, and desolation of the land far and wide. The colonists were driven back along the whole frontier. First and last there were said to have been two thousand whites killed or captured and as many families driven eastwardly from their homes, and this by the Indians of the lake regions, numbering in all not exceeding ten thousand warriors. The ferocity of the conflict is shown by the fact that a brave officer named Campbell was tortured and his heart cut out and eaten by the Indians to make them as brave as he,—reminding us of the old Hindoo custom of eating a tiger for the same purpose. And the ferocity was not all Indian. The British commander-in-chief wrote that he wanted to hear of no prisoners, an order which the soldiers carried out more than once, and afterward he even advocated that smallpox be spread among the savages to destroy them. Gladwyn, from Detroit, suggested the milder treatment—practically followed out from that time to this—of killing them off by the sale of rum. But the conspiracy had to be conquered into peace.

Henry Bouquet was a Swiss who had joined the Sixtieth Regiment, organized in compliment to the Duke of Cumberland and known as the Royal Americans. While colonel he was sent by Amherst to relieve Fort Pitt, and at Bushy Run in August, 1763, by a feigned retreat and actual advance he defeated the Indians in a pitched battle. Bradstreet, despatched along Lake Erie to relieve Detroit and other points, exceeded his instructions by a foolish treaty, promptly repudiated by Amherst, but Bouquet advanced steadily into the heart of the enemy's country. On Muskingum River, in October of the next year, he compelled the Shawnees and others to deliver up all prisoners and send delegates to meet Sir William Johnson at Niagara for a final treaty. There, in July, 1765, was made the submission of the western tribes, the old land route up Mohawk

River being not only confirmed but a strip four miles wide ceded alongside Niagara River to make sure for the future the communication with the west. This was a part of Croghan's scheme for buying land on the frontier for colonizing, and it has been the plan followed from that day.

Treaties were made with each tribe separately, following the old plan of *divide et impera*, and even Pontiac made a peace after his ambassadors to New Orleans learned from the dying D'Abbadie that their French father had indeed abandoned his red children in America. He himself lived some years longer, but was finally tomahawked in 1769 at Cahokia, and avenged at once by such a slaughter of the tribe of the murderer as practically to blot it out.

It was of the first importance for the British to take possession of the Illinois as soon as practicable, which movement Pontiac's war had prevented. This could be done by way of the Mississippi, by the Great Lakes, or by the Ohio, the two latter routes starting from Fort Pitt. Bouquet thought the natural way was up the Mississippi, and this was, in fact, first tried, for Major Arthur Loftus and the Twenty-second ascended that river, stopping first at New Orleans and receiving good advice from D'Abbadie. This in true British fashion he did not observe, with the result that on March 20, 1764, they were fired on from both banks at the place where the Tonikas used to live and Father Davion once exercised his sacred ministry. There were perhaps five or six killed and as many wounded, and this occurring at practically the outset of his journey, so to speak, in British territory, discouraged Loftus so much that he withdrew down the river, almost seeking the protection of the French, who with ironical politeness offered to give him a guard of French soldiers. Nothing more was attempted from either direction until next winter, when Alexander Frazer and deputy superintendent George Croghan made preparations at Fort Pitt to advance from there. Frazer seems to have been over zealous or anxious to have the glory himself, and so left Croghan and went, insufficiently guarded, down the Ohio to Fort Chartres. He was all but murdered,—in fact, it was reported to headquarters that he had been killed,—and was probably indebted to Saint-Ange for his life. He was not in condition to hold the post even if it had been surrendered, and as soon as he could he made his way down the Mississippi and finally reported to Farmar at Mobile. Croghan had hardly better success, for he was captured in June, 1765, in the Shawnee country, although soon rescued by friendly Indians, and after meeting Pontiac and receiving his submission he returned to Detroit, thinking it unnecessary to go further.

The actual surrender of Fort Chartres was not until the 10th of October, 1765, when Lieutenant Stirling pushed forward from Fort Pitt with one hundred Highlanders of the famous Forty-second Regiment and finally relieved Saint-Ange. This Frenchman, with grave courtesy, turned over the fort and its appurtenances and retired with his garrison across the Mississippi. Croghan while on his expedition had written to Farmar, supposing him to be on the way, but the Major, characteristically, would not start until everything was in prime military condition. On December 4th, he arrived at Fort Chartres with soldiers of the Thirty-fourth and relieved Stirling, who, with his men, went down the Mississippi and then by way of Pensacola to New York. Stirling lived to take part in other campaigns and to be not unknown to fame in different walks of life.

But for the promise of the future, it might be doubted if the Illinois were worth the trouble and expense of occupation. Fort Chartres, it is true, was a regular and well-built stone fortification, but there was not much of a settlement tributary to it. Not far off was a dependent Indian village, a windmill, and some creole inhabitants, while lower on Kaskaskia River, not far from where it emptied into the Mississippi, was an old fort and near it a grist mill and the homes of other settlers. Two or three times as far above Fort Chartres was the village of Cahokia, and all these settlements were connected by a road. The total creole population of these villages and of the country tributary was hardly two thousand, engaged in agriculture, trading, and furs. They could hardly be said to be an industrious race, and the Indians were, if anything, more worthless still,—the degenerate descendants of the tribes whom La Salle had first met, now debauched by decades of French brandy and paternalism. On the Wabash the post of Vincennes, sometimes called Post Vincent, was in better condition, for the Indians were braver and more warlike there and the environment made the white man more self-reliant. A number of titles still survive to show the hold which French institutions had taken upon this Illinois country, but the principal institution was the French military commandant himself, whose sway was fatherly enough but vigorous after its kind. The creoles did only enough work to keep them in food and clothes; their rulers attended to all public business, and the people were everywhere indifferent to all save the pleasures of the day. Further east the country now divided between the States of Ohio and Indiana was, after the Treaty of Paris as before, really occupied by the Delawares, Miamis or Twightwees, Shawnees, and other brave tribes, and one result of Pontiac's war was a mutual respect, causing a tacit understanding between them and the British that this was to be exempt from white colonization. Ultimately, what was called the Quebec Act was passed in 1774, with the design of making the lake region tributary to Canada, for the province of Quebec was extended to the Ohio, and this piece of legislation was to have great results in American history. At a time when railroads were not dreamed of and waterways were the principal means of communication, it was quite natural that the home authorities in planning for the future should adopt the French theory that all unsettled districts tributary to the Great Lakes should be made parts of the St. Lawrence country. It was in some sense a renewal of the old contest between Canada and Louisiana.

The territory south of the Ohio, and more particularly the mountain country which had so long bounded the

Atlantic colonies on the west, had also been included in the proclamation reserving the interior for the natives; but by another tacit understanding the proclamation was quietly superseded in this region by subsequent treaties with the Indians, and we thus have opened up one of the most fascinating chapters of American history.

Now that the British controlled the whole country, the policy on all the frontiers became somewhat changed. There was no longer a contest of French and English traders, no longer the same motive for conciliating the natives. The traders, licensed now and under bond, were fewer in number, and their calling less respected in proportion as the Indians themselves degenerated; and although the government strove to preserve the Indian territory, the boundary line was shadowy and often overstepped. This was not always by bad men, although it was necessarily by brave men. There was not an immediate general need for more territory to settle, although this was true in individual cases. The real frontiersman now was the hunter, for the supply of furs and skins was no longer bought from the Indians, but was the result of the efforts of British riflemen and trappers, who themselves killed the deer, the buffalo, the beaver, the otter, and other animals, whose skin or fur was valuable in the markets of the world. Englishmen took the place of the old *coureurs de bois.* Singly or in companies the hunters made excursions at appropriate times; some lived in the woods almost the year around, while others loaded trains of pack-horses in the fall or spring and drove them to the markets, towns, or trading posts where the furs were bought for export. As the game was exterminated or rendered scarce, the hunters pressed further inland, sometimes causing Indian wars and always gradually pushing on the frontier. Behind them many miles, but still following, and far away from the towns and centres of industry and exchange, came the true pioneers, accompanied by their wives and families.

The Appalachian range is rather a system than a range, for it is made up of the Blue Ridge toward the east, the

Cumberland toward the west, and intermediate chains of the Alleghanies between, with numerous subdivisions. The development which has heretofore interested us was all east of the Blue Ridge, along the watercourses rising at its foot and emptying into the Atlantic Ocean on one side, or was west along the Mississippi and the tributaries which take their origin beyond the Cumberland and Alleghany ranges. The mountains which had both attracted and deterred the Spaniards of Florida reach their loftiest summits or highest tableland in the district north and west of the Georgia and Carolina settlements, in what is not ill named the "Land of the Sky." This was the country of the Cherokees, who hemmed the advance of the French from the west and of the British from the east, influenced by both, and after the whole country had become nominally British commanded the passes from the Atlantic coast to the fair valleys draining into the Ohio and the Mississippi. We have seen how Fort Prince George near the Savannah and Fort Loudoun on the headwaters of the Tennessee were built; and despite the devastation about the one and the ruin of the other, they were the means of such chastisement of the Cherokees as put it out of their power to check further progress by the whites. We have now reached the time when even a mountain country no longer offered terrors, for it was the source of great rivers, and it was by river valleys that settlers advanced. There were no roads except Indian trails, and these, too, followed the river routes.

The colonies have heretofore presented each a separate individuality, varying with origin and location; those that we are now to trace have different seats, from which were built gradually their several commonwealths, but all had a common point of beginning. They may be traced to the entrance of settlers through one gateway from which they spread out in different directions. This point of departure was in that interesting mountain region about the sources of Tennessee River,—if not a Garden of Eden, in some sense an Ararat or a Hindu Kush; for it was the second

George Mason, of Virginia.

After the painting by Gilbert Stuart.

Peyton Randolph, of Virginia.

After the painting in possession of the Virginia Historical Society.

starting point of Americans. There we find the Little Tennessee coming in from Chota and old Fort Loudoun; the French Broad from the highlands of North Carolina; the Holston and the Clinch from the southwestern part of Virginia; while Powell's Valley and the Watauga are not far away.

All these streams are the headwaters of the Tennessee, earlier known as Cherokee River, or of the Cumberland. Of them the principal was the Holston, named for some early immigrant, but called Hogohegee by the Cherokees, and at first so little known was the geography of the country that Croghan thought that he saw where the Holston emptied into the Ohio. The country where they rose had now been reached by the immigration turned southwardly by the mountains and beckoned on by the valleys of Virginia's great Augusta County. The line between Virginia and North Carolina was run to the Holston in 1749, and hardly had Fort Dobbs been built upon the upper Yadkin than other forts, such as Lewis and Chissel, were to be found on the sources of the James or beyond.

Byrd's endeavor for the relief of Fort Loudoun was unsuccessful in its immediate object, for the massacre was not prevented, but as with all expeditions against the Indians it was a revelation to the tidewater Virginians, and even those from the valleys, of the beauties and possibilities of the mountain country further to the southwest. While Colonel Montgomery and Silouee were contending in the upper part of South Carolina, Daniel Boone was carving on a birch tree near Watauga that he had "cilled a bar." Indeed, Walker had seen something of the Kentucky region even a dozen years earlier, and we now find Cutbirth and others exploring to Mississippi River.

Heretofore it had been a question mainly of such adventurers, for there could be no definite settlement until some arrangement had been made with the Indians. The "dark and bloody ground" was claimed by Shawnees, Iroquois, and Cherokees. The Shawnees we saw subdued by Bouquet, and in 1768, at the great treaty of Fort Stanwix in New York, the Iroquois ceded all their rights by conquest and otherwise down to Holston River, while the same year the treaty of Hard Labor in South Carolina divested the claim of the Cherokees to its sources. The next year settlements began on the Watauga, and the expedition of Dr. Walker, the Virginia commissioner at Fort Stanwix, antedated that of Boone and Finley from the Yadkin only a little while. Providentially, at this time came such a crushing defeat by the Chickasaws of the Cherokees, who boasted that they could not live without war, that the whites, almost unnoticed, gained a foothold.

These Watauga settlers came largely from Virginia and imagined that they were locating within the limits of that province. They present an interesting instance of the bent of Anglo-Saxons for self-government. Far beyond the actual jurisdiction even of Augusta County they voluntarily formed an Association in 1772, adopting the old laws and constituting a new "court" having legislative, judicial, and executive powers. Among the members of this body were Robertson and Sevier, both able men, who were to make their imprint upon the future commonwealth for many years to come,—the one of Scotch, the other of French extraction, showing how the new country assimilated foreign blood to build up a State. The Association, on account of the jealousy of the Indians, at first only leased its lands at the source of the Holston, but in 1775 it bought the title, and, when eventually it was found that the Watauga was actually within the bounds of North Carolina instead of Virginia, became the beginning of the separate community which we call Tennessee.

Almost simultaneously there was an independent colonization to the northward. The river route down the Ohio to Limestone, now Maysville, was to play a great part in the development of what has since been called Kentucky, and the Ohio was in some sense the first road for incomers. Harrod and his friends came by this route from the older colonies to the falls of the Ohio, and striking across into the interior in 1774 built Harrodsburg. This was all but deserted during what is known as "Cresap's" or "Dunmore's" war,—the conflict with the Shawnees begun by the cruel murder of chief Logan's relatives, which was practically terminated by the expedition under Lewis from southwestern Virginia down the valley of Kanawha River. Then it was that Cornstalk and his Indians were defeated in the great pioneer battle at Point Pleasant where the Kanawha empties into the Ohio.

This made the frontiers more secure, and there was now to begin a considerable immigration, for settlers followed close upon the heels of the hunters. Their route now was not down Ohio River, but through a break in the western range of the Alleghanies, named by Thomas Walker in an early exploration for the Duke of Cumberland, and directed toward the river which in the absence of Indian traditions Walker had also named the Cumberland. There are other passes through the Alleghanies, some of which became noted, but, after all, the first in importance historically was Cumberland Gap. It was this that the early explorer Finley pointed out to the greater Boone; it was this that was used by the Long Hunters; and it was from here that Boone began his own explorations of the west. The Wilderness Road, which he blazed from Cumberland Gap, became as important in development here as Braddock's Road and Forbes's were north of the Potomac. Indeed, the Wilderness Road was the greatest of the three, for the other two were essentially military highways across the mountains to Fort Pitt, while the southern was from the first the route of thousands of immigrants.

In the year after the battle of Point Pleasant Colonel Henderson, of east Virginia, put in effect his Transylvania Company, and for £10,000 bought from the Cherokees seventeen million acres of land and established Boonesborough, which for some time remained a kind of capital. As the Watauga people had adopted articles of association, these more western colonists on May 23, 1775, held a convention there under a tree, and, after addresses from Henderson and the chairman, proceeded to pass nine laws, interesting as showing the needs and aspirations of the people. They established courts of judicature and their practice; regulated the militia; declared a criminal code; denounced profane swearing and Sabbath breaking; provided for writs of attachment; fixed clerk's and sheriff's fees; passed an act to preserve a public range or pasture, and, even before providing a game law, characteristically passed one to preserve the breed of horses. And yet, almost with the convention, the colony of Transylvania passed into history; for when in the same year eighty of the settlement prayed the protection of Virginia, and the proprietors on the other hand sought to have the Continental Congress recognize them as an independent colony, the Congress would not admit the delegate, and Virginia the next year constituted its over-mountain country into the County of Kentucky; for up to that time the district had been only a kind of fringe of Fincastle, the westernmost of the old counties. Although this attempt to establish a new proprietary government failed as completely as that of Carolina, Virginia at least recognized the equities of the case and compensated the would-be proprietors with two hundred thousand acres in lieu of the principality which they had sought to buy from the Cherokees. It may be questioned whether the Virginia system of land title was much superior to that of the Company, for all that the State required was the location and survey of a claim by someone holding military or other scrip and a return made to a State official. Boone made many of these surveys. Not being under any regulation as to size, shape, or location, the surveys frequently overlapped and as frequently left odd spaces unoccupied, defects which in some sense have left traces until this day. But at least it was an easy system, and, whatever its inconvenience now, it was probably the best fitted for the early circumstances of the country.

Such were the beginnings of Tennessee and Kentucky, and the movement once begun never ceased. In the mountain regions even south of Watauga development went on apace, although the Revolutionary struggle had the unfortunate result of somewhat dividing the whites and almost totally alienating the Cherokees from the Americans. The old superintendent, John Stuart, remained loyal to the crown, and is thought to have stirred up the Indians to murder and rapine by assuring them that a British army would come through West Florida and a fleet operate off the Carolina coast in conjunction with the Indians and conquer the Americans back to loyalty to good King George. Though we are not here concerned with the details of that struggle, we may look forward far enough to see the colonists accepting the challenge and entering on their side upon the conquest of the Cherokee country. They penetrated even to the site of old Fort Loudoun, whose tragic story Stuart could remember only too well; and the ultimate result was that the Cherokees were humbled, and the way was opened for a greater influx of westward immigrants to what North Carolina in 1777 named Washington County. Thus it was that Tennessee was one of the earliest monuments to the veneration which was to become universal for George Washington.

From these settlements immigration made its way further, and it was not many years before the new West began using the Mississippi to carry her products to sea. The English were pushing over the mountains, and on one side of the Mississippi, therefore, British territory extended or would in time extend from the Gulf to the frozen North, and on the other side Spain's right was equally undisputed from the sources of the Mississippi down to her old possessions in Mexico. As the British extended from the Atlantic to the Mississippi, the Spanish extended from the Mississippi to the Pacific Ocean. It was an interesting situation and one on which a historical student of the time might look and wonder as to the result. Heretofore the Spanish empire had been to all appearance wealthier and stronger than the little island kingdom beyond the Channel. Would Latin ports on the Pacific advance *pari passu* with the English ones on the Atlantic? Would the population west of the great river grow like that to the east? Would the trade of the great valley be divided equally between the rivals? And after development, what would be the political and commercial relations of the two halves of the continent? Would they be peaceful, or was the old conflict to be renewed between Latin and Teuton?

CHAPTER XXII

THE LATIN REMNANT

SIDE by side with the British growth was a national development of a very different kind. When the fortunes of war had shown the French minister, the Duc de Choiseul, that Canada was gone, he felt that Louisiana, interposed between the expanding British and the unyielding Spanish, could not be retained to advantage. Thus before peace was concluded the French monarch, on November 3, 1762, ceded to his "beloved cousin of Spain, without any reservation, from the pure impulse of the generous heart and sense of affection and friendship between the two sovereigns," all the country known as Louisiana. This was without consultation with Madrid, but the gift was accepted ten days later, although for the present it was to be kept secret. The French king continued to act as sovereign, appointing officers, as, for instance, Lafrénière the attorney-general and promoting Foucault the *intendant*. By the Treaty of Paris France ceded the east half of this territory to England, and Spain made no objection. She realized well enough that Louisiana had of late been only an expense to France, but being in better condition to stand the drain Spain embraced the opportunity to secure a fixed boundary like Mississippi River between her and the possessions of her inveterate enemy. Had all Louisiana been ceded to Great Britain, it is probable that there would have been no tacit agreement as to a boundary at Sabine River, and that the English, as did the United States afterward, would have maintained the extreme French claim to Matagorda Bay, if not to the Rio Grande. It was therefore no doubt with a feeling of relief that Spain realized the result of the Seven Years' War to be the extension of her Mexican possessions to the Mississippi, whose navigation was now open to her and whose mouth, with New Orleans, was within her own limits. This was the inducement to the Spaniards to accept the donation. They indulged in no illusions as to profit to be derived from Louisiana itself.

The cession was concealed for over a year and the French administration remained much as before, except that all expenses were reduced. Thus in March the king ordained that the troops should be disbanded and only a factory maintained, protected by four companies of infantry. D'Abbadie was appointed director, and on June 29th arrived at New Orleans and succeeded Kerlerec. Upon D'Abbadie fell the sad duty of surrendering the country east of the Mississippi, although troops were maintained in the Illinois district for some time to come on account of the trouble the English had with the Indians in consequence of Pontiac's conspiracy. The population of Latin Louisiana was increased by the accession of French inhabitants retiring from across the river, and also by the influx of a number of Indian tribes who followed the French flag rather than accept new masters. Two years later there came also over six hundred Acadians, who for ten years previously had been wandering about the British provinces, exiles whose pathetic story is told in *Evangeline*. They caused additional expenses to the government, but were successfully colonized in Attakapas and Opelousas, and others who followed were placed on the Mississippi from the German Coast even up beyond Bâton Rouge, so that in course of time parts of the river were known as the Acadian Coast. D'Abbadie found the colony in a state of complete destitution, and reported that it was a chaos of iniquities and that it would be necessary to resort to measures of an extreme character. All this made the French court the more willing to carry out the cession; so that on April 21, 1764, the French king finally notified D'Abbadie that he had ceded the country without reserve, and instructed him to put the Spanish governor and troops in possession as soon as they arrived. After the evacuation, government papers should be withdrawn except those with regard to boundaries, Indians, and the like, which should be turned over with all necessary information to the new governor. Louis closed with the expression of a hope that his Catholic majesty would respect religious privileges, that judges and the Superior Council would be permitted to administer justice according to the laws of the colony, and that all titles would be confirmed according to concessions previously made. This letter was registered by the Superior Council in October, and was to play an important part in the future. The cession had been suspected, but its confirmation was a hard blow. It no doubt hastened the death of D'Abbadie, which happened in the next February. He was succeeded by Aubry, who had been in command of the four French companies.

With a feeling perfectly natural, every parish of Louisiana sent delegates to a convention, among whom were many familiar names. Lafrénière, Villeré, D'Arensbourg, the Milhets, Saint-Maxent, and Braud were there, and Lafrénière, the attorney-general, eloquently presented a resolution supplicating Louis the Well-beloved not to cast them off. Jean Milhet was selected to present it and accordingly sailed for France, and on reaching Paris called on Bienville, then living in retirement at the ripe age of eighty-six. Together they secured an interview with the Duc de Choiseul and earnestly urged that the cession be annulled. Choiseul was affected and expressed himself with emotion, but replied that reconsideration was impossible.

Crowding fast upon Milhet's mission came a letter from Don Antonio de Ulloa to the Superior Council announcing that he would soon take possession of New Orleans, where he flattered himself that he would have opportunity to render all the services that they might desire, which would be his inclination no less than his duty. On March 5, 1766, he landed there with two companies of infantry under Piernas, and accompanied by Loyola, Gayarré, and Navarro, to act as *intendant*, *contador*, and treasurer, respectively. His reception was not reassuring, and it is said that, although a cultivated man, his manner was forbidding. He made a tour of the colony, spending a considerable time at Natchitoches in particular to study communications with Mexico. King Charles III. instructed him that Louisiana was to remain a separate colony, with its own laws, and was to have no commerce with his other American dominions. Louisiana affairs were to be managed by the ministry of State, and not by that of the Indies, which administered his older possessions.

The new officials from governor down were men of ability, and yet the natural hauteur of the Spaniards and the reluctance of the colonists resolved not to be satisfied soon produced an unfortunate state of affairs. Had Ulloa brought with him sufficient troops this would have made little difference; but the agreement was that to save time of transporting Spaniards the French military would be turned over to him. Aubry and many of the officers acted under these orders, but a number of the troops already behind in their pay and entitled to their discharge declined to continue. The question of money was pressing, and Ulloa's plan to buy up the currency in coin at seventy-five per cent of its face value, although really an improvement on the past, was opposed by the French and proved distasteful even to the Spaniards who were to be paid. In declining to recognize the authority of the Superior Council, Ulloa also made enemies, and on account of the tension he finally determined for the present not to take possession. A commercial decree gave further dissatisfaction. This permitted direct commerce between Louisiana and the French colonies in Spanish ships provided they carried back lumber and other products and the goods imported were sold at a reasonable price. This countervailed the freedom of trade which the inhabitants had long enjoyed, and was an act of paternal interference in favor of consumers resented by the merchants. Popular agitation began and even the suspension of the ordinance was insufficient. The people clung to the hopes expressed in the letter of Louis to D'Abbadie, as if it had been a treaty.

Ulloa left for the Balize, where he remained some time and had the Spanish flag hoisted. The real object of his visit there was to wait for his bride, a Peruvian lady, who finally arrived in March, 1767, when they were married at the Balize by his chaplain and thence came up to New Orleans. The latitude of Peru, however, was not that of Louisiana, and the lady speedily became, if anything, less of a favorite than her husband. A conqueror has never been well received in New Orleans, and in this case the people seemed utterly unable to realize that the cession to Spain was final, even though Milhet shortly afterward returned with his distressing confirmation. Although the French flag remained at the capital, the Spanish was flying at the Balize, on the Missouri, on the Iberville, and opposite Natchez, the four points where Ulloa established posts and distributed the Spanish troops whom he brought with him.

It is painful in history as in common life to notice the estrangement of those whom interest should hold together. People on the lookout for slights find them in the most innocent acts. Ulloa had nothing in mind but the good of the province, and yet seeking this good in a cold way not unnatural in a Spaniard he offended at every turn the susceptibilities of the French subjects. On the other hand, they were unwilling to recognize the transfer to Spain and interpreted every act and omission in the light of that unwillingness. If Ulloa did not hoist the Spanish flag at New Orleans, to their minds it was not because he had so few Spanish troops, but because he was not commissioned to take possession. If he had a chapel in his own house, it was a distinct violation of the customs of the province, which put all ecclesiastical matters under the supervision of the vicar-general of the Bishop of Canada. Beginning in this manner, it was no difficult thing for governor and people to get further and further apart, and on Ulloa's side the feeling was intensified by a letter of ex-Governor Kerlerec from the Bastille, pitying him from his heart for having been sent to such a country. There could be no doubt of the transfer. Ulloa assumed on account of Spain the administrative expenses from his arrival, and if Aubry still issued proclamations it was only as representing the governor.

Under the circumstances, it was no subject for surprise that an insurrection was hatched against the Spanish. Instead of being by the common people, however, it was by such men as Lafrénière the attorney-general, Foucault the *intendant*, the Milhets, and Villeré. It is said that they met at the house of Foucault's mistress, which was surrounded by a garden and trees in the suburbs of New Orleans. At all events, on the 28th of October, 1768, residents of the country parishes and many in New Orleans quietly made themselves masters of the city, and the Spanish frigate found it expedient to move from the shore and cast anchor in the stream. Aubry took such steps as were possible with only one hundred and ten men, and at his suggestion Ulloa and his wife retired on board the frigate. The Superior Council met and, in answer to a petition signed by six hundred people asking the restoration of ancient rights and the expulsion of Ulloa, considered the situation. Lafrénière the next day made an elaborate address, dwelling upon the letter of Louis XV. and that of Ulloa from Havana as showing that the ancient liberties of the colony were to be respected; and one part of his speech deserves to be remembered, even though the character of its author be not above reproach. "Without population," he said, "there can be no commerce, and without commerce no population. In proportion to the extent of both is the solidity of thrones; both are fed by liberty and competition, which are the nursing mothers of the State, of which the spirit of monopoly is the tyrant and stepmother. Without liberty, there are but few virtues. Despotism breeds pusillanimity and deepens the abyss of vices. Man is considered as sinning before God only because he retains his free will. Where is the liberty of our planters, our merchants, and our other inhabitants? Protection and benevolence have given way to despotism; a single authority would absorb and annihilate everything." The foregone conclusion was that the council on the 29th adopted a decree giving Ulloa three days to quit the colony. Aubry protested in vain, and the decree was received with great enthusiasm in the city.

Ulloa felt that it was useless to resist with his present force and retired to Havana without delay, and finding insufficient available troops there to take possession of the colony he returned to Spain. He had sent full reports, and Aubry on his side wrote similarly to the French ministry. The revolutionists organized themselves into a kind of government and flattered themselves that they would be sustained by the court of France, although they had even anterior to the revolution applied to the British for assistance, but had not received encouragement. While glad enough to see trouble for Spain, England was not prepared to intervene. This would mean war, and what was left of Louisiana was not thought worth that sacrifice. The different steps taken and the conduct of the people remind one of the great French Revolution which followed thirty years later, with the difference that the Louisianians soon realized their helplessness. They were not strong enough to form an independent State, and great was the disappointment when France made it known that she would not sustain them.

The effect in Spain can be well imagined. In a cabinet council opinions were given by different members at the request of the Marquis de Grimaldi, and it was the all but unanimous conclusion that possession must be retaken at once with an adequate force. Grimaldi notified the French court and requested disavowal of what had been done, making the characteristically Spanish remark that "the loss of great interests is looked upon in Spain with indifference, but that it is not so as to insults."

Alexander O'Reilly, an Irishman of ability, in the Spanish service, was appointed to proceed to take possession, and in July, 1769, he appeared in the Mississippi with a fleet and two thousand six hundred men, which made all resistance useless. The conspirators, with French versatility, made haste to placate the new governor, and Lafrénière was among the first to go down the river. O'Reilly received all graciously, but would make no definite promises. Soon the twenty-four vessels arrived at the city and the troops were landed. O'Reilly took possession in an elaborate manner, and the French flag made way for the Spanish on the staff in the *place d'armes*. New Orleans was completely overawed and all traces of the revolution disappeared.

O'Reilly's manner was pleasant, but he lost no time in having Lafrénière and others arrested and tried before a military tribunal. There could be no doubt as to the result, and eleven, Foucault included, were found guilty. Braud, the public printer, was acquitted because his duty compelled him to print all that was sent him by the commissary; but Lafrénière, Joseph Milhet, and three others were condemned to the gallows, and several to imprisonment, and in true Spanish fashion the memorial of the planters and other publications connected with the conspiracy were burned by the common hangman in a public *auto da fé*. There was difficulty in securing anyone to hang the distinguished prisoners, as it was not deemed proper for a negro, who ordinarily acted, to officiate. The method of punishment was therefore modified, and the condemned were escorted by grenadiers to the place of execution; and after hearing their sentence, they fell before a volley from the platoon, meeting death bravely. Much has been written as to this severity of O'Reilly, but considering the attitude of Spain toward all insurrections less harshness was exercised than might have been expected. Nothing further followed in the way of persecution, and it is said that those who were imprisoned were released, although they never returned to Louisiana. O'Reilly seems to have devoted himself earnestly to studying the needs of the colony, which he thought it his duty somewhat to remodel on the Spanish plan.

The rule of Spain in Louisiana was destined to be for the advantage of the colony. To what extent the peninsular government had learned experience with the passage of centuries may not be quite clear, but the monarch then occupying the throne was one who would have been the glory of any country. Perhaps it was the flashing up of an expiring flame, but, at all events, the reign of Charles III. was one of the brightest in Spanish annals. In one of the kaleidoscopic changes in Italy during the eighteenth century in the struggle between Spain, France, and Austria, he ruled Tuscany and not long after conquered Naples. His father, Philip V., was proud to confirm him on that throne and he added to it Sicily, and, insulted by an English fleet, he never forgot it. In 1759, he succeeded to the throne of Spain, and two years afterward formed the Bourbon Family Compact with Louis XV. The energy which he had displayed in Italy was transferred to the peninsula, where at first it was hardly relished. He even dared attack the custom of wearing large cloaks and broad hats, and showed himself sensible of the intrigues of the clergy. Charles remained on the throne for almost thirty years, and, as far as one man could, he arrested the decadence of his kingdom.

O'Reilly was worthy to serve such a master. His power was unlimited, his acts fully known and approved, and there could be little doubt that his severity saved Louisiana much subsequent trouble. She learned at last that the transfer to Spain was final, and accommodated herself to the new conditions. O'Reilly was soon able to send away over half of the troops with which he came, and in substituting the Cabildo for the Superior Council he not only took away a cause of disturbance but replaced it by an effective means of government. The Cabildo was made up of *regidores* who held honorary offices, of *alcades*, and an attorney-general syndic. They had both judicial and executive powers. The syndic was a kind of tribune supposed to represent the interest of the people, and the *intendant* had charge of the revenues, navy, and commerce, with some judicial functions. Ordinary judicial acts were performed by *alcades* throughout the province, and in each parish a commandant exercised police jurisdiction, subject to control from the capital. The colony was under the supervision of the captain-general in Cuba, to whom in some instances appeals lay and from him to the royal *audiencia* in Santo Domingo. Ultimately an appeal might lie to the Council of the Indies in Spain.

It was ordered that the Spanish language should be employed by public officials, although French was still permitted in judicial and notarial acts, at least in the parishes. Spanish jurisprudence was to be substituted for French, and, as an introduction, an abstract of law and procedure was made public, prescribing the duties of officials and citizens. This was something of a code in itself and just throughout,—the only criticism that could be made was that it was too just in that it prescribed everything, leaving nothing for local regulation. Indian slavery was no longer permitted, and special provisions were made for the different posts. Thus an end was put to the trade going on through Natchitoches with Mexico, and contraband intercourse with the English vessels on the Mississippi was prohibited. Economy was introduced and expenses cut down from $250,000 to $130,000. As if to show the good intentions of the government, Frenchmen were appointed to almost all offices and creole troops raised under the name of the Regiment of Louisiana. Regulations as to grants of land and commerce were especially important. At first lands were granted by the governor-general, but ultimately this was to be vested in the *intendant*.

According to our modern notions, it seems strange that offices should ever pass by sale. We think of it in the

Patrick Henry. *After the original painting by Thomas Sully, in possession of William Wirt Henry, Esq., of Richmond, Virginia.*

British army as destructive of all discipline, we remember it of the Roman Empire as a striking instance of both greed and anarchy; and yet, we find the same thing on a smaller scale in the Spanish government of Louisiana, for the places of the six perpetual *regidores* who were members of the Cabildo were at the first sold at auction and afterward transferred by the holders to others. This was no secret abuse, but was actually regulated by law, and it had its advantages. Theories of government have varied from time to time from that of an absolute monarchy to absolute democracy, with all shades of variation between, but the most autocratic government is modified by customs which cannot be infringed without danger to the State. Wealth often constitutes an important element. Commercial States have been powerful and trade has been the foundation of many others. A modified form of property influence may arise when a part of the legal machinery can fall to people of means through a system of purchase, and in this way the men of property in a community may acquire directly or indirectly an important voice in the management of affairs. So that even in this dependency of absolute Spain popular elements were not wanting, and the duties of the attorney-general syndic, who was chosen by the Cabildo, had a democratic side. This officer had nothing to do with prosecution or with legal affairs as such, but was a survival or imitation of the old Roman tribune. His duty was to propose to the Cabildo what he thought for the interest of the people, and on their behalf to oppose measures which he deemed contrary to their welfare. These popular elements might be almost *nil* under a governor determined to ignore them, but they at least supplied means by which under ordinary circumstances the general good could be protected.

Another popular feature in the actual administration was the Santa Hermandad. At the time when the central government was weak the institution grew up or, at all events, was developed by which the people of the several communities undertook the police of their own districts. It was of course, given a religious aspect, for the government prided itself on being called that of his Catholic majesty, and with a wisdom which is not always shown in Spanish history this local constabulary was recognized and adopted into the governmental system. In this way we find it introduced and working in Louisiana.

Regulations as to commerce caused the greatest inconvenience. Spain had never abandoned the idea that hers was a world empire, producing all that was necessary, so that no need could exist for trading outside its limits. As to Louisiana, there was the difficulty that the products, such as timber and peltries, could not be profitably imported into the peninsula and furthermore that the manufactured goods to which the colonists were accustomed were those produced in France or England and not those coming from Spain. The Spanish government had already confined the trade of the province to Seville, Alicante, Carthagena, Malaga, Barcelona, and Corunna and provided that no vessels except Spanish should ply even to these ports, and ships could not call at other Spanish-American ports. It was perhaps too much to expect even of the enlightened Charles III. to see how suicidal was such a policy. It was the policy of England also, and she only outgrew it by becoming the carrying nation of the world, so that such restrictions became meaningless. Spain was too conservative to change. The practical difficulty, however, was that Louisiana had become accustomed to free trade with France and that there grew up an illicit trade with West Florida. The English had equal right with the Spaniards to the navigation of Mississippi River, and under the mild rule of the Spanish governors English merchants established themselves even in New Orleans and soon absorbed a large part of the business of the place. The English in passing up and down the Mississippi found ready customers along the banks, and smuggling was winked at by the authorities. The English even had what are now called trade boats, fitted up with counters and shelves of goods, to which the planters resorted for their wants. It was not only impossible to prevent such commerce in a river equally open to the vessels of both nations, but restrictions imposed by Spain made such a trade essential to the very existence of the colony. Hence the governors, who were just and politic men, overlooked what they could hardly prevent. Oliver Pollock, during a season of distress, turned over to O'Reilly a brig loaded with flour and permitted him to pay what he thought best. The price was then twenty dollars a barrel, and Pollock's generosity, for he agreed to accept only fifteen dollars, was never forgotten and he was permitted to have free trade for his brig. Subsequently, from time to time, concessions were made in favor of French shipping, until finally there was almost free trade with the French islands, subject only to the imports being paid for by exports, to effect which local commissioners were appointed.

O'Reilly considered that the changes he had made had finished his mission, and on the 29th of October, 1770, turned the government of the province over to Don Luis de Unzaga. O'Reilly was a young man of thirty-four or thirty-five; his successor was somewhat older and proved to be an even more acceptable executive. He ruled almost as a father, with the result that Louisiana became thoroughly attached to the Spanish crown. In no way was his wisdom more manifest than in the attitude he assumed toward the quarrels of the priests. Louisiana had long been a Capuchin province, and the abolition of the Jesuits had removed the influence of that order. Father Dagobert was the Superior of the Capuchins and vicar-general of the Bishop of Quebec, and on the transfer of the province to Spain the question arose as to the ecclesiastical jurisdiction. Spanish Capuchins came, and one of them, Cirilo, moved heaven and earth to drive out the French priests, who were much loved, especially Dagobert. It is very likely that in easy-going creole style they omitted some of the unessential ceremonies and indulged their flock in some respects, but Cirilo reported many things amiss, and that Dagobert actually dispensed with more than the Pope might have done. Cirilo more than insinuates that the priests were unduly attached to mulattresses whom they had to take care of their house. Cirilo wrote all about it to the Bishop of Havana, and the bishop took up the matter. On the other hand Unzaga, after investigation, protected the French Capuchins to the extent of his ability, defending them to the bishop and to the Spanish court. He said it seemed to him that the common lot of humanity was for each one to judge for himself and act for the best, and that it was difficult to come to a correct appreciation of the true merits of men of the sacred calling when they chose to quarrel among themselves. At this the bishop took offence and the matter was referred to the home government. The final result was that while the bishop was in a way sustained, clear intimation was given that there must be harmony in the administration of affairs. After this some compromise was effected and the trouble largely abated.

The Spanish régime began in blood, but through the tact as well as the energy of O'Reilly and perhaps even more so of Unzaga, the creoles became thoroughly reconciled to their new allegiance. It might require another generation, it might require a war with some other power, to make the people attached to Spain, but when we recollect the Revolution of 1768 and the excitable character of the population it would seem that nine years had worked wonders. Unzaga thought his mission also accomplished and asked to retire to spend his remaining years at Malaga. This was at first refused, from the high appreciation in which he was held in both Louisiana and Spain. The court hardly knew whom to appoint in his stead. Finally his wish was granted as to removing him from Louisiana, although it was not to private life, and in 1776 he was promoted to be Captain-general of Caraccas. He departed amid universal regret, and the government was provisionally turned over to Don Bernardo de Galvez, a young man highly connected, who had recently come as colonel of the Regiment of Louisiana. Unzaga left the colony peaceful and satisfied; only the future could tell whether this boy of twenty-one would pursue the same policy or strike out a new one for himself.

Our attention has heretofore been directed mainly to that portion of Spanish Louisiana which was about New Orleans and the lower reaches of Mississippi River; but it must not be forgotten that the province extended, as under the French, far to the north and west, to the sources of the Mississippi and to the unknown beginnings of the Missouri, One might think that these wilds were of no value and would be neglected, the more especially as the Sioux to the north and the Comanches and other tribes to the south had never been brought even to the half-civilization prevailing east of the Mississippi. And yet this meant only that there was the better field for colonization, and when the French abandoned the older Illinois it was only to develop the more that part of the district west of the Mississippi, and seek to make it greater than before. It was a true colonization. Much of the later life of the settlements which we have studied has been an expansion from the centres established by European immigrants, so that it is perhaps rather colonial life than colonization proper. But now when, after the Peace of Paris, we cross the river with Saint-Ange it is to take up again the burden of settling a new country.

At the time of the Peace of Paris there was but one settlement to the west of the upper Mississippi, for those which we have known in the old French days had with the exception of Ste. Geneviève died out. And Saint-Ange was not the first pioneer under the new dispensation, for we recall that he was in command of Vincennes and Fort Chartres throughout Pontiac's war, and that far earlier Le Sueur and others had operated west of the Mississippi.

We again come face to face with that interesting industry which opened the French period a century before. The fur trade is a business that ministers to luxury and by means of romance and daring creates history. As relates to the beaver, it was the cause of the foundation of Canada and of the French *prise de possession* at Michilimackinac of the upper lake region. Du Lhut and Le Sueur became famous in its prosecution, and the jealousy which Canada felt for Louisiana was due to a well-grounded fear that skins would go down the Mississippi rather than down the St. Lawrence. The zeal of religion carried the Jesuits far into the Northwest, and voyageurs early explored in their tracks. We have seen how in other regions the *coureurs de bois* arose and swarmed in the woods. The love of freedom from all civilized restraints attracted them, and hunting supplied them not only with food but with skins and furs which they sold at the different trading posts. They were accused of selling to the English as readily as to the French, and no doubt the freedom of the woods developed a variety of freedom of trade. It is perhaps significant that the French had the same word, *course*, for the life of the *coureurs* in the woods and the life of the buccaneers on the ocean. The growth of Fort Chartres and the power of its commandant brought something of order into the fur trade of the Northwest, and it was well worth taking hold of. There was profit in it, and the future only could tell what developments might come from the partially explored Missouri. Beaver, bear, fox, and other fur-bearing animals abounded, and the severe winters had their redeeming side for the trapper and hunter. The Mississippi was still open toward the south, even if the British now controlled the route down the Great Lakes and the St. Lawrence. There was great promise for the first comers in the new Northwest, particularly if they could obtain something in the nature of a monopoly.

In the interregnum under D'Abbadie this was effected, and indeed there may be some question as to whether the arrangement of Maxent, La Clede and Company was not planned and even carried out before Kerlerec left. At all events, in the summer of 1763 the firm sent an expedition to the north under its junior partner, Pierre La Clede Ligueste, generally called "Laclede." By invitation they wintered at

Fort Chartres, and there prepared for the future. It was a disappointment when the Peace of Paris cut off half their proposed field, but it was necessary in any event to have a trading post on the west side of the river; and as the turbid Missouri was to be the scene of most of their operations, it was natural that the bluffs below the junction should be selected by Laclede. There in the early spring he sent Auguste Chouteau to clear away the forests, and just below the great Indian mound of unknown antiquity he built, in February and March, cabins and *magasins* for the business, and with them came a stone house for Laclede. With a mixture of religion and patriotism, and possibly a recollection of the old name for the Mississippi, they called the new post St. Louis. Indeed, they built better than they knew. As soon as peace came between the Briton and the Indian, Saint-Ange bowed himself across the Mississippi to the new post, where a fort was constructed, mills were built, land grants made, a church erected, and common fields enclosed. It became a great station for the fur trade and fully justified the choice. Ulloa appreciated the promise of the place, confirmed the monopoly, and hoisted the Spanish flag here even if he did not in New Orleans. O'Reilly sent Piernas to St. Louis and instructed the commandants of the posts of St. Louis and Ste. Geneviève to make it their special care that the rule of the king should be loved and respected, justice be administered promptly and impartially, and commerce be protected and extended; although he added some platitudes about monopolies. They were told that the Indians should be well treated, paid just prices for what they brought, and charged only a fair price for what they needed. In the time of O'Reilly the population of each of these two posts was made up of seventeen men and sixteen women, besides twelve male and six female negroes. His shrewd successors did all in their power to develop what began to be called Upper Louisiana. As the English took possession to the east, much of the French population migrated to the west, settling at Ste. Geneviève and especially at St. Louis, whose inhabitants were almost all French and so remained during the Spanish period. The officials held Spanish commissions, but in no way was the wisdom of the new rulers more manifest than in appointing Frenchmen to the different places of trust. A surveyor was provided, so that all grants could be confirmed. By 1769 the population had amounted to eight hundred and ninety-one, confined almost exclusively to St. Louis and Ste. Geneviève. From about this time Upper Louisiana, as it was called, had a lieutenant-governor holding directly from the crown, although subject in some sense to the governor-general and *intendant* at New Orleans. He was also sub-delegate of the *intendant* and thus superintended finances, Indians, commerce, and lands, while as lieutenant-governor he commanded the military at the different posts. Taxes were unknown except a duty of six per cent upon imports and exports and salaries and legacies, and there were license fees for the sale of liquors.

Saint-Ange died at St. Louis, universally regretted, in 1774. The lives of his friends Laclede and Chouteau have been a favorite theme, for these fur traders did much to develop the upper country as well as found what has become a great city. Laclede was born in the lower Pyrenees about 1724, and went to Louisiana at thirty-one. Chouteau was much younger, being born in 1750 at New Orleans, and long survived Laclede, who died on the Mississippi about 1778. Chouteau is not thought to have become his partner until a short time before this, and upon the death of Laclede succeeded to the business and built his mansion upon some of the old firm's lands. Maxent lived in New Orleans and seems to have been the well-known soldier of that name. Chouteau was a good business man and preserved his papers, but these only show that he applied himself strictly to his occupation of merchant and trader and operated the only mill in the country. Under the Spaniards he was never in office, but this was to be changed when the Americans came.

The foundation of a great city is always an interesting subject, although the event will generally be found to lack all elements of the spectacular. Peter the Great founded St. Petersburg of his own initiative, but no one knows who was the first to drive a post at Paris or put up a house at London. When Chouteau examined the Mississippi banks and made a clearing in the primeval forests for huts he failed to inscribe a date on any stone, but it is supposed to have been February 14, 1764. And yet he designed a city of some size, for its plan shows three blocks deep from the river and nine in each direction up and down from the church which soon came. In succession we have the river bank, Grande Rue or Rue Royale, Rue de l'Église, and Rue des Granges, and running perpendicular to the river were, among others, Rue de La Tour, Rue de La Place, and Rue Missouri, while around the whole settlement from Chouteau's Pond toward the great mound was soon a line of primitive fortifications, through which a few roads led toward the country. Gradually these blocks received houses and the population in Spanish times increased, living mainly upon trade with the Indians.

The fur trade was ultimately to make the Missouri known and to develop the whole Northwest, but under the Spaniards this result came slowly. Trading houses were of course established, but few of them were important, perhaps none have become the foundations of cities. Even New Madrid was of a later date. To the last, Ste. Geneviève and the ever increasing St. Louis remained the chief if not the only settlements of Upper Louisiana.

Across the river, George Rogers Clark and his militia conquered for Virginia the old Illinois formerly so well known to us, and for which even in British times a civil government had been proposed. In 1778 both Kaskaskia and Vincennes yielded to him, and in the same year Virginia established the County of Illinois and provided for its more effectual protection and defence. Clark had attempted to administer both the military and the civil departments of the government and was glad enough to welcome John Todd, appointed by Patrick Henry as the first governor. The officers were to be chosen by the people. So the courts of Kaskaskia, Cahokia, and Vincennes came into being, and strange enough the old Frenchmen thought it to be electing their own officials instead of having them appointed from abroad. One thus elected even refused to serve.

The administration of Illinois under the Americans does not at present concern us except in so far as it led to an effort on the part of the British to repossess themselves of the territory. For after Spain also declared war a comprehensive plan of campaign was devised against her Louisiana possessions by Lord George Germain, Secretary for the Colonies. Lieutenant-governor Sinclair, at Michilimackinac, was to be the principal agent in executing it, and Haldimand, from Quebec, was to supervise it in general. The only question might be whether the plan was not too far-reaching for execution in the wilds of the Mississippi valley. It covered a combined series of operations extending from the lakes to the Gulf and designed to result in the expulsion of the Spanish. Campbell and a fleet were apparently to go up the Mississippi to Natchez, and Sinclair was to descend the Mississippi, capturing St. Louis, and after joining Campbell the two should drive out the Spaniards from the lower posts, including New Orleans. As to the exact order of these proceedings there might be some doubt, but the idea seems to have been that Sinclair could operate in the north and Campbell in the south, unless Campbell preferred to wait until Sinclair joined him and both attack New Orleans. Before this George Rogers Clark had been active from the new settlements in Kentucky. He had, in 1778, founded Louisville on an island at the falls of the Ohio, and had not only Americanized Vincennes, but captured Governor Hamilton. He was, therefore, a factor to be dealt with in this extensive scheme, and so the Wabash Indians were to be despatched to keep him busy. What was done in the way of driving the Spaniards from the lower Mississippi will concern us in another chapter; for the present, we are interested in the attack on St. Louis from the north.

It would seem that so far from the new settlement of St. Louis having much influence up Missouri River, the Sioux were much relied upon to act against it. French traders were even to lead in this expedition, and Calvé and Ducharme were afterward much blamed in the matter. There is even a suspicion that the governor had sold much of the powder by agreement with the British. In point of fact, over one hundred whites and several hundred Indians marched southwardly from Michilimackinac and did some damage on the American side of the Mississippi. They crossed over and captured some whites west of the little town, but were frightened off by a cannon discharged by the alarmed garrison. It seems probable that Clark managed to come to the Mississippi in time for his presence and name also to alarm the savages, and yet return to the falls and "busy" himself with the Indians sent. The attack on St. Louis was a complete failure. This affair of 1780 is sometimes disguised under the name of the Indian attack on Pencour, for the inhabitants of St. Louis obtained their flour from Ste. Geneviève and were dubbed by the people of that settlement "Short-bread" [Pain-court]. A great stir this small event made, for potentially it was a great event, and it has been celebrated in local annals much as the unsuccessful Escalade at Geneva. If it had succeeded, the Indians would probably have exterminated the people, and the British gained a hold upon Spanish Upper Louisiana which they would have turned to good account when the treaty of peace was drawn.

The attempt led to the fortification of the town and also to unexpected results. In the first place, the Americans were strengthened in their determination and in their ability to hold their new County of Illinois, for George Rogers Clark was still at large and determined to keep all that he had conquered. Another result was one entirely unexpected, and which was to militate against the claims of the Americans.

The nearest post held by the British was that of St. Joseph, near present South Bend. It had been a garrison in earlier days and was now their westernmost post. During the year 1781, Don Francisco Cruzat, or Cruvat, who succeeded on the death of Leyba, determined to make a return visit to the enemy. Accordingly, in January, he sent Captain Pourré and sixty-five militiamen, French and Spanish, together with Indians, on an expedition of four hundred miles over a country covered with snow and ice. They had to carry their own subsistence and merchandise to secure favor with the Indians they might meet. Louis Chevalier acted as interpreter, and managed to persuade the Indians who were supposed to be allies of the British to remain neutral. Finally, St. Joseph was reached, taken by assault, and plundered, for it was a trading post also; what could not be taken away was destroyed, and the British flag was carried back and delivered to Cruzat. This would seem to be a strange venture, for it involved a long and terrible march to capture an insignificant post; yet it was possibly not without object. By a military fiction the capture of a post carries with it the title to all the surrounding or dependent country, and we find the Spaniards not slow to set up at the proper time that by this invasion they had made their own the whole territory from St. Louis to St. Joseph, if not beyond. If this was Spanish and West Florida was Spanish and there were no Americans between, it would seem as if the Spaniards were securing a hold upon the greater part of the Mississippi valley. It is quite possible that this was the object of the dash at Fort St. Joseph.

However, the claim was never admitted by the Americans, for the old conflict of Latin and Teuton which we have described had not closed without impressing the colonists with a feeling that what had been won was won for their own great future. It would be theirs if they had remained British, it must be theirs all the more if they were to become independent. So that their uniform contention was that the conquests of George Rogers Clark had won this whole country.

The public history of Upper Louisiana was as uneventful as the private life of its inhabitants. They went on in their easy-going way, content with what they had, envying no one, and rejoicing in the paternal government which saved them the trouble of doing anything. Cruzat remained governor until 1787, and our study of Upper Louisiana must leave him in charge. There were, indeed, only Perez, Trudeau, and Dellassus to come before the destiny of the country was entirely changed by a Louisiana Purchase of which the Spaniards did not dream.

CHAPTER XXIII

WIDENING THE SPANISH BOUNDARIES

THERE comes a time in the life of every people when the formal bands which have helped its growth become bonds in turn to retard its progress. If those in power are not able to accommodate the forms to new circumstances, if they attempt to retain the old bottles for the new wine, there is danger that everything will be rent asunder. Bluntschli truly says that every successful war not only settles the questions which gave rise to it but brings in new conditions and is a point of departure for future development. Such was the case with the British colonies in America. French authority had been extinguished and new conditions faced the colonies. The French conflicts had not only conquered the enemy but developed the English colonies themselves. If foreign affairs had been settled, domestic complications now ensued, and there resulted the American Revolution. That story comes later than the story of their colonization, but the colonial period of Spanish Louisiana to some extent overlaps the time of its neighbors' civil war, and so we must give it incidental consideration from the outside. While the thirteen colonies were invading the Latin province of Canada to the north and driving their own loyal inhabitants to the Floridas in the south, while Washington, with the help of France, was seeking from Boston to Yorktown to make the provinces free and independent States, the west bank of Mississippi River remained tranquil.

Neither France nor Spain would ordinarily have aided a revolution designed to increase the liberty of subjects; but on account of their fixed hostility to England, France was assisting the Atlantic colonies against the mother country, and Spain in endeavoring to mediate soon found herself involved in the struggle. She did not, however, enter into an alliance with the Americans as did France, although she was willing to aid them so far as it helped herself, and there was one direction in which she had already been aiding them without its being much observed by the British. Fort Pitt was, of course, in the possession of the insurgents and communication was not much obstructed from there down the Ohio and Mississippi to New Orleans, where Oliver Pollock was still influential. The English remained from the beginning in possession of Detroit, Michilimackinac, and a few other lake posts, for, as the water route was the principal mode of communication, these were practically then as before a part of Canada. There were some attempts to use these as bases of operations against the Virginians west of the Alleghanies, but practically George Rogers Clark made the Americans masters of the Ohio valley. In this way supplies could be brought up the Mississippi and Ohio in comparative safety, if only means could be found to pay for them. Both Patrick Henry and Thomas Jefferson when governors interested themselves in this subject and through Pollock in New Orleans much was effected. The details are obscure, but certain it is Pollock bought munitions of war and shipped them up to Fort Pitt and the other American posts. The great exploits of Clark would have been impossible without the supplies, and so Oliver Pollock and his work were among the causes which have enabled the United States to claim and hold the great Mississippi valley. Virginia in this way became indebted to Pollock in the amount of $65,814⅝, and in 1779 Governor Jefferson asked Galvez to advance this for Virginia. It would seem this was not done, as Galvez needed all the money and means he could command. Virginia paid Pollock in bills

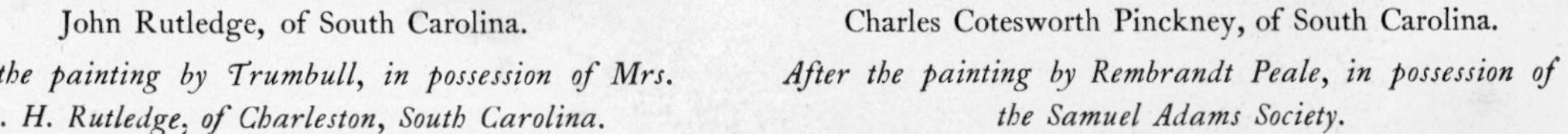

John Rutledge, of South Carolina.

After the painting by Trumbull, in possession of Mrs. B. H. Rutledge, of Charleston, South Carolina.

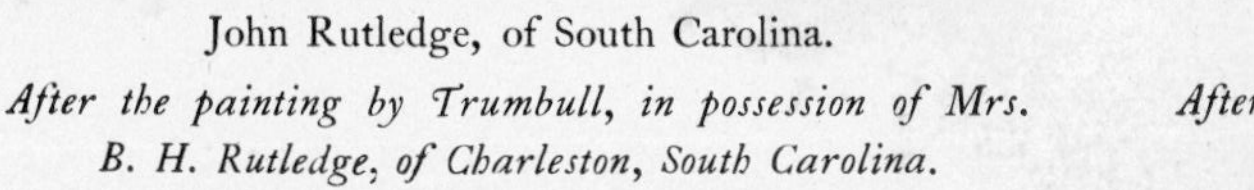

Charles Cotesworth Pinckney, of South Carolina.

After the painting by Rembrandt Peale, in possession of the Samuel Adams Society.

on Pinet, Da Costa and Company, of Nantes, drawn against tobacco shipped abroad. Unfortunately, the tobacco was captured by the British and the bill protested, with the result that Pollock was practically bankrupted. After the Revolution Virginia appointed commissioners, who upon investigation found that the State owed him $92,321, and tardy justice was done him.

Nor were the efforts of the American insurgents confined to securing munitions of war at New Orleans. Captain Willing came down the river from Philadelphia, made strenuous efforts to secure for the new republic adhesion of the inhabitants upon the east bank of the Mississippi, and sent emissaries over to Mobile for the same purpose. This was in vain, for West Florida remained loyal. Colonel Morgan, in command of Fort Pitt, wrote Galvez that he would like to secure transports at New Orleans so as to surprise Mobile and Pensacola, but Galvez had designs of his own in that direction and did not encourage the idea. In view of possible war Galvez placed gunboats upon the river, secured plans and descriptions of the forts and military in West Florida, and in some way even managed to secure the neutrality of the Choctaws and Chickasaws. In 1778 Willing made a descent upon the Mississippi posts of West Florida and captured Manchac and its vessels, with which he laid waste the country up to Natchez. Many of the inhabitants passed over to the Spanish side, where they received aid, and Willing helped not a little to alienate the creoles from the American cause.

War was finally declared by Spain against Great Britain in 1779, and Galvez took prompt steps to follow it up. He assembled the people of New Orleans in the public square, and in a vigorous address induced them to organize for the conflict. He left Piernas in command of the city, and despite a storm went up the river, his army growing as he went. In September he attacked Fort Bute, at Manchac, of which the British had repossessed themselves after Willing's raid, and took it by assault, there being but twenty privates in the fort. Galvez then marched to attack Bâton Rouge. With a Spanish force behind them, the British garrison were at a disadvantage despite the strength of their fort, which had high walls protected by a moat eighteen feet wide and nine feet deep, filled from the Mississippi; while the garrison consisted of four hundred regulars and one hundred militia, supported by thirteen pieces of heavy artillery. By a feint Galvez distracted attention from the position where he was erecting batteries within musket-shot of the fort, and on September 21st he compelled the British to surrender at discretion. This capitulation carried with it also Fort Panmure at Natchez.

Spanish vessels captured sundry British craft on the lakes and other waters, and Galvez was inspired to even greater exertion. In February of the next year he sailed from the Balize to invest Mobile, and in face of a disastrous storm landed at the mouth of the river. He had marched up the Mississippi despite storms, and the elements did not restrain him now, although his landing was made in such disorder that at first he felt inclined to retire temporarily. He soon learned, however, that there was even greater confusion in Mobile, and so pressed forward and erected six batteries to the north and west of the fort. He sent a summons to Durnford to surrender to his superior forces, adding that after the battle he might not be able to grant so favorable terms; and the amenities of war were shown by Durnford's reception to the bearer thereof, his old friend Colonel Bolyny, who dined and drank with him with great cordiality. Durnford's reply was memorable. He said: "My love for king and country and my own honor direct my heart to refuse to surrender this fort until resistance is in vain. A heart full of generosity and valor will ever consider men fighting for their country as objects of esteem and not of revenge." The battle began, and although Durnford received news that Campbell was coming with reinforcements, a breach was made, and it became necessary to surrender on March 14th. The total garrison was under three hundred men, and they marched out with flags and drums, and grounded arms outside the forts, the officers retaining their swords. It is said that Galvez was mortified when he saw how few they were, but he kept his word to take them to a British port upon their promise not to serve against Spain or her allies for eighteen months. Campbell arrived too late and could only return to Pensacola in heavy rains and over swollen streams.

Pensacola yet remained, and Galvez, keeping Mobile under military rule, spent a year in preparation. He went to Havana and secured aid which letters could not bring. Meantime, the English sent Von Hanxleden with Waldeckers to drive the Spaniards out of their intrenchments on the east side of Mobile Bay, and they charged bravely with the bayonet, but in vain. Von Hanxleden was killed and buried on the field of battle. In March, 1781, Galvez was ready and landed his one thousand four hundred soldiers and artillery on the island of Santa Rosa, and directed the fleet to proceed across the bar. The naval officers replied that they had no chart, and that soundings seemed to show the channel was too shallow, whereupon Galvez had the entrance sounded by his own brig, when plenty of water was found; but the navy still refused to proceed, although troops had already arrived by land from Mobile, and Galvez was anxious to attack. Nothing daunted, he threw himself into the brig, and, with the flag of Castile at the masthead and his Louisiana vessels following, swept past the fort into the bay. Galvez's feat was admired by friend and foe alike, and Admiral Irizibar was shamed into action.

It will be recalled that the principal defence of Pensacola was Fort St. George upon a hill overlooking the town, and this was now regularly invested, although to silence the fleet the British built a fort on the shore and drove them across the bay. Galvez actively superintended operations from the sand hills north of the town, but without the aid of the fleet he was at a disadvantage. In the first days of May, however, he dropped a shell into the powder magazine of Fort St. George and after the explosion the Spaniards succeeded in getting possession of a wrecked redoubt, whence they turned field pieces upon the interior of the fort. Even while the Spaniards were preparing to deliver a final assault the white flag was run up. The terms of capitulation were signed on May 9th, and by them eight hundred men were made prisoners and the province of West Florida surrendered. These troops also were to be transported to an English port, and the rule of the Briton in Florida came to an end. Governor Chester, General Campbell, and the legislature at last found something in common, and if they still quarrelled it was without arms and without office, aboard an enemy's vessel bearing them to New York.

The results of this campaign were so striking as to be celebrated by Poydras in a poem, the earliest in Louisiana literature. The British were at first unable to realize them. On the Mississippi the soldiers had surrendered, but the colonists at Natchez were so satisfied that the reverse was temporary that in April they undertook to recapture Fort Panmure. They invested it, and by threat of mines managed to secure its surrender, but when they learned that all West Florida had really become Spanish they remembered Lafrénière and fled eastwardly toward Savannah, which was then in British hands. Their sufferings were indescribable, and all the fugitives did not survive. They had with them their wives and children, and those who did not die or were not captured by the American insurgents finally arrived at Savannah in the fall.

In coming into possession of West Florida, Spain had to determine what method of organization was to be pursued. Mobile had heretofore never been Spanish. It had been British for eighteen years, but in population was still largely creole, and there was no great difficulty in reconciling its inhabitants to accept the rule which the other parts of old Louisiana had found acceptable. Indeed, the Louisiana troops that had come to Mobile had found not a few friends, if not kindred. At Pensacola the case was different, for even if the place was Spanish in name, the Spanish had migrated and the British had practically built the town over again. The cases were now reversed, although some British still remained in both places. The treaty of peace which followed in 1782 allowed them to remain if they chose to become Spanish subjects or within a certain length of time to sell their goods and retire. The Spanish government did not restore the old French boundaries of the country. Not even the Mobile district reverted to Louisiana, and West Florida remained under the Spaniards, as under the British, a separate province, and Pensacola was still a quasi-capital, although the governor-general had his headquarters at New Orleans.

Spanish institutions were gradually introduced in the conquered provinces, Spanish customs superseded the English; and as many of the English had fled in consequence of the war, much land reverted to the government and was granted out anew. The commandants at Mobile and Pensacola had semi-independent powers and performed many of the functions of the old governors. But the main problem facing the new conquerors, as it did the earlier, was the Indian question, and it was not long before great congresses at Pensacola and Mobile gave the Spaniards as complete an influence and perhaps as great a power over the Creeks, Choctaws, and Chickasaws as had been enjoyed by the English before them.

As to the rest, West Florida became thoroughly Spanish, and yet if we could look forward into the future we should find that it did not prosper after the death of Charles III. Louisiana did, for it was fortunate enough finally to discover a way of utilizing the sugar cane. This had earlier produced only *tafia*, a cheap alcoholic drink hardly improving the morals of the country, and a coarse sugar which deliquesced too easily to admit of export. But at last Étienne de Boré discovered the process of crystallization, immortalizing himself and enriching his country.

Thus did the Latins enlarge their bounds, and when the Americans sought the aid of the court of Madrid they found that it could be purchased only at the cost of abandoning all right to the Mississippi. So far as Spain was concerned, the new republic was to be little more than what Iberville had earlier permitted; for West Florida had been conquered from the British, and the Americans had nothing to do with it one way or the other. The dominion of Spain once again swept around the Gulf of Mexico, and when Great Britain in 1783 surrendered East Florida also St. Augustine and the Atlantic coast up to the St. Mary's became Spanish once more. Only the claim to the Illinois was given up by Spain.

It looked as if the days of autocracy had returned. A paternal government may be strong in that it protects the rights of citizens and aids the development of the country, and this was the aim of the Spanish system; and still, like all others of its class, it was bound in the course of time to decay at the heart or give way to the rising popular tide. The only true strong government is that which rests not merely upon the consent of the people, but is really through representative forms carrying out the will of the people themselves. This will may be crude, but the whole people feel that it is their own will and in course of time they rise equal to their duties. This latter was the case with the English colonies on the Atlantic, the former that of Louisiana. The popular element in the Spanish colonial system of which we have spoken was not such as to grow into a consciousness of participation in the government itself. It did not ripen into political rights, but left the people with a feeling that they had a way of addressing their sovereign, without any way of governing themselves. It produced, as was intended, a spirit of dependency. The French rule has been thought of as a bureaucracy, a kind of official aristocracy, in which absence from central control, aided by a division of authority in the province, developed a spirit of peculation and, toward the last, almost of anarchy; the

Spanish in its outward manifestations was much more of a success. The people were content, and that was the difference between them and their Atlantic contemporaries. The British colonists were not content. They long anticipated Tennyson in preferring "fifty years of Europe to a cycle of Cathay." It was the secret of their progress.

Thus the Latin stood facing the Teuton. It was no longer across Mississippi and Iberville Rivers, for the Spanish conquest extended in an indefinite line from the Mississippi to the Atlantic. Great Britain in recognizing the independence of the United States was to name the line of thirty-one degrees as bounding them on the south, while Spain said that her conquest of West Florida carried the northern line above Natchez. With a Charles III. in Europe and a Galvez in Louisiana the claim would be maintained. On the other hand, if the United States were to be kept off Mississippi River and Georgia denied expansion to the west similar to that of Carolina and Virginia, the future was less promising. Much was to depend upon the growth of population. The English had outgrown England, and occupied the American coast. They seemed now about to outgrow the Atlantic coast, and, indeed, the interior up to the mountains, and but for the American Revolution, really an English civil war, there would have been no question as to the result. But again the map was changed. At the beginning Canada and Florida had been in alien hands, and after they had been conquered now again by results of this civil war they had come into alien hands, and the United States were bounded by foreign dominions to the north and foreign dominions to the south just as when they were colonies. Independence was a great boon, but it had apparently been purchased at great cost. The friendship which had arisen with Spain had helped the United States to attain their independence; but the claim of Spain to the Mississippi and to Florida contained the germs of future conflict.

Spain went even further at first, and claimed that she had conquered the east half of the Mississippi valley and stood in the position which France had occupied before the Treaty of Paris. Remembering what the Board of Trade had declared to be the policy of the crown under the proclamation of 1763, we cannot wonder that Spain should adopt the same view and consider the thirteen Atlantic colonies as bounded by the Alleghanies. England had fixed that western limit for her own purposes, and in capturing the leading posts west of the mountains Spain could fairly contend that she had conquered up to the limits recognized by Great Britain herself for her coast provinces. But if this obtained, the French wars had, so far as the American colonies were concerned, been fought in vain. This was to some extent adjusted by the treaties ending the American Revolution, but it was to revive under new forms. First was to come a dispute over the limits of West Florida, and then a long drawn out attempt by smiles and favors to seduce the trans-Alleghany settlements from their loyalty to the United States. We cannot follow these and can only notice here again a chance, if not a necessity, for future misunderstanding. In point of fact, America could not ultimately be half Latin and half Teuton. The wars with France must be carried to a legitimate conclusion. America must be either wholly Latin or wholly Anglo-Saxon.

CHAPTER XXIV

AMERICAN TENDENCIES

EXCEPT with regard to the help given to the Virginians, Louisiana was not concerned in the American Revolution, and in considering the Latins and their growth we had to go beyond that period in order to find a proper resting place. We must leave Latin facing Teuton, for the question of supremacy was not settled until long afterward. Even taking the later date, the French and Spanish can hardly be said to have become American. They were rather Europeans in America than strictly Americans themselves. On the other hand, among the Atlantic colonies we find a different feeling and find it at an earlier date. At the end of the colonial period was the beginning of the change, for circumstances were then making for a different goal. In beginning to realize that they were no longer colonists of a European power, but people born in America and interested only there, those whom we have heretofore known as colonists were taking a great step forward. It might lead to a difference in their relations to the mother country; it might lead to a difference in their relations to the colonists of Louisiana and Florida, who still kept so closely in touch with European traditions. Let us see how this came about.

The colonies of America as now portrayed have been the resultant of settlements by Spain, Great Britain, and France. It would seem that for three countries taking up not half of Europe there was ample room to expand themselves on a new continent as large as the old; but this was not the view of the nations concerned. Instead of holding an international congress and defining their spheres of influence, as would perhaps be done nowadays, all three selected territory and proceeded to settle it, despite overlapping boundaries. Spain early occupied the West Indies and Mexico and, under the name of Indies, much of North America. The mainland to the north she had called Florida from the time of Ponce de Leon, De Ayllon, and De Soto, and through her explorations and settlements claimed up to what we name the Chesapeake, if not further. The English under Elizabeth and James settled Virginia, fixing temporarily the south line at thirty-four degrees and running north to where the French had already occupied Canada, and not without conflict even in that direction. Lastly the French, under La Salle and Iberville, discovered and occupied Louisiana, including under that name everything west of the Alleghanies. The powers did not even wait for their colonies to grow to a point when it might become important to define limits, but began with conflicting claims, and also because of wars that arose from European questions further mixed up American boundaries. The key to the interminable tangle is found in hanging the history of America on the three names, Florida, Virginia, and Louisiana. Gradually the respective claims are reduced until the north line of Florida is thirty-one degrees, practically the east line of Louisiana is the Alleghany ridge, and Virginia and her daughters Carolina and Georgia occupy the Atlantic coast. It was characteristic of colonies of the more successful colonizing races that they progressed because of separation, and found their strength therein and not in union. There was not even a single generic word under which the British colonies were known. Virginia was in some sense the mother of them all, and she long remained the most important, but Virginia ceased to be the common name, and no other took its place. At the close of the colonial period we use the term "America," but that embraces Louisiana, Canada, and

Florida, as well as the original English settlements on the Atlantic. Spanish Florida was also subdivided, for Florida at first embraced everything west to Mexico; but, strictly, this was less an instance of subdivision than of conquest by other nations. Louisiana was, so to speak, carved out of Florida, but the carving was done by the French against the protest of the Spanish. To the Spaniards Florida was at first almost synonymous with what we call America, and to the Englishmen the same was true of Virginia, saving an indefinite recognition of the peninsula of Florida and of Canada. But ultimately matters settled down so that Florida was one thing, Louisiana another, and Virginia was subdivided until the colony of that name was but one of several.

It is not quite clear that colonization covers all we have studied, and yet it may be questioned if any other word would be suitable if we take the process as meaning the transfer of more or less of a country's population to a new soil, with the result of bringing the territory within the sphere of the mother country's influence, for settlement or for exploitation. A settlement colony would be where the population was transferred from an old to a new country for purposes of growth, with the incidental effect of driving out or absorbing the aborigines. This was essentially the case with the British in North America. An exploitation colony, on the other hand, is where the newcomers are interested more in developing the resources of the new territory than in populating it, and will be found to result, as a rule, in their dominating rather than exterminating the natives. Such was the case with most of the Spanish colonies, and indeed is true of all European colonies in tropical regions to this day, and results from the fact that Aryans attain their mental and physical vigor in cool climates and do not retain it in hot ones. They may for a season live in the tropics as masters, but must, as a rule, return to the old country for recuperation. From causes heretofore studied, the French colonization, even in Louisiana, assumed somewhat of an exploitation form, and the French led rather than exterminated the Indians. The Latins in the tropics have shown more disposition than the Teutons to assimilate with the natives, although French experience in North Africa is now tending the other way; for the most diplomatic of colonizers are becoming the most exclusive, if not oppressive, in dealing with the darker races. In the past, however, with the growth of population in the case of settlement colonies, and assimilation with the natives in the case of exploitation ones, both kinds assume a civilized appearance, although climatic and racial conditions never wholly lose their strength. The mother country, if she pays any attention to the matter at all, thinks of either kind of colony as a place from which is to be drawn raw material, such as precious metals, timber, or agricultural products, and then, as the people develop in number, she thinks of them as consumers of her own manufactures. When, in course of time, the dependencies become strong enough to manufacture for themselves there is apt to be friction, especially in the more homogeneous settlements. In the meantime there might arise another form of colonization, that of emigration from one colony to another, or to new territories adjacent to the older provinces. Thus we saw the Scotch-Irish emigrating from northern regions to the south, and in Carolina, Georgia, and Florida found immigrants even from the upper Southern colonies. More important yet, we have studied the western movement down the Ohio and through Cumberland Gap, which was adding two new commonwealths to the original thirteen. This might be called internal colonization, and was a process which was to continue with ever increasing rapidity as the means of transportation improved.

The real beginnings of American colonization had not been governmental. With the British this was beyond doubt, for these had begun with individuals or companies, and we recall that only Crozat and the French Compagnie had given life to Louisiana. The commercial company had in America proved its value for colonization purposes, as it has in our own day in Africa and Asia, and then as now when the government interfered to sustain the venture, it changed a business enterprise into a political commonwealth. The Seven Years' War had been a struggle for existence between the two exponents of this method of colonization, and the Peace of Paris declared the survival of the fittest. Spain, on the other hand, had never encouraged individual initiative, and her method was now to be tested over against the British. The result had been with Spaniard and Frenchman to make the colonists dependents of the home country, and emasculate such mixed population as arose, while the British had tended more and more toward autonomy.

The British colonies were sparsely settled and were separated from each other by great distances. In the far North there was nothing but an occasional fort to protect the fur trade, and in Canada as well as in Florida there was much alien population. In the great Mississippi valley, over which had been the main conflict, the Indians were still masters, and the intruding communities of white men had dangers before them. And yet, it was plain that the seed sown through two hundred years had taken firm root. The east half of North America was on the way toward becoming British, and from Hudson Bay to the Gulf the English language and institutions were supreme.

We have seen how the population planted originally upon the seacoast spread from there over the tidewater of the country, how even during the French wars, and more particularly after the Peace of Paris, it expanded from the tidewater to the foot of the mountains, and was now occupying the Appalachian valleys and pressing through Cumberland Gap over into the beautiful country watered by the Ohio. In this part of America the Anglo-Saxon was supreme. Trouble there doubtless would be with the Indians, but it would be trouble which could be overcome. The future would be one of development.

And yet, we are looking backward at the movement from a height which enables us to understand it more clearly than did the men who themselves were making the history. To them it was the growth of their respective colonies. The increasing population west of the Susquehanna was to them the growth of Pennsylvania. The settlement of the Shenandoah and Watauga valleys was the expansion of Virginia and North Carolina. The people of one knew little and cared less about the people of even an adjacent province. In time of Indian invasion humanity might compel assistance to be sent outside of the boundaries, but sometimes even then the troops were hired rather than loaned. No money would be given to help to build forts on the frontier of New York, even if they did protect against the French, and when Virginia built one on the upper Ohio it was because the junction of the Alleghany and the Monongahela was thought to be within its own limits. Devotion to the little commonwealths of Greece was not more intense than that in America to the respective colonies, and the reason was much the same. Each had its own governor, each its own legislature chosen by its citizens, and the interests of the several colonies were separate. Even the home government, which sent out the governors and superintended the affairs of all, saw no necessity for a governor-general, and left each colony to its own particularistic growth.

There was also unknown to the people themselves a line of cleavage between the Northern and Southern provinces. The boundary run between Pennsylvania and Maryland was to become much more famous than Mason and Dixon imagined, although the distinction was more accentuated in the next century than in the eighteenth. Ultimately the difference was one of temperament, customs, and institutions, but the causes were simple. These were originally probably two in number,—the climate of the two sections, and the difference in origin of their immigrants. Of course, no one contends now that the Virginians were all Cavaliers, or that the New Englanders were all Roundheads; still, as a generic division this is a more convenient form of expression than any other. And yet, the Southern colonies were not founded to carry out any theory, for although Carolina was an apparent exception the vision of Locke soon disappeared, leaving the colony to work out its own salvation along the same lines as all the others. Georgia, it is true, was intended as a home for the distressed, and its chief city was built on a peculiar plan, but this dream also faded away; and the three or four Southern colonies, recruited from among the same class of people and having almost the same products, became homogeneous, and this all unrealized by themselves. We have seen that even the form assumed by the dwelling house showed the difference, and it was to be more and more marked as the years rolled on. Climate made the main difference in that toward the north it not only necessitated greater exertion on the part of the people, but induced them to live closer together in villages, and thus ultimately produced communities where civic life was more intense. In Virginia, and certainly further to the south, the reverse was true, for a highly individualistic type was produced, and the introduction of African slavery had a far-reaching effect.

The laborers at the beginning were indentured white servants brought over from England, and who in course of time would, under ordinary circumstances, have developed into a peasant class. We have seen how this growth was arrested and finally blotted out by the growth of African slavery, induced by competition with the adjacent Spanish colonies, and assuming such a hold on the colonial civilization that it would have been impossible to abandon it even if the people had so wished. There was every disposition to limit the institution. Even in South Carolina the provincial Assembly imposed a duty on every slave imported, which would have been prohibitory, but this was promptly vetoed by the royal government; for long after the death of James and Charles, who had originated the Royal African Company to supply America with negroes, this corporation remained in favor in England, and the governors were instructed to see that its operations were aided. Negro slavery was thus riveted upon the Southern colonies. Slavery was recognized everywhere, but in the North the climate was unfavorable to the negro and economic conditions prevented the growth of the institution. Slavery existed throughout the whole country, but ultimately there resulted a gradual drift of the negroes through sale or otherwise to the South. Negroes could work in the swamps and low countries where the white man would die out, and the institution was an economic blessing in the beginning. More land was reclaimed and more crops were raised than would have been possible otherwise. Evils connected with slavery were in a new country not so apparent. That it confined the people principally to agricultural pursuits was not appreciated at first, and when this was recognized it was not regarded as a disadvantage, for it was felt also that agriculture is the foundation of everything else. Even Thomas Jefferson was to decry manufactures, and we must remember that it was not until late during the Seven Years' War, and consequently almost the time of the Peace of Paris, that the great economic change from agriculture to manufactures and commerce was fully established in England. It often happens that colonies perpetuate conditions existing when they were founded. The New England colonists on account of the sterility of their soil and the bleakness of their climate turned early to other pursuits than agriculture, while the Southern for converse reasons remained agriculturists, especially after African slavery was introduced and had accentuated the situation. The Southern colonies, making allowance for difference of flora and labor, continued to be largely what the home country was when they were founded, while those to the north met with different conditions and struck out new paths. These considerations come to us as we now look back with the better perspective given by time, but to the men of that day they were not so plain.

The differences are not to be ignored. They were real and they caused differences of fact and of feeling to prevail for a long time, in some respects to exist even now. And yet, when the fear of the Spaniards on the south and the

Frenchmen on the west was removed, when the Indian was felt to be either a ward or an enemy who would at some future time be displaced, room was made for the growth of other feelings than those peculiar to a time of colonization. Generations had grown up loving the New World. Travel and commercial intercourse between the settlements were increasing, and, all unobserved as it was, the colonies were gradually drawing closer to each other.

During the several wars with France the common interest was better appreciated. We have noticed a convention of the Southern governors with Loudoun at Philadelphia. Something similar occurred at Alexandria when Braddock undertook his fatal campaign, and the most important of such congresses was that held at Albany in 1754. It was famous more especially for a plan of union advocated by Benjamin Franklin, which did not suit the colonies because giving too much authority to the crown, and was rejected by the crown because it gave too great freedom to the colonies. In one sense it indicated that the colonies were not yet much inclined toward union which involved general supervision from without, but the fact that there was a congress at all was something. The stimulus of foreign danger was removed by the complete expulsion of the French. There was less need for united action when the borders were not threatened, and yet the fact was that there was more danger to British supremacy than to the idea of colonial union. The New England colonies had united more than once, even had had a common governor, and had been able to capture Louisburg. The example was not lost, although imitation did not come for some time.

Although there was no governor-general of the American colonies, they were under one supervision, that of the Board of Trade, so that corresponding laws were suggested in all so far as their circumstances admitted. The home government became accustomed to considering them together, although not yet by any means as a unity, and in the same way the colonies became used to looking to one general head. Governors like Andros and Nicholson were changed from one capital to another at will. The institution of a post office tended no little also toward Americanization. Spotswood as postmaster-general worked, although unconsciously, for the unification of all the colonies. Intelligent men could not but feel that the development even in regard to government was along the same lines in all. There was no longer the distinction of proprietary, corporate, and royal colonies, for all had become royal, with definite charters or something equivalent, governed by an appointed governor with his council and an assembly elected by freeholders or other electors. There was not one in which there had not been a dispute between the executive and the assembly, and these disputes, taking out the personal elements, were strikingly alike. The governors, often instigated from England, desired a larger revenue either to support the officials or to carry into effect some measure nominally for the public benefit. Frequently it was a proper measure, but sometimes it was not suited to the existing conditions, and almost always it was a measure for which the people were expected to pay and which the people thought either unimportant or one which should be paid for by the imperial government. And these quarrels of the assemblies with the governors tended toward a feeling of common interests. The occasions were different, but almost everywhere the cause was the same, and that was jealousy by the people of the royal prerogative. The people were sometimes ignorant of their own good, but the royal executives were carrying out orders given on behalf of a government thousands of miles away which often could not appreciate the actual conditions in America. The newspapers and news letters, the correspondence of leading citizens, made the people of one province acquainted with the affairs of another, and these were seen to become increasingly analogous. Men could not help feeling that it was the battle of people against king fought out by their ancestors at Runnymede and in the Revolution of 1688,—an old foe with a new face. Centuries of conflict had worked into the very marrow of the English race the conviction that eternal vigilance is the price of political safety.

It seems to us now monstrous that a country should seek to exploit colonies for its own good and not for that of the dependent people, and yet our study has been in vain if we do not realize that this was, and is, the object of colonization in the beginning and the practice of all countries throughout history. Great Britain was perhaps the most enlightened nation, because its people were the freest, and yet the same spirit there prevailed. Indeed, it was not until the famous *Report* of Lord Durham after the Canadian rebellion in the nineteenth century that the idea of ruling colonies for the benefit of the colonies themselves was made a basis of official action. The proclamation of 1763 has been considered in regard to its proposed effect upon the Indians, but it had a deeper meaning. A report by Lord Hillsborough, president of the Lords Commissioners for Trade and Plantations, made in 1772, throws another light upon it, for he "took leave to remind their lordships that the principle adopted by this board and confirmed by his Majesty immediately after the Treaty of Paris was to confine the western extent of settlements to such limits that they would lie within reach of the trade and commerce of the kingdom and also of the exercise of that authority which was conceived to be necessary for their preservation in due subordination to the mother country." He even declared that these were "the two capital objects of the proclamation and that the great object of colonizing North America had been to improve and extend the commerce, navigation, and manufactures of the kingdom." The protection of the Indians was only so that they would remain undisturbed and contented and thus extend the fur trade, and only on this account was it that the savages were to enjoy their deserts in quiet.

The first settler had always ties in the home country, and it was several generations before his descendants forgot them. All institutions at home were looked up to with reverence, and even the rule of Parliament was disputed only by advanced thinkers. And yet, in time the people caught up with those who were in advance, and it began to be felt that the colonies in America had rights of their own. There was some selfishness in this, for it cannot be denied that the mother country had expended far more in its wars for the colonies than it ever got back. It was not an unfair claim that the colonists should help to pay in one form or other some portion of the cost of their defence against the Spaniards, French, and Indians. And yet, this claim for past favors was resented and the fitness of the French for influencing the world of thought and of letters was never more apparent than in the feeling soon entertained in America toward former foes. The fear of conquest removed, the tact and charm of the French and of French institutions had full sway. And in saying "French" we mean "Latin," for it must not be forgotten that the French remained predominant in Louisiana, including West Florida, even after the change of flag. The influence which the Frenchman had exercised upon the Indians was measurably transferred to the English colonists, and there gradually grew up among these a greater friendliness toward their Latin neighbors, with whom now there was no dispute, than toward the Englishmen of the mother country, whose representatives were officials representing taxes and other burdens.

Such was the general feeling in the Southern provinces. It is true the importance of Charlestown as a port tended to unite its mercantile classes to the mother country. Those of New England might become dissatisfied, but the merchants of Charlestown were prosperous, despite all exactions, and remained loyal. And yet there was another side to this. Carolinians not only frequently went to England on business, but, as in the case of Henry Laurens and the Pinckneys, left or sent their sons there to be educated. The bar of Carolina, and, to some extent, of Virginia, was made up of those who had learned or practised at Westminster.

When the debates on the American questions began in Parliament, not a few of the audience were Southerners, and what was often only the insincere play of the Opposition was by them taken literally. When these young men returned home and found even judicial offices filled by such pimps as Shinner, rewarded in the colonies for services which could not be recognized at home, or saw reform blocked because placemen in England held sinecures in America which conflicted, or their own kindred displaced from office to make room for foreigners, it was felt that something was wrong. An English education accustomed them to better things, and, furthermore, showed how to attain these. And the same was true in the army. Everyone could see that Braddock knew less about colonial fighting than Washington. It might be questioned whether Oglethorpe was as well posted as Palmer, and even when the army officers were efficient as well as brave they were disposed to be supercilious to provincials. Men who had built up the British Empire in America and felt equal to greater things were not disposed to yield to inferiors, even if these were clothed in ermine or scarlet. Quincy heard Carolinians lament that honors were not for them, but for sycophants. The feeling of injustice rankled deep, and if opportunity came for righting the wrong it might be welcomed.

As a result, the feeling toward Great Britain became somewhat strained. There was the same love for the old traditions, the same loyalty to the common sovereign, but less regard for England as the home country. Virginia, Carolina, and Georgia were the only homes they knew now, and England was where other people lived, kindred, but nothing more. The sentiment was that the future of the colonists was bound up with America; and now that the French had ceased to be enemies, even the creoles were in some respects nearer than the people over in England, for at least all colonists lived in one atmosphere, all were confronted by much the same conditions. Those at Natchez felt quite at home across the river, and when the bitterness of war died out the word "America" was claimed by colonists whose ancestors came from England and by colonists whose ancestors came from France. The colonies were separate, patriotism was local; but it was gradually realized that there were colonial interests, a similar past, possibly a common future. There came the use of the word "Continental" as well as the word "Colonial,"—the growth, in fact, of an American sentiment. The popular impression is that the colonies had flourished under a salutary neglect by the home government, and in a sense this is true, for there was no such minute supervision as in Louisiana and Florida. But in a very important sense the British government took a deep interest in and kept a full oversight over them. We have seen how the Privy Council as representing the king had charge of colonial matters, and with the close of the French war the system was made even more complete. A colonial secretary was appointed, and in many respects the governmental institutions of all the colonies were moulded alike. In 1763 Charles Townshend became the first lord of trade, and inaugurated the great change from requisitions upon the colonial governments to taxation of the individual colonists. Officials were to be paid by the crown and supported by a standing army, and all this was to be provided from taxation. This was a most important step toward unification of the colonies, and was to be copied by them when years afterward they discarded the system of requisition upon the several States and substituted immediate taxation by the general government, directed to individual citizens and their property. In this shape it was to cause great opposition to the ratification of the present constitution, and now, years in advance, it was to cause the storm associated with the name of the Stamp Act.

Not only were the relations of colonies to the mother country imperfectly understood at that day, but the whole nature of taxation was in an experimental stage. It was not appreciated that there is less objection to indirect duties than to direct taxes, and yet since 1733 there had been an import duty on foreign sugar, coffee, wine, cloth, and the like. The fact is, however, that these duties were prohibitory and there was little collected from them. Grenville adopted Townshend's plan, but gave time for the colonial agents to devise something more acceptable, if possible. All they could do was to present remonstrances, which were not considered, and the act passed both Houses of Parliament almost unanimously and received the royal assent March 22, 1765. It imposed a stamp duty on every skin or piece of vellum or parchment or sheet or piece of paper on which shall be engrossed, written, or printed legal proceedings, note, bill of lading, franchise, license for retailing spirituous liquors, bonds, warrant of survey, deed, lease, contract, power of attorney, newspaper, advertisement, pamphlet, almanac, and other things,—extending through sixty-two sections. As a supplement there was passed the next month a Quartering Act, providing for the billeting in public houses, or, in lack of these, in private houses, of the army which was to be needed in America, with other incidental rights found only in martial law. The effect can be imagined of such measures, which were not only direct taxation falling upon every business man, but at a high rate and to be enforced with a high hand. Public meetings and private disturbances swept the country from Boston to Savannah. The principle declared in Virginia's early charters and enforced in the province from the time of the Great Charter down was found in almost every subsequent fundamental law, and was now claimed as a birthright of Englishmen. There could be no taxation without representation; taxes could only be imposed by the provincial assemblies.

These legislatures took up the matter. In the Virginia Burgesses, Patrick Henry, translating the argument that won in the Parsons case into parliamentary forms, proposed five resolutions. The last declared: "The General Assembly of this colony have the sole right and power to lay taxes and impositions upon the inhabitants of this colony; and that every attempt to vest such power in any person or persons whatsoever other than the General Assembly aforesaid has a manifest tendency to destroy British as well as American freedom." There was no real difference in feeling between the tidewater Virginian, in his wig and powder, and the Scotch-Irishman of the interior, clothed in homespun; but the former was the more conservative, as they both sat there in the old State House at Williamsburg, looking out upon the college, church, and palace connecting them through so long a past with the mother country. It was then that Henry, as if inspired, delivered the magnificent address in which he referred to Cæsar as having his Brutus, Charles I. his Cromwell, and, despite the cries of "treason" from the speaker in the high crimson chair, added that George III. might profit by their example. The resolutions were carried, the last one by a majority of only one, and the Old Dominion swept into the current of the Continental policy.

The feeling of loyalty to their several colonies gave way to the feeling of a common danger to all the colonies. South Carolina adopted Virginia's resolutions, and it was not three months after the passage of the act that the Massachusetts Assembly proposed the appointment of representatives to meet in New York to consult on the present circumstances. The congress accordingly met in October. Delegates were there from Delaware, Maryland, and South Carolina of the Southern colonies, as well as those from Massachusetts, Rhode Island, Connecticut, New York, New Jersey, and Pennsylvania; Virginia, Georgia, and North Carolina were not represented only because the governors prevented it. Professing the warmest sentiments of affection and duty to his majesty's person and government, they, nevertheless, esteemed it their "indispensible duty" to declare on October 19th that liege subjects in the colonies "are intitled to all the inherent rights and liberties of his natural born subjects within the kingdom of Great Britain," and continued through thirteen articles to make clear that they would only be taxed with their own consent, given personally or by their representatives in their respective legislatures, and denouncing the Stamp Act and the extension of admiralty jurisdiction to punish infringements thereof.

In Virginia Patrick Henry was not the only man active in resistance, although it was his eloquence that carried the day. Peyton Randolph, George Mason, John Page, Cyrus Griffin, Edmund Pendleton, and others, although more conservative, were prominent in those trying times. In South Carolina Christopher Gadsden then and later led the opposition. He was radical in his actions, and among the less extreme leaders of the people were John Rutledge, Charles Cotesworth Pinckney, and David Ramsey.

Resistance in America was not confined to resolutions. From the northernmost to the southernmost province different organizations were formed, generally called Liberty Boys, who, by threats and overt acts, compelled stamp distributors to resign and naval officers bringing stamps to keep them on board. Possibly the earliest and most serious of these disturbances was that at Cape Fear River in North Carolina on November 16, 1765, when the people, under the lead of Colonel George Ashe, the speaker of the Assembly, went to Governor Tryon's house and compelled stamp master Houston to promise not to receive stamp paper or act in its distribution. A few days afterward the *Diligence* brought the stamps to Brunswick, near Wilmington, but, despite her frowning cannon, could not unload them on account of armed men occupying streets and shore. Not long after, the organized citizens compelled the release of vessels seized by the government for violating the law. At Savannah in December the stamps were taken out of the ship *Speedwell* and guarded, but Governor Wright received threatening letters and Colonel James Habersham was waylaid, and it seemed expedient to send the stamps to a fort and afterward to a ship. The only ones used were to clear vessels in the harbor, so as to prevent their arrest upon the high seas. One of the leaders in Georgia was Noble Wimberley Jones, who was so obnoxious to royalty that the House was forbidden to choose him speaker. Similar resistance occurred or was threatened everywhere, and the law was practically a dead letter.

Meantime, in England had come a change. Rockingham succeeded Grenville, and Conway, who had charge of colonial matters, was opposed to taxation against the consent of the colonies. Conway directed the governors to preserve order, and, after some indecision, on May 18, 1766, the Stamp Act was repealed, although at the same time a Declaratory Act was passed affirming that the colonies are "subordinate to the crown and parliament, who have full power and authority to make laws and statutes to bind them and the people of America in all cases whatsoever." Thus the immediate cause of dissatisfaction was removed, for the Declaratory Act carried no penalty and the colonies were still as free as the Parliament to think what they pleased.

Universally there was rejoicing, and people could once more breathe freely. The royal governors, Botetourt in Virginia, Tryon in North Carolina, and Wright in Georgia, were all good and able men, and resumed much of their old influence. Grateful Virginia could erect at Williamsburg a monument to Botetourt on his untimely death, and North Carolina a splendid palace for Tryon.

In South Carolina feeling had run as high as anywhere, and upon the repeal of the Stamp Act the Commons House of Assembly voted to erect a marble statue of William Pitt on account of his opposition to the act. Samuel Wragg wished it to be a statue of the king, but found himself alone. The sculptor Wilton accordingly set to work in England, and in 1770 the statue arrived in Charlestown, where it was received with processions, salutes, and the ringing of St. Michael's bells. As soon as the pedestal could be prepared, the statue was erected at the intersection of Broad and Meeting Streets, probably the most prominent place in the city, in full view from the government buildings, the Exchange,

St. Michael's, and the western fortifications, and was there long to remain—the guardian angel of Charlestown.

The spectre of revolution was removed. The drift of circumstances, the tendency of events, the acts of the home government, had indeed created an American feeling; but, after all, might it not be a feeling which would lead to a closer union with the mother country? Men of that day could not look upon events in the light in which we view them. To them the Seven Years' War was the most glorious in the history of the world in that it had changed Great Britain from an insular kingdom with a few outlying dependencies into the greatest empire of history. Surely the recent mistake as to taxing America would not be repeated. A vast dominion had been acquired in the Orient, and through the old East India Company England had become an Asiatic power. Perhaps the work of colonization, which had been too great for the Virginia Company, which had been perfected by proprietors, kings, and peoples, reinforced by accessions from France and Germany, would in the west build up a corresponding dominion, greater as its foundations were deeper and broader. Perhaps London would be the capital of an empire greater than any yet imagined, one not only world-wide in its membership, but one to influence and inspire all other peoples and races on the globe. Granted that in America the Spaniard was to the west and south. Menendez, Iberville, and Galvez were potent names; but their scheme of civilization, their final attempt to lead the natives rather than to supersede them by more advanced races, even the growth of the Latins who had come over,—these might seem to a philosophical observer not to possess the promise and potency which would resist the Anglo-Saxon advance. Or if the statesmen of that day could not see so far into the future, at least the Latin was separated from the Anglo-Saxon by vast spaces which it would take long to fill. The battle had been won as to the east half of the Mississippi valley, and the question of the remainder might well be left to the future.

And yet, might not the danger of disruption come again? Was this time of rejoicing the lull before the storm? Possibly the American feeling was something which was not to advance the British Empire; perhaps the foreign observer was right who said that colonial growth was like that of fruit, that the colonies must eventually fall ripe from the parent stem. But, even if this proved true, in dropping the seed might take root and an offshoot grow up as great as the older tree. And come what might, the Southern colonies would do their part. In the South had been the earliest English settlements; and should independence be necessary, not only would a Southerner be ready to move its declaration in a Continental Congress, but a Scotch-Irish county like Mecklenburg in North Carolina would be the first community in the New World to renounce allegiance to the British crown!

CHRONOLOGICAL TABLE

DATE		PAGE
1607.	The London Adventurers' expedition under Newport reached Chesapeake Bay . .	63
	Spain endeavored to check the colonization of Virginia by England	94
1609.	Newport arrived at Jamestown with reinforcements for the colony	68
	The Virginia colony dispersed	70
	New charter for Virginia granted by King James	71
	Lord De la Warr arrived at Jamestown as the governor of the colony	75
	Rights of English colonists in Virginia . .	158
1610.	Expedition under Gates and Somers sailed for Virginia	74
1612.	New charter granted to the Virginia Company	77
	First shipment of tobacco from Virginia sent to England	78
	Captain John Smith's Oxford Tract published	101
1615.	Last of the "ancient planters" arrived in Virginia in the *Treasurer*	81
1617.	Samuel Argall arrived at Jamestown as governor	81
	Pocahontas died in England	98
1618.	Guinea slave trade privilege granted to the Earl of Warwick and others	113
1619.	Slavery introduced in Virginia	82, 112
	The first legislative body of Virginia met at Jamestown	85
	Indented servants sent to Virginia	111
1620.	Friction manifested between the colonizing Company and the king	96
1621.	Lotteries in aid of Virginia colonies abolished	90
1622.	The Indians of Virginia perpetrated a general massacre of the settlers	99
	Royal African Company chartered to import slaves into the colonies	113

DATE		PAGE
1623.	The Privy Council investigated the Virginia Company's affairs	101
	Captain John Smith's *True Historie* appeared	101
1624.	The Virginia Company's charter annulled	102
	Tobacco exports from Virginia restricted to England	115
1625.	Census of white servants and negroes in Virginia	112
1628.	Children sent as colonists to Virginia	111
1629.	Annual expeditions against the Indians ordained by law in Virginia	123
1630.	First general inspection law enacted as to Virginia tobacco	116
	Charter of Carolina granted to Sir Robert Heath	135
1631.	Legislation enacted requiring Virginia lands to be enclosed against cattle	117
1632.	System of road building established in Virginia	117
	Charter of Maryland granted to Lord Baltimore	135
1633.	Virginia Dissenters made first settlement in Carolina	137
1634.	Shires named in Virginia	120
	Privy Council empowered to govern the English colonies in America	163
1637.	Office of treasurer instituted in Virginia	110
	Custom house established in Virginia	116
1639.	Patent of Maine granted to Sir Ferdinando Gorges	135
1640.	Ferries in Virginia first mentioned	118
	Virginia colonists massacred by Indians	123
1642.	Restrictions enacted in Virginia against lawyers	120
1644.	Opechancanough attacked the Virginians on the upper York and Pamunkey Rivers	123
1649.	Declaration of Virginia in favor of Charles II.	119

DATE		PAGE
1679.	La Salle ascended the Great Lakes . . .	188
1680.	Carolina's population	143
1682.	Tobacco riots in Virginia	128
	La Salle reached the mouth of the Mississippi and claimed Louisiana	190
1683.	Presbyterianism introduced in eastern Virginia	353
1684.	Stuarttown founded by Lord Cardross . .	145
1685.	La Salle landed at Matagorda Bay	194
1686.	Spanish attack on Port Royal	145
	Spaniards attacked the Scotch settlement at Port Royal	292
1687.	Huguenot church erected in Carolina . . .	144
	La Salle assassinated near Trinity River, Texas	195
1690.	Williamsburg, Virginia, founded	130
1691.	College of William and Mary founded at Williamsburg, Virginia	130
	North Carolina so designated	359
1693.	Pensacola settled by Spaniards	284
1696.	Board of Trade instituted to control colonial affairs	163
	Santa Maria (Pensacola) Bay occupied by Spain	204
1698.	Post office established at Charlestown . . .	149
	The first Chief Justice of Carolina appointed	149
	First free public library in America established at Charlestown	149, 370
1699.	African freedmen legally banished from Virginia	114
	Hennepin's map of America published . . .	200
1700.	Census of African slaves in Virginia . . .	113
	Iberville explored Mobile Bay	204
	Le Sueur explored the Mississippi to the Sioux country	249
	Spanish mission established near the Rio Grande	281
	The Shawnees located on the lower Tennessee and the Cumberland	325

DATE		PAGE
1715.	Massacre of Carolina colonists by allied Indians	152
	Edenton the recognized capital of North Carolina	152
	Natchez founded	243
1716.	Governor Spotswood discovered the Shenandoah valley	320
1717.	Carolina suppressed piracy	154
	Louisiana granted to Law's Compagnie d'Occident	228
1718.	Fort Chartres, in the Illinois, established by Boisbriant	252
1719.	Traffic in negro slaves established in Louisiana	231
	Pensacola surrendered to the French and restored to the Spaniards	232
	New Orleans pictured	238
	The Missouri explored by Du Tisné	257
	English traders on the Wabash and in the Illinois territory	324
	The proprietary rule overthrown in South Carolina	361
1721.	The population of Louisiana enumerated	235
	Treaty made between the colonists of Carolina and the Creeks	325
1722.	La Harpe explored the Arkansas	242
	Navigation of the Mississippi effected	267
1723.	Right of suffrage legally denied to black freedmen of Virginia	114
1724.	Charlevoix attempted the discovery of the Pacific by way of the Missouri	257
1725.	English post established at Oswego	338
1726.	The French erected Fort Niagara	338
1727.	Arrival in Louisiana of the Ursulines and the Jesuits	240
1728.	Norfolk noted as a place of prominence	357

DATE		PAGE
1728–1729.	Boundaries of Virginia and North Carolina revised	358
1729.	Proprietary rule ended in North Carolina	360
	Population of North Carolina	360
1730.	Cherokee chiefs visited England	325
	The Shenandoah valley claimed by Lord Fairfax	353
	Alliance entered into between the British and the Cherokee nation	362
1731.	First newspaper established in South Carolina	369
1732.	Free trade established between France and Louisiana	270
	Oglethorpe received charter for colony of Georgia	303
1733.	Savannah founded	304
	Richmond laid out	357
	Swiss colony settled in Carolina	363
	Independence of judiciary asserted in Carolina	367
1734.	Lutheran colony established at Ebenezer, Georgia	306
	The Carolina colonists menaced by the growing influence of the French	325
1735.	Mobile and Dauphine Island devastated by a hurricane	263
	English influence, through Adair, acquired over the Cherokees and the Chickasaws	323
	Charlestown's theatre	371
	Fire insurance organization established in Charlestown	371
1736.	Louisiana harassed by the Chickasaws	262
	John and Charles Wesley arrived in Georgia	307
	A Moravian colony established in Georgia	307
	The French defeated by the Chickasaws and their British allies at the battle of Ackia	329
	Virginia *Gazette* founded	369
1738.	Augusta County constituted	353

DATE		PAGE
1738.	Negro insurrection in Carolina	363
1740.	Cotton grown in Louisiana	269
	Oglethorpe invaded Florida	309
	Whitefield visited Georgia	314
	French expedition made against the Chickasaws and a truce agreed upon	330
1742.	Spanish attack on Frederica repulsed	312
1744.	La Vérendrye reached the Rocky Mountain district	258
	The Six Nations recognized at Lancaster the sweeping territorial claims of the British within Virginia colony	333
1745.	Census of the population of Louisiana taken	265
	Census of the population of Mobile taken	331
	Judiciary system established in Virginia	354
1746.	Sir William Johnson appointed superintendent of Indian affairs in the colonies	322
1747.	Value of peltries exported from South Carolina	373
1748.	Louisburg restored to France by the Peace of Aix-la-Chapelle	337
1749.	Céloron took formal possession of the Ohio valley for France	340
	North Carolina *Gazette* first published	369
	Boundary line established between Virginia and North Carolina	417
1750.	The Choctaws brought into friendship with the French	265
1750–1751.	Gist explored the Ohio and the Roanoke	333
1751.	Sugar cane first planted in Louisiana	269
	Georgia's first Assembly met at Savannah	315
	French fort erected at Sandusky	340
1752.	The charter of Georgia surrendered to the crown	315
	Third French expedition against the Chickasaws ended in failure	331

DATE		PAGE
1770.	British settlement on the Mississippi began	402
	South Carolina erected a statue to Pitt in recognition of his opposition to the Stamp Act	474
1774.	A Chamber of Commerce established in Charlestown	372
	Province of Quebec extended to the Ohio	414
	Harrodsburg built	419
1775.	New England colonists settled at Natchez	402
	The Transylvania Company founded Boonesborough (the beginning of Kentucky)	419
1777.	Washington County, North Carolina, constituted	421
1778.	Clark conquered for Virginia the old Illinois	441
	Louisville founded	442
	The Americans under Willing captured Manchac	449
1780.	St. Louis attacked by the Sioux	443
1781.	First East Florida Assembly met	408
	St. Joseph captured by the Spaniards	444
	West Florida surrendered to Spain	452
1783.	East Florida surrendered to Spain	454

LIST OF ILLUSTRATIONS

VOLUME III

FACING PAGE